Mach

Machiavelli in Love

Sex, Self, and Society in the Italian Renaissance

GUIDO RUGGIERO

The Johns Hopkins University Press

Baltimore

© 2007 The Johns Hopkins University Press
All rights reserved. Published 2007
Printed in the United States of America on acid-free paper

Johns Hopkins Paperback edition, 2010
2   4   6   8   9   7   5   3   1

The Johns Hopkins University Press
2715 North Charles Street
Baltimore, Maryland 21218-4363
www.press.jhu.edu

The Library of Congress has catalogued the hardcover edition of this book as follows:

Ruggiero, Guido, 1944–
Machiavelli in love : sex, self, and society in the Italian Renaissance / Guido Ruggiero.
p.   cm.
Includes bibliographical references and index.
ISBN-13: 978-0-8018-8516-7 (hardcover : alk. paper)
ISBN-10: 0-8018-8516-7 (hardcover : alk. paper)
1. Sex customs—Italy—History. 2. Renaissance—Italy.
3. Sex—Social aspects—Italy—History. 4. Sex role—Italy—History.
5. Sex in literature. I. Title.
HQ18.I8I834 2006
306.70945'09024–dc22
2006015555

A catalog record for this book is available from the British Library.

ISBN 13: 978-0-8018-9835-8
ISBN 10: 0-8018-9835-8

For Laura
"e come sare' io sanza te corso?
chi m'avria tratto su per la montagna?"
(adapted from Purgatorio *III:5 — 6)*

CONTENTS

ACKNOWLEDGMENTS

Although this book is the product of a career of research, discussions with students, colleagues, and friends, and reading widely in the literature of the Renaissance, it began to come together in a more serious way in the early 1990s thanks to fellowship support from the John Simon Guggenheim Foundation and the National Endowment for the Humanities. Much-appreciated stays at Harvard's Villa I Tatti and the Institute for Advanced Study at Princeton in that same period of time allowed me to make the most of those grants. But crucial for the project were my years as Josephine Berry Weiss Chair in the Humanities at the Pennsylvania State University from 1997 to 2003. That handsomely endowed chair and the Weiss family's generous support enabled me to read much more widely and make this book much more ambitious than would have otherwise been possible. Similar support from the University of Miami allowed me to finish writing the book even while serving as chair of a rapidly growing, exciting department of history there.

I would also like to thank John Paoletti, Roger Crum, and Cambridge University Press for allowing me to publish here in an expanded and revised form as Chapter 4 an essay published in 2006 as "Mean Streets, Familiar Streets, or The Fat Woodcarver and the Masculine Spaces of Florence" in Crum and Paoletti's coedited volume *Renaissance Florence: A Social History*. Similar thanks are in order to Ellen Kittell, Thomas Madden, and the University of Illinois Press for allowing me to publish as Chapter 3 a revised version of the essay "The Abbot's Concubine: Lies, Literature and Power at the End of the Renaissance" in Kittell and Madden's coedited volume *Medieval and Renaissance Venice* (1999).

As this book is truly the product of a career, however, I owe too many debts of gratitude to list here all the fine people who have helped along the way. Colleagues, students, and staff at all the universities where I have taught over the years—whether as a visiting professor (the University of Tennessee and the University of Syracuse in Florence) or as a regular member of the faculty (the University of Cincinnati, the University of Connecticut, the Pennsylvania State University, and the University of Miami)—have been most helpful and generous of their time and friendship. Equally important have been the colleagues in the broader profession who have encouraged, stimulated, and supported this project over the years. And although I cannot thank everyone, I would like to thank at least a few of the most important: Ed Muir, Claudio Povolo, Jim Farr, John Martin, Geoffrey Symcox, Ronnie Po-chia Hsia, Matthew Restall, Karen Kupperman, Richard Brown, Peter Burke, Joanne Ferraro, Londa Schiebinger, Robert Proctor, A. Gregg Roeber, Donald Spivey, Linda Woodbridge, Konrad Eisenbichler, Martin Elsky, Ian Frederick Moulton, Meg Gallucci, Deanna Shemek, Tita Rosenthal, Bette Talvacchia, Ann Rosalyn Jones, Peter Stallybrass, Valeria Finucci, and Albert Ascoli. Four senior supporters and intellectual role models also deserve special mention and thanks: Natalie Zemon Davis, Gene Brucker, the late Gaetano Cozzi, and most especially Lauro Martines; all four have written more letters for me and given more good advice than any scholar could rightly expect.

Special thanks are in order to my Miami colleagues Mary Lindemann and Richard Godbeer, who read and commented on early drafts of the book, as well as the readers for the Johns Hopkins University Press and my most supportive and helpful editor there, Henry Tom. But I am most indebted to Laura Giannetti, who truly was a Virgil to this project, even if I regularly fell far short of playing a Dante in return; nonetheless, her thoughtful readings, comments, and critiques have made this a stronger book and undoubtedly would have made it stronger yet if I had taken them all. Thus I dedicate this book to her—friend, teacher, guide, and partner.

Machiavelli in Love

"Given that el Machia [Machiavelli] is a relative of yours and a very good friend of mine, I cannot refrain from taking this occasion that you have given me to write to you and to commiserate with you about the things that I am hearing daily about him. . . . And if it were not for the great, virtually terrible events that are happening in this poor region [of Modena] which have given people other things to talk about than gossip, I am certain that no one would be talking about anything else besides him [Machiavelli]."[1] Thus did Filippo de' Nerli write his friend Francesco del Nero during carnival season in 1525 about the gossip that was making the rounds in Modena concerning Niccolò Machiavelli.

The "great, virtually terrible" events to which Filippo referred were the famous Battle of Pavia of 24 February 1525 and its aftermath. At nearby Pavia the French army had suffered a major defeat, and the French king Francis I had been captured by the emperor Charles V and carried off to Madrid as his prisoner. For the moment the battle seemed to mark the final demise of French pretensions in Italy and a future dominance of the peninsula by Charles V. After a generation of war that had disrupted the hegemony and relative peace that had allowed five powers to dominate Italy following the Peace of Lodi in 1454—the city-states of Venice, Milan, and Florence; the kingdom of Naples; and territories of Italy ruled by the pope, the Papal States—a Spanish-German domination of the peninsula seemed assured. Things would not be that simple, however. The famous Sack of Rome by Charles's troops in 1527 was just around the corner, and the sixteenth century would continue to be a century of turmoil in both political and religious terms which would effectively close the most brilliant days of the Italian Renaissance. Yet in the days following Pavia the fate of the city-states of Italy seemed sealed, and it is no wonder that gossip in Modena about Machiavelli was limited by discussion of that impending fate and that battle.

But still one is moved to wonder what the Florentine politician and political thinker Machiavelli could have done even to begin to compete with discussions in relatively distant Modena about the Battle of Pavia and the dark future that seemed to loom for the Italian peninsula. At the time, his fame (or infamy) was already established and growing as the controversial author of *The Prince,* and he was also busy corresponding with friends and the powerful about the travails of Italy and the best strategies to adopt in the face of the foreign armies that had overrun the peninsula. He was even beginning to regain some weight after his fall from power in 1512 in Florence as a friend of and correspondent with several of the key leaders and thinkers of the day (men like the noted Florentine ambassador and political thinker Francesco Guicciardini). Thus it would be easy to assume that the gossip about el Machia had something to do with his political or military ideas or advice on how to defend Italy from foreign invaders.

Nothing could be further from the truth. Nerli completed his thought "I am certain that no one would be talking about anything else besides him" by adding: "considering that a patriarch of that fame has fallen head over heels [*andare alla staffa*] for someone who I don't want to name."[2] The gossip that had reached Modena was that in his mid-fifties Machiavelli, long married (1501) to Marietta di Luigi Corsini, had developed yet another adulterous passion for a much younger and reportedly beautiful woman, Barbara Raffacani Salutati, a noted singer, poet, and personality who shared her favors at times with the rich and powerful. Machiavelli was in love. Again.

And Modena was abuzz with the news, for, as was usual with el Machia, it was not a quiet affair. In fact, he had recently written a comedy, *La Clizia,* about an old man, married and a patriarch of a substantial Florentine family, who had fallen madly in love with a younger woman and made a fool and a spectacle of himself in the process. Significantly, the old man's name, Nicomaco, seems to have the ring of Machiavelli's own name. That comedy was first performed with great success at the country villa of his good friend Jacobo di Filippo Falconetti, where he may have first met Barbara, and even our concerned letter writer Nerli associated the play with the gossip that was circulating about Machiavelli's affair as far away as Modena. In fact, in a rather different vein he had written to Machiavelli himself a little less than a week earlier complimenting him on the success of that performance and claiming with evident hyperbole that he had heard that it "was presented in such a [successful] way that not only in Tuscany, but also in Lombardy the reputation of your magnificence has spread rapidly." Nerli wrote further: "The fame of your comedy has flown everywhere [*è volata per tutto*]; and don't think I have heard this from letters from friends, for I have heard it [even] from wayfarers who go up and down all the highways preaching 'the glorious richness and proud festivities' of the gate of San Frediano."[3]

Reports that his mistress had actually sung the songs that filled the breaks between the acts in the comedy almost certainly added to Machiavelli's notoriety. But apparently el Machia was not troubled by his fame or notoriety, for less than a year later, in January 1526, we find him corresponding with his friend Francesco Guiccardini, who was at the time ruling the Romagna for Pope Clement VII, about a performance they were planning to stage of Machiavelli's earlier and ultimately more famous and successful comedy about love and adultery, *La mandragola*, during carnival that year in Faenza. Machiavelli wrote, "I want to assure you that I will come [for the performance] whatever happens." But he admitted that he was less sure about bringing along Barbara and the other singers for the performance "because she has certain lovers, who might block her from coming; nonetheless with a certain diligence they may be quieted." Still, he wanted to assure Guiccardini that the two of them had planned to come, and to reassure him, he revealed that he and Barbara had written five new songs "precisely for this performance."[4]

Although the ongoing political troubles of Italy eventually caused the performance planned by Guiccardini and Machiavelli to be canceled, the songs that Machiavelli and his young mistress wrote for it have survived and suggest a rather different Machiavelli from the dour, Machiavellian political thinker and practitioner often imagined by later commentators on his political writings. The song following the first act, for all its nods to Petrarchian conceits typical of Renaissance love poetry, literally seems to sing of a different Machiavelli:

Love, the person who doesn't try
Your great power, hopes in vain
Ever to truly witness
What may be heaven's highest merit.
Nor will such a person know what it means in the same instant
To live and die, to seek evil and flee the good,
To love themselves less than others.

And they'll never know how often
Fear and hope freeze and burn our hearts,
Or understand how both men and gods
Tremble before the arrows with which you're armed.[5]

Or again the song that opens the last act of the comedy where, thanks to a truly Machiavellian ploy, adultery finally wins out with a happy night in bed together for young lovers at the expense of a foolish old husband:

O sweet night, O holy
Hours, dark and quiet,
Who accompany yearning lovers,
You carry with you such
Happiness wherever you rest
That all alone you make souls blessed.
You give worthy prizes
To bands of lovers
For their long trials;
You make, O happy hours,
Every cold heart burn with love![6]

Machiavelli in love? What are we encountering here? Who was this Machiavelli? What was he doing wishing to sing with his mistress in his fifty-seventh year the praises of a God who swept one away and left one passively pierced with his pleasurable arrows? Was this other Machiavelli, the lover, a chimera? Was he merely an intimate footnote of no significance for the life of the real Machiavelli or his thought? Was he merely a passing moment of his life imitating art and the topoi of love and sex in the literature of the period which he enjoyed? Or was this other Machiavelli a minor aberration of his deeply troubled later years?

Perhaps this was just a playful side of that dark thinker in a society that saw such affairs with young mistresses as insignificant "affairs of the night." Perhaps it was a form of Renaissance self-fashioning in which Machiavelli refashioned himself as a lover in his later years. In fact, it could be any, all, or none of the above. But these questions nonetheless are interesting, and they lead to more significant and perhaps more answerable ones about how sex, self, and society interrelated in the Renaissance, questions that it would be unwise to dismiss as merely sidelights on the Renaissance, as I hope *Machiavelli in Love* will demonstrate. In this book, then, I have written a series of essays about sex, self, and society across the Italian Renaissance and how all three interacted with a broadly shared everyday culture and the values and concerns of the time to create a rather different world where Machiavelli in love takes on a richer meaning and provides material for thinking more deeply not just about that distant intriguing time but, in a way, perhaps the present as well.

My interest in the history of sex in the Renaissance is not a new one. My first published essay in the *Journal of Social History,* "Sexual Criminality in the Early Renaissance" (1975), dealt with the topic using crime data from the fourteenth century in Venice to probe the way violent sexuality was policed and perceived.[7] In my second book, *The Boundaries of Eros: Sex Crime and Sexuality in Renaissance Venice* (1985), I used similar but richer documentation to attempt to construct an overview of the way society perceived sex both licit and illicit over the fourteenth and fifteenth centuries in that same city and to construct some hypotheses about the sexual life of Renaissance Italy in general.[8] Then, in writing *Binding Passions: Tales of Magic, Marriage and Power at the End of the Renaissance* (1993), I used another type of documentation—the extremely rich records of the Venetian Holy Office. Reading them against the grain as it were—not so much for the heresies or feared heresies that were being investigated by that Venetian branch of the Roman Inquisition as for the revealing and highly detailed testimonies from people of all social levels collected there on sexual practice and everyday perceptions of Renaissance sexual life—I used these records to write narratives that both illustrated and analyzed the role such passions played at the end of the sixteenth century in Italy. In the end that book was concerned with much more, attempting in many ways to be a different history of late Renaissance society and the end of the Renaissance from the perspective of passion: a history of how individuals in late Renaissance society saw themselves as bound by their passions more generally and in turn how they saw their passions being bound to create a relatively ordered and viable society. The narrative format—the analysis was incorporated into a series of tales about everyday life drawn from Inquisition testimonies—hopefully worked to allow readers not just to read about how everyday life was supposed to be lived but actually to read human stories that gave a sense and a feeling for that life and the role sex and passion played in it.[9] Finally, I published *Five Comedies from the Italian Renaissance* (2003), translated and edited with Laura Giannetti, a sampling of the most important Renaissance comedies selected at least in part for the revealing ways they presented gender and sex on stage.[10]

Needless to say, as I have been working on the subject of Renaissance sex, the field has literally exploded, owing in large part to the pathbreaking scholarship done in the context of gay, feminist, and cultural studies and the new social and cultural history. Yet I feel as if the topic is still in its exploratory stages and still highly hypothetical. At the least, much as is the case for the more general history of sexuality, it is still highly controversial with much exciting work being done. There is not the space to review that literature here, especially as much of it will be explicitly or implicitly discussed in the essays that follow. Still, perhaps the most important and controversial work in the area has been done by Michel Foucault and his followers, and at times the chapters of this book may read like an extended and critical review of his most important ideas and those of his disciples on the history of sex. Such a reading would be true to my intentions in this work with two important caveats. First, it is accurate if it is kept to the fore that a "critique" can be positive as well as negative, for many of my critiques are meant to enrich and make more complex, in the context of Renaissance Italy, Foucault's often pathbreaking and prescient hypotheses. Second, just as Foucault saw his work as essays, and highly hypothetical essays at that, on the role sex played or did not play in the past, my critiques are in turn highly hypothetical essays focused primarily in the narrower yet richly documented frame of Renaissance Italy.

More pertinent, perhaps much of what has been most revolutionary and suggestive in Foucault's work hangs on his amazingly fertile way of redefining key terms to literally deconstruct what seemed like certainties about the past—and the present for that matter. Of course, that fecundity has a potential weakness as well, for one has only to disallow his definitions or even slightly adjust them and the ground quickly slides away under his most intriguing and challenging arguments. Unfortunately, this potential has been exploited by many of Foucault's critics, with the result that potentially rich historical debates have often been largely conducted in terms of theoretical definitions and redefinitions that preordain the outcome of those debates. Clearly avoiding rewriting history by simply rewriting definitions is a broader problem, and, of course, Foucault himself as just noted was one of the boldest practitioners of and at times one of the biggest sinners in this. But when he was at his best in redefining the past, his new definitions were built upon a dialogue with that past rather than created out of theoretical necessity or paradigmatic concerns. To me that is the key: from a historical perspective the most useful redefining is that which is the most constrained by the past, where theory is forced to give its due to past texts, be they archival, literary, or prescriptive. And thus, while the chapters in this book also at times redefine the ground out from under the feet of Foucault and his followers, I have attempted to do so always limited by what the documentation of the period allows and with an eye to how such redefinitions open old texts to new and richer readings.

Two of Foucault's most controversial redefinitions are at the heart of these essays: his apparent insistence that sex is a modern invention, a product of the disciplining discourses that in many ways set apart and define the modern world developed primarily in the nineteenth and twentieth centuries; and his closely related claim that a sense of sexual identity is again a modern invention and that in the premodern world there were merely practices and uses of the body which had no relationship to a personal sense of identity. Foucault provocatively claimed, then, that before the modern world there was no sex and no sexual identity. My goal is not to overthrow these powerful and often telling hypotheses but rather to drop their teleological dimension (the way that the past of sex and identity is defined by the way it leads to the present), which often warps our discussions, and to attempt to clarify what sex and identity meant and did not mean in the Renaissance. To simplify greatly and get ahead of the arguments necessary to make my points more effectively, this book argues that although Foucault's hypotheses and definitions have great weight from a modern perspective, neither Renaissance sex nor gender fits well with the modern definitions that underlie his arguments.

Certainly neither sex nor identity existed or functioned in the Renaissance as they do today or as they did in the nineteenth century, and in many ways before Foucault's pioneering work that "certainly" would have been a great deal less certain for most people. Nonetheless, both did exist in the Renaissance in an often very different Renaissance way and were extremely important factors in the way life was led at the time across the social spectrum. Speaking very broadly, both Renaissance sex and identity were practices as Foucault suggested, in a way performances (reflected and unreflected) and negotiations with the broader groups in society with which a person interacted and were seen as such at the time. Both also had a private and personal dimension that cannot be entirely overlooked, but once again as Foucault and his followers have amply demonstrated, that dimension was more secondary and less developed than in modern society. Still, one may be allowed the suspicion that their claims about how powerful an inner sense of sexual identity is today may be overstated for large parts of the population and in turn are perhaps undermined a bit by an ongoing emphasis on the external performance of self suggested by the apparently strong necessity to display and negotiate identity and to a degree sexuality through social markers such as clothing and behavioral codes.

Ultimately, however, if my hypothesis about the Renaissance is correct, sexual identity and identity more broadly at the time were what might be called "consensus realities": imagined realities, but no less real for that, which were shared within the various groups with which an individual lived and interacted, groups such as family, neighbors, friends, social peers, fellow workers, fellow confraternity members, and broader communities and solidarities. These consensus realities, as they were shared understandings within a group, were not necessarily tightly structured; nor were they the same from group to group. As we will see, for example, Machiavelli's identity as a lover had rather different meanings for the consensus reality of his family than it did for his circle of close friends and again a different valence for the broader communities in which he was known. Thus Filippo de' Nerli could commiserate with Machiavelli's relative Francesco del Nero about the gossip concerning Machiavelli's affair which was making the rounds in Modena, while at the same time Machiavelli and his friends, as will become clear, were treating it positively. But the point is that to a great extent Machiavelli was known in terms of these consensus realities, and in turn, because they were flexible and socially maintained, Machiavelli could have an impact on them. With self-presentation, with self-performance he could negotiate to a degree his identity, a perhaps more complex and nuanced refashioning of what Stephen Greenblatt labeled so brilliantly Renaissance self-fashioning. At the same time, in this process of social identity negotiation and maintenance there was a powerful potential for social discipline, for binding passions and behavior in general, as the judging power of the groups that surrounded one in society had a weight in the Renaissance that is difficult to appreciate from a modern perspective. Tellingly, however, this disciplining potential was somewhat balanced by an ability to perform (or not to perform) self and sex in the Renaissance, making "negotiating" a crucial concept in the process and leaving some space for individual agency in the performance of self.

The problem, of course, is how to get at such complex processes. Few archival documents deal directly with such concerns. Prescriptive literature provides some useful information, but it is evidently often heavily skewed especially when it comes to sex and sexual practices. Renaissance literature, although clearly difficult to use, seems in many ways to be one of the best sources because often it focuses on the presentation and negotiation of self and sex in order to identify and make sense of characters in ways that made sense to Renaissance readers. Thus it offers the opportunity to tease out the way those things worked or at least how they were perceived as working. Significantly, both sex and self in Renaissance literature tended to be established with a few broad strokes that could be quickly appreciated by audiences or readers and which allow us also to quickly identify broad stereotypical perceptions before attempting to probe more deeply.

In part this rapid sketching was due to genre considerations. The novella or short story was one of the most popular forms of literature in the period in large part because it could move back and forth easily between an oral format of storytelling that was still a prominent part of everyday life and a written form that was fairly easily disseminated and read. This genre placed a heavy emphasis on action over description, with the result that there was less description of character and what there was often tended to be stereotypical. The handsome, noble young lover; the evil old father; the young beautiful girl to be loved; the tricky friar or priest; the kind nurse or *balia;* the foolish tutor or pedant—these types of characters appear over and over again and in their repetitions allow one to reconstruct their imaginary range. But beyond these often fairly stereotypical descriptions, deeper qualities tended to be marked out in the novella with deeds that provided the crucial signs of more complex identity. Significantly, these deeds or practices that served as signs to mark deeper aspects of identity functioned in literature, I would suggest, much as deeds or practices in daily life served to construct identity for the groups within which a person lived and negotiated identity. For the more social performative nature of Renaissance identity relied on exactly such signs, and thus, on reflection, it is hardly surprising that the Renaissance novella would rely on that same system of deeds-as-signs to establish identity. Sex, on the other hand, as it could be presented in terms of deeds, in a way was more privileged and more directly described, at least by those writers of short stories who described it directly. Some, however, preferred to allude to it playfully, and in those allusions and metaphors there is a rich discourse of deeper meaning to be read. Those who were more direct in their descriptions were seldom as direct as in modern literature, but again their quick compressed descriptions often distill the essence of what the sex described was seen as meaning at the time.

A second form of literature that speaks often of sex and identity is the "erudite" comedy that was particularly popular in the first half of the sixteenth century, only to slowly lose place to the more informal and popular commedia dell'arte toward the end of the century. Often based more or less closely on clas-

sical models (hence the name "erudite"), these comedies virtually always re-
set the scene and the characters in a Renaissance context so they would make
immediate sense to a Renaissance audience, and at times they even changed
the action and the plot line drastically to suit a Renaissance sense of action and
humor. In their quick action; clever, slapstick, and often erotic humor; and fine
sense of everyday life, these comedies are anything but erudite and often seem
closer to the novella tradition staged. In a few cases they were actually drawn
from that tradition, but more tellingly, once again as in the novella, characters
were rapidly sketched often in a stereotypical fashion and then fleshed out with
deeds that gave them more individual characteristics. And following that
process, one can begin to trace out how identity was established in the Renaissance. One problem for the presentation of sex, however, is that almost all
comedies were set in the streets and squares of Renaissance cities; thus sex with
rare exceptions had to be reported, and for once deeds were replaced with descriptions. Still, once again these descriptions are quick and usually aim at presenting sex in a pleasurable and titillating manner; thus what little is described
is often highly revealing.

It is important to remember, however, that these comedies come down to us
not as they were performed but as they were written down for publication.
While from many perspectives, especially the perspective of understanding the
comedy as a performance, this is a problem, it may actually be a plus for considering the way sex and gender were understood at the time: for although we
cannot know what the audience's response was to certain characters or their
deeds on stage except in rare instances in which letters or chronicles record
this, what we may have in the final written form of these comedies is a rewriting of them which has responded to the audience's responses. Obviously this
is highly hypothetical, but still it is worth considering that the authors of such
works in rewriting them for publication had the opportunity to adjust characters to make their identity clearer and to portray their sexuality in ways that
worked better for the time. What seems clear, however, is that in rewriting
many authors developed a more clever play of words and metaphors that explored more deeply both the meaning of sex and character for the time.

Finally, letters—especially Renaissance letters that were consciously more
literary—offer another fascinating perspective on identity and sex in the period. Significantly, like the "erudite" comedies, letters that were more literary
often consciously paralleled the novella form, as was the case for some of Machiavelli's most interesting letters, as we will see. Thus one more time, in a
slightly different context, with usually more pretense of describing true events,

we have the quick bold sketching of character and the action-oriented descriptions of deeds to add greater individuality or even at times to overturn stereotypes. Nicely, however, with this genre we also frequently have the response of the person to whom the letter was written. When that is the case, we can get a sense of how the deeds and signs reported in a letter were read and understood—a rare opportunity to apply and test reception theory in the Renaissance. Although letters could be quickly copied and circulated widely, even published, in the Renaissance, normally their audience was more restricted, and thus one can begin to appreciate how self-presentation and self-negotiation could be tailored to the individual or groups to whom letters were addressed and once again their responses. In sum, in letters we have an opportunity to see the performances and negotiations of self that went into establishing and maintaining identity written out, and often written out from various perspectives within a group.

Although in this book I have used other literary forms as well, my primary focus has been on these three genres. Obviously all three have very real dangers and limits as historical sources, which are discussed in greater detail in the chapters that follow. Yet when one is trying to use such texts not to establish what actually happened but rather to explore the perceptions of the time, they also offer real advantages because, in order to be understood, they usually had to speak to those perceptions. Perhaps the most problematic exception to this in the Renaissance was the literary fascination with classical topoi and earlier forms of representing passions such as love. At times this literate practice of what today might be labeled plagiarizing the past is so evident—even highlighted to reveal an author's erudition or cleverness—that it is easily identified. At other times, however, things are considerably less clear and leave room for a troubling uncertainty about whether one is discovering Renaissance perceptions or Renaissance re-representations of the perceptions of earlier periods. And while uncertainty is a necessary virtue for historians and all historical analysis of literature for that matter, one way to limit that uncertainty is to move across genres and beyond literary sources to other texts from the period which provide other perspectives on the same issues. The more overlapping we have across different textual forms, the more certain will be our explanations. In turn, it is in the disjunctures between various textual traditions that we can discover some of the more telling fault lines in our interpretations and hypotheses.

Of course, there is another type of difficulty in dealing with literary texts from the Renaissance, ironically a modern one. Given the literary turn of cultural studies and the proliferation of literary theory over the past few decades, the reading of literary texts has become much more sophisticated, exciting, and dangerous. It is especially dangerous for historians, who have enough trouble keeping up with their own theoretical discussions, mastering their own archives and printed texts, and following the burgeoning new literature on topics as diverse as the new social history of warfare, the new cultural history, or good old political or social history, never mind embarking on reading Renaissance literature and the fascinating but rapidly growing critical literature on the same. A little more than a decade ago, however, I published an article originally titled "Re-Reading the Renaissance: Civic Morality and the World of Marriage, Love and Sex," which suggested that historians and literary scholars needed to work together to reread the literature of the Renaissance using the best of the new insights of both disciplines to gain a deeper understanding of the Renaissance and Renaissance literature.[11] Needless to say, many scholars in both fields were already doing that, and a fruitful rereading is well under way. Led more by literary scholars than historians perhaps, it has generated new readings of classic Renaissance texts and rediscovered many rich but forgotten ones as well. In this book I have tried to use the insights of this new scholarship to reread a range of literary texts and meld them with more traditionally archival-based historical scholarship to understand how sex, self, and society interrelated in the Renaissance. But hopefully in the process of looking closely at literary texts some suggestive new readings of well-known Renaissance literary works have emerged here as well—so at their best my rereadings may be fruitful both for history and for literature. Although it would be difficult to claim that one is saying anything new about literary works by Machiavelli, Boccaccio, Castiglione, or Aretino, I hope readers will find some interesting new ways of seeing some of their more important works— and if not always new, at least momentarily out of fashion, irreverent, and challenging ways of rereading and rethinking them.

Chapter 1, "Of Birds, Figs, and Sexual Identity in the Renaissance, or The Marescalco's Boy Bride," focuses on a rereading of one of Pietro Aretino's (1492–1556) most interesting comedies, *Il marescalco* (*The Master of the Horse*), completed in the late 1520s in Venice after he had fled Rome (reportedly to escape prosecution for his obscene verses written to accompany Giulio Romano's infamous erotic engravings of sexual positions) and wandered Italy for a while in search of new patrons. *Il marescalco* is often interpreted as an attack on court life (the Marescalco's problems turn in part on his being a courtier in Mantua) or a humorous reprise of the Renaissance debate on the marriage, or a closely related laughing replay of the Renaissance *querelle des femmes* from a largely misogynist perspective, yet until recently there has been a surprising tendency to understate the central role that male-male sexuality plays in the comedy. My rereading, then, attempts to move Aretino's defense of male-male sexual relations, which seems to be at the heart of this comedy, back to center stage by reading the comedy against what we know from other sources about such relationships in the Renaissance. In the process we get a clearer picture of the way the Renaissance could view the theoretically heinous sin of sodomy (male-male sexuality was labeled unnatural and hence fell under the rubric of sodomy in legal and moral literature) in daily practice in a more positive light. In fact, we see the outlines of an ideal of a more positive male-male sexuality and at the same time get a glimpse of a perhaps deeper sense of personal sexual identity. In that context a relatively unnoticed subplot emerges which turns on the maturing of the Marescalco's young lover, Giannicco, and we get a clearer picture of the way male sexual identity was perceived as ideally developing across the stages of a man's life in the Renaissance. That picture takes us to the central theme of the chapter: the way male sexual identity was perceived as evolving over the life span of a man in the Renaissance in contrast to an apparently more static vision of sexual identity for women. Thus in the end, from a rereading of Aretino's comedy, the chapter spirals out to consider male-male sexuality, Renaissance perceptions of the stages of life, and aspects of the sexual and gendered determinations of identity in the Renaissance, all essential for understanding Machiavelli in love.

"Playing with the Devil: The Pleasures and Dangers of Sex and Play," Chapter 2, examines one of Giovanni Boccaccio's most humorous and apparently blasphemous novelle, the famous story of Rustico and Alibech told at the end of the third day of tales in the *Decameron*, and contrasts it with a case drawn from the records of the Venetian Holy Office (a special local branch of the Roman Inquistion) of a certain Suor Mansueta, who had accused herself of having given herself to the Devil because of the great sexual pleasure she enjoyed with him. The contrasts between an imaginary tale told in the middle of the fourteenth century by one of Italy's most enjoyed *novellieri* and the virtually unknown account of a late sixteenth-century nun are rich with suggestive insights about the way play and the pleasures of sex were associated in the Renaissance and the way perceptions of both changed across the period. Suor Mansueta's narrative of herself as the playmate of the Devil is also rich with suggestive material about identity and sexual identity, as in many ways her presentation of that relationship with the Devil turned on the ultimate evil of sexual identity, an evil that was so devastating that she could claim that she had lost her identity and the Venetian clerics and laymen who heard her testimony concurred and responded accordingly with a long series of exorcisms to reclaim her for herself. In contrast, the tale of Alibech's adventures in search of the true meaning of Christianity, which turns on a playful metaphoric understanding of the resurrection of the flesh and putting the Devil back in hell, allows us once again to see more easily and more humorously the way play and pleasure were associated in an earlier period. At the same time it also allows us to follow the logic of the blasphemous depiction of sexual delights in the service of the Christian God to several provocative hypotheses about Boccaccio's deeper meanings. And although the author has been proclaimed dead, those rereadings are too much fun not to resurrect Boccaccio—especially as he has been condemned in recent times as a misogynist and even portrayed as a pessimistic moralist—as a laughing celebrator of life, women, and sex for a moment at least.

In Chapter 3, "The Abbot's Concubine: Renaissance Lies, Literature, and Power," another contrast between literature and archival texts is explored. In this case the contrast is between Captain Fear, a popular late sixteenth-century stock character in commedia dell'arte, and a certain Abbot Ruis, who was tried by the Holy Office of Venice for his strange claims about his relationship with his concubine in the little village of Summaga in Friuli. At one level, both tales turn on what it meant in the Renaissance to be a concubine. Captain Fear, a stereotypically aggressive and fecund male lover, had been taken on by the Amazons to literally inject some new military valor into their blood line by serving as their male concubine and impregnating as many of them as he could in as short a time as possible. His initial successes, although impressive, were quickly undercut by the stereotypical unlimited desire of his female employers, and he was soon reduced to a drooping and useless state. Abbot Ruis, at much the same time and in much the same area, was also telling a tale of his sexual demise at the hands of a woman, but she was his concubine, and she had unmanned him using sexual magic that made it impossible to function or to find peace without her. These stories of masculine demise at the hands of dangerous females—the literal loss of self that evil women and excessive passion could entail—again provide an interesting perspective on sexual identity in the Renaissance. But perhaps more interesting, especially in the tale of the demise of Abbot Ruis, is the way we can see how in daily life presentations of self and the portrayal of others sexually could be used to create significant microstrategies of power—strategies that operated below the more formally recognized macrosystems of patriarchy and government and which created a much more complex and richer play of forces in daily life in the Renaissance.

"Brunelleschi's First Masterpiece, or Mean Streets, Familiar Streets, Masculine Spaces, and Identity in Renaissance Florence," Chapter 4, plots literally on the map of Renaissance Florence a less well known late fifteenth-century novella, the tale of a cruel joke played on a woodcarver known as Il Grasso (The Fat One) by the famous architect and "Renaissance man" Filippo Brunelleschi. The heart of the tale, as it is told by Antonio Manetti, turns on the way Brunelleschi cleverly punished his friend Il Grasso for a slight by using the spaces of the city, especially the masculine spaces, to literally take away his identity. Following the unfolding of that clever plot, we see how identity was once again primarily social and in many ways mapped out and read in terms of the masculine terrain of the city. A cleverly literary letter of Machiavelli allows us to voyage deeper into the illicit masculine spaces at the heart of the city to examine how they also contributed to the performance and negotiation of identity, especially once again sexual identity, and to eventually circle back to a highly speculative rereading of Manetti's tale which turns on the sexual identity of Il Grasso and Brunelleschi and which adds a rather provocative dimension to the title of the chapter. But behind these speculative adventures, the more serious focus of the chapter is again masculine identity and its close relationship to the intimate spaces of urban life in the Renaissance.

In Chapter 5, "Machiavelli in Love: The Self-Presentation of an Aging Lover," el Machia, who has been looming in the background, comes to the fore with a long analysis of his correspondence with his friend and sometimes patron Francesco Vettori and with a challenging and irreverent reading of his two most important comedies, *La mandragola* and *La Clizia*. The focus of the discussion is on the way Machiavelli presents his own approach to love, lust, and sex from the more personal perspective of letters exchanged with Vettori and his circle of closer friends and in the more public forum of his comedies—both revealing instances of self-presentation and self-negotiation. Once more I have sinned perhaps too boldly in resurrecting an author and another canonical author at that, but again my goal has been to attempt to open up for a rereading and a rethinking the canonical Machiavelli—suggesting a considerably less Machiavellian Machiavelli. My reading of his letters presents a Machiavelli in his forties, fallen from political power, who playfully portrayed himself to his friends as at once a sorry old man and a successful lover of younger women, a passive victim of his passions, loves, and lusts, rather than as an aggressive master of his passions, love, and women, which one might expect given his idealization of an active, aggressive, and masculine persona in his political writings. And tellingly Vettori and his other correspondents not only accepted that self-presentation but regularly confirmed and reinforced it. In turn, for his comedies I suggest a rereading that reemphasizes their comic and again self-referential nature. While it is difficult to say anything that has not already been said about Machiavelli, the melding of these rereadings with the discussion of Renaissance ideas of sexual identity and Renaissance sexual practices developed in earlier chapters hopefully will present a Machiavelli that is suggestive and good to think about anew.

That contextualization of Machiavelli's letters and comedies in terms of a Renaissance understanding of sexual identity and sexual practice allows the chapter also to serve as an example of and in a way a conclusion to the earlier discussions of these themes. And that in turn leads to the last chapter, "Death and Resurrection and the Regime of *Virtù*, or Of Princes, Lovers, and Prickly Pears." In tribute to the Baktinian vision of the premodern grotesque body and its cycle of life, death, decay, and rebirth, a discussion of death and resurrection in terms of identity both sexual and more general seems an ideal way to end the body of this book. And at a slightly deeper level this chapter serves to close the book by reopening—resurrecting as it were—an old question that still lacks an adequate answer or even an adequate recognition as a particularly important issue. In *Binding Passions* I asked a question that I have been asking across the span of my career in various ways: How were Renaissance passions bound, and, to the degree that they were bound, how did that binding work in the practices of daily life to create a relatively tranquil and ordered society?

Behind that question lies a conviction that today we are in many ways the victims of a modern fallacy that sees government and the state as much more important and powerful than they actually are or can be, especially in everyday life and even more especially in things sexual. This fallacy, in fact, may in some ways be traced back to Machiavelli and his Renaissance vision of government and an ideal state that could create and defend a civic morality and order that would sustain an honest, loyal, and ultimately virtuous citizenry, as this chapter briefly suggests following in the footsteps of a much more developed scholarship. Given the strong desire of Machiavelli and Renaissance governments to control urban society and to contain the feared strong passions of the time, what stands out, however, is their actual limited ability to do so. Simply put, they lacked the effective bureaucracies or the technologies of government to do so, and this should come as no surprise, for when we drop our modern statist blinders, current events demonstrate clearly and often tragically that even modern governments equipped with computers, virtually limitless paper, fearless and aggressive bureaucrats, and frightening force are incapable of containing violent passions—or more secret sexual ones, either.

If this reasoning is correct, the question becomes, What were the significant disciplining and ordering mechanisms of Renaissance society, or to put it another way, How were passions bound in the Renaissance? This last chapter resurrects this question by looking at the nexus between a very powerful disciplining concept in the Renaissance *virtù* and Renaissance identity. Provocatively, it puts forth the idea that much more important than government in ruling was what I have labeled the regime of *virtù*: a regime that turned on the social disciplining of individuals—once again by the groups within which one lived, worked, and played in the Renaissance—in terms of *virtù*. In this the regime functioned much like the consensus realities that stood behind a Renaissance sense of sexual identity and broader senses of identity, for ultimately *virtù*, because it was socially judged, turned on self-presentation and self-negotiation. To argue this the chapter then traces the trajectory of *virtù* across the Renaissance beginning with a brief quotation from Machiavelli ruing the lack of *virtù* in contemporary society and blaming the current turmoil and tribulations of Italy in the face of foreign invasions directly on its lack. Anyone who has read his political writings will be aware of how central the concept was in his thinking about the current problems and past successes of governments and societies.

To trace the complex trajectory of the term and to suggest the significance of the regime of *virtù* across the Renaissance, the chapter considers three lesser known literary texts that deal with death, a last judgment, and ultimately resurrection in terms of *virtù*, the richest and most complex of which is the tale of the metaphoric death of the virtually stereotypical evil peasant Scopone (Prickly Pear) and his resurrection as the virtually reversed stereotypical good peasant Salice (Pliant Willow), a death and resurrection that turn not only on his submitting to the regime of *virtù* but also on his lord and master giving up his youthful pleasures for *virtù* as well—shades of the Marescalco and Chapter 1. The heart of the chapter deals with more canonical literary texts again—first, a rereading of another fascinatingly rich tale of Boccaccio's from the early Renaissance, the story of the tragic love and demise of Gismonda and Guiscardo at the hands of her father, Tancredi, the prince of Salerno—a tale whose moral turns on the *virtù* of the young lovers and the lack of same demonstrated by the prince in the face of their secret affair; and second, a rereading of Castiglione's *Book of the Courtier* from the perspective of sexual identity and *virtù* which reveals a set of deep parallels with Machiavelli's contemporary presentation of *virtù*. In fact, Machiavelli's vision of *virtù* is a continuing point of reference throughout the chapter, primarily to give context to the other Renaissance discussions of the term but also to suggest that his own vision of *virtù* was very much a product of his time and less a transfer of an ancient Roman ideal than is often claimed and clearly not an evocation of a universal political truth as some modern political thinkers have asserted. In sum, this book opens with Machiavelli in love and closes with Machiavelli still in love, but rather than ending there, it reopens in this last chapter an issue that is at the heart of his vision and a Renaissance vision of a social organization that can control human desires and passions, a vision that turns on ultimately once again the judgment of identity in terms of *virtù* by the groups within which one lived, worked, and played.

Finally, let me say that I hope I have presented Machiavelli in love and the other literary texts used here sinning boldly—writing essaylike chapters that in the mold of Montaigne's essays (although clearly less personal and much less elegant) wind through the complexities of the issues discussed without closure or final pronouncements. These are essays that are meant to suggest much but claim little and, more important, essays that are meant to be challenging and challenged, to be thought with rather than close thought or be accepted. Thus in these essays I have mixed an intentionally playful and often irreverent analysis of Renaissance literature, both canonical and obscure, with my own archival research and my understanding of current historical scholarship. And although I have tried to come to grips with the exciting range of theories and critical approaches that have enlivened recent literary scholarship without redebating them here, I have been dangerously eclectic in my approach. The same is undoubtedly true of the voluminous historical scholarship on these topics, but I would like to think that there my knowledge and reading have ranged more widely. Yet in the end I fear that rather than robbing the infidels as Augustine recommended, I have been the infidel robbing the truly consistent and original thinkers in my own and other disciplines. Still, to begin rereading the past and to enjoy the project of considering Machiavelli in love in the context of Renaissance sexual identity and sexual practice, one must sin boldly, and I confess to having done so. Hopefully readers will find that sinning at least interesting and perhaps even a pleasure to think.

Of Birds, Figs, and Sexual Identity in the Renaissance, or The Marescalco's Boy Bride

As this book and this essay mean to play with ideas and concepts that we hold dear, I thought that I might begin with a game that was listed by Tomaso Garzoni as one of the more popular games played in upper-class circles in Renaissance Italy. It is a game that in its own way seems to play with what we might expect of polite society in that time and place. It was called "Letting the Bird [*uccello*] Peck at the Fig [*fico*]" and was described as follows: "[in this game] each woman takes a certain fig . . . and each man a certain bird and one man says, 'I would like my bird to peck such and such fig.' And the woman who hears her fig named answers, 'My fig will not be pecked by that bird. And when it is . . . pecked, I would like it to be pecked by that other bird.'"[1]

To understand this game one needs to know that bird/*uccello* and fig/*fico* had the same double meaning in the Renaissance that they do today in Italian—an *uccello* signifies a phallus as well as a bird and a *fico* a vagina as well as a fig. Letting the Bird Peck at the Fig, then, was a game that allowed young members of polite society to play at sex in a social setting in that tantalizingly safe way of many games in which one names and does not name, in which one agrees to everything but actually commits to nothing—here, a game in which one agrees to sexual intercourse, but only rhetorically. Without considering the many ramifications of birds pecking at figs in polite society, let me suggest that this game was about sexual identity—it was a way of publicly displaying Renaissance "heterosexuality."[2]

In the present scholarly debates over the history of sexuality, my claim that playing "Letting the Bird Peck at the Fig" involved sexual identity may well be dismissed as a mistaken play itself, for, as most people are aware, it is widely held that Michel Foucault in his seminal works on the history of sexuality argued that sexual identity is only a modern phenomenon. According to this understanding of Foucault, sexual identity is the product of a deployment of sexuality developed in the discourses that spun out around the new disciplines of the modern period, disciplinary discourses that created what they named—modern-disciplined individuals, individuals who viewed themselves as identified at a deep, virtually ontological level by their sexuality. One was literally a homosexual, a heterosexual, or a myriad of other sexual beings on a range of possibilities defined by disciplines.[3]

A crucial component of Foucault's hypothesis about modern sexual identity was the vision that sex and sexual practices changed in dramatic and largely unrecognized ways over time—a healthy corrective to those who had assumed that sex was an unchanging biological given. That problematization of the history of sexuality has been very useful for historians, but Foucault's discourse on the modernity of sexual identity has been picked up and reified into a virtual paradigm that is less useful, I would argue.[4] In a way it is ironic that the followers of a thinker like Foucault, who emphasized the fluidity of every discourse including his own, have taken this particular discourse and transformed it into a disciplinary structure that limits what can be said about the history of sexuality in a way that undermines the richness and complexity of that history and the richness of Foucault's own vision.

My goal in this chapter is merely to suggest that we pay a little more attention to the figs and birds of the Renaissance and consider the possibility that although neither the sexual practices nor the ways of understanding identity of the period were modern—which should come as no great surprise—we can and should look at how the two worked together to gain an understanding of the interesting and suggestively different nature of life in the period. Returning to the game "Letting the Bird Peck at the Fig," one thing that stands out immediately is the social context of the sexual play, for I want to argue that Renaissance perceptions and constructions of identity were highly social: they were perceptual realities created in crucial ways in external social spaces. This is not to argue, as have some, that they were wholly external and that there was no personal psychic space where they could be or were deployed. Such hypotheses, while suggestive, take a perceptive reading of an important difference of the premodern world—that much more of life was lived in an external social space—and push it too far, I fear. There are too many discussions of the interior life of individuals in the Renaissance at every level, from humanist discourse to the testimony of common people about their inner thoughts and feelings before criminal and inquisitional tribunals, to contend that interiority did not exist.

Nevertheless, the heavier emphasis on the social/external measure of identity, especially sexual identity, in the Renaissance means that if we look for identity in the expected places from a modern perspective we simply may not find it.[5] Rather, I would suggest that we need to look for it in what I will label "consensus realities"—imagined realities that were built up, reinforced (or disciplined), and shared by the various social groups with which an individual interacted in the Renaissance. Family, friends, neighbors, fellow citizens, and other social solidarities such as guilds and confraternities each constructed in dialogue with a person a socially recognized personal identity for that individual. Identities based upon "consensus realities" could be quite different for the same person depending upon the group that shared them; thus within a family a man could be viewed as honorable, just, and loyal, whereas within the broader community he could be viewed as violent and dangerous precisely because he defended his family's prerogatives aggressively. Or, as a starker example perhaps, a married poor women who occasionally earned money as prostitute to sustain her family could be viewed by her neighbors as honorable and a *donna da bene* but viewed by most other groups as without honor.

As will become apparent, the relativity of such socially shared "consensus realities" explains much about the apparently fluid nature of Renaissance identity and what has been labeled Renaissance self-fashioning. In the end, as we shall see, there was perhaps less of the latter and more identity negotiation by individuals in dialogue with the various social groups with which they lived, played, and worked. In fact, we might see the game of "Letting the Bird Peck at the Fig" as a social performance that turned on the building or reinforcing of a consensus reality about the sexual identity of its players—individuals within a social group essentially acting out an agreed-upon reality that all desired sexual intercourse with the opposite sex, something by no means given in the Renaissance.

Perhaps the most important and unlikely-seeming social space where sexual identity was assayed and confirmed was the marital bed. Most people are aware of the tradition of bedding newlyweds with public and often bawdy ceremonies and the examination and display of bed sheets the morning after.[6] Here we have a crucial evaluation of a couple's sexual identity carried out by and for some of the most important groups that sustained that couple's identity: an erotically charged bedding and the public display of freshly washed bed sheets helped mark the correct sexual identity for newlyweds for family, neighbors, and broader solidarities—male as functioning phallus and woman as former virgin and now sexual wife on the road to childbearing.[7]

A nicely irreverent refashioning of this theme can be found in Pietro Aretino's *Dialogues*, set in Rome but written in Venice in the 1530s. Nanna, the autobiographical narrator of the early books of this work, provides a revealing account of her marriage night. The potential problems in her marriage with a rich old man whose sexual identity was quickly laid out as being largely impotent were myriad, but the immediate problem was that Nanna was no longer a virgin owing to her earlier adventures in a convent. Fortunately for the plot at least, the only group that was aware of her changed sexual status was her former sisters in the convent and their clerical partners in crime, and as they were not involved in her marriage or conveniently in the tale of Nanna's exploits any longer, their knowledge did not condition the shared consensus reality of her future family or neighbors, who still identified her as a virgin. There was, however, the more significant matter that the consensus reality of virginity, crucial for marriage, could be undermined by the simple reality of her body—at least as far as the Renaissance idea of a virgin's body was concerned. But her mother solved that problem with a ruse designed to deal with the public needs of her wedding night: "There came the night of the sexual coupling, which [her future spouse] . . . awaited like the harvest awaits the farmer; and my sweet mother's cleverness was beautiful: she, knowing that my virginity had left me in the lurch, killed one of the chickens for the wedding and filled an eggshell with the blood; showing me how to fool him."[8]

That evening in bed with her husband she played the required virginal role—it took all the old man's strength and stored-up desire plus her mother's aid to actually consummate the union. But that coupling concluded *publicly* with her artful use of the chicken's blood playing a central role: "It was then that my screams made all the neighbors come to their windows and my mother rushed back to the bedroom: there seeing the blood of the chicken that had dyed the sheets . . . she convinced him that I should sleep the rest of the night with her. In the morning all the neighbors were discussing my honesty and in the neighborhood they did not speak of anything else."[9] Humorous and cynical as this account of Nanna's wedding night is, it turns on the Renaissance understanding of how crucial that moment of sexual identification was— Nanna's whole neighborhood approved of what occurred sexually in her marriage bed. Her honesty and virginity had been made public along with her aged

husband's sexual functioning, and everyone was happy at least in part because the correct sexual identities of the newlyweds had been confirmed. Even
though Nanna was not a virgin and her husband was barely capable of functioning sexually, the required consensus reality had been confirmed for them
as newlyweds for family and neighbors.

Yet if one looks more closely at the wedding-bedding scene, there is a hint
of something deeper, more personal about young Nanna's sexual identity. In
the midst of retelling how she successfully fooled her husband, Nanna admitted, "Tasting that hot joint I could not hold myself back from letting myself
go . . . and I did not yell [anymore] until his wilted flower fell from my vase."[10]
Nanna reveals here that she was not entirely the master manipulator of men
that she is often portrayed as being by modern critics. Aretino fashioned her to
be that, clearly, but part of the erotic quality of the *Dialogues* stems from the
fact that she cannot resist enjoying her sexual encounters. This suggests, however, a more internal sexual identity that Aretino had created for his character—not only did she use sex, but she enjoyed it and could not resist enjoying
it. And, significantly, we cannot see this solely in terms of external acts or practice; Aretino needs to have his character report it to us even in the unexpected
moment when it takes over with her largely ineffective husband.[11] For our purposes it does not matter that Aretino was probably creating a negative identity
for his Nanna, perhaps a reassuringly negative identity—a whore is always a
whore even before she becomes one; what matters is that he was creating an
internal identity and anticipates that his Renaissance audience will be able to
understand it. In the end this internal self melds well with Nanna's external
self—after all, she is a fiction—and she decides that she can lead an honest
life only by becoming what she is: a whore, or as she puts it, "selling what her
shop has to sell." And when she openly becomes a whore and sells what her
shop has to sell, tellingly those groups with whom she interacts will form a consensus reality that she *is a whore*, exactly what Aretino is claiming she is.

Returning to marital beds, less noted perhaps than the community evaluation of the first night's sex were the ongoing anxieties about sexual identity
which could beleaguer them. In Venice as elsewhere in the Renaissance, there
was a wide range of magic concerned with punishing enemies and forcing others to act in accordance with one's wishes which I studied for an earlier book.[12]
One of the most popular forms of that magic was binding or hammering magic
that made men incapable of performing their marital duties on that fateful
first night and often thereafter.[13] It appears there was an active business in
such magic, precisely because male sexual performance was such an important

part of consensus reality of sexual identity, and lack of performance was widely discussed. In 1588, for example, the Venetian Holy Office heard a case involving a friar, Gabriele Garofolo, accused of teaching magic to unbind the phalluses of newlywed males. Tellingly, Fra Gabriele did not deny the accusation; rather, he presented himself as providing a much needed service to the poor men of his parish who were unable to perform sexually. He informed the Holy Office that in his parish, there were many men who were "bound," who could not "consummate their marriages." His cure was a nice blend of the holy and the profane: "Against such binding ties," he reported, "it is effective to dissolve some dust from a church bell and drink it with an egg or broth while saying a psalm." And he claimed proudly that his public service had worked in consummating many marriages and curing many men.[14]

Fra Gabriele's service to the men of his parish brings us back to Foucault, for although Foucault denied that there was a sense of sexual identity in the premodern world, he did perceptively see that sex was deployed in a discursive system that he labeled "Alliance." A cornerstone of that system of Alliance was family; in turn, a central moment in the forming of families was marriage, and, as we have seen, a crucial aspect of marriage was the successful sexual functioning of males in the marriage bed. Unconsummated marriages were essentially not marriages.[15] All this might be reduced to Alliance, but it seems to me truer to the complexities of the situation to recognize the significant role that consensus realities of sexual identity played in the formation of a marriage and afterward in the organization and disciplining of a family, as well as in the relationship of the new couple—both as individuals and as a couple—with the broader groups with which they interacted. Alliance and sexual identity as formed in and disciplined by consensus realities are both significant factors in understanding what occurred in the Renaissance marriage bed and beyond.[16]

Clearly such sexual distinctions were closely tied also to gender distinctions, which were also closely monitored and disciplined by consensus realities. The Renaissance discourse about the differences between men and women had many elements that turned on sexual identity, and in turn many elements of sexual identity could be partially understood in terms of gender. Significantly, however, gender seems to have implied sexuality more explicitly for women. Females were viewed first as asexual children, then sexually possible and marriageable with their first period, then sexually potent and realized as wives producing legitimate children, and finally sexually dangerous as widows. Tellingly, those who did not marry were also identified sexually—nuns, as brides of Christ (a sexual relationship whose rich discursive territory has been largely overlooked), or *zitelle,* a term that signified an unmarried adult woman capable of sex but who did not participate in it.[17] And, of course, illicit categories such as whore and concubine were primarily sexual. Thus a woman's sexuality was ideally always labeled and central to her status and identity.[18]

Significantly, there are a host of signs that a woman became truly a woman only at marriage and perhaps once again at a deeper level when she had her first child—signs that were easily read by the various groups of which she was a member and thus crucial for reconstructing her identity as wife and mother. Most important throughout Renaissance Italy, when a woman married, she went through a series of defining rites of passage that differed a bit from place to place but which normally included moving to a new residence, often with elaborate ceremonies; and, of course, she took a new name. In turn, she went from being formally powerless and officially a child to being officially, at least, an adult with all that that implied. And most significantly from a Renaissance perspective, she became sexual in the context of a family goal of producing its own next generation. Perhaps one reason the followers of Foucauldian orthodoxy have overlooked this close association of sex and female identity in the Renaissance is that their studies have tended to focus on males and on male-male relationships at the expense of women's experiences.

When we turn to males, one must concede that the centrality of sex to Renaissance notions of identity seems less clear. A closer look at the expected course of male sexual development suggests, however, that this is partially an illusion caused by the fact that sexual identity for males changed across the span of a life and thus might seem less prescriptive. Young males, like females, were presumed to be sexually innocent, but once they reached puberty, they were seen as losing their asexual status without gaining adult status. Rather, they embarked upon a long period of what might be labeled adolescence. That term, however, is so freighted with modern meanings and that span of years had so many valences specific to the Renaissance that I prefer using the term often used at the time to describe it, *gioventù,* and the related terms *giovane* (for a male in that age range) and *giovanile* (as an adjective describing that age). At the highest social levels a male could remain a *giovane* until well into his thirties.[19] Artisans and lower-level workers moved through this period of life more rapidly, but it appears that they did not gain adulthood in the eyes of contemporaries until their early twenties.

This long *gioventù,* stretching to twenty years for the upper classes and six to ten years for the lower classes, was a crucial period of transition for males and a crucial period of rather nebulous sexual identity as well.[20] In fact, one reason *gioventù* garnered so much attention in the Renaissance is that it was seen as a highly problematic period not only in terms of behavior and social placement for males but also in terms of sexual identity. *Giovani*, for example, could display themselves as quite feminine with homoerotic innuendos, as both feminine and masculine with a corresponding sexual ambivalence, or as decidedly masculine; thus in Venice, while adult males of the upper classes usually wore black, formless, asexual robes, young males more regularly opted for showy tights that displayed legs and bottoms in all their ambivalent splendor and magnificent codpieces often of contrasting color and impressive dimensions.[21] This ambivalence was played with on the stage, recognized in literature, disciplined by complex laws and traditions, but it was eliminated only with time as a *giovane* grew up, married, and became a "man." At marriage sexual ambiguity ended, and crucially for our argument that moment of fixing of adult identity turned on sex—a male took on the full adult role by demonstrating through his sexual performance in marriage that he deserved to be an adult first by consummating the marriage, then by producing children.[22]

What, we might ask, was sexually different about that long period of *gioventù* that preceded adulthood? In *The Boundaries of Eros* I argued that in Venice this long period was one in which many *giovani* experimented with sexual roles, moving ideally, however, from roles that assumed sexual passivity to an adultlike role that required an active sexuality, even with other males. This active/passive division of sexual identity may be the deepest form of sexual distinction in the Renaissance. It was used widely in Venice and beyond, and it served to characterize at a basic level virtually all forms of sexual relations. In that complex period of *gioventù*, however, there was room for considerable play, especially in the area of male-male sexual relations. These relationships were conceptualized as involving an older *giovane* taking an active role in sex with a younger partner who was passive. As I argued in *Boundaries*, this was clearly not modern homosexuality for a host of reasons, but perhaps most tellingly because it implied for neither partner the fixed identity that modern disciplines have associated with homosexuality and most simply because it was embedded in a world and discursive systems that were decidedly nonmodern.

I would suggest that this long period of indeterminate sexuality for males has contributed to the perception that sexual identity did not exist in the Renaissance. And while it is true that this period of indeterminacy meant that

Renaissance males did not define their sexual identity in terms of a binary division of either heterosexuality or homosexuality, there is every indication that there was an ideal path that a male was to traverse in his sexual maturation. This path was inscribed in a host of disciplining discourses, internalized to a degree, and, more important, traveled by a youth as a social performance of self—a performance of identity before the groups that a male lived and worked with in order to construct, negotiate, and maintain with each a consensus reality about his developing sexuality. Considerable uncertainty remains, however, about how this period of *gioventù* fit into the sexual and social dynamic of Renaissance society. Some have claimed that male-male sexuality, legally defined as a subset of sodomy, was a virtually normal feature of everyday life for *giovani*, widely practiced and generally accepted although occasionally punished with mild penalties. Those who sustain this position argue that serious punishment of such activity was reserved for atypical violent acts, such as rape or assault. Normally, however, such activity was accepted and often subsumed under the rubric of male friendship. In this vision Florence has become a near utopia from a homoerotic perspective, with a large percentage of the *giovani* there participating at one time or another in such relationships while their elders looked on in bemused toleration.[23]

Cities like Venice, however, suggest a somewhat less rosy picture. There across the fifteenth and sixteenth centuries sodomy was punished irregularly but severely. A typical example is the prosecution of a group of male "sodomites" denounced to the feared secret police of Venice, the Council of Ten, in 1474. The Ten's rhetoric figured sodomy as a sexual crime that threatened God's wrath against the city itself. And the council acted on that rhetoric with secret and aggressive trials that ended with a brutal death for active sodomites, who were executed between the Columns of Justice at the ceremonial center of the city, *even nonviolent giovani.* But following the distinction noted above, the Ten assumed that males were either active or passive, reserving the death penalty only for the active partners—again here the Renaissance perception of sexual identity was a marker, a most deadly one.

Two active members of the 1474 group were executed with relative dispatch.[24] Two passive members, perhaps warned in advance of their impending arrest, had fled the city. But the Ten was most concerned about a pair identified as "lovers": Simeone and Marino. The problem in the council members' eyes was that Simeone at eighteen was getting to be too old to be accepted as a passive partner; he did not seem to be following the correct path of sexual development. Thus they contemplated an unusual penalty for him—cutting off his nose and then forcing him to stand by and watch the decapitation and burning of his lover, Marino.[25] After considerable debate carried out by some of the most important men in Venice sitting on the Ten, they merely ordered that Simeone receive twenty-five lashes and be banished for five years. His older, active lover, however, *was* decapitated and burned before his eyes between the Columns of Justice.

Clearly, Venetian justice seems much sterner than Florentine. It should be noted, however, that in Florence, as in Venice and elsewhere, the discourses of law and traditional morality never lost their apocalyptic flavor with dire warnings that such activity threatened the wrath of God and the punishments of Sodom and Gomorrah. Significantly, however, in Renaissance Venice prosecutions tended to focus on either groups of young sodomites or older men who could no longer be considered *giovani*. Thus it may be that although penalties were more severe in Venice, there was still a tacit acceptance of *giovanile* sodomy which fit in a more widely accepted vision of sexual development for males. It may be also that the apparent contrast between Florence and Venice turns more on which group's consensus reality about sexual identity dominated at any particular moment. In Venice, where a communal sense of civic morality appears to have been stronger, smaller-group evaluations of family and peers may well have been overwhelmed from time to time by a push to burn sodomy out of society. In Florence, where family and clan and personal ties appear to have dominated, smaller-group consensus realities that saw male-male sodomy as a passing and not particularly problematic stage on the way to "correct" adult sexuality may well have won out. In the end, however, only further research will tell if there is some intermediate ground between the vision of a wide sexual freedom for males in Florence and a more restricted situation in Venice, where nonetheless *giovani* had considerable room for discreet ambivalence.

Suggestive of this contrast in interpretation and apparently contemporary perceptions of sodomy as well is the contrast one finds in Venice between the punishment of young men like Simeone and Marino and Pietro Aretino's fascinating comedy *Il marescalco*. Although set in Mantua at the court of Federico Gonzaga, this comedy, completed in Venice in the late 1520s, is rich with references to Venice and was clearly designed to please a specifically Venetian audience as well as a wider Renaissance one.[26] When the play opens, the lead character, the Marescalco (or Master of the Horse; like several other characters in the comedy, he is always identified by his title), has learned that the

Duke has promised to marry him to a beautiful young woman who comes complete with a handsome dowry of 4,000 ducats. This clearly is the dream of every right-thinking *giovane* ready to take on his correct adult sexual identity in the Renaissance—a marriage to a rich and beautiful woman. But it is the Marescalco's nightmare, for he hates the idea of marriage, wishing to remain in his *giovanile* world of male-male sexuality. And his vocal resistance allows Aretino to adroitly develop several themes: first, a series of laments about life at court; second, a brief but humorous reprise of the Renaissance debate over marriage; and third, a slightly veiled but ultimately triumphant defense of sodomy—a defense that turns on Renaissance sexual identity. In the end the Marescalco discovers to his delight that he has been the victim of a joke (*burla*) constructed by the Duke: his beautiful bride is none other than a comely young page—the ideal sexual partner for his tastes. The Marescalco thus has a boy bride and presumably lives happily ever after.

Here we seem to be in that utopian world of Florence where even a ruler can joke with one of his subjects about his sexual practices with *giovani* and actually cater to them. Yet if we look deeper, it might be argued that this comedy creates problems for that Foucauldian vision: for rather than treating male-male sexual relations as mere sexual practices—an insignificant passing phase on the way to correct male sexuality—the Duke constructs an elaborate joke that turns on the fact that the Marescalco has a different sexual identity than the norm. His practices have become his social identity—a consensus reality—recognized by the other players at court and by a Renaissance audience as well. And more significant yet, his practices are a sexual identity that the Marescalco defends aggressively to the other individuals and social groups with which he interacts and has no intention of giving up under any circumstances.

Early in the comedy there is a humorous discussion between the Marescalco and his Balia, who is anxious to see her onetime charge honorably married.[27] But he resists all her blandishments, and as he gruffly does so, he creates a sustained attack on marriage, women, and the ideal Renaissance sexual identity for men. The give-and-take begins with a vague attack on the Marescalco's life which circles around his continued attraction to *giovani* to drive straight toward the Balia's vision of a better life as a husband and father. She pleads with him, "Come, come now, wake up and throw off your blasphemy and sinful ways." The Marescalco queries, echoing our own curiosity at this stage, "What do you mean blasphemy and sinful ways?" Teasingly the moment of ambiguity is drawn out with her allusive and elusive response: "You know what I am

talking about." And clearly the Marescalco knows what sexual sin she is referring to, for he fires back angrily, "What, have I crucified Christ?" The Balia
continues to evade with a "No, but . . . " Still the Marescalco presses on, pushing at the Balia's evident reluctance to name what she is referring to when she
labels his ways "blasphemy and sinful."[28] The dance of the unsaid continues
for a few more lines, until finally the Balia comes as close to saying what she
is trying not to say as she is willing: "You know very well what. Now it's time
to follow my advice: take a wife, my son, and establish some honor for yourself.
Stop running after youthful pleasures [*gioventudini*] and begin your family and
household."[29]

Do we need to ask what youthful pleasures, *gioventudini*, would come close
to crucifying Christ, threaten the Marescalco's honor, and virtually silence the
normally loquacious Balia? Evidently, and it will become ever more evident as
the comedy progresses, she is attacking his incorrect sexual identity, his interest in *giovani*, and his desire to continue his life of youthful sodomy as an adult
without taking on a wife and a family. The Balia tries to lure him away from
all this and into his correct sexual identity—and his destiny it appears, given
the Duke's commitment to marry him—with a series of laudatory claims
about the sweetness of married life. Aretino, ever the playful manipulator of
language, however, undercuts her blissful depiction of marital felicity by humorously sliding her encomium from the sublime to the prosaic and on to the
ridiculous, punctuating her unwitting descent from the positive to the laughable with the occasional harshly negative comments of the Marescalco. For example, the Balia begins by explaining that taking a wife is like gaining paradise on earth: "It's paradise, simply heaven, to take a wife. . . . You return
home, and your good wife comes to greet you at the top of the stairs. Laughing and with a loving heart, she gives you a welcome that touches your very
soul. She helps you off with your jacket and then, full of joy, she turns to you,
and noting that you're all sweaty and tired, she dries you off with some towels
so white and so delicate that they soak up all your cares. Then she puts the wine
to cool and sets the table and fans you for a bit. And then she has you pee."[30]
The Marescalco's response is a telling laugh that presumably would have been
echoed by the audience and which aptly punctuates the Balia's descent from
promised pleasures to the mundanely ridiculous, literally from enjoying paradise to urinating.

After describing the sweet welcome he will have when he returns home as
a husband, the Balia turns to the evening meal that will follow, full of caresses
and wifely services, "Once you've peed, she sits you down to dinner, and she

excites your appetite with certain little sauces and little dishes that would rouse the dead. And while you eat, she never stops bringing you, with her sweetest little ways, now this plate and now that one and she offers you every tasty mouthful, saying, 'Taste this, taste that, try a bit of this, for my love, or if you love me taste this.' With such words all honeyed and sugarcoated, she'll send you not just to paradise, but several thousand miles at least above it."[31] The sugarcoated sweetness of marital bliss begins to cloy as Aretino's clever send-up of the pleasures of marriage continues with the Balia moving on to his bed-ding replete with his being washed by his loving mate with perfumed waters and ensconced between the sheets with many sweet kisses and words. Then the Balia promises that the good wife, after saying her prayers and climbing into bed next to him, "embracing him and kissing him all over," will say, "My heart, my soul, dear hope, dear life blood, sweet son, handsome father, am I your little girl? Your joy, your daughter?" And she concludes once again as-serting the sweet heavenliness of marriage: "When a man is treated like that, isn't he in paradise?" Given the Marescalco's sexual desires, his gruff "It doesn't seem so to me" is hardly surprising and once again punctuates Aretino's play-ful send-up of the Balia's enthusiastic encomium of marriage. But nicely the Marescalco opens the door for the central act of marital paradise from a Re-naissance perspective by asking her, "What's the point of all those kisses?" "They serve," she pounces, "to sweetly plant the seeds of little babies in a holy way."[32] Marriage, marital bed, sex, reproduction: here we are again at the heart of our Renaissance discourse of adult masculine identity—a discourse, a dis-cipline, and an identity that Aretino's hero violently rejects.

Later in the play the Pedant, already a stock character of learned foolish-ness, provides a similar defense of marriage and a thinly veiled warning about sodomy replete with echoes of the penalties that such transgressions could en-gender. With his typical pompous and unrestrained verbosity he informs the Marescalco, "His Excellency, His Most Illustrious Lordship loves you and thusly this very evening, gathering you to the matrimonial yoke, he will join you to such a well set-up *puella* [lit. a young girl who has not yet reached pu-berty] that *totum orbem* will envy you." Faced by the Marescalco's hostility and lack of enthusiasm for marriage, the Pedant advises him that he should recall what the Gospels have to say on the matter. The Marescalco inquires hopefully, "Are the Gospels against taking wives?" But, of course, his hopes for a biblical escape from his impending marital demise are quickly dashed. "Against?" the Pedant pontificates. "*Imo*, the opposite, and you should listen to their words . . . the Gospels say that the tree that does not bear fruit should be cut down and burned." Cut down and burned like Simeone's lover between the Columns of Justice, we and a Venetian audience know. And to make the point more clearly Aretino has the Pedant continue, "Based on this wisdom, so that you like the tree should make fruit and so that the human race should grow and multiply, our most magnificent Duke has chosen you to glory in a most uprighteous consort."[33] The Marescalco is the dangerously barren tree, whom the Duke will save from the fate of Sodom and Gomorrah by forcing him to marry and accept his required identity as husband and adult male—an identity that requires making fruit, that is, the heterosexual sexual intercourse necessary for reproduction.

Returning to the Balia's ongoing arguments in favor of leaving behind his dangerous *giovanile* pursuits and taking up the required sexual identity for adult males as husband and father, she continues to describe a host of other marital pleasures—all sweet and filled with Italian diminutives that seem unlikely to attract the gruff Marescalco. Tellingly, however, she concludes with the pleasures that grow out of the joys of becoming a father, the fruitful tree of the Pedant: "Then there come the little babies, little pets, little playthings." She gushes, "Oh God, what content, what sweetness a father feels when his little boy touches his face and his breast with those tender little hands, saying, 'Papa, my Papa, oh Papa.' And I've seen harder men then you wilt at the sound of that 'Papa.'" But significantly she concludes her long celebration of marriage with the key question of male Renaissance sexual identity: "Oh, when will I see you in that state?" The Marescalco's response is short but not so sweet: "On the feast day of Saint Con-Man, which falls three days after the Last Judgment."[34]

The Marescalco has rejected her cloyingly sweet vision of marital bliss from the first, and after comparing unfavorably having a wife with having syphilis, he insists: "A male servant is good enough to do all those things that you have taken so long to describe. And whenever you get tired of him, you can send him off to the whorehouse—something that you can't do with a wife."[35] Of course, his point is not entirely on the mark, for, evidently, male servants could not supply one of the essential objects of Renaissance marriage and heterosexual intercourse—children. But once again what is not quite said is telling, for it has already been established that the Marescalco's young servant, Giannicco, is not merely his sexual partner but his lover as well. Any doubt on the matter was cleared up early on in the comedy, in act 1, scene 2, when the friendly Messer Jacopo points out in passing that the two were always talking together and bickering and refers to Giannicco as the Marescalco's *pivo*—a term used at the time to refer to the younger male passive partner in a sexual relationship with an older male.[36] And I use the term *lover* advisedly, for as the play progresses, the playful banter between Giannicco and his master suggests a type of sentimental attachment. Sex and affection without children, without reproduction and continuation of the family line—this was no simple practice or pleasure but something that, if it endured beyond *gioventù*, as it appeared to be doing for the Marescalco, implied the rejection of the correct adult male sexual identity at the very heart of Renaissance social organization and continuity. And in Foucauldian terms it meant that in the Renaissance a man could reject Alliance (and sex whose goal was merely reproduction) for pleasure and masculine love.

These issues are underlined and taken deeper by the Balia relating to the Marescalco a dream that she had had the night before—a dream that turns on a suggestive echo of the game "Letting the Bird Peck at the Fig." "It seemed to me last night that near dawn I was in the garden sitting at the foot of the fig tree," she began, "and while I was listening to a little bird that was improvising a song, along came a bestial man who found the singing of the little bird annoying. He threw stones at it. But the little bird kept singing, and he kept throwing stones. And while that bird sang and he threw, I argued with the man and he argued with me. But in the end the little bird was allowed to stay on the fig. Have you understood my dream?"[37] What was the audience (or more likely the reader) of Aretino's comedy to make of this dream? How would they have understood it? If they had played the game "Letting the Bird Peck at the Fig" (or if they merely considered the popular double meanings of *bird* and *fig*), their expectations almost certainly would have set them up for the clever joke that was to follow.

Even without that context one would be tempted to immediately assume that the Balia's dream reflected a fulfillment of the wish that the Marescalco would soon succumb to marriage, albeit reluctantly, for as the Master of the Horse, the Marescalco was one of the people at court whose life brought him closest to the animal realm; thus, his gruff temper and rude manners are often labeled beastly by the other characters, and it was easy to identify him with the beastly man of the Balia's dream. In fact, it was that gruffness or beastliness that allowed him to throw stones and refuse the figs offered him so courteously by his Lord, in life and presumably in the Balia's dream as well. More important, perhaps, it was that lack of courtly polish, those bestial ways that allowed him to say clearly and directly the "truth" about women and marriage.

Still, for all his gruffness and ill-mannered directness, his Balia could have dreamed that hidden behind his beastly nature lay the good person whom she had nursed and loved as a *giovane,* in spite of his youthful "sins and blas-phemies." In that good man surely was well hidden a little bird who longed to sing, marry as an adult male should, and peck happily on a fig of his own. Thus, the Balia's dream probably would have been quickly understood by Aretino's audience, readers, and perhaps the Marescalco as well as a wish-fulfilling prog-nostication that his better side would win out over his beastly ways. In sum, the dream seemed to promise that after ineffectively throwing his stones at het-erosexual desires, settling onto his fig, he would learn the sweet pleasures of marriage and sing happily ever after—a perfect metaphor for the Renaissance ideal of the progressive sexual development of young men toward an active heterosexual identity expressed in marriage and producing children—main-taining the correct consensus reality of sexual practice for family, friends, court, and audience.

But Renaissance humor was built not only with such canny double mean-ings and wordplay; one of the favorite ploys for a well-turned joke, or *burla,* was the sudden, unexpected, and well-turned reversal—especially when that unexpected reversal left one shaking one's head ruefully at how completely one had missed the logic of what had been laid out leading up to it. And that is ex-actly what Aretino had set his Renaissance audience up for, for when the Balia asks, "Have you understood my dream?" the Marescalco replies, "Sure. But the real issue is to understand how you've understood it." Then, with perfect comic timing, the Balia overturns all expectations, explaining quickly, "The little bird that was singing is your boy, Giannicco."[38] Giannicco is the singing phal-lus, not the Marescalco!

This surprise reading of her dream creates that abrupt break in our fantasies of *uccelli*/phalluses, *fichi*/vaginas, and marital bliss, a break that creates, if not laughter, at least a bemused smile at how well Aretino and his innocent, paradise-dreaming, Balia have set us up and played with our expectations. But it also stops us to ask a crucial question that underlies the joke and, I would suggest, the very plot of the comedy that has been largely missed by modern readers. For to understand the full richness of Aretino's humor we have to un-derstand that Giannicco was also at a crucial turning point in his sexual iden-tity: his bird was beginning to sing, and he was ready to go in search of figs of his own, as the Balia's dream reveals. A Renaissance audience would have im-mediately seen the issue: Giannicco had reached an age at which he was no longer content to be merely the Marescalco's *pivo,* and that meant that the Marescalco's happy sexual life without women was in danger from that angle as well. From this perspective a happy ending for the Marescalco, as required by the comedic genre, would necessitate not only avoiding a marriage to a woman but also finding a new lover, and Aretino cleverly provides us with a happy ending that fulfills both needs—a boy bride for his protagonist who fulfills his desires and frees Giannicco to go hunting figs of his own.

To return to the fig tree of the Balia's dream, although she does not suggest that it refers to the genitals of the Marescalco's future wife, as we might have at first expected, the fact that the bird sitting on it is only Giannicco does not necessarily disqualify it as a metaphor for that future wife. Given Aretino's playful humor, the idea of Giannicco sitting on the Marescalco's fig tree, having sexual relations with his wife, is not as outlandish as it at first sounds. In fact, it anticipates a witty joke and a theme that will return. Later in the comedy Giannicco tells the Count and the Knight, representatives of the Lord of Mantua and his court, of a ploy that he has dreamed up which he hopes will convince the Marescalco to take a wife.

As the Count and the Knight have just been gruffly rebuffed by the Marescalco when they congratulated him on his impending marriage, they are all ears as Giannicco explains, "I told him that if she was beautiful and rich, he should take her the Half Way, and that way we would all luck out." Puzzled by this strange suggestion, the Count asks, "What are you talking about?" Enthusiastically Giannicco clarifies: "It's like this, sir: he'll have to put out for a few days after the marriage, but soon the usual handsome young guys will begin flocking around [his wife] like roosters; then he will have his fill of the cocks and I'll have my fill of the hen. What do you think?" One is tempted to agree with the Count's laughing reply: "Solomon himself couldn't have given better advice."[39] And tellingly the singing bird, Giannicco, leaves them and ends this scene with yet another song. "The young widow, when she sleeps alone, / Has no reason to complain of me. / She has no reason. / She has no reason." Of course not—for exactly as the Balia's dream has innocently revealed, Giannicco's bird is beginning to sing, and even young widows will have no reason to complain about him.

But returning to the Balia's explanation of her dream, she, of course, is not yet in on the final joke of the comedy, and thus she still sees it as foretelling the eventual correct marriage of the Marescalco. Actually she claims that Giannicco's singing bird advises the bestial man to marry. But, as noted above, the fig may not be the Marescalco's future wife or her genitals, and if the bird is a phallus, it is the phallus of his young male lover, not his. In essence Giannicco is a youth on the correct path of sexual identity, moving from a passive to an active role that would prepare him for marriage and adulthood—his bird had begun to sing, and suggestively in virtually every scene in which he appears, Giannicco himself sings as if telling us something about his correctly developing sexual identity. The Marescalco, in contrast, was risking his honor, his place at court, and his adult male status by refusing to move on to marriage—refusing, we might say, to play the game "Letting the Bird Peck at the Fig."

In real life in Venice this could be the stuff of tragedy ending between the Columns of Justice, but Aretino turns it to comedy: when we come to the scene in which the bride is being dressed for the wedding, it is finally revealed to the audience that she is he—the Marescalco's bride-to-be is the young page Carlo—a perfectly perverse and humorous reversal of the usual happy ending of Renaissance comedies. Thus the audience and readers learn that they will have their wedding as the genre requires. But, fittingly, it will not be the wedding that the main character fears and detests but a wedding that he will appreciate and which, at least in theory, the audience might well fear if it were not so funny and so truly an Aretine ending. Aretino was clearly playing on (and with) the ambiguity that surrounded such male-male relationships at the time at the very least for laughter and, at a deeper level it might be argued, to underline the illogic of the Renaissance ideal of sex limited to marriage and reproduction. Perhaps, in the end, he was even attempting to defend a different ideal of sodomy—a warm, affectionate relationship between an older, but not yet fully adult, male and a willing youth, like the earlier relationship between the Marescalco and Giannicco.[40]

Suggestively, in tune with the expectations of the time, Aretino presents the bride-to-be, the young page Carlo, as making the transition from being a male youth to a beautiful young woman effortlessly, for Carlo is in that androgynous period of male life: the first years of *gioventù*, when his passivity, lack of a beard, and youthful figure allow him a perfect ambivalence. On one level Carlo's transformation into a young bride was a gender switch, a realigning of the cultural signs that marked him as male. The young page quickly learned to imitate the cultural cues of femininity, as one of the matrons who is dressing him points out approvingly: "By my faith, anyone would believe that you're a young girl. . . . You have the airs, the speech, the manner, and the walk." But at the same time it was also a sexual transition that turned on a deeper sexual flexibility—an as-yet-unformed adult male sexuality—which allowed the youth to be sexually passive like a woman on his way to eventually becoming fully sexually active as an adult. Young Carlo expresses it best when, dressed as the bride, he boasts of his new sexuality, "I am a miracle! Once a man, I've become a woman, and the Marescalco will marry me."[41]

Such were the sexual miracles of Renaissance *giovani.* They could be laugh-ingly celebrated, as in this comedy, and they could be feared, as they were in the harsh laws of Venice and other cities. But for the youths of the time, such "miracles" could be both empowering, leaving considerable room for Renais-sance sexual self-fashioning, and difficult, opening the door for numerous doubts about achieving sexual adulthood and adult status in general. It has of-ten been noted that the transition to full adult male status was a long and diffi-cult one in the Renaissance and one that created a wide range of discourses from the humorous to the disciplinary. And certainly there was much more than sex and gender involved, but to miss the central role that both played would be to miss some of the most important keys to male identity and sense of self in the period.

The miracle of Carlo's literal reformation as a bride has one last scene rich with reversals and revelations, the long-awaited marriage scene. Physically threatened, the Marescalco is pushed along despite his fainting at the sight of his bride, despite his claims that he has a hernia that prevents him from per-forming sexually, despite his travesty of the Petrarchian language of love—he "sweats and is frozen" at the same time, his heart beats wildly, he pales be-fore his bride, he is close to passing out, not because of true love but rather the opposite.[42] Still, the marriage goes ahead typically, but tellingly, garbled by the Pedant who performs the ceremony and in doing so pontificates on the key sex-ual significance of marriage for the Renaissance formulated in both religious and secular terms: on the religious side the Pedant notes that sexual intercourse was initiated by the Lord God to produce children and fill the earth, his cre-ation, with subjects, just as on the secular side it is being initiated by the Lord of Mantua, Duke Federico, to fill his realm with subjects. The Pedant, more-over, in his learned confusion manages to recall that man is different from beasts not only because of his reason but also because of a social sensibility that moves him to marry and produce children—something, of course, that hu-morously recalls the beastly nature of the Marescalco with his refusal to marry. His speech, richly larded with Latinate foolishness, is worth quoting more fully:

In principio creavit Deus caelum et terram. Praeterea, He made *pisces per aequora, et inter aves turdos, et inter quadrupedes Gloria prima lepus.* I have been saying that God the Father, after He created heaven and earth, created fish for the sea and birds for the air and for the woods deer and bucks. *Ulterius, ad similitudinem suam* he mixed up from clay the masculine and the feminine, *postea* he bound them, *idest,*

He coupled them together so that they would grow and multiply *sine* adultery *usquequo* they *filled up the seats* that the overweeningly proud and ungodly followers of Lucifer had emptied. And the Lord made man *principaliter* to trample [*conculcante*] *leonem et draconem*, and He made him a rational animal with his sight, his touch, and his other faculties *solum* so that his desires would be different from those of the beasts, *et ideo* so that he would copulate with women, as is shown in Genesis, where Adam and Eve are discussed.[43]

Once again here the Pedant transforms into humor what could well have been a serious discussion of contemporary marital and sexual values by quickly sliding from the high to the low and undercutting even his potentially serious theological points with laughter. As a result, what were widely held Renaissance views of marriage become dangerously laughable and even ridiculous. Marriage and sexual reproduction to "fill up" the "seats" that Lucifer and his followers have left unfilled has a perhaps unintentional but decidedly sodomitic ring. But more telling yet, the claim that God made man primarily to trample lions and dragons signals strongly the foolishness of the Pedant's arguments, especially with the strange verb *conculcante*—with the syllable *cul* (ass) in the middle—mocking the argument and itself suggesting sodomy. Throughout the comedy Aretino has formulated a host of original words in Italian based on *cul* or incorporating the term to suggest humorously sodomy and sodomites; here in the midst of a supposedly theological discussion of the benefits of marriage and reproduction he places one of his most subversive usages of the term.

What follows in this speech, however, is the final ridiculing blow, for he has the Pedant claim that God made man different from beasts—and by implication the beastly Marescalco—"solum" (only) so that he could copulate with women. That sexual intercourse between males and females is what separates humans from beasts is obviously in and of itself ridiculous. That this is somehow associated with the only reason men were given rationality again in its illogic seems to mock the standard arguments that God made the sexes for marriage and reproduction. In fact, we find the Pedant inadvertently rehearsing a fairly widespread medieval belief that animals were sexually polyvalent—in distinction to the clearly inaccurate argument occasionally advanced today that same-sex sexuality is not encountered among animals and thus unnatural—and contrasting it with the idea that humans were given reason so that men would copulate with women.

It might well be that in addition to the Pedant's usual erudite foolishness there was a reversal here which would have appealed to the social biases of the Renaissance upper classes, the anticipated readers and audiences of this comedy. Male-male sex was often associated with upper-class learning and academic settings (both positively and negatively); thus, asserting that such behavior went against reason reversed the obvious and once more appeared ridiculous. Whether this reading is accurate or not, in the midst of mocking the strictures against sodomy and the labeling of sodomites as beastlike, Aretino is clearly harking back to our beastly Marescalco and apparently defending his "beastly" ways once again. In sum, the arguments in favor of traditional marriage and sexuality and against sodomy as they appear more and more foolish coming from the mouth of the Pedant open the way for a rethinking of the Marescalco's commitment to sodomy—a rethinking that the whole comedy laughingly proposes.

Yet for all that, the beastly Marescalco does finally marry. After the bride gives her carefully practiced and maidenly "Sìiii" to the Pedant's "Are you willing, most delicious lady, to take for your perpetual husband the personal Marescalco of the Most Excellent and Illustrious Lord Duke Federico, First Duke of Mantua?" the Marescalco tries one last time to claim a hernia as a medical excuse. But in the face of the quick denial of Giannicco ("Rubbish. He is totally closed up!") and the threats of the Count, who draws a knife ("Either you decide to say yes or you decide to have me finish you off right here"), he finally blurts out, "Yes, sir. I want her. I'm willing. Mercy!"[44] And they kiss—another public moment of display of sexual identity, nicely reversed by Aretino for humorous effect, as, of course, we and the audience know that this is a marital kiss between two males. Moreover, it was no ordinary marital kiss at another, more titillating level, as the Marescalco makes bitterly clear, "Your tongue, eh? Already the fun begins. God might be able to make her a martyr, but neither God nor her mother can make this one a virgin. O horns, I haven't been able to avoid your sad tune! Give me patience!"[45]

The Marescalco's bride had revealed with a clearly nonvirginal kiss that *her* sexual identity was wrong—the consensus reality of her virginity and chastity conveyed to the Marescalco by friends and fellow courtiers is belied by her erotic kiss. The Marescalco's worse fears seem to be true, and that, of course, makes the timing right for the central reversal of the comedy—the stage discovery that his bride's sexual identity *is* wrong, but right for him. Determined to see how bad things really are, he begins to examine his mate: "Hold still, don't wiggle so. Move a little this way. Come a little closer . . . closer yet." And as his hands discover the page's masculinity: "Oh my! This is really wonderful!"[46] All the cast members, who have come together on stage for the wedding scene, gather around laughing, discovering that they too have been fooled and that the bride is actually Carlo, that the Marescalco has a boy bride.[47]

The comedy quickly closes with the happily married couple being whisked offstage to celebrate and the Pedant tarrying a moment to promise the audience that he will soon compose a work that will attack marriage and show that those who escape it are truly the happiest of men. The brisk pace of these last moments and their laughter sweep one along so smoothly that one may miss the true bite of Aretino's humor. The Duke has promised the Marescalco a typical Renaissance happy ending to his comedy—a bride. And with one last joke on us all, Aretino has made the Duke deliver. Reading correctly the sexual identity of the Marescalco—as do the other players—the Duke has selected in the *giovane*, Carlo, someone with the perfect sexual identity for him, a young passive youth. This is a comedy that plays with the Renaissance sense of sexual identity, not a modern sense surely, but one that would work for a sixteenth-century audience in Italy. Aretino's last laugh turns on his happy ending—the Marescalco has his boy bride, and it might be suggested that now even Giannicco will be happy, as his singing bird finally will have a chance to play "Letting the Bird Peck at the Fig."

CHAPTER 2

Playing with the Devil

The Pleasures and Dangers of Sex and Play

It was a winter's evening in the 1540s. January. Florence. Four aristocratic young men ("de i primi e più gentili della terra") were playing instruments and singing after dinner at the home of their hostess, a rich and noble widow. One of these youths was the widow's brother, which suggests that she was still young, much the same age as her guests, as was not uncommon in a time when young women often married much older men. Outside the sky grew gray and laden with snow, which began to fall silently, heavily. Within an hour the snow had built up in the courtyard, and the young men left their music to go outside and play in the newly fallen snow ("a trastullare colla neve"). As they laughed and threw snowballs, the well-mannered ("manierosa") young widow watching from the window decided to join the fun and attack her brother and the other youths with the help of her female guests, four equally aristocratic and well-mannered young women.

With her friends she planned a lightheartedly traitorous attack. Quietly they gathered the snow that had collected on the roof of her villa and built a stockpile of snowballs with the aid of several female servants. Then from the windows that faced the courtyard they launched their attack on the youths playing in the snow below. Snowballs rained down on the young men. Taken by surprise, they playfully tried to counterattack, but the women had by far the best of the battle of the sexes, given their superior strategic position and preparation. For a third of an hour, as long as the snow lasted, the women had a wonderful time, a marvelous game/play ("meravigliosa festa"), and for once the young aristocratic males had by far the worst of the action. In the end they were left lamenting their defeat, wet, and bedraggled ("imbrodolati e molli") in the courtyard as the women, laughing, shut the windows and went off to change and warm themselves by the fire.

This playful snowball fight of a winter's evening, this idyllic aristocratic moment, this brief battle of the sexes, evokes nicely a theme that is often overlooked when historians consider the history of sex and gender—the way play is regularly deeply intertwined with the construction and understanding of both in many societies and cultures, much as we saw in Chapter 1 with another aristocratic game, "Letting the Bird Peck at the Fig." No matter that this moment of play between the sexes was formally a fiction—it served as the opening for the story that in a Renaissance tradition, following the lead of Boccaccio, framed a mid-sixteenth-century collection of novelle, *Le cene*, by Anton Francesco Grazzini, called Il Lasca—for it has the necessary ring of veracity to make the frame story work for a late Renaissance audience.[1] Of course, it may well be that aristocratic youth were not so well mannered or fine, yet that playful moment evokes an ideal that suggests that we need to look more closely at how play, sex, and gender interacted in the Renaissance.

This is especially the case because, even with all the recent excellent studies of sex and gender, few have considered sex, or gender for that matter, in terms of play. Troublingly also when I turned from literature, where references to play and specifically sexual play are relatively easily found, to archival documents, I could think of relatively few that referred to sex and play together. But I was unsure whether this was because there were few or whether I had been blinded in my own research by the concerns of recent historiography, which, given the vicissitudes of our times, seem focused on returning inexorably to politics and power.[2] In addition, in looking for sex as play in archival texts, a more basic problem arose—what exactly was I looking for? What do we mean by play and, more important, what was the meaning of play at the time? Johan Huizinga in his famous book on play, *Homo Ludens: A Study of the Play Element in Culture*, provided a definition that has become classic: "Summing up the formal characteristics of play we might call it a free activity standing quite consciously outside 'ordinary' life as being 'not serious,' but at the same time absorbing the player intensely and utterly. It is an activity connected with no material interest. . . . It proceeds within its own proper boundaries of time and space according to fixed rules and in an orderly manner."[3]

Suggestively, Huizinga, as he considered the broader implications of this definition, rather quickly expanded it to include virtually all of life under the rubric of play, including a wide range of things that on the surface do not appear to be particularly playful, such as ritual and most of high culture. At the same time, however, he also managed to eliminate sex from his world of play.[4] Today it seems curious that on the one hand Huizinga appears to have included too much in his definition and on the other excluded a whole range of activity that might seem central to play, such as sex. Perhaps the underlying paradox of Huizinga's exclusion of sex from his definition of play turns on the perennial scholarly difficulty of constructing definitions that are free of the values and perceptions of a particular time and place. Huizinga, writing a serious book on play in the midyears of the twentieth century, wanted his subject to be at once playful and serious (the mid-1940s were clearly a most serious time, and *Homo Ludens* was first published in 1944). And while he may well have been aware of the paradoxical, virtually quixotic, nature of his desire, in the end he wrote a book about the serious work of play.[5]

Looking more closely at the way play was described in the Renaissance itself, one finds significantly that play (*gioco*) was a concept of great and expanding interest in fifteenth- and sixteenth-century Italy.[6] A host of works examined the subject, and just as the sixteenth century saw a series of compendiums (or protoencyclopedic texts) on things as diverse as fashion, professions, and manners, it also provided some of the first attempts at collecting and describing large numbers of games. Girolamo Bargagli's *Dialogo de'giuochi che nelle vegghie sanese si usano di fare* (Dialogue on the Games That Are Played at Sienese Evening Gatherings), written about 1563 and first published in 1572, is perhaps the best-known example. It collected 130 games, giving a brief description of how each should be played.[7] But a quick glance at Bargagli's work suggests that it provides a very specific view of what gaming and play should involve. It is more prescriptive than descriptive, and its explicit aim was to catalog and explain the *aristocratic* games that could be played with "honesty" and good manners by the youths of Siena and presumably other youths of similar social status elsewhere. For that reason he focused on more formal games rather than on play, games that were usually played with witty and clever wordplay, tactfully competitive storytelling, or agonistic discussions. In sum, these were games that turned more on verbal skills, quick wit, and a ready ability to spin an intriguing tale which displayed one's aristocratic graces and sensibility, games that were suited to an evening's gathering of aristocrats, as his title promised.[8] After their momentary play in the snow, Grazzini's aristocratic band of youths turned to just such gaming, for their opening snowball fight was merely part of the frame story that enfolded their ongoing evenings of playful storytelling.

The strongly aristocratic tone of both Grazzini's and Bargagli's presentation of play calls to mind Castiglione's *The Book of the Courtier*, a work obviously also much concerned with aristocratic play and gaming. In a concrete sense

Castiglione's work is nothing but another more complex form of the gaming/play that Bargagli recommended: another aristocratic group of men and women agreeing to discuss in a playful yet competitive fashion a series of questions about court life, *virtù* (what made one person better than another), and love. Their game required members of the group, in this case primarily the male members, to demonstrate their quick wit, their *sprezzatura,* (effortless skill) and their manners in a special time and space (court) following special rules agreed upon by the group in an agonistic fashion that allowed participants (and readers of the work) to identify who played in a most pleasing and winning fashion. Within the context of this frame game, not surprisingly, Castiglione's players returned over and over again to the issue of gaming and play in more specific contexts. And as in Bargagli's work, the concern with classifying and separating out the correct forms of aristocratic play and gaming was crucial. This is perhaps best illustrated in *The Book of the Courtier* in the well-known discussion between Federico Fregoso and Gaspare Pallavicino about athletic contests of strength and prowess: there Federico warns that it is unwise for aristocrats to play such games with commoners, expressing the concern that such play is demeaning and, implicitly at least, the deeper fear that defeat at the hands of commoners might create riffs in what might be called the Great Chain of Status.[9]

In many ways these works have a common message: that society (much like reality and nature) is ultimately ordered as a hierarchy—in this case a Great Chain of Status—and play and games should not move up or down that chain mixing participants or players of different social levels.[10] Aristocrats must play only with aristocrats and commoners with others of their own status; mixing threatened not just the social order but in a very deep way the very order of things. But this hierarchical vision of players had a significant corollary. Some games and some play were labeled inappropriate for the upper classes and the aristocracy because games and play had the potential to reflect these hierarchical categories as well. Certain forms of games and play were crude, common, and "dishonest" and thus suited only to the lower orders of society and to be avoided by those who laid claims to higher status;[11] in turn, refined and elegant games, much like refined and elegant manners, were yet another way of demonstrating social place. It may well be that in the longer term these distinctions served to render certain games, among them games with stronger sexual innuendos, unacceptable and to limit more generally the range of play in daily life.

At the least Bargagli and Castiglione, along with many of their contemporaries, were anxious to separate out games that were suitable for the upper classes and at the same time were suspicious and usually quite negative about any aspect of *gioco* that seemed to smack of the lower classes or the common. As a result, much of the literary discussion of play and gaming tends to have a strong aristocratic bias that to a degree undercuts its usefulness for defining play in the Renaissance. Yet at the same time that very bias alerts us to a crucial aspect of play in the Renaissance: its importance in defining social distinctions in a society in which play was viewed as an important aspect of everyday life. In fact, it might be argued that as the Renaissance progressed and became increasingly aristocratic, not only did aristocratic play become more aristocratic and closely monitored for its refinement and honesty, but representations of lower-class play and gaming became more common and unseemly, more negative caricatures than descriptions.

And in dangerously spinning hypothesis on hypothesis, it might be suggested that a mounting emphasis on the commonness and coarseness of lower-class play in a society increasingly focused on morality and moral reform could transform what was originally primarily a social distinction about play into a moral restriction on play deemed common and vile. In a more concrete way, this rethinking and restriction of play might be associated with contemporary reforming agendas that sought to limit lower-class play to certain specific times like carnival and special festive occasions and even at those times to limit its license and coarseness—in other words, seeking to make it once again less common and vile in favor of making it finer and ultimately more disciplined. If these admittedly hypothetical factors were beginning to come into play at the end of the Renaissance, *gioco*, like manners, would have had an extremely important role to play in the "civilizing process" first suggested by Nobert Elias and the social and moral restructuring of early modern society.[12]

With such claims, however, we are coming close to repeating Huizinga's misstep of making play too serious a business. And in the end what we need is a general definition of play that will work for the Renaissance—neutralizing as much as possible the aristocratic bias of contemporary literature (without losing sight of it)—and which will also allow us to speak more generally of play as a category of activity that transcends its local cultural and social dimensions.

A contemporary Renaissance text that stresses many of the things that Huizinga stressed perhaps helps meet this difficult double goal. Tomaso Garzoni, another sixteenth-century protoencyclopedist, wrote on professions and work in his *La piazza universale di tutte le professioni del mondo* (The Universal Piazza of All the Professions of the World). In a chapter titled "On Players [*Giocatori*] in General and Particular," following the lead of Torquato Tasso, Garzoni opened his discussion defining play as follows: "Play [*gioco*] . . . is defined as being a trying of fortune and cleverness between two or more people. . . . [It was] developed . . . as a diversion and *pleasure* for souls worn out by the hard responsibilities of serious concerns. All of which required that such people *enjoy* themselves a bit and revive themselves with some *pleasant diversion*."[13] In this definition there is a clear sense of the double meaning that *gioco* had in Renaissance Italian (and retains today), for it combines both a sense of play and the more structured form of play that in English is referred to with the noun *game*. Yet for all that, nicely, both Garzoni's sixteenth-century definition and Huizinga's mid-twentieth-century one contain elements that seem to ring true across time and which might be used as a broad working definition.

Play (as well as gaming) we might define, then, as a special kind of activity that (1) emphasizes pleasure and pleasant diversions; (2) deemphasizes practical goals, especially those related to work; (3) has its own special times and spaces; and (4) follows its own rules different from those of everyday life (even if they often reflect or build upon those rules). In the end, this definition must be considered merely a broad set of parameters, a framing point of departure—perhaps an ideal for all definitions used in historical discussions—for in every culture, if we are to talk about a history of play, our definition will have to be adjusted to the particular practices and discourses of that culture. But what stands out in this definition is the close relationship between pleasure and play in the context of time—play is a pleasurable diversion from the practical time of adult daily life, as Garzoni points out, and that seems the essence of play across diverse societies and cultures.

Returning with this definition to the interrelationship of sex and play in the Renaissance, the dominant prescriptive discourses tended to ignore any play element in sex to focus on the ideal role of sex in family continuity and civic morality. In other words, they emphasized the importance of sex within marriage for the purpose of procreation and the creation of the next generation of an ongoing family—ideally sex in the Renaissance was a serious business.[14] Nonetheless, one does not have to look far, especially in Renaissance literature, to escape family and civic morality and find a strong play element in descriptions of sex. The novella tradition immediately comes to mind. But the portrayals of courtship in romance and the Petrarchian conceits of much love poetry also evoke significant play elements.[15]

Yet, as noted, literature does not present an unproblematic picture of sex and play in the Renaissance. Along with the aristocratic bias of much literature and a moralistic and disciplining tone that grew in league with the reforming tendencies of the late Renaissance, there are the classic problems of using literature for historical analysis. Most pertinent, so much of Renaissance literature was derivative from earlier periods that in matters sexual it is frequently difficult to identify what reflects the period and what reflects an earlier time that the Renaissance admired or desired to emulate. With regard to play and sex this is especially a problem, for it might well be posited that in a period that saw sex as primarily a duty in terms of procreation and maintaining a family line, literature that drew on ancient examples of a more perfect age might be an attractive vehicle for imagining a more pleasurable, playful approach to sex.[16] A related problem stems from the fact that "good" literature, if we mean by that literature that has endured and still speaks to us today, often speaks with a different voice today; thus, it is dangerously easy to read apparent continuities or similarities between the Renaissance and today as real ones—simply put, it is too easy to find sex as play in the great works of Renaissance literature to feel secure that we are not reading modern concerns and values into those past texts.

Ultimately, such doubts must always haunt the study of the past, but shifting from one form of text that might be labeled as more imaginatively based, like literature, to another set of texts that might be viewed as more pragmatically based (or at the least seen as constructed with a different set of presuppositions and goals), like judicial texts, provides another perspective on issues of sex and play. Once again, then, a wedding of archival texts and literary texts opens interesting possibilities. And judicial documents, especially case records, have unusual potential for developing a richer understanding of the issues involved. First, once one moves beyond the legal requirements of a case, the documentation often speaks directly about the concerns of the period, naming and renaming the central issues of contemporary concern. Second, if the case is rich in detail, especially if it includes testimony, one may be able to identify more than one contemporary perspective on the issues involved. Almost certainly there will be the perspective of the legal tradition and that of the males who staff a court, but the often extensive repetition within cases and between them allows one to chart the structure of those perspectives and eventually move beyond them to discover some of the other visions to be found in the testimonies collected. Moreover, the repetition of material in criminal cases can often alert the attentive reader to the blind spots in his or her own understanding of the past.[17]

So what do Renaissance criminal cases say about play and sex? At first glance disappointingly little. We might, in fact, stop right there—arguing that the play element in Renaissance sex was so insignificant that the criminal records of the time were unconcerned about it, the law largely ignored it, and the courts did not deal with it or discuss it—and return to literary texts. But that would be too easy. First it would be too easy because rulers, the law, and courts did associate play with sex in a number of significant ways in the Renaissance, as the case of Venice reveals particularly well. Laws in that city were particularly concerned about the association of prostitution and gambling; as is well known, play and sex in that area were seen as particularly dangerous.[18] Less well known but very evident in the fifteenth- and sixteenth-century campaign to eliminate the vice of sodomy—led by the famous (or infamous) and extremely powerful Venetian Council of Ten—was the attempt to limit both association and play among males of different ages.[19] This was done in part at least to restrict familiar contacts associated with games and play which it was feared might lead to sexual contact.

Criminal cases reveal that play was associated with sex in other significant ways, as well. For example, at the higher levels of prostitution courtesans in the major cities of northern Italy sold not only sex but a package of activities that often included various forms of what might be labeled play: gambling (playing cards or dice), music (playing instruments), witty conversation (playing with words), and even poetry and literature (at least in theory playing more seriously with words).[20] This range of types of play associated with sex (which we have only begun to sketch) suggests that there was a deep association between play and sex, especially in areas in which pleasure rather than procreation was the primary goal. And I would argue that the association went deep in part because pleasurable sex (in distinction to sex as a duty to a spouse, a family, or a lineage) was seen in very significant ways as being play also. This is difficult to see, however, in criminal cases in large part because the legal issues involved seldom turned on play or playful sex; most cases dealt with the duty aspects of sex, and, of course, sex that was prosecuted had to be portrayed almost by definition as serious.

Still, occasionally we do see language that directly describes aspects of play in sex, as in the 1487 case heard in Venice prosecuted by the Avogadori di Comun—a small committee of important men responsible for prosecuting many of the more important crimes committed in the city—involving the noble Domenico Contarini and a young Greek prostitute named Gratiosa. The case turned on the love magic used by Gratiosa to engender a mad love in Contarini, but the sexual play in bed (referred to virtually as an aside) gave the case a rather different cast. "One day when the aforementioned Gratiosa was in bed with Ser Domenico and they were playing together [*et luderent simul*] Gratiosa took some of that material that accumulates there from the navel of Domenico and some from her own navel." Or again, "playing with and sexually enjoying [*ludendo et trepudiando*] the said Domenico, she took a candle and measured his virile member."[21]

Both the navel lint and the candle were used to bind the love of Domenico, and with impressive effect: "The result of this magic was that the said Ser Domenico was rendered insane and mad . . . so that he committed the most strange and sad excesses."[22] Suggestively, by reformulating this playful sex as engendered by magic, these criminal records rendered it less dangerous to think about and, of course, easier to prosecute in a way that was less dangerous for this young noble as well. It explained why Contarini had been literally bound by his mad passion to a lower-class woman and why he committed those unnamed "strange and sad" excesses. It was not due to that sexual play between a noble and a commoner; it was not mere play and pleasure; it was magic. In a way this case and its language were actually unnaming play to find binding magic.

It might well be argued that it was one thing to play with a courtesan—a play that was already becoming aristocratic and refined at least in appearance—but what may appear largely harmless play was particularly dangerous with a more humble prostitute because of its cross-class elements. According to Renaissance ideals of prostitution (a rationale that rendered it relatively safe for a society based on family and patriarchy), Contarini should have been engaging merely in another form of economic exploitation, "renting" the prostitute's body. Magic, in a way, explained and excused his dangerous involvement and play with a lower-class woman which went too far beyond mere renting to seem acceptable to his family and the courts that adjudicated his "excesses."[23]

Ludendo in bed is a phrase that recurs irregularly in Venetian court cases and continues on as *giocando a letto* when they are written in the vernacular. But usually, as in the case of Domenico and Gratiosa, such play is referred to so briefly that it is difficult to say much with assurance about it. Yet Domenico and Gratiosa's fifteenth-century play in bed has interesting resonances with Renaissance literature. It brings to mind, for example, the unusually explicit scene of lovemaking in the sixteenth-century anonymous comedy *La venex-iana* in which the young dandy, Giulio, and the young widow, Angela, play and joke amorously about her breasts between bouts of lovemaking in bed to-gether. Giulio declares with a witty courtesy that recalls the ideal courtier, "I came to visit your Ladyship a free man, but now I'm chained more tightly than a criminal in your prison—the prison of these sweet breasts." Picking up smoothly on the metaphor of crime and her "sweet breasts," Angela replies: "Ah my sweet little thief, you kiss them, eh? Don't squeeze them too hard, or they'll cry out!"[24]

What impresses is the way play and pleasure are quite literally intertwined in this scene and others in the comedy. Giulio playfully asks if he can have An-gela's left breast to keep, and the courteous banter continues:

> *Angela:* That's good, because it is the one over my heart.
> *Giulio:* May I say a few words to my sweet little breast?
> *Angela:* Yes, say whatever you want. Oh, oh, you're breaking my heart! Wait
>   a second, I want you to feel the same sweet pain.
> *Giulio:* Do you know what my little apple says? That she's happy.
> *Angela:* Tell me what you asked her.
> *Giulio:* If that was sweet for her and if she wanted to do it again.
> *Angela:* She is sure she does, my sweet treasure.[25]

And the scene fades out almost cinematically as they return to their lovemak-ing. But the playful pleasure of sex here emerges from the unsaid for a mo-ment even in their overly arch speeches, and it is clear that there was a sense of mutual sexual pleasure in the Renaissance which was associated with the same playing in bed that we saw in Gratiosa and Domenico's case of fifteenth-century play.

One of the most intriguing and revealing literary Renaissance scenes of sex-ual play and pleasure, however, is the famous tale of Rustico and Alibech in Boccaccio's *Decameron*, and, nicely, it turns on what might be seen as the truly ultimate form of dangerous play, playing with the Devil. Narrated by the ever irreverent Dioneo, the narrator who seems to be always pushing the sexual edge of the ten storytellers who have come together in the hills above Florence to escape the plague of 1348, the tale is the last told on the third day of the ten dedicated to storytelling, a day dedicated to stories that end with much desired things gained or regained by dint of great effort.

In Dioneo's tale pleasure and play come together with the Devil in the hard, small bed of the desert hermit Rustico, a bed that blossoms with pleasure when he kindly shares it with the naive young pagan Alibech in order to help her find the true path to the Christian God that she seeks and true, ultimate pleasure. In most of the stories related on the third day the object desired is sexual pleasure, and both in the playfulness of the tales themselves and in the sexual play described, play is closely associated with pleasure and sexual pleasure closely associated with play. Rustico and Alibech's tale, however, stands out for its playfulness and its explicit association of playing in bed, pleasure, and sex. It is also simply a very funny and clever story that still works well, even if much of its truly transgressive nature is lost today.

Dioneo began his story pointing out that although love's pleasures were well suited to the soft beds and luxury of palaces and the riches of an aristocratic life, love was by no means limited to such ambiences; for Love's power was so great that it was felt even in "the deep forests, the frozen Alps and desert caves."[26] To exemplify the truth of this claim he turned to the case of the "young," "beautiful," "courteous," and "rich" pagan Alibech, a naive girl of about 14 who lived in the city of Gafsa in Tunisia. Youth, beauty, courtesy, and wealth, of course, were necessary to make this love story important for his aristocrat listeners, but a certain naïveté was necessary as well, as will become clear, to make Alibech an attractive and humorous victim/beneficiary of the tale. This tale-worthy Alibech, then, moved by a youthful desire—in contradistinction to a more consciously formed adult desire[27]—had formulated the desire to serve the Christian God inspired by the highly positive things she had heard about such service from the Christians of her city. When she pressed these Christians about how best to accomplish this, they assured her that he was best served by those who fled the things of this world and retired to the solitude of the desert to live as hermits.

As a result, she fled the comforts of her home and her father's riches and journeyed to the nearby desert in search of the promised pleasures of serving the Christian God. Fortunately, although she suffered "great fatigue" traveling alone, she didn't lose her desire or her way, and after a few days wandering in the desert she came upon a holy man at the door of his poor hut. Amazed to find such a young and beautiful girl alone at his door, he asked her what she was doing, and she explained that she had come to the desert to learn how to serve the Christian God. Fearing the temptation of the Devil, this holy man provided her with the meager hospitality of his hovel, a quick meal of "roots of herbs, wild melons, dates and water," and then sped her on her way to another hermit perhaps less tempted by his devils and more capable of teaching her how to serve his God.[28]

But the next hermit she found, presumably troubled by similar concerns about her youthful beauty and his own devils, sent her on her way to yet another. Dioneo's tale might well have ended there, with Alibech wandering the desert unable to find a hermit to help her serve the Christian God—a humorous comment on the problems that even desert hermits had resisting sexual temptation which would have fit in well with the anticlerical tone of many of Boccaccio's tales. But the tales of the third day were ones in which people found what they were seeking by dint of their efforts, so Alibech was destined to find what she sought with such danger and constancy, yet humorously not quite as she or Dioneo's audience might have imagined at first.

Finally, she found a desert hermit who was willing to take her in, Rustico, "young, quite holy and good." Alibech's dangerous beauty was not lost on the young man, "but unlike the others in order to make a great trial of his prowess [implying his prowess as a holy man, but, as we shall see, perhaps with a humorous double meaning] he did not send her away . . . but kept her with him in his cell."[29] Of course, true to Boccaccio's and Dioneo's humor, poor Rustico's "prowess" in self-denial failed almost immediately, but his failure manifested itself in a rather original way that made his fall particularly laughable. With oblique questions he confirmed his suspicion that this young girl was as innocent as she seemed and knew nothing about sexual intercourse; and thus he decided that "she ought to give him his [desired] pleasures, under the pretense of serving God."[30]

He began his conquest, then, with a short sermon on how the Devil was the enemy of the Christian God and how the best service to God was to help him put the Devil back in hell, where God had damned him. Quickly taking the bait, Alibech innocently and enthusiastically asked how one could provide this aid to God. And, of course, Rustico, more than willing to be her guide, instructed her to begin by undressing as he did so. Naked and unwittingly returned to the original prelapsarian state of Adam and Eve in the Garden of Eden, "Rustico more than ever burning with desire now that he saw her so beautiful experienced *the resurrection of the flesh.*" The innocent Alibech, seeing his "resurrection," asked innocently the obvious question, "What is that thing that I see sticking out in front of you that I don't have?" "Oh my dear child," Rustico replied with perfect guile, but also with a ring of everyday poetic truth, "this is the devil about which I was telling you just now. And do you see that now he is giving me great tribulations, so much that I can hardly stand it."

Without the slightest trace of pre-Freudian penis envy, Alibech exclaimed, "Oh thank God, for I see that I am better off than you for I don't have that devil myself."[31] But Rustico was ready to spring his neat little theological/sexual trap, pointing out promptly that while she did not have the Devil she had the other part of the holy equation, hell: "You have Hell and I say that I believe that God sent you here for the good of my soul, given that this devil gives me so much pain. For if you were willing to take pity on me and let me put my devil back in your hell, you would give me the greatest consolation and at the same time give God the greatest service and pleasure."[32]

Thus it was that Alibech learned to her great pleasure how to serve the Christian God and put the Devil back in hell. At first, given her lack of experience and Renaissance assumptions about sex, she found Rustico's devil rather demanding and rather painful, as a devil returning to hell might be expected to be. But Rustico assured her with his male self-confidence, perhaps augmented by the fact that he was a fiction in a happy tale in which the pleasure of sex was bound to succeed, that "the Devil will not always be so [painful and demanding]." And that indeed was the case, for young Alibech was assiduous in her service to God, and "it came to pass that the game/play [*giuoco*] began to give her *pleasure*."[33]

Here once again play and pleasure come together in a vision of sex that satisfied both partners in the relationship. And although in the beginning Alibech was the innocent victim of Rustico's plot, the transition to this pleasurable sex for both partners was signaled by the introduction of the concept of play. Alibech believed that she was still serving God, but now it was not a duty, not something that was demanding; rather, it had become play and a pleasure, as she made perfectly clear: "I see clearly the truth of what those good men told me in Gafsa, that serving God is such a sweet thing: certainly I don't know of any other thing that I have ever done that gives me so much *pleasure* as putting the devil back in hell."[34] For Alibech playing with the Devil of Rustico literally was the ultimate pleasure, and with a humorous reversal of formal orthodoxy it was the most satisfactory and pleasurable way of serving God as well.

Beyond its humor and its nice evocation of the way play, pleasure, and sex went together in the early Renaissance, this tale suggests that if we shift our approach slightly to look at sex more broadly in its pleasurable aspects as well, we can greatly expand the amount of information to be found about play. Clearly not all pleasure may be considered play, not even in sex, but as pleasure seems to be so closely connected with play both in general and in the Renaissance vision of playful sex, we may be able to work our way back to the play of sex in the Renaissance by evaluating sexual activities labeled pleasurable which reveal an element of play and gain a larger understanding of the meaning and dangers of sexual play.

Certainly sex as a pleasure of the body was much more regularly discussed in a wide range of Renaissance texts, and its dangers were much more clearly detailed. Sex as pleasure could misguide young people into mistaken relationships, lead to unwanted and illegitimate children, disrupt marriages and families, engender a wide range of violence, break social boundaries, overthrow Christian and social values, and destroy *virtù*, honor, and reputation, to name only the most obvious Renaissance dangers. Thus it required careful regulation through a wide range of magistracies and courts. Moreover, sex as a pleasure of the body was perceived as so dangerous that it mobilized far wider disciplining mechanisms—a whole range of techniques deployed to bind the dangerous passions associated with such pleasure—which we are just beginning to study.

But rather than tackling all of that in this chapter, I would like to look at a less happy case of playing with the Devil drawn from the Venetian archives to attempt to analyze more closely the fears such play and pleasures could create. Heard by the Holy Office of Venice in 1574, more than two centuries after Boccaccio's tale, the case involved the love affair between Suor Mansueta of the convent of Santa Croce and the Devil.[35] It was an affair that was highly physical and involved both great pleasure and great pain. And there is a strong probability that it may have been a wholly imaginary affair invented by Mansueta, rather than one she believed she had experienced, invented to try to force her superiors to allow her to leave the convent. But even if it was a fiction, a tragedy to balance Dioneo's comedy, in order for it to work or even gain the attention of the Holy Office, it had to have the ring of veracity, the feel of the possible (much like the literary texts discussed earlier); simply put, it had to have enough sixteenth-century reality—yet another consensus reality—in it to worry her superiors and the officials of the Holy Office. Significantly, they took her claims seriously enough to investigate them in minute detail and act on them. Thus, whether her tale was true or not, it is the way it worked and the way in which the authorities took it seriously that warrants study and reveals the deep and dangerous interconnections between pleasure, sex, and play.

Of course affairs with the Devil were nothing new in the Renaissance, and they have been analyzed from a number of perspectives.[36] But this is less true in terms of an analysis of the pleasures of the body involved in such affairs and certainly less true in terms of play. And given the stakes involved, sex with the

Devil might seem to have virtually nothing of the play element in it. Clearly it was an extreme and morally loaded form of sex, for in a deep and troubling way it marked the ultimate form of incorrect sexual intercourse. Thus we might say it had the potential of marking much more, especially for the very dialectical way of looking at such things exhibited by the clerics who staffed the Holy Office of Venice. For them, the dangers of that sex if associated with pleasure may well have marked the extremes of the danger of sexual pleasure and play, as well as perhaps play in general. At the same time and complicating the picture, however, as the Devil was often associated in his evilness with the pleasures of this world, the dialectical extreme of physical intercourse with him could mark some of the ultimate pleasures of this world as well. In a theological vision this coming together of ultimate pleasures was quite logical and negative, even if not everyone was aware of or shared that logic.

Suor Mansueta's case in its complexity suggests all this and much more. In her first testimony before the Holy Office she quickly admitted both her desire to return to the world outside the convent and her sexual affair with the Devil. "I have been a religious in the convent for twelve years. I have always stayed there unhappily, with my body in the convent and my heart in the secular world." Her twelve years in the convent suggests that she was still relatively young. As most women entered the convent in their early teens when it became clear that marriage was not in their future, Mansueta was probably still in her mid- to late twenties.[37] "From the first," she continued, "I said prayers frequently asking God that He grant me the grace to allow me to leave the convent. But the more I prayed the more there grew in me temptations, to such a degree that I was in such a state that one day I went into the garden . . . and called the devil with all my heart to come and take me away. And I gave myself to him in body and soul."[38]

To this point Suor Mansueta's account could hardly be more standard; she had prayed to the Devil for something that she wanted very badly—to leave the convent—and in return she had offered herself body and soul to him.[39] But as she moved on to explain what that meant, especially the giving of her body to the Devil, her account took on more detail and color. "[The Devil] did not appear to me visibly, but I unquestionably felt my hair stand on end. Actually the devil never appeared before me visibly so that I could see him with the eyes of the body, as I see each of you, but I did see him clearly with the eyes of the mind [*con gli occhi della mente*]. And he talked to me and I heard his voice and words with the ears of the body, like I hear your Lordships' words. [His words] always excited and tempted me especially when I was in bed. And he revealed himself to the eyes of my mind with a rough and commanding face and in the dress of a porter or chimney sweep."[40]

The Devil, although seen by Mansueta only "with the eyes of the mind," had a real physical presence for her, one that she felt with her "hair stand[ing] on end" and one that had an intriguingly common demeanor—he was seen dressed as a "porter and chimney sweep." But it was evident that one of the most important aspects of the Devil (or at least her specific devil, for she, like many others, seemed to make a distinction between her devil or demon and the Devil) was his sexual attraction, which "always excited and tempted" her. Certainly part of that attraction was the general expectation that the Devil in his mastery of evil knew how to tempt even the best of Christians, but one of the keys to his ability to tempt Suor Mansueta was the sexual pleasure he offered her. "He had sexual relations with me [*far meco carnalmente*] so that *I felt that pleasure* in my sleep. But this sleep is not real sleep, but rather as in a vision; thus I touched him as if he was in fact a man and *I felt great pleasure*."[41]

It would be interesting to consider Suor Mansueta's careful distinctions concerning her modes and states of perceiving reality, but that would lead us too far from the matter at hand—her pleasure. That pleasure, as she makes perfectly clear, was "great," and at least from her perspective it was a pleasure of the body ("far meco carnalmente"). In fact, touching the Devil "as if he was a man" was one of the sources of that great delight. Here we are very close to the pleasures of Gratiosa and Domenico Contarini in bed and perhaps to their play as well, for even if one of Suor Mansueta's prime motives in confessing her pleasure with the Devil was to secure her release from the convent, her way of telling her story stressed her physical pleasure in intercourse with him. It was not that this was something that she had to suffer in order to gain his aid; it was something that she literally could not resist because it gave her physical pleasure. In this her experience with the Devil was not shared by all women who described such relationships. Many described their intercourse either in terms of worship or as a form of exchange for power or favors without reference to pleasure, presumably frequently following the suggestions of their interrogators, who were theologically more concerned with such issues. Still, there were a number of women who stressed the role of pleasure and play in such intercourse.[42]

But when it was associated with sex and the Devil, that pleasurable aspect of play clearly had negative dimensions as well, which Suor Mansueta's description of her continuing pleasure with the Devil highlighted: "And I felt great pleasure and I corrupted myself and I touched his shameful parts as he did mine. Moreover he did evil things with me from in front naturally and against nature and I did the same things to myself with my own hands. After I was in prison I would have done the same if my hands had not been in chains."[43] Among other things Suor Mansueta's physical pleasure had a dangerous addictive element that the Renaissance also seemed to associate with play when viewed in a negative light. Playing cards or dice, for example, involved a host of moral dangers—frittering away limited family resources, the drunkenness and immoral environment of tavern gambling, brawls over cheating and winnings, to name only the most obvious—but increasingly such activities garnered a negative valence in part because of what might be called their addictive quality. They lured good men away from the positive activities of everyday life and took them away to a special time and space—a gaming/ play space often associated with taverns—to their detriment. While there was probably not yet a clear distinction between work time and play time, increasing suspicions about the appropriateness of play and certain addictive forms of play especially for the lower classes seem to point in the direction of later hard distinctions between positive work time and questionable play time.

In fact, in a very hierarchical society like that of the late Renaissance, as noted above, certain games were meant to be played by the upper classes and were refined when played by them. Cards and games of chance provide a good example. Played at court by aristocrats, they were idealized as refined and noble; played in the tavern by commoners, they were increasing low, common, and dangerously addictive, much like Suor Mansueta's addictive sexual play with her coarse common devil, who appeared to her as a porter or chimney sweep. Eventually in the civilizing process of play it would come to pass that common people—born to work rather than play—when they played, were not merely wasting their time; they were going against the very nature of society and the correct order of things tempted by an addiction that led them away from that correct order to a negative time and space of damning pleasure where ultimately the Devil ruled. In her play with the Devil, then, Mansueta was perhaps literally ahead of her time. For common people, however, gradually play time would be limited to the special times set aside for play—carnival, feast days, and ultimately the "weekend"—by the disciplining authorities of society, authorities like governments, churches, and businesses which increasingly arrogated to themselves the control of all time.[44]

Although Suor Mansueta was no commoner, her pleasures with the Devil, reflecting the ultimate negative level of pleasure, were common and mean even in her own descriptions of them. As she described it—perhaps to play on the fears of her judges and secure her release from the convent—her pleasure was a dangerous addiction that took her away from the tasks that, in the natural order of things, were hers as a nun and a bride of Christ. Crucially, her sexual identity could no longer be seen as a bride of Christ but rather as the mistress of the Devil. The shared vision of Renaissance sexual identity—the consensus reality shared by Suor Mansueta and her inquisitors—meant that she was involved in an adulterous relationship with the Devil in which God himself was the victim.[45] As she made perfectly clear: "If I remain in the convent I will lose my soul and I will never do well. . . . Thus I pray your Lordships . . . that you allow me [to live] in the secular world because I have always wished to be there and have a man for a husband."[46] Leaving the convent would allow her to take a husband and escape the temptations of the Devil, the pleasure of the body that he offered. Her distinction is also worthy of more careful consideration. With her future husband the uses of her body would be licit, and perhaps it would not be pushing it too far to suggest that in a way they would not be play. Rather, she would be moving from the special time and pleasures of play with the Devil to the regular time and ways for Renaissance women of marriage and family; for in marriage the sexual uses of the body had a regular socially productive goal—the procreation of children and the continuation of a male-dominated family lineage.

With the Devil the end of her pleasure was pleasure itself beyond the confines of the everyday world—the ultimate evil when taken with the Devil and the ultimate danger of play. Suor Mansueta's pleasures with the Devil could be read as a virtual definition of play taken to its most negative extreme from the perspective of church authorities. As argued above, play was an activity whose primary goal was pleasure. It was an activity, moreover, that stood outside the regular order and time of things. For Mansueta this was so true that beyond occurring in a convent and with the Devil—both an unusual place and a most unacceptable partner for such deeds—her pleasure even occurred in a different psychic state, seen as it was by her with her "eyes of the mind" while actually being experienced ("carnalmente"). It operated with different rules than those of everyday life and often played on the pleasures that breaking the rules could involve. Sex "against nature," "evil," and her masturbation were all imperatives of her sex with the Devil; they were the rules of their game of pleasure and not the rules of the everyday world which the Holy Office was willing to countenance and certainly not for a nun. In sum, Suor Mansuetta in her pleasure, in her special time and space, and with her special rules and imperatives was not just finding pleasure with the Devil; she was playing with him, and it was a very dangerous game indeed, the absolute negative limit of sexual pleasure and play.

Clearly the literary playing with the Devil of Alibech and Rustico seems much less dangerous and in its ways much more pleasurable than Suor Mansueta's play. In part this may be traced to the fact that the sexual world of the early Renaissance—before syphilis, before the religious reform movements of the fifteenth and sixteenth centuries, and before the advancing initiatives of church, state, and the leading families of the period (if not all their male members) to confine sex safely within matrimony—began to make sex a little less the easy "natural" sin it was considered by Boccaccio. Speaking very generally and very broadly, sex had become a more serious matter by the late sixteenth century. But in part this lighter tone may be traced also to the fact that in literature when a tale is told by someone like Dioneo—a fictional character himself crafted to elicit laughter and press the limits of the boundaries of *eros* in his storytelling—play and pleasure tend to go together, as they should ideally largely for the logic of the tale itself. Nonetheless, the adventures of Alibech and Rustico playing in their hard little bed in the desert suggest that, not surprisingly, literature has no lack of potential to be polyvalent, equivocal in the sense of speaking with more than one voice and to more than one end. And in the end I would suggest that this apparently clever little tale of playing with the Devil was virtually as dangerous and subversive in its sexual play as that of Suor Mansueta and perhaps more so.

The first suggestion of this is to be found in the seemingly charming and clever but evidently blasphemous metaphors that underlay the humor of Boccaccio's prose. Labeling their sexual intercourse "putting the Devil back in Hell," as noted in the tale itself, was a reference to a contemporary clever euphemism for sexual intercourse.[47] Nonetheless, for all its humor as it is used in Dioneo's story, it equates sex, illicit sex at that, explicitly with one of the central goals of God: confining the fallen angel Lucifer to hell. And this blasphemous metaphor does so in a way that has deep and potentially dangerous resonances with many of the most traditional theological concerns about the dangers of sex, even if it does so in an apparently playful and lighthearted manner, for the Devil himself was often portrayed as highly phallic, a sexual and aggressively penetrating master, as Suor Mansueta's testimony confirmed.

Moreover, as the church father Saint Augustine stressed in his *Confessions*, the primary danger of sex was that it made humans turn from the pleasure of God—the only real pleasure—to seek the false pleasures of the body. This rejecting what does truly exist—the pleasure of seeking and finding God—for what ultimately is only a passing and hardly real thing at all (in this case sexual pleasure) is the ultimate basis of all sin. For Augustine sin is choosing what does not exist over what does, which is exactly what Alibech innocently did as she playfully turned the desert into a momentary sexual paradise, putting the Devil back in hell. Clearly in this vision the phallus could well be viewed as a primary agent of the Devil, as it could easily be seen as the active force that leads men away from God. And, in fact, Suor Mansueta was claiming that it had a similar valence for women as well; only within marriage and outside the convent could she find a safe haven from her devil and his phallic temptations.

At a deeper level yet, what caused the fall of Lucifer himself was his turning away from the truth of God, and thus one might see an even stronger connection between the Devil and the phallus—the phallus in its capacity to make one turn away from God might be seen as a personal devil exactly as Rustico portrayed it to the innocent Alibech. Turning to Alibech's hell, one also could find suggestive deeper theological resonances. The essence of hell is absence—the absence of God. And, of course, a woman's genitals for all their real physical presence were in the Renaissance (and often still are) represented as an absence, a void. Paradoxically, it is an absence that has great power, like the absence that is sin, and again the parallel is intriguing. Yet hell, for all its emptiness of God and lack of true being, is also a place of great power and danger for humans and this world. Putting the Devil back in hell and finding pleasure in doing so from this perspective seems a little less like humorous light play. But it may well be that this is claiming too much theology for Boccaccio and too deep a range of metaphors for a simple little clever story.

Yet the sense that there is a deeper blasphemous core to the story is strengthened by the other famous metaphor of the tale, Rustico's infamous "resurrection of the flesh." The outrageousness of the scene of Rustico's "resurrection" before the naked Alibech may so catch the modern imagination that one misses the simple fact that here we are faced with a playful sexual metaphor that turns on and seemingly mocks the central mystery of Christianity. Although the theological context has moved away from Old Testament teachings about the punishment of Lucifer and the ultimate conflict between evil and good, nonbeing and being, Devil and God, we are still in the realm of Saint Augustine—since for him, and what would become the mainstream of Christian theology, the key to the message of the New Testament was that Christ had come to save humanity as both fully God and fully man, as the Nicene Creed proclaimed. And Christ in one of the deepest mysteries of the faith was therefore resurrected in the flesh, as all who are saved will be resurrected thanks to his sacrifice.

But here in Boccaccio's tale we have the resurrection of the flesh turned to a completely different end, to enjoying illicit sexual intercourse with the innocent Alibech. Moreover, all this was done under apparently false pretenses and in the name of leading her to the Christian God and his service when it was instead presumably misleading her to her fall—again from Saint Augustine's perspective, the ultimate evil. Evidently in the process she also lost her virginity, and in the pleasures of her play with Rustico's devil she clearly forgot about any chastity that she may have had or valued before her trip to the desert. In the end, one might even be tempted to argue that Rustico's devil with his false resurrection that tempted poor Alibech to sin was a real devil much like Suor Mansueta's devil was real, for both were an absence and an antithesis of God, literally false gods that led to their fall.

But I am more tempted by a different argument, and the thing that draws me in that direction is once again the issue of playing with the Devil. For Alibech does not fall as a result of her play; in fact, there is no indication that she is a victim or even a sinner in any way. She never becomes pregnant; she never loses face or honor; she is never punished or chastised in the tale for her pleasures. At the conclusion of the tale, she returns to civilization, marries, and lives happily ever after putting the Devil back in hell with her new husband, who presumably is happily unaware of the full range of her earlier theological pursuits. There is nothing in the story to indicate that she is any the worse off for her adventures or her blasphemous service to God and Rustico.

Actually, there is only one blemish on her happy and pleasurable adventure, and that was the inability of Rustico's devil to live up to the demands of her hell, for in a typically Renaissance vision of female sexual desire Boccaccio portrays the young girl's desire for the Devil as insatiable and thus maliciously her desire to serve God as well. "Rustico," she implores as his virility begins to fail him, "if your Devil is now chastened and does not trouble you, my Hell still does not give me peace, so you would do me a favor if you with your Devil would help quiet the rage of my Hell as I helped you subdue the pride of your Devil."[48] In turn, in what might be labeled a moment of masculine solidarity, Boccaccio provides a convenient excuse for the failure of Rustico's devil: "Rustico, who lived on the roots of herbs and water, had trouble meeting her demands; so he told her that it would take too many devils to take care of her Hell, but that he would do what he could."[49]

Yet significantly the comic failure of Rustico's devil underlines the humor of this tale, a fact that is confirmed by the laughter of the entire band of aristocratic youths at its conclusion, both the young men and women. In the face of that laughter and the happy play of the story, I would suggest that once again we have a tale that turns on a clever reversal of the accepted vision of things, so typical of Renaissance humor.

But this is a reversal with a deeply significant twist: it presents a playfully pseudo-Christian mythic rationale for an everyday poetic vision of sex which is at the heart of Boccaccio's portrayal of sexual intercourse and the pleasures of the flesh throughout the *Decameron*. And in this context Rustico and Alibech's blasphemous search for the pleasures of serving the Christian God in putting the Devil back in hell may also be reread as a wistful rewriting and reversal of the story of the Fall and the Garden of Eden.

In the regular theological vision, with their first sin Adam and Eve were thrown out of the terrestrial paradise, discovered shame, were burdened by sin, and knew all the negatives of the binary sexual division imposed upon them as punishment for their Fall from grace. This order of things—the First Age of Man—endured until the *resurrection of the flesh* that was brought by Christ's suffering and death on the Cross, which heralded the opening of a new era and a new order in the Christian vision of history as revealed in the New Testament. With the resurrection of Christ in the flesh, humanity's relationship with God changed in a fundamental way; the punishment and alienation that followed the expulsion from the Garden of Eden were replaced by love and the possibility of salvation—the Second Age of Man—and all this turned crucially on the suffering of Christ and on the resurrection of the flesh.

If we can leave aside the blasphemy of the concept of Rustico's own resurrection of the flesh for a moment, it is interesting to note that that resurrection also provided a crucial turning point in the young couple's microhistory. It initiated the sexual intercourse that turned their hard desert into a new Garden of Eden where the young and innocent Alibech willingly serves God and not only enjoys that service but finds it the ultimate, virtually transcendent pleasure that she innocently assumes Christianity as a superior religion provided. While other desert hermits in contrast led a hard life of suffering and privation in searching for their Christian God—and the tale has taken us to their bleak huts, which seemed to have little in the way of true Christian love to offer—Alibech in her innocence found pleasure in the Christian God almost immediately, and for her the desert bloomed. To return to Alibech's happy proclamation, noted earlier, as she learned to appreciate the pleasures of sexual play, hers was an innocent and pure claim of ultimate pleasure: "I see clearly the truth of what those good men told me in Gafsa, that serving God is such a sweet thing: certainly I don't know of any other thing that I have ever done that gives me so much pleasure as putting the devil back in hell."[50]

Suggestively, although the reversal was not as neat and perfect as it might have been, this return to the Garden of Eden was predicated also upon undoing the temptations of the Devil—Rustico's devil forced into serving God by going back to hell. And while Rustico in his clever misuse of the language of Christianity was consciously misleading the innocent Alibech to what might seem to be her private Fall, in fact, such a reading appears incorrect as the desert blossomed for her in her service to God and she concluded with a virtually beatific vision, "And because of this [pleasure to be found in the service of God] I hold that anyone who does anything else than serve God is not human."[51] In a striking fashion she had indeed returned to the Garden of Eden, and, as was the case for Adam and Eve, there she was perfectly content to only serve God—and even if we must remember that her service was not quite what was portrayed in the biblical tale, it was a pleasurable service and literally outside the time and space of this post-Fall world. Was this again ultimate play?

In the Garden of Eden, Adam and Eve innocently knew God as the source of their pleasure, and certainly the innocent Alibech did so as well. Yet it might well be objected that in the Garden of Eden there was no knowledge of sex and that that knowledge was one of the punishments inflicted upon humanity following the Fall. But in a curious way, as Foucault and his followers would point out, of course, Alibech in her innocence did not know sex, either, in her Garden of Eden, only the pleasure of her service to God. Her sexual intercourse was simply the playful pleasure that one dedicated to a loving God in the name of an ongoing metaquest to return the Devil to hell and perhaps bring love and happiness to all in an innocent return to a prelapsarian world. In fact, the point might be pressed further by noting that in the original biblical story of the Fall it was the woman, Eve, who pressed Adam to eat the apple—and, of course, as the story was portrayed in the Renaissance, Eve was the one held normally responsible for the Fall—whereas in this story it was the man, Rustico, who pressed the woman, Alibech, to put the Devil back in hell and thus undo the Fall. Alibech, the counterwoman to Eve, then, by innocently accepting his request, undid the knowledge of sin, made the desert bloom with love and pleasure in a pure service to God, and regained admission to the Garden of Eden.

The reversal is not a perfect one, however, for Rustico lacked Alibech's saving innocence. Clearly, part of the humor of the story is found in the fact that while he enjoyed for a while the results of his irreverent deceits—he too enjoyed newfound sexual pleasures and his desert bloomed for a moment—rather quickly the desert reasserted itself in the form of his inadequate diet and his inability to serve God as Alibech did and perhaps most tellingly in his desire to escape Alibech's demands. As a result, he seems more trapped than saved by his own misuse of the Christian myth and his multiplying lies. In the end, while the story focuses on Alibech living happily ever after in her return to the world, Rustico was left behind in the desert, although admittedly "with great pleasure" at having escaped Alibech's hard demands for serving God.[52] Still, of course, there is a certain logic in the fact that those who cannot serve God like Alibech with an innocent and sin-free play and pleasure are not qualified to return to the Garden of Eden and ultimately must be left in the desert as anti-Adams to her anti-Eve.

Yet in an abstract way, rather like Rustico the sinner left in the desert, sinning boldly, this suggests a still more blasphemous and irreverent rereading of the tale too playful and intriguingly too much in the spirit of Dioneo/Boccaccio to ignore. For if instead of suggesting a mere reversal of the Garden of Eden story we posit a fundamental reversal of the underlying myth of Christianity, some additional elements of the story fall suggestively into place. Rustico, for example, might actually be seen as the Antichrist who used the central tenets of the church in an ultimately evil way—the battle of God with the Devil and the resurrection of the flesh—to seduce a young woman away from the church and destroy it. But in the process of seeking the ultimate evil, inadvertently he fulfilled God's master plan and ushered in a new, last age and a new, last dispensation, just as it was promised that the Antichrist would do.

According to Renaissance theology, that third and last promised age, much like the age that preceded it, ushered in by Christ, would change in fundamental ways humanity's relationship with God. And certainly Alibech's approach to serving God was fundamentally different from that of the age of the New Testament, at least as interpreted by Saint Augustine and the church. Sex in Alibech's new last age would no longer be in the service of procreation (in pain and suffering) and family but would be in the service of a playful and pleasure-giving God whereby innocent pleasure truly led to the negation of the Devil happily returned to hell and ultimately the end of time itself.

Many expected a new age and a new dispensation in the fourteenth century, an age to be ushered in by an Antichrist, a third and final age before the Last Judgment and the End of Time. Although there was considerable uncertainty about what that last age would be like, it must be admitted that virtually no one thought it would be an age of happy, playful, innocent sex in the service of a loving, smiling God in a new blossoming Garden of Eden. Probably not even Boccaccio or his fictional storyteller Dioneo. Yet one might still wonder why in the frame story of the *Decameron* the queen of the third day, Neifile (identified by some commentators as "New-in-Love" or "New-Love" from the Greek), decided to move the storytellers to a new garden that day, a garden explicitly identified with the Garden of Eden. Or why, for that matter, Dioneo told his tale of resurrections on Sunday as the last tale of the third day—the day of resurrections, resurrections and the beginning of new, last dispensations it should be recalled. And, of course, one might also wonder a bit about Dioneo's name, as it conjures up the image of a very different age and the Greek god of play, pleasure, and sex—Dionysius.

Perhaps, for all its improbability Boccaccio/Dioneo as the prophet of a new dispensation of a more playful, happy sexuality warrants consideration also in light of the portrayal throughout the *Decameron* of youthful, formally illicit sexuality as a minor natural sin easily forgiven.[53] Be that as it may, clearly the pleasures of playing with the Devil were dangerous pleasures indeed, whether they led merely to the blasphemous and irreverent surface humor of Dioneo's tale or to deeper reveries that playfully (or maybe not) undercut the traditional Christian vision of sex and sexual relations. Interestingly and not surprisingly, Alibech's playing with the Devil was one of the first stories eliminated in the sixteenth-century expurgated versions of the *Decameron*.[54] Even without deeper readings the tale's blasphemy was evident, and its playful humor was no longer seen as innocent or acceptable play. Which brings us back to Suor Mansueta, for her tale of her play with the Devil brought her into the hands of much the same sixteenth-century censoring ecclesiastical authorities, now reorganized and rearmed with an eye to combat all blasphemy and to limit sex to the acceptable realm of matrimony and procreation. Even if in the long run those authorities failed in both aims, certainly playing with the Devil and the pleasures of same were at the extreme end of the unacceptable at the end of the sixteenth century, and Suor Mansueta, having fallen into their hands, was in serious trouble.

But the Holy Office of Venice had a deeper problem with her case because Suor Mansueta in her play with the Devil had given herself up body and soul to him and thus was literally possessed by him. Possessed and thus no longer under her own control, she could not be punished or held accountable for her deeds—as the essence of sin and crime was the willing of them in ecclesiastical courts as well as secular ones. But, of course, she did not will her deeds because, as she was possessed by the Devil, her deeds were actually the Devil's. In fact, as the notary's account of her possession reveals, it was often unclear to the Holy Office whom they were actually dealing with, Suor Mansueta or the Devil—a suggestive problem of identity that implies once again that an internal sense of self was not irrelevant in the Renaissance even if the more social consensus reality aspect of self and personality was normally more significant. Tellingly, the scribe even slid uneasily back and forth between using the pronouns *she* and *he* when describing her interactions with the tribunal and her/his words and deeds. Clearly, then, the first necessity in ending her play with the Devil and determining which punishable deeds were hers and which the Devil's required eliminating the Devil as a player—in other words, exorcism to give her back her very self. And although the procedures of exorcism have been often described, those procedures take on a slightly richer meaning when they are viewed in terms of play and self in the Renaissance.

"On Monday the eighth [1574] Suor Mansueta's exorcism was begun," the scribe coolly began his account, "and once some exorcisms were done her body began to shake *and it did not want to obey* orders, or at best it did so badly. . . . And the priest said 'tell me your name.' But she did not want to say anything except, 'No, no.' And she grabbed the stole [that she had tied at her neck] with one hand and then the other and pulled it around her neck to strangle herself with a frightening fluttering and turning up of her eyes, then she threw down the stole and scrambled away."[55] One thing is immediately clear here: Suor Mansueta's body was literally out of control, at least the normal controls of the everyday world of Renaissance Christians. Of course the implication was that it was in the hands of the Devil. But taking matters a bit further, we might say that it was also following a different discipline than that of the everyday Christian world—in playing with the Devil this body had accepted another set of rules, another discipline: the Devil's.

Thus the exorcist's goal in making her body "obey" (*obedire*) was to bring that body back under the discipline of the Christian world and the everyday and subtract it from the Devil's discipline with its corporal pleasures of "ultimate" play and its potential for "ultimate" pain and eternal damnation. To this end those involved in the exorcism had to gauge every sign of Suor Mansueta's body with care and in terms of its obedience to authority, first, in order to free it from play and, second, in order to assure that when she regained control she would be able to resist the urge to play again.[56] That was no easy task, but the exorcist and the Holy Office were prepared to try. After all, this was not any play, not just any game; it was the ultimate contest fought out over Suor Mansueta's very self, her body, and her sexual pleasure.[57]

But, of course, the Devil was not prepared to give up his playmate easily.

> Tuesday after dinner . . . the priest began to preach to her. She began to shake and the spirits came upon her, *and they did not want to obey* at all. The priest blessed the place *and the body* cursing all the spirits that had come in aid of those who had possessed the body of that poor woman. After he had done that he began to read the exorcisms and . . . *demand obedience* which required a great deal of effort. Still she began to obey. . . . The first sign was that she was forced to move that body with cries, tears and sighs. She made quite a few signs such as several times throwing herself on the ground with her eyes rolled up most fearfully; finally reduced by the exorcisms, with Holy Water, and the sound of the bell—that bell is greatly feared by this spirit—she threw herself on the ground crying and sighing mightily with tears at her eyes. The priest ordered that that body stand up and it did so and it made an impressive number of other *signs.*[58]

The battle for Suor Mansueta's body was one fought out in terms of commands, obedience, and control; the language of the scribe is eloquent on this point. Once again the "signs" (*segni*) were physical and suggest that the goal was to transform her body from the Devil's plaything into a disciplined Christian body.

But the battle to discipline that body and stop its play with the Devil required a certain cleverness as well. The Devil could make her body obey his rules still, returning to their old games, even forcing it to laugh and be unmaidenly frank and physical at the most inappropriate moments. The exorcist, however, countered by playing on the Devil's pride in his ability to play with that body, and, of course, the cleric could use the power of the ultimate things of God such as Holy Water, incense, or the Sign of the Cross to counterattack.

> Wednesday morning . . . he began to read and having read a good bit [Suor Mansueta] just laughed not saying anything. The priest exorcized her and at a certain moment she began to tremble. The priest commanded him that if he were a real devil he should make the whole body tremble from head to toe and he [the Devil] made it happen to such a degree that I believed that it [her body] was going to break apart so great was the fury. He ordered that he stop it and immediately it stopped always however [with the priest] adding punishment to punishment otherwise it did not obey. . . . He commanded him [the Devil] that if he were a true devil that

he give a sign of it by violently throwing off the sandals of Suor Mansueta. With a great roar and other signs . . . [and] with great violence he threw them off and that body lay on the floor as if dead. . . . As the body was on the floor, first the priest, than I held the sacred beads [the rosary] under her nose so that she could smell them. She always crying out and complaining exclaimed "What a stink" and threw off her stole. He ordered her and she went to pick it up on her knees with her mouth. . . . And he bound it in her mouth where she kept it until he unbound it.

The exorcist then taunted her spirits with holy incense, causing her/them to cry out, "I don't ever want incense." After a short battle of wills he forced her to accept it, but immediately "she scampered away and went out into the courtyard. The priest, without moving, still reading and adding punishment to punishment, made her return, tied the stole around her neck and *ordered her that she put herself under his foot.* She did not want to do so but she was pressed and she put herself down. Then the priest put his foot on her saying the *Qui Habitat* and she remained quiet."[59] What more perfect sign that her play with the Devil was coming to an end than placing her body literally under the feet of the church in the form of the foot of her exorcist. Her body had been forced to accept the discipline of the church, and with perfect symmetry, leaving her play behind, she returned to normal behavior thanking all for their help, asking for their forgiveness for her untoward actions, and begging that they pray for her.[60] Across the day she had gone from laughing at their attempts to save her to acting just as a good Christian woman should, laying at the foot of the church, asking for forgiveness and reclaiming her Christian self.

Friday, the last day planned for her exorcism, brought out the ultimate weapons of the church—relics and a piece of the True Cross—to reclaim Suor Mansueta's body and soul.

Friday morning . . . the priest . . . ordered the devil to show a sign of himself in that part of her body. Thus obeying he made the chief devil go into her tongue and there he bound him so that he/she could not speak. . . . The priest always reading psalms or other prayers held a box of relics over the body. As it was time to speak with this head spirit, he unbound him . . . and the spirit began to complain [about the relics, which he in the meantime had thrown on the floor]. The priest ordered him . . . to show reverence and humility by picking them up with his mouth while on his knees with his hands tied behind his back. . . . The spirit scooped them up in one sweep with his mouth and put them in their box with a great ease that I could never have matched even with my hands.

Clearly the exorcist had become the master by this point, but now it was his turn to play with the Devil—he was ready to use his own special Christian rules, his own special Christian time, to reveal his faith's ultimate pleasures. He continued:

> "I want to see if you can stand up to a very great mystery." Then he put a cross on his/her shoulder and he began to read the Passion [Christ's suffering that led ultimately to the resurrection of the flesh]. Immediately that body began to tremble . . . with cries, sighs, and very distorted eyes, it became so agitated to throw off [the cross] that it was frightening. It threw itself on the ground as if dead or in death throes. And the exorcist put on him/her a box that contained some of the wood of the Holy Cross which put him/her in the greatest rage saying "What stink is this" and he/she wanted to take it up in his/her hands. But his/her hands were forcibly tied behind him/her *not with rope but with prayers.*

The Devil (now reduced to a mere head spirit) had been bound with prayers, and the exorcism of Suor Mansueta had become a theater of Christianity triumphant, as not only had her body and her self been reclaimed from their blasphemous play, but the transcendent discipline of Christianity had triumphed over the minions of the Devil and by implication the Devil himself.

The last recorded act of the passion of Suor Mansueta and the triumphant theater of the church was at hand. The scribe, apparently ever more in awe, reported, "With that body lying as if dead on a chair, the priest signed it and ordered the spirits to go down into the bottom of the left foot . . . with a manifest *sign.* . . . The body seemed to come to a rolling boil even in the foot. It kicked off its sandal and distorted the foot as the rest of the body became as if dead and smiled. But the chief spirit remained bound in the tongue. The priest noticed this and he unbound him and ordered him down [to the foot] with the same *signs. And the body returned to itself.*"[61]

Suor Mansueta's play with the Devil was for her most costly and for us most revealing. In the beginning she claimed it brought her pleasure and an escape from the everyday world of the convent which she disliked so much. In sexual play with the Devil, however, the different rules of life and the body which she accepted in order to play, the different space and time she played in, and the pleasure that was a primary goal of her play became much more dangerous than the special rules, time, space, and pleasures of more normal play. In the Renaissance the latter could be dangerous and required increasing control as well, but the former in terms of Suor Mansueta's play with the Devil presented the ultimate extreme of the danger of play. And as the site of that play was the body of Suor Mansueta, it was the body that had to be reconquered and returned to a Christian discipline. Ultimately, of course, it was her soul that was at stake, but significantly it was her body that was the primary field of conflict, the prize to be won, the thing to be brought back under the discipline of the church. Justice, not merely the justice of the state through the Holy Office or the justice of the church through the procedures of exorcism but Eternal Justice—the very order that underlay the universe—required that Suor Mansueta's body give up its play with the Devil.

In the end, however, it is unclear whether the attempt to stop that play ever really worked for Suor Mansueta. The last reference we have to her is a brief note from 17 February 1575 which prescribed continued exorcism for her in the convent because she "remain[ed] possessed by demons."[62] As she was forced to remain in the convent, it appears her sexual play with the Devil continued. In the world sexual play also remained suspect and may well have become more so, as both ecclesiastical and secular authorities in the early modern period seem to have tried harder to hem in this form of bodily play by enforcing more aggressively well-established theological and secular traditions that saw sex as a duty in marriage (the marital debt) and as serving family and societal goals (procreation). This effort to confine sexual play also required a much closer examination of motive and self in the private evaluation of the pleasures of the body which was monitored with increasing rigor in confession. Toward the end of the Renaissance all this may have helped to create a major divide in the way people perceived themselves, their bodies, and their pleasures. And, in fact, this may have been one of the most significant divides on the uneven road to the modern body and the modern sense of self. In the end, whether or not Dioneo or Boccaccio ever conceived of it as such, the new, modern age was not to be the age of sexual play and pleasure that Alibech innocently found in serving the Christian God in her blossoming desert thanks to the resurrection of the flesh; rather, it was to be the age of the modern self-disciplined body and self and modern sex. Playing with the Devil would be the ultimate evil rather than the ultimate good.

CHAPTER 3

The Abbot's Concubine

Renaissance Lies, Literature, and Power

In 1573 the abbot of Sumaga, Alessandro Ruis, was going around the little village where he lived—and to some extent ruled as the leading ecclesiastical figure—regaling his neighbors with a tale about his problems with his former concubine, Cecilia Padovana. Cecilia, he was complaining, had used some very troubling magic to bind to her the love of the men she desired including himself. His story may have seemed particularly credible to many, for the abbot was merely the shadow of his former self. Broken and bitter, he appeared to have been devastated by his separation from Cecilia, and, as much love magic was designed to "hammer" and punish its victims if they did not yield to love, his demise and literal unmanning must have seemed to many an impressive testimony to the power of the woman who had once been the abbot's concubine.

At much the same time in much the same area another man was in a way regaling a similar audience with virtually the reverse of the abbot's story. That practically no one remembers him today detracts little from his notoriety at the time, for he was the widely known warrior-hero Captain Fear, and he was traveling around regaling the locals with, among other tales, a revealing account of his unhappy unmanning as the male concubine of the Amazons. It seemed, he explained to his listeners, that the peace and prosperity of the once warlike Amazons had changed them and that lately "there had been born many, many Amazons who were not inclined towards . . . war, but instead preferred the needle, the distaff, and the spindle. . . . The wise and valorous Queens of the Amazons, seeing that, concluded that their subjects were no longer worth a damn either in making love or war."[1]

One can well imagine the plight of the Amazon queens from the sixteenth-century male perspective of Captain Fear and his listeners. With peace those once fearsome and powerful warriors had slowly fallen back to their "true natures," their true gendered identities, finding spinning and weaving more satisfying than war. Fortunately, the Amazon queens had long ago forsaken nature for nurture and had, according to the modest captain, an ingenious plan for reinvigorating their troops. "Realizing that something must be done they decided to send for me, having heard already about my reputation which convinced them that I alone was capable of impregnating them all."[2]

Captain Fear's listeners were certainly aware of that reputation, that consensus reality about his sexual identity. In a no longer famous contest with Hercules over who could impregnate more virgins in one night, had he not managed to impregnate two hundred by midnight while poor old Hercules had taken the whole night to impregnate only fifty?[3] And when Zeus had flooded the earth killing off everyone except Deucalion and Pyrrha, had not he, Captain Fear, stepped in for the former, fearlessly cuckolding him to repopulate the earth single-handedly with Pyrrha? Why, he had even slept with Death and impregnated her—their children were the Guelf and Ghibelline parties.[4] No, Captain Fear was not merely a great male warrior—the quintessential *miles gloriosus*—with his violent and indiscriminate slaughter of men and gods, his close friendship with the Devil, and his literal love of Death (a particularly good mistress because she was always quick to finish); he was also the consummate and consummating male sexual actor, as most of his listeners were well aware.

But one must not overlook the fact that this great warrior and gallant, who had defeated most of the gods in battle and cuckolded them as well, as concubine to the Amazons had played a decidedly different role. His world of male fantasy had been literally turned upside down, for the Amazons, of course, were ultimately the warriors in his story (even if he provided the warrior seed), and he was their sexual servant, their male concubine. Tellingly, this reversal of identities ultimately reversed the very nature of the captain himself, changing him from the one feared to the one who feared, and that necessitated a shameful admission.

Things certainly had started well with the Amazons. Given as great a triumphal welcome as any conquering hero, even if he was to be a sexual object, he quickly impregnated the two queens, who as quickly gave birth "to 365 Amazonettes who were born all armed in the Scithian manner."[5] Then working at the modest but sustainable pace of "impregnating 300 Amazons a day," he quickly repopulated the Amazon race with warlike women—an impressive moment of sexual performance if ever there was one!

But Captain Fear's servant and buddy interrupted his fearfully fruitful tale with a question: "My dear master how were you able to stand up to so many women and satisfy so many insatiable natures for it is often said that three things are insatiable: the earth for cadavers, Hell for souls, and women for lovers."[6] Captain Fear had to confess, "To tell the truth I began to droop, and I slowed down my pace, and shortly I became such that I appeared to them a broken down stud, old, weak, and a sluggard."[7] More heroically than Rustico perhaps, the magnificent Captain Fear had nonetheless ultimately fallen before the Renaissance stereotype of female desire. From the gloriously fertile and irresistible male stud of fantasy, he had become at the hands of his Amazons a totally different person; lack of sexual performance, an inability to live up to his sexual reputation, had finally undone even the indomitable Captain Fear.

What, you might well ask, do these two characters have in common? Captain Fear was the braggadocio creation of Francesco Andreini and his troop of itinerant actors known as the Comici Gelosi, who toured the late Renaissance spoofing the conceits of the heroes of chivalrous romance—the captain played by Andreini himself was the deliciously outrageous embodiment of the male ideal of that genre.[8] Abbot Ruis on the other hand was merely a small, unknown local figure fallen from power. One evidently was a creation of fiction; the other actually lived.

But those seemingly self-evident distinctions begin to fade when one looks more closely at the abbot and his concubine, for in the end their story becomes more and more clearly a set of artfully constructed fictions that turn on microstrategies of power, and Captain Fear was first and foremost an artfully constructed mocking of often real and similar strategies of power. In both cases, moreover, whether mockingly or seriously, those microstrategies of power that were deployed turned on creating and manipulating what I have been calling consensus realities about sexual identity. Captain Fear evoked laughter by playing off widely shared visions of male sexuality taken to their ultimately absurd but cleverly logical conclusions; Abbot Ruis played a harder game that attempted to use consensus realities about his own sexuality and that of his concubine to force her to return to him. At a more immediate level each case also illuminates assumptions about the powerlessness of concubines and at a deeper level turns around sexual fears about male potency and female sexual power over men.

In an article by Oscar Di Simplicio about priests and their concubine/servants, while ruing the lack of detailed information about such relationships in the early modern period, the author notes that the strategies and dynamics of power in such situations could be extremely complex, especially when servants were female and served as concubines as well.[9] It was not unusual for such women, especially in the countryside, to become matriarchs of the church, running its daily affairs, serving as intermediaries between the priest and the community, at times taking on spiritual functions, and even producing priestly heirs.

Shifting the ground of Di Simplicio's argument just slightly, returning to the heart of the captain's boasting and Abbot Ruis's problems, it seems to me that each in its way suggests that sexual relationships and specifically those concerned with concubinage were rife with the possibilities for what I would like to call microstrategies and systems of power. These were webs of power often invisible to the great sweep of more traditional history but which none-theless were extremely important for the daily living of life, webs that in our cases turned upon the complex negotiations of sexual identity. And they were important especially because they opened up for everyday people a significant range of strategies that provided both the illusion and the reality of wielding power in situations often dismissed today as powerless. As will become clear, in this play of microstrategies we catch a glimpse of that much sought after and much debated question of individual determinacy in the Renaissance: agency. Actually, one of the more promising microstrategies of power available at the time—more self-negotiation than self-fashioning—was the ability to ma-nipulate consensus realities with self-presentation, self-performance, and self-display in order to create spaces for action and realizing personal goals.[10]

Returning to Captain Fear's sexual failure at the hands of the Amazons, for example, although such misogynistic topoi have often been pointed out and analyzed for what they reveal about gender stereotypes and desires to discipline society sexually, his demise suggests deeper issues. If we take Captain Fear's self-presentation of his failure seriously, something that is admittedly hard to do, it suggests that behind the laughter he and his traveling troop of players were trying to elicit there lurked a shared fear about sexual identity—that men were not as powerful as they claimed to be and that even the most pow-erful could be unmanned, especially by powerful women.

And although that fear often has been dismissed, I would suggest that it reveals a shared reality—a widely shared consensus reality—for men and women perceived that men had been unmanned by powerful women often enough and in a wide enough range of ways to sustain a real concern about woman's sexual prowess, demands, and illicit powers. In turn that meant con-trolling women in a number of well-discussed ways in the Renaissance, but it also meant in ways little discussed that those uncertainties about male prowess created fissures in the dominant male discourses of power and in the practical webs of power that seemed to dominate daily life, fissures where other webs of power could be spun, other microstrategies followed even by those who were officially limited to needle, distaff, and spindle.

Rather than attempting to lay out here an overview of the microstrategies of power that I have discussed in some detail elsewhere,[11] I want to look at the tale of Abbot Ruis to suggest some strategies that were constructed around a particular case of clerical concubinage reported with the kind of detail that Di Simplicio did not find and which turned on the fear of being unmanned by a woman.

The checkered career of the abbot from Sumaga, a small town of about five hundred inhabitants in Friuli, a rather poor and undeveloped region in north-eastern Italy, provides a good indication of the complex nature of concubinage, power, and passion in the countryside.[12] Alessandro Ruis came to the attention of the Holy Office of Venice because of what today seems clearly a lie—the stories that he was telling locally about Cecilia Padovana's love magic. In 1573 he was questioned about those stories by an official of the bishop of Concordia, at the behest of the Holy Office. This Holy Office was officially a Venetian secular magistracy staffed in part by clerics and in part by nobles to repress heresy. By the 1570s it was widely respected and feared for its power and its aggressive pursuit of heresy and was just beginning a period of active investigation of those who practiced magic deemed to be black not only in Venice but in the countryside as well; it was in this context that the abbot's tales had caught the office's attention.[13]

Ruis was evidently very nervous about discussing his stories with an agent of that powerful body. Under questioning he repeatedly asked for a delay so that he could have time to order his thoughts, claiming that he could not remember the particulars of his stories or who was involved and that he did not want to testify inaccurately before such an important person. This was so patently false that his objections were brushed aside,[14] and finally, his examiner literally gave him back the heart of the story that he had been telling locally: "Don't you remember that you said . . . that the matter was the following: that there was a woman who had Holy Oil and with that Holy Oil she oiled the palm of her hand and being in bed, with that hand . . . she took the virile member of the man . . . and holding it in her hand she said the words of the consecration of the Most Holy Host, saying 'for this is my body' in order to bind his love?"[15]

Although this story of yet another resurrection of the flesh was apparently a lie, it fitted well enough with love magic as it was practiced at the time to have caught the attention of the Holy Office. Much magic used holy things to bind, and even if it is not stated how it could have worked, what is significant is that the abbot could report such magic and expect it to be believed. Recognizing that such beliefs were shared, he had constructed a strategy of power that had served his interests well at least until he was forced to reveal it to higher authorities.[16] Up to that point Ruis's strategy had been relatively straightforward. He had been using this accusation of a likely-sounding type of magic as a form of blackmail to try to force his concubine, Cecilia Padovana, to return to him. Building upon a shared community perception—a consensus reality again—that such magic existed and was used by certain women to dominate men sexually, he could claim that he was a victim of it, and if he could make the claim stick, in the end both community pressure and the fear of higher authorities being brought into the case would force Cecilia to return to him.

In fact, it appears he had first tried the strategy a few years earlier when Cecilia had fled. At that time he had complained to a few people about that magic and threatened to take the matter to higher authorities who also shared the perception that such magic existed and was effective. And his microstrategy of power had delivered; Cecilia had returned. But the abbot was clearly uneasy about actually making it work in a formal case heard before the Holy Office of Venice. There other powers were at play apparently well beyond the level at which he could manipulate them. It appears, however, that he hoped that with a delay he could once again secure Cecilia's return in exchange for not testifying. Once he testified, obviously, that possibility was lost. Thus, even faced directly with his own story, Abbot Ruis at first tried to avoid it: "I did not say this nor could I have said it, because this one cannot know unless one had been in the bed [where it was done]. But I did say a great deal and if you would give me a recess to remember, [I could tell you] both names and other things that I do not now remember."[17]

In the end, however, finally understanding his examiners' resolve, he did reluctantly outline the story that he was again circulating. It was very similar to the story given to him by his examiners, with a few details altered presumably to help his case. Several years earlier Cecilia had lived in a house in Venice kept by a certain Madonna Medea and her daughter Orsetta, who was a courtesan. One day when Cecilia returned to the house, however, the servants would not let her enter, saying that their mistress did not want her to live there anymore. Abbot Ruis, who just happened to be in Venice at the time, hearing about the incident, went to talk with Medea. "Talking with the said Madonna Medea and asking her why she had kicked out Cecilia," Ruis related, "she said, 'I threw her out because she is a lewd woman and she taught my daughter some witchcraft [*stregarie*] to make herself loved [*farsi voler bene*].' . . . According to what Madonna Medea said there was some Holy Oil with which she [Cecilia] said one had to oil her genitals and her hand and then saying certain words one touched the member of the man." [18]

Finally Abbot Ruis had laid his cards on the table; his bluff had been called. Almost immediately his examiners began to pick at those cards, asking him why he had not reported the matter at once to the bishop of Venice. One answer, of course, might have been because that was not part of his strategy of blackmail. But instead his explanation turned on his earlier relationship with the young woman: "As Cecilia was the daughter of that Lucia who was the nurse of my child and as she stayed sometimes in my house I reproached her for this. She denied that this [story] was true. But I continued to reprove her and threaten her and she said to me that that woman from Saletto, whose name I do not remember . . . had taught her this thing; thus as Saletto was under this Bishopric I told it to the [local] Bishop." [19]

As the abbot's tale grows, it opens what must have been for the authorities a familiar-sounding world of local women's networks and love magic. That world may have been largely imagined to support the cards Ruis had been forced finally to play, but even so it could ring true to his listeners, for it referred to systems of power that women were believed to be manipulating at the time—a vision shared by the nobles and ecclesiastics who heard Ruis's case, many of his local contemporaries, and even Captain Fear's listeners.

"I asked Cecilia 'where did you get that oil?' She replied, 'I got it from that woman who taught me the magic.' Cecilia explained to me that that woman had gotten it from her own mother [Cecilia's] . . . who was then the housekeeper of the priest of Morsana. . . . Cecilia said that her mother had been asked repeatedly by the woman from Saletto to have some Holy Oil in order to oil a child of hers who suffered from epilepsy." Powerful women using holy oil to heal and to bind love suggests another microsystem of power that was widely relied upon and perhaps as widely feared. [20] Without such real fears Ruis's apparently false claims would not have had a chance to work.

Although this detail fleshed out Ruis's hand nicely, there were potential dangers in such particulars, for they opened the door to further questions that led to the issue of clerics keeping concubines. In theory, by the 1570s the reforms of the Council of Trent which had been aimed at breaking the habit of clerics keeping concubines should have been reaching the countryside. In fact, the Venetian Holy Office along with Venetian authorities was just beginning to look into the most egregious clerical misuses both in Venice itself and in their mainland territories. The question remains, however, whether the abbot's misuse was egregious enough to warrant their concern once it had been brought to their attention by claims much more troubling and sacrilegious about holy oil and phallic love magic. It may have been that in the abbot's desire to regain control of his concubine his microstrategy of power had come face to face with a macrostrategy of power concerned with revitalizing the church by breaking a cycle of concubinage that seemed to threaten the moral quality and commitment of the clergy.

Whether or not that was the case, as his questioning continued, we find him quickly revealing rather nonchalantly the dangers of clerical concubinage not for himself but for a friend. Ruis noted that Cecilia's mother, Lucia, who had nursed his own child, had also been for years the servant (*massara*) of the priest of Morsana (a nearby village), and in his second testimony he further admitted that she had been, like many such women, much more than a servant. The issue had been raised because the Holy Office, following up on his claims about holy oil, was concerned about who had provided the oil and suspected that the priest of Morsana, Domenigo Borgana, had given it to his servant, who in turn had given it to her daughter. But Ruis stoutly denied that, labeling the priest "his friend" and "a good man [*un homo da bene*]."[21] That led to questions about the relationship between the priest and Lucia. "Lucia stayed with the said priest as his servant," he reiterated, but then admitted, "She stayed with him for many years from what I have heard and I believe that she was also his concubine. This is because I know and I have seen that he had with her five or six children. The oldest among them is called Zamphilo and is about nineteen or twenty years old. I have heard the priest call him son and also Lucia call him son. I have also heard this for the other small boy and the girls."[22]

This description of the priest of Morsana is particularly interesting given the pose that Abbot Ruis was attempting to maintain before his examiners and ecclesiastical superiors. Domenigo Borgana was "a good man" and a reliable priest who would not do something as awful as allow the holy oil under his care to fall into the hands of local women. But Ruis admitted that this "good" priest had kept his servant as his concubine for many years and that they had produced five publicly acknowledged children together; evidently local consensus realities about this priest's sexual identity were more accepting than the reforms of the Council of Trent would lead one to anticipate—but of course those reforms were long in reaching the countryside, if they ever did.

Interestingly, this case includes quite a bit of material about Lucia herself and suggests that she was an unusually well established woman for a former concubine getting on in years. As noted earlier, for a time she had lived in the abbot's house as nurse to his son. At that time she had already had Cecilia, who was "seven or eight," and to have been able to nurse, she had recently been pregnant; thus, given that she had recently been pregnant, was apparently on her own, and was selling her milk and perhaps her body as well, her prospects might not have seemed very promising. But her strategies appear to have worked out well in the end.

Shortly after leaving Ruis's service she went to live with the priest Domenigo. There she stayed for many years and, as noted, produced five more children. When she left the priest, she moved around some but eventually settled back in Morsana. Abbot Ruis reported, "I do not know how many years ago it would be that she left [the priest of Morsana], however, two months ago she came to visit me at my house in Venice . . . and she told me that she had come from Padua, where she had a certain income which she had gone to collect. As she was leaving without wishing to stay for dinner or anything else, she explained that she was in a rush because the boat for Portogruaro was about to leave and she wanted to catch it to go to Morsana. There, she explained, she was living in a house that she had bought herself."[23]

Thus in 1573, at the time of the case, she was about 48 years old, living in a house of her own surrounded by her children and traveling about the countryside to collect her revenues. Even allowing for exaggeration, Lucia had done much better than one might expect for a servant, wet nurse, and concubine with a raft of illegitimate children from the village of Morsana. It appears her own microstrategies of power had brought her a certain wealth and position.

But the details of Lucia's life did not distract those interrogating Abbot Ruis from pursuing their interest in her daughter, Cecilia. The abbot was asked to describe her in his second testimony: "Cecilia, as I have said, is a young woman of about thirty-two, more pretty than ugly, pleasantly fair in complexion, of medium height, neither fat nor thin."[24] More pertinent, he was asked: "This Cecilia before she decided to commit this evil act did she live in your house? And after? And for how many years?" The abbot confessed, "When her mother was nursing my son . . . the said Cecilia was about seven or eight and she lived with her in my house. When her mother left . . . she took with her this young girl who had to have been about ten. . . . About five years later she returned to my house . . . and following that she has always lived in my house." The abbot did qualify his "always" by admitting that she had left him at times to go to "Venice and diverse places staying in rooms and renting lodgings together with diverse women . . . like that madonna Medea" and that she had finally left him for good "about ten or eleven months ago" to flee with a doctor.

The notary of the Holy Office moralized in the margin of his notes at this point, "Cecilia lived in the house of the accused and in diverse places without her mother and she was not married."[25] Intentionally or not, the movement of his mistress and her living on her own without her mother had helped to demonstrate to him and most likely the Holy Office as well that she was a loose woman perhaps capable of the deeds that Ruis had claimed. The power in such assumptions about a woman's sexual identity is clear; women on their own were evil, and that meant that women who valued their reputation could not be on their own. But beyond that, once again here the mobility of this young woman from the countryside stands out. Like many other women who had accepted sexually identifying labels like "concubine" or "prostitute" or who had been forced to do so and thus lost their honor, young Cecilia had been empowered as well as demeaned and seemed to move at least around the Veneto with impressive ease—essentially by opting out of community evaluations of her sexual identity at one level Cecilia had gained the ability to negotiate a more complex identity and way of life, not necessarily a better or happier one, but more complex certainly.

It is also interesting to note the age at which Cecilia was brought to Abbot Ruis—15. This, of course, was considered a good age for marriage and also a good age for becoming a prostitute or a concubine. That she had been his concubine no one who knew them doubted, and neither Cecilia nor her mother denied it. The abbot's friend Domenigo Borgana summed it up well when he testified, "It would be about fourteen years that this Cecilia has been continuously with this Abbot as his concubine and this is widely known [*et questo è notorio*]," or again when he affirmed, "The love which the said Abbot had for this Cecilia, his concubine, was a thing known to all."[26] Here again we see how sexual identity falls back upon a group judgment—a consensus reality—"widely known" or "known to all."

Both Cecilia and her mother, Lucia, were less enthusiastic about the love involved, as one might expect. Lucia in her first testimony wasted no time in revealing her counterstrategy against the abbot's claims, and it too turned upon group judgments and consensus reality. After describing her daughter's relationship with him—"Cecilia has been with the Abbot Ruis . . . for about fourteen years as his woman and concubine"—she struck out with: "I hold this Abbot Ruis to be a loud-mouthed-fool [*sbaiaffon*] and a fraud [*busardo*] and *he is held as such and for such by all those who know him.* Moreover what he has said in this case, he has said completely from rage and jealousy because Cecilia my daughter has left him. Already once earlier when she left him he went about saying similar fantasies and then when Cecilia returned to stay with him he ceased. Now that she has left again he has begun again his lies and false fantasies as a hammer [*per martello*]."[27] Behind the insults, Lucia's blackmail defense is clear. Essentially Abbot Ruis's accusations were "false fantasies" motivated by a desire to force her daughter to return to him. Such a strategy had worked before, and now he was attempting it again.

If blackmail was to be a main line of defense against Abbot Ruis's accusation, character assassination aimed at destroying his honor and reputation would play a major role as well, as the colorful epithets applied to him and "known to all" suggested right from the start. Thus Lucia continued, "While Cecilia, my daughter, lived in his house he did not even give her one penny or even a blouse." Obviously this did not fit the expectations about concubinage of those who were hearing Lucia's testimony, for they asked immediately: "How can you say this, given that your daughter lived in the house of this Abbot and went about nobly and honorably dressed?"

Her response reads as if it was quick and heated. "If she went around [dressed] nobly, others had given her the clothes, for that Abbot kept her in his house for his profit. That is others went to her carnally and they dressed her and gave her money and this Abbot sold the clothing and also took from her the money that she had earned."[28] One begins to understand why the abbot Ruis had been anxious to keep his story of Cecilia's love magic out of the hands of the Holy Office, for in her mother he had a powerful adversary, who with her testimony was prepared to try to turn the tables on him by creating another vision of how he kept his concubine and of the man himself—another identity for Ruis himself.

And that, in fact, was what was happening—the case was rapidly changing from one concerning the love magic of a young concubine to one concerning the evil life and nature of the abbot himself, an evil life that went well beyond merely keeping a concubine like the "good priest" of Morsana. One set of apparent lies was being replaced by what in all likelihood was another.

But again, as lies the counterattack of Cecilia and her mother provide interesting suggestions about the strategies of power that underlay the relationship between the abbot and his concubine. In her testimony Cecilia talked first about the times she tried to leave the abbot to live on her own or with a lover. The first time she fled she was about 19. She reported that she had gone to Venice, where she had been helped by the wife of an herb dealer, who had sent her on to the house of Medea. Her account is too brief to know if this was some sort of women's recruitment network for prostitution. But as several witnesses had reported that Medea's daughter was a courtesan, that may have been the case—Cecilia may have been escaping to try her hand as a high-class prostitute in Venice (a potentially more lucrative venture then being the concubine of Ruis).

If that was true, at 19 with Medea as her manager, she might have had an excellent chance to do well. Although she was from the provinces, she had grown up in the households of clerics and apparently had some education and some exposure to the manners and graces of life at higher social levels, all of which might have qualified her to be a courtesan. But if her strategy of escape had hinged on that, it was cut short by the abbot, for after about ten days at Medea's house he came for her and carried her off by force, at least in her telling of the tale.[29]

The second time she fled, she was about 29. Theoretically love was her motive, love for a certain Messer Zuan Battista Pilato of Padua, who had fallen in love with her as well. "Love," it should be noted, also served as one of the most complex and promising microstrategies of power in the Renaissance, and her love in this instance may well have been fortified by a desire to escape the abbot and find a rich protector. She had run off with her lover to his house, but again Ruis interfered, this time with his blackmail strategy.

The third time was Cecilia's charm. She ran off with a doctor and changed her name to avoid being traced. She had managed to stay free from the abbot for almost a year at the time of her testimony.[30] But when Ruis had discovered where she was, once again he had begun his campaign to force her to return. This time, however, his strategy escaped his control, as it had come to the attention of higher authorities before the blackmail could work.

Beyond the abbot's reluctance to testify, a key to this reading of the case for those authorities, at least, was his attempt to pressure Cecilia and her mother not to testify. Apparently he had hoped that he might be able to regain command of the situation by playing on their fear of appearing before the authorities. Thus he sent the *gastaldo* of Sumaga, who was his man, to warn the women that they should flee rather than testify. But it was too little and too late. The women were ready to take on their abbot and try their own strategies on the Holy Office of Venice. In the end even his *gastaldo* deserted him, admitting the abbot's ploy when questioned and also his desperation.

Abbot Ruis, deserted by his supporters and onetime friends in large part because of his almost demented drive to take back his concubine, by this stage could almost seem a tragic character. In fact, many locals suggested just that in their testimony. A once powerful man, he was now viewed in his community as a slightly mad loudmouth who had sacrificed everything that he had built up in his futile quest to regain his mistress, undone by a powerful woman and his own sexual desires. If one believed in love magic, one could almost believe that Cecilia *had* used the holy oil to bind his love to her—as his behavior was virtually what was claimed for such magic. But it should not be forgotten that for much of Cecilia's life Abbot Ruis had been in control, able to force her to return to his home and bend to his will in large part because in his small community he was a powerful, dominant male and she was not. Clearly Cecilia put that situation in its most negative light in her testimony, but it was a vision that was echoed in most of the testimony heard by the authorities and echoed in many lives of women in similar situations.

Near the end of her testimony she was asked, "What did you do in the house of the Abbot all those years?" She replied, "I went to his house when I was very little [*picinina*] and it's true that he took me on as a maid. But from being a maid I became his companion in bed and I have always been with him for about fourteen years." She then added on her own, "He never gave me much of anything significant as a reward; but such things were done by a lover of mine." When asked if the abbot knew about this, she replied, "Yes sir. The said Abbot took both my virtue and the money that I had from my lover."[31]

Was Cecilia actually prostituted by the abbot, who kept her as his concubine, or was this merely another front in the campaign to paint the abbot in as negative a light as possible? Had he in the end become a pimp as well as a man broken by his sexual desire for his young concubine? If it was a lie, at least it was not so outrageous a one that it could not be given credence by both the locals who testified and the ecclesiastical authorities. Without going that far, however, it appears that the tale of the abbot and his concubine reveals a countryside in the 1570s where clerical concubinage was still widely practiced and perceived as unexceptional. It was necessary to accuse the abbot of prostituting his concubine and keeping the profits to add the required weight to the charge to make it have an impact. The priest of Morsana, who everyone admitted had kept Lucia as his concubine and fathered at least five children with her, was essentially ignored once it was ascertained that he had kept his holy oil safely locked away from his women. He also appears to have been more open-handed with his concubine, allowing and perhaps even aiding Lucia when she decided to move out into a house of her own. Needless to say, there is not enough information to be sure about the nature of either relationship, but the testimony about both suggests an interesting range of arrangements in rural clerical concubinage.

In the end it appears that Cecilia escaped the abbot and that he escaped ecclesiastical punishment. The last material contained in his file with the Holy Office is a letter from him sent from his home and dated 18 June 1575 asking the office to expedite his case, as the false accusations involved were causing him undue hardship. Four months earlier the Holy Office had written to Rome asking for a decision on the matter, but if authorities in Rome replied, they had not done so by June, and their response is not recorded in the files of the Holy Office.

Thus for us, the abbot, his concubine, and their lies once again become invisible to history. Captain Fear, in turn, if you were worried, escaped his unmanning as male concubine of the Amazons to live on in literature, on the stage, and in the imagination of the time as a "true" masculine warrior hero, still echoing and reversing in this the abbot and his concubine. And nicely, all escaped the dangerous implications of their untruths to live on in this microhistory, if only for a moment, and suggest some different perspectives on self-negotiation, masculine identity, and microstrategies of power at the end of the Renaissance.

Brunelleschi's First Masterpiece, or Mean Streets, Familiar Streets, Masculine Spaces, and Identity in Renaissance Florence

"At the heart of the city there is a place full of joy. . . . Seek the grandeur of the high dome of Santa Reparata [the cathedral] or ask for the magnificent church of God that shows the Lamb [the Baptistery]. Once there bear to the right a few paces . . . and ask for the Mercato Vecchio. There half way down the street stands a happy whorehouse which you will know by the very smell of the place. Enter and give my greetings to the whores and madams. . . . The blond Helena and the sweet Matilda will greet you. . . . You will see Giannetta and . . . the naked and painted breasts of Claudia. . . . Here . . . you can find anything that is illicit."[1] This description of the heart of Florence written in the early fifteenth century by Antonio Beccadelli, known as Il Panormita, and dedicated to Cosimo de' Medici might seem largely alien to the brilliant early Renaissance flourishing of art and humanistic culture that we associate with the city. Certainly the spaces of Renaissance Florence were alive with a cultural and artistic excitement that was crucial for what has been labeled the Renaissance, but Panormita's equally lively description suggests many questions about how contemporaries actually lived in that cityscape.

One thing seems clear, however: Renaissance Florence, much like a Renaissance text, had many ways of being read and lived. For the upper classes, for example, the city was to a great degree a creation of their wealth, power, and imagination and both consciously and unconsciously incorporated, reflected, and reinforced their customs, values, and culture.[2] For others (the lower classes, marginal people, transients, perhaps women) there were other readings, other lives, other consensus realities about the city's identity and significance. And this suggests once again that the modern understanding of public space and the distinction between public and private spaces does not work well in the Renaissance; what we would label today public space was for the upper and middling classes of the time at least more masculine and identity-giving (in the sense of providing a sense of being a member of a civic community and the groups of that community) than public. Yet, as we shall see, it was also full of special meanings for these different groups and solidarities, thus rife with what might be considered more private readings as well. In this chapter, however, I would like to go beyond social readings and anachronistic distinctions like public and private to follow the smell of flesh in Panormita's streets, for that very smell suggests that Florence, like other Renaissance cities, was built primarily by and for men, their pleasures, play, work, desires, fears; in that light we should expect that it has Renaissance readings that are particularly conditioned by their values, visions, and ways of thinking, especially about themselves.

One way of rethinking the spaces of Florence in the Renaissance, then, is considering the way in which the city was lived, thought, and formed using what might be labeled its masculine culture—rethinking its spaces in terms of gender and male sexuality. To a degree virtually all culture in the Renaissance was marked by masculine values and vision,[3] and in turn it is clear that "masculine culture" regularly was intertwined with broader values and visions that it would be reductionist to treat as merely male. Nonetheless, there are certain strains of the broader culture of the Renaissance that might be fruitfully separated out and examined from the perspective of gender or sex—specifically masculine—if we keep in mind that what we are creating are largely artificial categories.

Especially important perhaps were three discourses for the masculine spaces of the Renaissance city: one on male friendship, a second on male honor, and a third on male pleasure. These discourses melded together (not without conflict and contradictions, however) to make up a central component of a broader regime of social organization and discipline in the Renaissance which I will call the regime of *virtù*—an ongoing display of male power, rationality, and control which was central to adult masculine identity, status, and discipline.[4] Of course, the very etymology of the term *virtù* turns on its Latin root *vir,* meaning male, and suggests its intimate connection with male culture.[5] At one level, in the Renaissance the meaning of *virtù* was simple: in virtually every context it marked out those characteristics that set one man (*vir*) above another. But what those characteristics were was often hotly contested and changed over time, with Boccaccio finding *virtù* in the fourteenth century in the cunning rationality of his clever tricksters in the *Decameron;* fifteenth century humanists finding it in a rational, controlled, classical approach to life and, for a time, service to the state; and courtiers of the fifteenth and sixteenth centuries finding it in the blending of service to a prince, manners, grace, and *sprezzatura* that entailed a delicate balance of aggression and passivity reflected in Ariosto's male heroes, Orlando and Ruggiero, and in Castiglione's vision of a perfect courtier.

Now it might seem that a concept as hotly debated and contested as *virtù* would not serve well for a regime, but in fact it was so hotly contested precisely because its rule was so omnipresent. If one could capture the definition of *virtù*—or more pertinent the consensus reality of it—one could control real power; thus debates about *virtù* cut to the heart of how life should be organized and lived. And as a result the regime of *virtù* was ubiquitous in the Renaissance—humanist ideals and writing, governmental forms, social concepts and norms, art, literature, religion, even commercial organization and methods all to a degree turned on (and in a real way were ruled by) its imperatives. Significantly, however, this regime was not merely verbal; nor was it internalized to the same extent or in the same way as modern disciplining discourses seem to be.

For this essay I want to suggest that much of its weight was carried by the physical spaces of the city, by the sights, sounds, and smells of the familiar spaces of Florence. This regime of *virtù*, along with maleness, male culture, and masculinity, was literally thought through and written out on the spaces of Renaissance cities like Florence. Males discovered, negotiated, and lived a masculine culture in large part in a city that was rich with signs and reflections of that culture and that regime of *virtù*—a cityscape that played a crucial role in sustaining the consensus reality of ideal masculine identity and male sexuality. Even the Mercato Vecchio smelled of the flesh of their sexual desires, and Panormita could celebrate that, expecting other men to share his enthusiasm and Cosimo de' Medici's approval.

But rather than continue in this theoretical fashion in this chapter, I would like to use a novella set in Quattrocento Florence, "The Fat Woodcarver" by Antonio Manetti, as a concrete example for exploring the power of this way of looking at the city and the regime of *virtù* there. Actually, the tale has been looked at extensively both by art historians interested in the famous characters involved and by literary scholars interested in the claim that it is a literary description of real historical events. Much of that scholarship has been summed up by Lauro Martines in *An Italian Renaissance Sextet*—a volume that provides translations and a cutting-edge analysis of six Renaissance novelle, including this tale.[6]

As Martines impressively demonstrates, it is a fascinating tale on many levels: first, simply as the story of a cruel joke that at the time seemed uproariously funny, even if it no longer seems so today. Robert Darnton has pointed out that such moments of "dead" humor can be most revealing for discovering the distance of the past and its distinct meanings. Few today would laugh at the conceit of a group of friends who convince one of their number that he has been transformed into another person, especially when the joke's victim, Manetto, called Grasso (the fat woodcarver of the tale's title), comes close to going mad and eventually flees the city in dishonor as a result of their complex scam. But the story is also interesting because of its claims to be true, and the characters involved include some of the most famous artists and artisans of the period including Filippo Brunelleschi, who was the mastermind of the joke. In a way, then, we have in this story a fifteenth-century representation of the masculine culture of some of the people who were crucial for the building of Florence and that very culture in the Renaissance. Notably, it is also a tale that turns on Renaissance identity and one might say its "unperformance," as the fat woodcarver literally loses his identity at the hands of a group of his friends and their cruel joke. And finally, and most important, the story is interesting because it speaks clearly the three discourses noted above and stages them in the spaces of Florence as an emblematic tale of the regime of *virtù* and its power.

Another significant aspect of the tale is that although it was written down in the form discussed here in the 1480s by the Florentine architect and writer Antonio di Tuccio Manetti (1423–97), the events were reported to have taken place in 1409, well before he was born. Manetti, however, knew Brunelleschi, even wrote an account of his life, and thus could claim to have heard the story from the master artificer of the cruel joke himself.[7] Moreover, it was a story whose fame had grown over the years largely because it was too good an exemplar of *virtù* in action not to have captured the Florentine imagination; thus, it reflected a lively oral tradition as well. And like all good stories—even when heard from the mouth of one of the protagonists—we may assume that it had a tendency to grow and become more perfect and, in a way, truer as it was retold and committed to writing. Truer, in that presumably details that did not add to the central themes had dropped away and nuances that enhanced those themes had been highlighted; if that was the case, the tale had become truer to its themes and the cultural values of its time as it had become more false to actual events—literally it had gained strength as a deeper set of truths about identity and life in the masculine spaces of the city as it lost its conformity to actual events.

Nonetheless, one must not be too positive about the way in which its re-telling enhanced its truth, for even approximately seventy years of remem-bering it meant refashioning it over more than two generations of vibrant changes—changes whose impact on the tale are difficult to judge today. Per-haps most pertinent, over that period many of the characters went from being promising young artisans and intellectuals to the Florentine heroes of a great generation of artistic and intellectual creation, arguably one of the most cre-ative and successful in the Renaissance. Still, thinking about the story of the fat woodcarver as a tale about identity (and an emblematic moment of the regime of *virtù*) which grew across the fifteenth century in Florence rather than as a mere account of an event in 1409 in a way makes it richer yet.[8]

The tale begins with a group of young friends gathered one evening for din-ner at the house of Tomaso Pecori, a prominent Florentine of good family. A congenial group, they were drawn, as the narrator notes, "from the governing class and from among the masters of the more intellectual and imaginative crafts, such as painters, goldsmiths, woodcarvers, and the like."[9] After dinner, as it was a cold winter night, the group gathered around the hearth to continue their conversation. Already several things stand out which relate to masculine culture and the use of space in Florence. First, of course, is that these friends are all male. Women may have prepared and served the meal, but they are in-visible. Second, male friendship here reaches across formal class boundaries: chatting together are artisans and members of the governing class, men of more important old families and some newer men as well.[10]

In a socially sensitive age in which arguably social boundaries were being more strongly marked out and a new aristocratic ethos was gaining ground, one might wonder what the basis for friendship was in such a diverse group. The key, at least in Manetti's telling, seems to be a respect for talent and intellec-tual accomplishment, a respect for *virtù*. Significantly, it is not just any artisan who is admitted to this circle of friends but those dedicated to "the more in-tellectual and imaginative of the crafts" along with men "from the governing class"—men who were superior to others because of their skill (*virtù*) or their standing socially or in government (again *virtù*). Here, then, before the fire of Pecori's home, men gathered together to enjoy themselves in conversation united by friendship and a common respect for each other's *virtù*. A third thing one might note is how hearth and table had, for the evening at least, ceased being a "private" or even domestic space. What might have been labeled such with a wife and family gathered around on a similar winter night had become a masculine, virtually civic, space where male friendship dominated. Hearth and table were transformed from domestic space to civic/masculine space by male use; and the tale makes this perfectly clear, briefly noting that the conversation turned on matters of the men's crafts and professions. How space was used, then, could transform it profoundly, and here the gendered use of space breaks down the modern concept of public versus private space which seems in part to turn around the home and the domestic.[11]

After a while, however, the conversation turned to the fact that one regular member of the company was not there, Grasso the woodcarver. Tellingly, the tale in part identified Grasso, as many men were still identified in the fifteenth century, by his physical place in the city: not only was he labeled a skilled craftsman and a heavy young man of 28, but he was identified by the location of his shop, "in the Piazza di San Giovanni."[12] That location was revealing: it suggested that he was an artisan of some stature, for his workshop occupied a central location—the Piazza di San Giovanni was the site of the Baptistery and stood before the main cathedral of the city, a short stroll from the Mercato Vecchio and on the edge of Panormita's fleshy "place full of joy." Already a Renaissance man would begin to know Grasso by the space his workshop occupied.

Although Grasso's friends, his space, and the compliments in the tale about his skill as an artisan served to confirm his importance—his place in the regime of *virtù*—his friends were about to radically reposition him. His rejection of their dinner, upon reflection, was interpreted as a snub that reflected on their honor. Snubs may be a crucial trial for friendship in any culture, but the context of this snub begins to reveal something of the different flavor of male friendship in Renaissance Florence. The tale lets the cat out of the bag rather quietly, noting that this snub was particularly galling because his friends "were almost all of a higher rank and station."[13] Now *virtù* could overcome a degree of social disparity, but rank had its weight even in friendship—in fact, one might argue that it was crucial, for friendship implied support, and socially superior friends had patronlike qualities. But, of course, superior men (especially patrons) required a respect and consideration that made Grasso's refusal to attend dinner a serious matter indeed. Attendance marked in the quasi-public space of Pecori's dinner table Grasso's participation in the group's friendship, patronage, honor, and *virtù*; his absence could be seen as marking a rejection of the same—a most serious matter in the regime of *virtù*.[14]

The response of Grasso's friends to his snub was one that Florentines were famous for: a *beffa*, a cruel trick or joke that dishonored the victim and, to a degree, restored the honor of those who had been dishonored. Interestingly, while truly great *beffe* like the one played on Grasso had to demonstrate a maximum amount of ingenuity and *virtù*, they served to bind groups together and discipline male relationships as well—in sum, they served as crucial moments of the regime of *virtù*.[15] And for our discussion it is suggestive that most *beffe*, like this one, turned on the clever use of the masculine spaces of the Renaissance city. Filippo Brunelleschi, the architect of the trick, suggested: "In revenge for his not coming this evening . . . we'll make him believe that he has become someone else."[16] In sum, the group that sustained many of the most important components of Grasso's identity, that played a crucial role in the negotiation and maintenance of his sense of self, would repay his snub by taking that very self away and replacing it with another—a virtually perfect poetic justice.

The plot was launched the next evening, when Brunelleschi visited Grasso in his shop as he had done "a thousand times before." This was not by accident, for artisans' shops were important spaces for male sociability; premodern work habits made for a workplace radically different from the modern one. With Grasso's shop at the center of the city, friends and acquaintances moved in and out maintaining the networks that made the social, political, and economic world of Florence work, networks that for the most part were viewed within the framework of friendship and *virtù*. Grasso could in turn step out to lounge in the street before his shop and encounter passing friends, visit the shops of his compatriots, or even stroll on with comrades for a drink to the nearby taverns the Porco and the Malvagia (just a few paces from his shop in the warren of streets dominated by the palaces of the Adimari and Medici families)—for in many ways Renaissance Florence was a small, intimate space where friendship was constantly being demonstrated and vetted in its streets and shops and meaning and identity were found in such quotidian encounters.[17]

With a fifteenth-century vision of work that still saw work time and social time as integrated rather than distinct, Grasso would have been free to maintain his contacts largely because of that intimate space, which made it possible to do so traveling short distances on foot. One needs, then, to think of a workday that had the potential at least to be highly social and the shop again not simply as a place of production. Or perhaps it would be better to think of the shop as a place that produced more than products; it produced identity (as noted earlier), and it helped to produce the networks, friendships, and contacts central to the male world of Florence. This was so much the case that shops could even take friendship to an erotic level, as Michael Rocke has pointed out in his work on sodomy and homosocial relationships in Renaissance Florence: "Often it was the sociable bonds forged in the all-male environment of neighboring shops that provided both companionship and a supportive environment for sodomy." In fact, one of the areas of workshops heavily identified with this activity was the famed Ponte Vecchio, again right at the heart of the Renaissance city. There the butcher shop of the Del Mazzante brothers was virtually a hotbed of such activities.[18]

So Brunelleschi visited Grasso in his shop as a friend ordinarily would, but the familiar security of this space and their friendship was quickly overturned. With the pretense that his mother had fallen ill unexpectedly, Brunelleschi used Grasso's offer of aid—an offer that *virtù* and friendship led him to expect—to hold Grasso in his shop by asking him to wait there in case he needed to call for his help when he returned home. But rather than returning home, Brunelleschi circled back to Grasso's home near the cathedral, just a short walk away. Knowing that Grasso still lived with his mother, who was off in the countryside, Brunelleschi broke in and bolted the door behind him. Later, when Grasso arrived home after waiting long enough to be sure that his friend would not call for his aid, finding the door bolted, he assumed that his mother had returned and called her to let him in. Brunelleschi, waiting inside and expecting just this behavior from his friend, imitating his voice, responded, calling him Matteo. Brunelleschi's *beffa* had begun; he had taken Grasso's most secure place in Florence—his home—and his voice and was now using them to undermine Grasso himself. When Grasso insisted that he was Grasso and not the voice he heard coming from his house, Brunelleschi, again imitating his voice, dismissed him, saying he did not have time for jokes—a nice irony lost on Grasso increasingly caught up in exactly that, Brunelleschi's cruel joke.

The importance of place in all this is underlined by Grasso's reported thought process in the face of this spatial deconstruction of self. "What does this mean?" he asked himself. "That fellow up there [in my house] seems to be me ... and his voice sounds just like mine. Am I losing my mind?"[19] We might reply that he was not so much losing it as it was being stolen by Filippo, who was literally taking away the places by which Grasso thought himself in

Renaissance Florence—his home and his shop—and thus his identity and sense of self. When Grasso stepped back into the street, another friend and conspirator, the sculptor Donatello, sauntered by as if by accident and remarked, "Good evening, Matteo, are you looking for Grasso? He went into his house a little while ago" and continued on his way.[20] Again we see the close familiarity of the city, but once more Donatello was deconstructing it, informing Grasso that he was some unknown Matteo and that the real Grasso was already in his house.

Increasingly lost, Grasso decided to use the familiar spaces of Florence to relocate himself. "Startled and stunned . . . Grasso set off toward the Piazza di San Giovanni, saying to himself: 'I'll stay here until someone who knows me passes by and says who I am.'"[21] The Piazza di San Giovanni was the square of the Baptistery, the very center of Grasso's world hard by his home and his shop. Walking through his familiar masculine world, Grasso should have quickly refound himself in his daily spaces encountering the male friends and acquaintances that in many ways made him Grasso, but Brunelleschi's *beffa* was just taking shape, and the familiar streets suddenly turned mean when a group of officials from the Merchant's Court appeared, suborned by Brunelleschi, who arrested him for his debts, not as Grasso but rather once again as that unknown Matteo. Protests that he was not Matteo were ignored as a particularly inept, perhaps even deranged, attempt to avoid arrest. Hauled before a clerk of the court, he was registered as Matteo and thrown in jail. Fortunately for the plot, the other prisoners knew Grasso and this Matteo only by reputation; thus, hearing him referred to as Matteo, they accepted him as Matteo.

Now the very space of his city was conspiring against Grasso, for although men from all stations in life found themselves at one time or another in prison, especially debtors' prison, it was for men of Grasso's status a dishonorable space and hence relatively unfamiliar. As a result Grasso/Matteo was faced with a particularly difficult problem—in this alien space how was he to find the friendship and support to refind himself and gain his release? He saw two options: he could accept his new identity and seek out the help of Matteo's family and friends, or he could insist that he was Grasso and use his old friends to prove it. Both options crucially turned on the use of perhaps the two most important groups that defined and monitored identity in the Renaissance, family and friends. The latter strategy was more appealing to him—suggesting the strength of his inner conviction that he was Grasso.

But again place conspired against him as he reasoned, "If I send word home to my mother, and Grasso is at home (for I heard him there), *they'll make a laughing stock out of me.*"²² His inner sense of self was struggling with the much stronger Renaissance sense of self as negotiated and maintained by the groups with which one interacted. In essence Grasso had come to fear that the crucial group—his family—would not come to his aid, for he had heard for himself that as far as his family was concerned he was already at home and he would become "a laughing stock" if he tried to insist otherwise. Ultimately, then, the intimacy of Florence and the ties of friendship seemed to offer his best hope: he decided to stay by the window of the jail next morning until some friend passed by who would recognize him—a member of another group who could give him back his identity by proclaiming that he was Grasso and not Matteo. As the Merchant Court and its jail lay near the northeast corner of the Piazza della Signoria, a place of heavy foot traffic, his plan based upon the spaces of Florence seemed to offer a good chance for success.

The *virtù* of the plotters, however, thwarted his hopes: for in the morning, per Brunelleschi's plan, another conspirator, the powerful Giovanni di Messer Francesco Rucellai, showed up at the jail. Rucellai was from a noted Florentine family, and his friendship with Grasso had strong overtones of patronage, as Grasso often had carried out commissions for him. Thus, when he saw a powerful friend and patron like Rucellai at the jail glancing around, he had every reason to smile hopefully—he fully expected that the traditional alliances of friendship and power would reidentify him. Such hopes were quickly dashed, however, when Rucellai pretended not to know him. Crushed, Grasso was forced to conclude, "Giovanni Rucellai . . . didn't recognize me—he who's always in my shop. . . . It's certain that *I'm no longer Grasso and have become Matteo.*"²³ Just as the social space of Grasso's shop and his friendships were central in how he thought himself, now they had become crucial in how he was unthinking himself, losing his identity and becoming Matteo.

As Martines notes in his discussion of this tale, more telling yet was an apparent detail in the anxious self-examination that followed. Grasso worried that if he had lost his mind along with his identity—as seemed the case—he would be chased after and ridiculed by children in the streets of Florence. Such fears suggest that not only were streets and city spaces familiar stages to display male friendship and connectedness, but they also could be cruel courts trying honor and *virtù*. Insults, threats, and merely dishonoring gestures were carefully noted and evaluated. Violence, for which Florence was famous in the Renaissance, was often the only acceptable response—even the psychological violence of a cruel *beffa*. But violence had to be carefully applied in a way that could be evaluated socially within the masculine world of violence itself and within the context of family and group. And the price of violence or vendetta miscalculated was often escalating violence and the breaking of ties of friendship and group solidarity—a cruel spiral whereby those very ties that bound society together became what dissolved it.[24] Thus the streets of Florence had a rather Manichaean quality: they could be warm and familiar with the smiles of friends, or they could be cold, cruel, and physically dangerous for those who had lost honor and friendship. Grasso's position was worse yet, as he saw all too clearly, for not only had he lost his friends and in a very real way through that lost his identity, but he was also losing his mind, which meant that even little children could dishonor him in the streets—ultimately even madness threatened his place in the regime of *virtù.* And crucially all this was thought through and understood within the context of the masculine spaces of the city.

Grasso in jail, denied access to the spaces and connections of Florence, found that his day went from bad to worse. But finally Matteo's brothers showed up there to move the *beffa* on to its final phase. They had Grasso called over as Matteo and, when he accepted that identity, bawled him out for his foolish wasting of his wealth in gambling and evil living—the origin of Matteo's debts that had led to his arrest. Significantly, their complaints centered on the fact that he was no longer a youth—much like the Marescalco in Aretino's comedy discussed in Chapter 1—and they insisted that it was high time that he grew up and started living honorably. Honor and shame, maturity and immaturity, responsibility and pleasure provide the positive and negative poles of their complaints—certainly a quotidian lament that explained the indebtedness of many a young Florentine, for another significant area of male friendship and sociability was the illicit world of the city that focused on drinking, gambling, and sex, the very world that Panormita celebrated. All three were closely associated in Renaissance Florence, and all three were a prominent feature of the center of the city where Grasso lived and worked and where, as Matteo, he had supposedly fallen into debt and eventually really into jail.

It is worth pausing for a moment in our tale of Grasso's unmaking to look more closely at this other crucial aspect of the masculine spaces at the heart of Renaissance Florence. The narrow warren of streets leading off from the Mercato Vecchio and surrounding the old Roman and medieval heart of the city were loaded with small-scale prostitution, taverns, baths, and inns that offered a fairly complete, if largely illicit, package of wine, women, gambling, and perhaps even song (as music was often associated with Renaissance prostitution) contributing to the smell of flesh in the area that Panormita lauded. There one could find also a public brothel—set up by Florence's government to try to contain the dangers of prostitution and perhaps turn a profit for the city as well. This zone and its immediately surrounding area contained a host of taverns including the Bertuccie, Chiassolino, Fico, Malvagia, Panico, and Porco, names that in themselves virtually promised the whole program of the illicit world (respectively: the Monkey/Pussy/Ugly Whore; the Little Whore House/Little Confusion/Little Out House; the Fig/Cunt; The Wicked Woman; The Panic; and the Pig/Depraved).[25] There, beyond wine, men could find prostitutes, both female and male, gambling, drink, and apparently plenty of trouble to go along with masculine conviviality.[26]

Suggestively, however, Grasso's new brothers bawled him out because he was no longer a youth, implying that maturity meant that he should no longer be frequenting this area of the city for illicit pastimes.[27] Implicit in their complaint was an important distinction between youthfulness and maturity, for at least ideally this illicit world at the heart of Florence turned on a specific period in the life course of males which stretched from the early teens to about 30 years of age. Although this period is occasionally referred to as adolescence in Renaissance texts, as discussed in Chapter 1, it is perhaps more appropriate to use the terminology used more regularly at the time, *gioventù*, for this age period in order to stress that Renaissance *gioventù* was culturally constructed in ways that were decidedly different from modern adolescence. Most obvious, as noted earlier, it involved a longer period of years and, given shorter life expectancies, constituted a larger portion of a male's life, but, perhaps most significant, it was virtually entirely a masculine phenomenon. In Renaissance Florence women, especially upper-class women, married ideally in their early teens and entered almost immediately into their adult world of maternity and domesticity. Males instead passed a long *gioventù* that could stretch out to fifteen, even twenty years, a fact that both fascinated and troubled the Renaissance.

For our discussion, however, such young men, *giovani*, were the ideal denizens of the illicit spaces at the heart of Florence. Sex there was intertwined with a host of other activities attractive to this largely illicit masculine youth culture, including gambling (not just with cards and dice but also turning on general fisticuffs, cockfights, and other forms of microviolence, plus early forms of lotteries and numbers scams), hard drinking, and cons of every type. Less noted but nonetheless important were the services that this illicit world furnished for the perceived needs of such young men—loans, love magic,

magic to gain friends, cures for sexual disease, and various scams to help the young lighten the purses of their fathers to finance illicit pleasures.[28]

Some have been unwilling to see the significance of or even see this illicit world at the heart of Renaissance Florence and other Renaissance cities, it should be noted. And to some extent their reservations are well taken. It clearly would be wrong to think of the heart of Renaissance Florence in terms of the red-light districts or degraded centers of many modern cities. At the simplest level the life of the city coursed through these same streets, and the illicit was not cut off from the everyday. In fact, across the Renaissance the illicit world continuously spilled out from the center along commercial routes and even beyond the gates of the city at the same time that the government launched a series of failing initiatives to contain the illicit in specific areas or at least isolate it from the ceremonial and spiritual centers of urban life.[29] In addition, the strong disciplining forces of honor and shame had not yet been fully mobilized to isolate the illicit world or the men, especially young men, who frequented it—in a way we could say that illicit masculine pleasures still had their place in the regime of *virtù*.

But having said that, we have merely said that the illicit world of Renaissance Florence is not to be confused with modern illicit spaces and cultures. And while that is clear, it does not mean that we should ignore the fact that there was a formally illicit world at the heart of Renaissance cities like Florence largely created and maintained for male sociability and pleasure. Although women played a role in this world, it was theoretically at least merely as objects of male desire, and even though that theory was much belied by actual practice, it was a crucial shared vision. Moreover, what most significantly distinguished this illicit world from other places and forms of male pleasure was that those central building blocks of Renaissance society—the family and the church—were largely ignored there. The world of family and church was a different one with different rules, different goals, and a different ethic. Also tellingly, social hierarchy broke down in this world, gentlemen associated with lower-class women; males of the lower classes made love to males of the upper and visa versa; male groups formed and reformed around pleasures and vices rather than around issues of work or politics or more recognized forms of power. But evidently the separation was not complete: it may well be that the illicit heart of the city helped to create not only the masculine social networks that made the city function but also an emotional attachment to the city in an age before nationalism and the social and cultural construction of national loyalties. Could it be that Panormita's celebration of Florence dedicated to Cosimo de' Medici was intended also to play on such sentiments?

Clearly, however, this illicit world at the heart of Florence often functioned to reinforce or even build masculine lines of friendship and comradery, especially for young men. And at times those relationships involved more, for as Rocke argued in *Forbidden Friendships,* in Florence male friendship had an important sexual dimension, and this too was intimately related to *gioventù.* In fact, Rocke contends that such sexual relations were largely confined to that period of life and that they were so common then that they were virtually a normal part of life—a point that is well taken.[30] But it needs to be remembered that much of this activity was, in the eyes of the church, sinful; in the eyes of contemporaries, formally illicit; and in the eyes of Florentine government, illegal as well. Here we see how discourse and the practice of living often part ways: in grammar and language opposites do not go together, whereas in everyday life and sex they frequently do; thus, the illicit world of Renaissance Florence shared the same spaces and in some ways reinforced and interacted with the city's licit world and culture.

A particularly rich and rather literary example of the way these illicit spaces were understood and played a role in male sociability in Florence can be found in the letters of Machiavelli to his friend and hoped-for patron Francesco Vettori. In 1514, shortly after he had informed Vettori that he had completed *The Prince,* he exchanged a series of letters with Francesco, who was serving as Florentine ambassador in Rome at the time, about the sexual predilections and exploits of two of their circle of close friends, Guiliano Brancacci and Filippo Casavecchia. It seems that the two had visited Vettori in Rome for a while and had complicated his life with their opposing sexual tastes and values: Casavecchia preferring young males as sexual partners and disdaining the company of women, especially the courtesans who frequented Vettori's house and gardens, and Brancacci preferring courtesans and young women while being especially troubled about gaining the reputation of associating in any way with male-male sexual relations. But when shortly thereafter Brancacci and Casavecchia returned to Florence during the carnival season, Machiavelli wrote his friend with an amusing story (a "novella," which can be read as simply "news" or as a "short story") of a ridiculous sexual "metamorphosis" that had occurred involving their two friends.[31]

Machiavelli began his account in a metaphoric vein, relating that their friend Brancacci one night decided that he wanted to go hunting for birds in Florence—"andare alla macchia," literally beating the bushes for them. Beating the bushes for birds, given the Renaissance double sense of bird, as phallus, from the start suggests the direction in which this story was headed. But given Brancacci's reputation in their circle of friends as someone who was troubled by sodomy and sodomites and uninterested in young boys, that direction seems decidedly wrong. How could Brancacci, back in Florence during the carnival season, suddenly be hunting for phalluses when in Rome he had done nothing but preach to Vettori against even the least appearance of association with this "vice"? Machiavelli provided a possible escape when he promised that his tale would hide things behind metaphors, and thus one might suppose that Brancacci's name was a cover for someone else; but, as we shall see, he soon dropped out of the metaphoric mode and named clearly the characters involved, and Brancacci remained Brancacci throughout. The answer to this dilemma seems to lie instead in the "ridiculous metamorphosis" promised, for the humor of the tale turns on the fact that their common friend had suddenly changed the object of his sexual desires and decided to go hunting birds.

And that the birds he had decided to hunt were phallic was made clear while Machiavelli was still in the humorously metaphoric vein by the place where he decided to beat the bushes. "He crossed the bridge of the Carraia [one of the bridges that crosses the Arno] and went along the street of the Canto de'-Mozzi [probably now Via del Parione] which leads to Santa Trinita, and entering Borgo Santo Apostolo, he wandered about a bit through those narrow allies [*chiasci*] that are in between; and not finding any birds in waiting ... he moved on past the headquarters of the Guelf party, through the Mercato Nuovo and along the street of the Calimala he came to the Tetto de'Pisani where looking carefully through all those hiding places he found a little thrush."[32] Tellingly, this itinerary took Brancacci hunting for birds through the heart of the district of Florence dedicated to illicit sex—the area just discussed, where the former Grasso, now Matteo, had run up his debts following his desires of *gioventù*—a place rich in bordellos, baths, inns, and prostitutes offering a whole range of sexual services, including male prostitutes and *giovani* available for sexual encounters. If Machiavelli's story of Brancacci's bird hunting is merely a story, he nonetheless took care to give it the correct setting, a setting that his reader, Vettori, would have understood immediately as true, as these were the shared masculine spaces of illicit sex at the heart of the city. Brancacci then took his prize bird into a nearby alleyway in a dark place near where Frosino da Panzano—an acquaintance of Machaivelli's and Vettori's mentioned occasionally in their letters—had lived at one time and after "kissing" and "petting" him a bit had sexual relations with him.

Machiavelli then switched from the metaphoric mode of the bird hunt to a more direct narrative to explain the complex unfolding of the joke (*burla*) that was at the heart of his tale. Brancacci, when he found out that his partner was a certain Michele, "the son of an important man," decided that his bird required more tending than he originally anticipated and promised to pay him for his services. But as he did not have the money with him, still in the dark of the alley he decided to trick the lad, and in a move that echoes curiously Brunelleschi's cruel joke on Grasso, he changed his own identity, telling the youth that he was Filippo Casavecchia—a likely-sounding lie given Casavecchia's apparently fairly widely known sexual tastes—and asked him to send someone to his shop the next morning for the money. Here perhaps was the second metamorphosis in Machiavelli's story, for in a way not only had Brancacci taken Casavecchia's sexual identity and made it his own by going bird hunting in the heart of the illicit sex district of Florence, but in the end he had taken his name and his formal identity as well. Needless to say, the next morning, when confronted by a messenger from the youngster demanding money for sexual services rendered, Casavecchia did not find the joke (*burla*) at his expense amusing in the least and sent the messenger away claiming to never have heard of this Michele and demanding that if the boy wanted anything from him he should come and see him himself. When Michele heard this, "the boy, being afraid of nothing," went to Filippo and, reproving him, promised that "if he [Casavecchia] had no compunction about tricking him, he had no compunction about defaming him."[33] Once again the streets of masculine friendship showed their disarming potential to turn rapidly dangerous and mean.

Realizing that the youth meant business, Filippo took him aside, and while he agreed that the lad had been tricked, he insisted that he was not the one who had done the tricking. He claimed, "I am a well behaved man [*molto costumato*] and I do not get involved in such evil affairs [*tristizie*]."[34] The way Machiavelli develops his story here is once again revealing for attitudes toward illicit sex, especially sodomy. Among their circle of friends Casavecchia openly had quite a different reputation—he projected and accepted a sexual persona as one who exclusively preferred male youths—and seemingly was untroubled by it within that group. From the perspective of the group's consensus reality about Casavecchia's sexual identity, his adventures with boys were seen not as something negative but as something that made him a good fellow and one of the group, virtually all of whom vaunted their participation in the world of illicit sex in one way or another.[35] But in the broader social world of Florence, Casavecchia had another reputation, another sexual identity to defend as "a well behaved man" who did "not get involved in such evil affairs." Of course, there was also the matter that such behavior in older men was officially much frowned upon in Florence and the penalties could be quite stiff; thus Casavecchia was threatened not just with a loss of reputation but also with potentially serious criminal penalties if this young man with a powerful father decided to pursue the matter, taking it from the arena of male friendship to that of civic reputation and morality. Fortunately for Machiavelli's humorous account of the affair, Michele agreed to keep things quiet and to allow Casavecchia to discover what had actually happened.

Machiavelli perfectly depicted Casavecchia's dilemma at this point—a dilemma not unlike Grasso's when he was in jail and could not decide whether to accept his new name and identity—reporting what their friend had supposedly said to himself: "If I keep quiet and pay off Michele with a florin I become his source of income, I become his debtor, confess my sin, and instead of being innocent I become a criminal; if I deny everything without finding out the truth I have to become involved in a dispute with a boy, I will have to justify my behavior with him and with others and all the blame will fall on me; if I try to find out the truth, I will have to put the blame on someone, perhaps incorrectly, and make an enemy and for all this I will still not be justified."[36] Behind the wit of Machiavelli's report, Casavecchia's dilemma comes through clearly, and we get a good sense of how tricky the world beyond Machiavelli's letters and his circle of good friends could be for older men who were interested in sex with youths. But once again Machiavelli's narrative was a laughing one about a "ridiculous metamorphosis," and when Casavecchia put aside his fears for a moment and began to think seriously about who might have played this trick on him, "he immediately hit the target," guessing that Brancacci was exactly the type of person who would do such a thing.

He then enlisted the aid of Alberto Lotto, a friend of his and a relative of young Michele's—Florence once again demonstrating how small and intimate a Renaissance city could be for men of the upper classes—asking him to see whether he could get the youth to recognize Brancacci as the true culprit. Lotto, in turn, convinced Michele to go with him to the square of Santo Ilario (Saint Hilarious, a most fitting place again to bring this joke to its conclusion at Brancacci's expense, but even with its perfect metaphoric quality a place that actually existed), where, coming up on Brancacci from behind while he was regaling a group of friends with stories, the boy was able to recognize his voice as the one belonging to the man who had claimed to be Casavecchia in the dark. When Brancacci turned around and recognized the youth, he realized that he had been found out and ran off, thus admitting his guilt and winning public scorn ("vituperato") while Filippo escaped from that same fate and his dilemma. Machiavelli concluded his tale noting that the affair had spawned a new saying in Florence that carnival season, "Are you Brancacci or are you Casa[vecchia]?" and then tied the whole story together with a reference to Ovid's *Metamorphosis* by claiming humorously, "[And this tale] was told by all [the gods] in heaven."[37] This classical reference harked back to Machiavelli's original "ridiculous metamorphosis" and underlined the storylike quality of his letter by paralleling the way all Florence was talking about the transformation of Brancacci into Casavecchia with the way all the gods in heaven, according to Ovid, talked about how Vulcan displayed his wife, Venus, and Mars caught in adultery.

But behind that classical and learned reference and just beneath Brancacci's metamorphosis into Casavecchia, there may have been another "ridiculous" metamorphosis that worked for a laugh only in the context of the ongoing sexual themes of the letters exchanged between Vettori and Machiavelli. In beating the bushes of Florence for young birds, Brancacci had changed an important element of his identity in those letters and in the context of their circle of male friends—he had gone from being a man attracted exclusively to young women and uninterested in boys, even at times condemning such relationships, to one who secretly hunted them in the illicit night zones of Florence. Now all this may have been a mere joke, a fiction, a learned reference to the classics, or it may well have been an elaborate metaphor to discreetly discuss politics, language, or power—all have been suggested. Still, two things seem necessary to make any of these interpretations work: first, both Machiavelli and Vettori had to recognize the Renaissance sexual identities of Brancacci and Casavecchia to make his tale work—if it was of no significance who Brancacci penetrated sexually, there was no metamorphosis in his picking a boy; second, Machiavelli had to be able to re-create the actual sexual world of the streets of Florence to give his narrative and the metamorphoses he described the ring of truth.

Simply put, whether "true" or not—in the sense of whether it actually happened or not—this tale was "true" to the sexual world and masculine spaces of Renaissance Florence and the way they worked, a world where men hunted birds through the streets known for illicit sex at the center of the city; where Casavecchia was known at least by his friends as a man who preferred sex with boys and was uninterested in sex with women; where Brancacci had the exact opposite reputation; where both men were concerned about their sexual reputation in the broader community, while they could be and were more open and relaxed within their circle of closer friends; where this group of friends could laugh in their letters at sexual practices that were formally illegal; and where a clever Machiavelli could transform whatever actually happened into a novella about a "ridiculous metamorphosis." In the end it seems that Machiavelli did not entirely make up this story and that perhaps Brancacci had undergone a metamorphosis, as claimed, to go out beating the bushes of Florence for thrushes during the carnival of 1514, for Machiavelli concluded this section of the letter noting, "I believe that you may have heard this news from others, still I wanted to tell you about it in more detail, because I thought I owed it to you."[38]

In sum, this world of male friendship and sexuality was written across the city, especially its heart. Those same streets and alleys that hosted inns and female prostitutes were frequented by males seeking partners for sodomy; in fact, female partners or male partners were apparently often viewed as interchangeable in the many taverns, inns, and houses of prostitution. Still, some areas in the city were more associated with sodomy, and males who sought those particular pleasures knew where to find them. The Via dei Pellicciai, running from the west side of the Mercato Vecchio south past the Via Porta Rossa, for example, was a famous haunt at the end of the fifteenth century. And the two taverns most noted for sodomy, the Buco (near the Ponte Vecchio in an alley that still bears its name) and the Sant'Andrea or del Lino (located behind the church of the same name not far from the Mercato Vecchio and just east of the Via dei Pellicciai), were apparently solely for males and not frequented by female prostitutes. Some, perhaps seeking a bit more privacy, abandoned the city center for the open spaces just beyond the walls. And finally, rather fittingly given our tale, Brunelleschi's dome itself became so noted for such activity that in the sixteenth century young males were banned from the area![39]

As Casavecchia's fears about Michele's accusations becoming more generally known suggest, however, across the fifteenth and sixteenth centuries, it seems that older men's participation in the illicit world became progressively more questionable—owing in part, I would suggest, to the logic of the regime of *virtù*. For mature men the ideal was increasingly that *virtù* should dominate passion, which is not to argue that it did but rather to suggest that an important split was developing between the ideals of masculine sexual control in maturity and a broader freedom of action in *gioventù*. Yet for young men the illicit world of sex may have been seen as offering an opportunity to build networks based on friendship—a hypothesis supported by fears expressed that the process could go wrong and that some contacts formed in the illicit world might be counterproductive. Friendship, after all, was fine up to a point, but one needed the right friends for success. Close ties based on sex and friendship with the right males could build the basis for a successful life; ties to the wrong individuals could spell disaster. This may help explain Rocke's interesting finding that some families actually encouraged their young sons' sexual relationships with older men. When their partners were important, parents could hope that their children were in good hands in the illicit world and building the networks of friendship that would lead to success.[40]

Be that as it may, and returning to Grasso's metamorphosis into Matteo, it is suggestive that the characters of our tale are themselves either *giovani* or just leaving that period behind. Brunelleschi, the master plotter, not yet the master architect, is in his early thirties. In the tale's retelling Grasso has become 28, although contemporary documentation suggests that he was actually closer to 24 in 1409, the year in which the tale is set.[41] Moreover, the older males in the story seem much more the masters of *virtù*. Led by that master plotter Brunelleschi, they control the action with mature male rationality and power—they work the streets and institutions of the city masterfully to make their *beffa* work. Grasso, in contrast, is still not beyond the passions of youth and thus stands as an easy mark. In this vision of the tale Brunelleschi's evident *virtù* might be seen not as a premonition of his later artistic accomplishments but as a proof of his newly attained adult male status: cool, rational, calculating, and in control; thus, with his *beffa* he demonstrated for his contemporaries that he had mastered the regime of *virtù* and become a mature male adult—in a way this cruel joke at his young friend Grasso's expense was his first masterpiece, a masterwork of *virtù* that marked his passage to adulthood.

There may be yet a deeper level that has to some extent dropped out of the later telling of the story that we are working with. If Rocke is right in asserting that a very high proportion of Florentine males during *gioventù* participated at one time or another in sodomy often subsumed under the rubric of friendship, the close friendship of Brunelleschi and Grasso might be read in another way. In fact, this whole grouping of young friends so relaxed about status might be read differently. Could it be that the *virtù* of the members of the group which helped to explain their egalitarian friendships was a later addition to make the story work better as a tale about the cleverness of the great artist and architect Brunelleschi and that a more significant reason for the group was the cross-class sexual attractions common within the illicit world of Florence? And could it be that Grasso, several years younger than his close

friend Brunelleschi, was once his lover, reflecting the classic age patterns of
Renaissance homoerotic relationships? In this interpretation both men had
now grown too old for their relationship: Brunelleschi in his early thirties was
ready for adult male status; Grasso in his early twenties was ready for taking
at the very least the active role in sex with other younger males or women.[42]
Could it be that this cruel joke, motivated so thinly in this retelling, masked a
different original *beffa* that also turned on friendship—an aggressive shift
from a sexually based youthful friendship between Grasso and Brunelleschi to
a mature nonsexual relationship initiated by Brunelleschi? Certainly in that
context Grasso's emotional flight from the city and his old friend and their
eventual reestablishment of a relationship on other terms, discussed below,
makes eminent sense.

Whether this sexual reading is true or not, young Grasso languished in jail
for the supposed sins of Matteo until his brothers returned after dark to free
him. The rationale was that darkness would protect honor—the return of the
prodigal son would go unnoticed in the mean streets of Florence. Thus, after
nightfall they took Grasso/Matteo home; now his place was in the Oltrarno
district just across the Ponte Vecchio "near the church of Santa Felicita, at the
beginning of the Costa San Giorgio."[43] Re-placed as Matteo, Grasso was virtually Matteo. Home at last, he sat down to dinner with his brothers, almost as
if the social moment of male kin eating together confirmed his new identity
and the success of Brunelleschi's *beffa.*

But, of course, his brothers were not kin, and they immediately betrayed
him by slipping him a powerful sleeping potion. As he was dropping off, the
last words he heard were a report of a conversation they claimed they had overheard walking through the Mercato Nuovo. Someone behind them had said,
"Do you see that fellow who's lost his memory and forgotten who he is?" To
which his friend replied, "That's not the fellow, it's his brother."[44] The shame
and dishonor of the mean streets of Florence were always at work, and it
seemed that there would be no real rest for Grasso/Matteo. More accurate, in
the imaginary streets of Brunelleshi's clever *beffa*, Grasso was being continu-
ally remade as Matteo—but those streets worked in Grasso's imagination only
because they mirrored the fact that exactly such masculine evaluation of *virtù*,
honor, and shame in the streets of Florence worked continuously in forming
and disciplining men. There, without laws, without formal pronouncements
or policing, men were formed and reformed by the regime of *virtù.*

Deeply drugged, the former Grasso was ready for the climax of his trials.

Brunelleschi arrived with six of the original group of plotters, loaded their sleeping victim into a hamper, and carried him back across the Arno to Grasso's home. There they put him in his bed and placed his clothes where he normally left them, but to complete their joke they could not resist putting his feet where his head normally lay. Renaissance humor, as we have seen, was fascinated by and heavily reliant on reversals; reversing their victim in perhaps the most personal space he had, his bed, was one last trick too good to pass up. Then, "they took the key to his workshop . . . went there, entered, and moved all the tools . . . turning the blades upside down, and the same with the handles of his hammers . . . and they did this to all the tools that lent themselves to such reversing, and turned the whole workshop topsy turvy."[45] Thus in a way his most familiar spaces, bed and workshop, were reversed one last time.

The morning of the third day brought the resurrection of Grasso, and once again the places of Florence were so central that the tale speaks for itself: "Awakening to the sound of the Angelus from Santa Maria del Fiore . . . he recognized the sound of the bell, and opening his eyes . . . realized that he was in his own house, and his heart was suddenly filled with great joy, for it seemed he had become Grasso again."[46] In a walking city (like Renaissance Florence), without the roar of traffic, waking in the morning to the familiar local sounds of church bells and the familiar voices of passersby and familiar shops opening, the city truly does whisper in the sleeper's ear place and identity. Grasso's return to himself was marked by hearing his bells from his bed in his house on his street in his city, and the tale evokes that once common measure of place and self perfectly to re-place and reaffirm Grasso as Grasso.

The *beffa* was still not complete, however: first, finding everything reversed in his familiar spaces kindled Grasso's doubts; then, Matteo's brothers arrived and, no longer recognizing him as Matteo, asked for their brother who had disappeared; and finally, Brunelleschi and Donatello worked him over one last time in public aided by the reappearance of the real Matteo. But tellingly Grasso, back in his places and recognized in the streets as himself again, had used the spaces of Florence to become himself once more. One last detail is worth noting: as Grasso left Brunelleschi and Donatello, Filippo brought his *beffa* full circle. The whole plot had been set in motion by a snub—Grasso's refusing to dine with his friends; now Brunelleschi turned to him and offered, "We must have supper together one evening."[47] Friends had been rejected, the price had been paid, and now mockingly or seriously the circle had been completed with a new offer of dinner and friendship.[48] Tellingly for the future, however, Grasso left without responding; he soon learned that he had been the victim of his friends, and with that realization came a cruel understanding: although he had not gone mad and had always really been Grasso, it really did not matter—the regime of *virtù* ruled. He had become in the consensus reality of the populace of Florence the infamous victim of a famous *beffa*, and that meant that not only had he been publicly dishonored by his friends, but in the end even children would mock him in the streets: his worse fear had come true in the mean streets of Florence.

As all this turned on the spaces of Florence and their use by a masculine culture of friendship, honor, and *virtù*, a change of space was a virtually necessary response. And although it might seem like an overreaction from a modern perspective, in the Renaissance with a Renaissance sense of identity, that is exactly what Grasso opted for: he sold his shop and left Florence, accepting the offer of a friend to go with him to serve the king of Hungary. With perfect timing as he was leaving the city, the tale confirmed one last time his worse fear: "Before mounting the horse [to leave], as he was walking through Florence . . . he happened to go by several places where he heard people talking about what had happened to him, and everyone was laughing and joking about it."[49] Mean streets indeed.

Fortunately for Grasso, escape from those streets of Florence made his fortune. Leaving behind his shame and the friends who had made him infamous with their cruel *beffa*, Grasso, because of his woodcarving skills (*virtù*), became a valued retainer of the king of Hungary, and that in turn made him a rich and noted craftsman, who many years later could return to Florence and laugh with Brunelleschi about the cruel joke—for in a way what the regime of *virtù* had taken away Grasso's own *virtù* had regained. In fact, on later visits Brunelleschi and Grasso often talked about how Grasso had experienced the *beffa*, and the storyteller, Manetti, pauses to note that this was crucial for the tale's richness, as "most of the funny things had happened, so to speak, in Grasso's mind."[50] At one level that is true, of course; the internal workings of Grasso's mind are developed in this tale as in few other Renaissance *novelle*. But it is interesting to note how intimately intertwined Grasso's thoughts were with the spaces of his city, Florence. Home, shop, streets; hearth, dining table, bed; Bapistery, cathedral, Mercato Vecchio, Mercato Nuovo; church bells, familiar sights and sounds: all were tools in Grasso's thinking of himself and important elements in the masculine world of Florence and its culture. Honor, friendship, pleasure—all played a role in a regime of *virtù* that truly ruled there, a rule that was deeply intertwined with the spaces of an intimate city and its familiar, mean streets.

CHAPTER 5

Machiavelli in Love
The Self-Presentation of an Aging Lover

In 1512, following his fall from political power in Florence, Niccolò Machiavelli found himself exiled from the world of political power and intrigue with which we usually associate him. Yet in that period of unhappy exile, Machiavelli not only wrote his greatest political works but also savored other passions and presented another persona that is rather surprising given the traditional stereotype of the man as a dour, cold, and ultimately Machiavellian figure. In fact, from 1512 until his death in 1527, Machiavelli—continuing with a theme expressed in his earlier years in his letters to his friends and colleagues—enjoyed and cultivated a reputation as a lover, a lusty advocate of erotic pleasure, and a witty observer as well as a participant in the world of illicit sex, a reputation that he not only encouraged but was ready to exploit for humor, friendship, and power.

If, as has been suggested in these essays, sexual identity and identity itself were mainly played out in public—to a degree a public performance of self—in many ways for Machiavelli his self-proclaimed passions were a significant aspect of his self-presentation and self-negotiation with the groups with which he interacted in society, especially with his circle of friends and his potential political patrons. It is not surprising, then, that we find that in these years of exile from political power Machiavelli wrote two rollicking comedies that turned on sex and seduction—*La mandragola* and *La Clizia*—as well as a number of love poems and lyrics and a fascinating series of letters that mix politics, love, and sex with a revealing verve, humor, and element of self-revelation that has often troubled modern commentators.

PART I. WRITING A SEXUAL SELF AND MASCULINE FRIENDSHIP: LETTERS WITH VETTORI

Early in 1515 Machiavelli—about to turn 46, already referring to himself as "almost 50" and "old"—was involved in an oft cited correspondence with Francesco Vettori, a Florentine aristocrat and friend who shared Niccolò's sense of impending old age. In that correspondence, as commentators have pointed out frequently, Machiavelli tried out and refined many of the political ideas that are to be found in his more widely read political works: *The Prince* and *The Discourses*. The sexual side of that correspondence, however, has been frequently overlooked or commented upon with embarrassment. Yet sex played a major role in that correspondence as well. Often dismissed as a light diversion, as an attempt to escape the brutal realities of the political struggles of the time, or as a way of relieving and avoiding the tensions of the political disagreements that divided the two friends, this playful no-holds-barred sexual exchange evidently touched on all these things, but what shines through is the fact that it was a central part of a much broader social performance of self in which Machiavelli used his correspondence with his friends to construct a strong personal portrait of himself as a committed, if aging, lover and a passionate pursuer of sexual pleasure and love.[1]

So it was in this context of Machiavelli's ongoing self-portrayal as a lover that on 16 January 1515 Vettori wrote Machiavelli a letter that might sound like the typical letter of one old man to another complaining about the immorality and lust of the youth of the day: "Today's world is totally taken up with love, or actually to say it straight out, lust."[2] And as was typical of the correspondence between these two acute observers of the contemporary scene, Vettori continued to analyze the origins of the problem. "A father has a son and he says that he wants to raise him honestly: nonetheless . . . he gives him a tutor who is with him the whole day and who is allowed to do with him whatever he wishes and that tutor is allowed to have him read things that would arouse the dead."[3] Reading things that would "arouse the dead" clearly Vettori did not see as contributing to the "honesty" of youth; but perhaps he was suggesting more, as the stereotype of the tutor or pedant who educates his pupils not just in the classics but in the homoerotic pleasures of the day while giving them a classical polish was virtually a topos of Renaissance literature, both prescriptive and humorous. And as we have seen, the early years of *gioventù* were a period when males were assumed to be quite passive across the board, but especially in things sexual; from that perspective the stereotypical interests of clichéd tutors could fulfill the expectations and fears of the age. Thus, allowing a tutor "to do with him [one's son]" whatever he wished may well have implied much more than merely having him read erotically charged classical literature.

"As the boy gets older," Vettori continued, "[his mother] gives him a room on the ground floor with an independent entrance and all the other things useful so that he can do as he pleases, bringing in and sending out whomever he wishes."[4] Such permissiveness and independence from parental supervision, Vettori implied, literally opened the door to youthful lust. And it seems that here Vettori may well have been referring to that next stage of sexual development that arrived in the late teens, when a Renaissance youth began to move toward a more aggressive sexuality and transformed himself from being the object of the passions of others, like tutors, to being the person who actively sought out others as sexual objects, whether younger male partners or women. "Thus," he concludes, "one should not be surprised that our youth [*giovani*] are as lascivious as they are, for this is a result of this terrible upbringing."[5] These laments could hardly seem more prosaic and typical of the complaints that old men make against the young in every age—aside from some allusions to the homoerotic tendencies of Renaissance young men perhaps.

Vettori, however, from the first was aiming these traditional-sounding complaints at a rather surprising conclusion, for the actual targets of his attack were he himself and his good and intimate friend Niccolò Machiavelli. He continued immediately, "And you and I, even though *we are old men*, we retain to a degree the [bad] habits we took up as youths [*giovani*] and there's no escaping it."[6] In fact, Vettori began this letter noting that he had been thinking about Machiavelli and his love life for the past few months and was deeply troubled by the way that Machiavelli let himself be swept up and transformed by love—hardly the Machiavellian master planner and manipulator one might expect. Rather, Vettori seems to have seen Machiavelli in love as someone who wore his passionate loves on his sleeve and who took a troublingly passive approach to his desires.

Referring to this, he quoted a line from Virgil, "Oh Coridon, Coridon, why do you let yourself be overwhelmed by such madness?"[7] Interestingly, this classical reference draws on the tale of the pastoral love of Coridon for a young male shepherd, but Vettori transforms this male-male love into a reflection of Machiavelli's passion for women without hesitation; the interchangeability of the Renaissance object of desire seems unconsciously reflected in this classical allusion without value judgments on that desire. Love/lust for a young male shepherd in the ancient world could serve as a model for thinking about the love/lust of Machiavelli in Renaissance Florence for his current courtesan flame, la Riccia, and in both cases the troubling aspect was the way in which the older male was swept away by his desire, much more than the object of that passion. The correct control or binding of an adult male's passions rather than the object of those passions was the issue for Vettori.

And, of course, here love (*amore*) and lust (*foia*) were very close: overwhelming passions that easily coexisted, a fact made clear by the next line in Vettori's letter, "Today's world is totally taken up with love, or actually to say it straight out, lust."[8] In fact, Machiavelli understood Vettori's comment about his approach to love in just that vein, for a little more than a week later he replied to Vettori's letter: "I don't know how to respond to your last letter about lust [*foia*] with other words . . . than with this sonnet which will show you what great effort and cleverness that thief Love [*Amore*] has used to enchain me." Machiavelli then turned to verse:

That youthful archer [Love]
Has often tried to wound my breast
With his arrows, for he enjoys
The injury and suffering of others;
And even if [those arrows] were so sharp and cruel,
That even a diamond would not withstand them,
Still they have found such a powerful resistance [in my breast]
That all their power was of little note.
So he, charged with outrage and wrath,
To demonstrate his excellence,
Changed quiver, his arrows, his bow;
And he transfixed me with one [arrow] with such violence
That I still am suffering from the wound
And I confess and recognize his power.[9]

Machiavelli's love sonnet expresses fairly typical Petrarchian conceits about the power of Love's arrows, conceits that he often returned to in his poetry. In this case, however, he refers to his own strength and his ability to resist those arrows, only to overturn his claim of resistance and control, lamenting sweetly that Love, outraged by his defiance, changed his weapons and wounded him so gravely that he is still suffering and is forced to "confess and recognize his [Love's] power."

The Petrarchian topos of suffering clearly at play here does not exhaust the range of Machiavelli's portrayal of his love life; it perhaps enriches it and gives it a deeper resonance in the often highly literate correspondence with his friend—but let me repeat, it does not exhaust it. Like most learned men of the Renaissance, Machiavelli could not resist translating his feelings into allusions to classical and Renaissance literature, so much so that one must always wonder how much of what he wrote about himself and others was literary topoi and how much was actually felt.

A fascinating and ultimately unanswerable question, but fortunately, for the purpose of this chapter we do not have to confront that issue. In this essay how Machiavelli portrayed himself in love is what matters, for if my underlying premise is correct—that identity in the Renaissance was to a great degree based upon a performance of self and a negotiation of self with the groups with which a person interacted—it is that performance and those negotiations that we need to understand more than anything else. And in transforming his love life into Petrarchian conceits or classical allusions for his correspondents and his friend Vettori he was writing out a sexual self: helping to create and sustain a consensus reality, a Renaissance sexual identity that to a great degree was Machiavelli for them all.

Having said that, however, I want to stress that even literary topoi are not timeless. They are limited to a degree by the extent to which they make sense in the cultural world in which they are deployed. To appreciate the love of Shakespeare's Romeo and Juliet we need to forget that their love today might well be viewed as statutory rape or perhaps even as child pornography; at the least we need to recognize its culturally specific locations in a period when female "children" were considered "adults" in their early teens and capable of having loving sexual relationships and marrying as "adults." More pertinent, if one was to transfer the topos of the love of young teenage girls directly without mediation into modern literature, one would find oneself labeled, much like Nabokov with *Lolita*, as someone working on the margins of the acceptable at best. This is merely to say the obvious, that Machiavelli, like all other writers who wished to be understood by their contemporaries, had to measure his topoi against the cultural world of his readers, and that was especially true in the two genres in which he wrote extensively about sex and sexual identity: his letters and his comedies. Significantly, in both genres he had regular feedback on the way in which his use of classical and literary allusions was received: in letters he, and we, regularly have the responses of his readers (something that in other genres is relatively rare for the period), and in his comedies we can often judge where he was trying to elicit laughter from a Renaissance audience.[10]

As a result we need to measure the sexual self that Machiavelli presented both within the context of literary topoi and contemporary sexual mores and that of the larger everyday world in which all of the above were represented and articulated. From these perspectives the conceit of being wounded and bound by love has strong resonances with the Renaissance vision of love as a binding passion which I have discussed elsewhere.[11] And Machiavelli continued with this theme, apparently breaking free from his literary topoi to create a more personalized self-portrait, noting: "Those chains with which he [Love] has bound me are so strong that I have given up completely on being free, nor can I conceive of a way that I could free myself."[12] Machiavelli in love, he claimed, was incapable of breaking free from that binding passion, like many others in the Renaissance. But he took this idea deeper, noting that while he was so bound by love that he had lost his freedom, still if he could be free from those chains he would choose not to be, preferring his life as a lover. "If, however, chance or other human intrigues opened for me an escape I would not want to take it because I am so attracted to those chains: now sweet, now light, now heavy."[13] Still in the realm of literary conceits perhaps, Machiavelli portrayed himself as one who enjoyed this type of life and concludes: "They [these chains] weave a sort of web that forces me to conclude that I cannot live happily without that quality of life."[14]

Quickly, he took this vision of himself to the actual specifics of his life: "And because I know how much you [Vettori] enjoy such pleasures and understand similar aspects of life, I am sorry that you are not here [in Florence] to laugh, first at my tears and then at my laughter."[15] And he noted that if Vettori were to visit him there with their common friend Donato del Corno and Machiavelli's current love, the courtesan la Riccia, Machiavelli himself would find a happy refuge for his "boat," which had been lost in this "storm [of passionate love] without rudder or sail."[16] His boat ("legno") has regularly and justly been read as a clever double entendre referring both to Machiavelli the individual as a boat lost in the storm of love's passion and to his phallus similarly lost—a loss that presumably a visit from la Riccia would bring to one happy, safe harbor at least.[17] Self and sex here informed evocatively the same metaphor. And with a clever wordplay Machiavelli brought his literary reflections down to the level of his own erotic self-portrayal. Machiavelli the poet and echoer of literary conceits became the self-proclaimed lover of the courtesan la Riccia and friend of men who, like himself, moved in the world of illicit sex. And, of course, not to be overlooked, he became in this self-portrayal literally an erect phallus as well, wishing to sail lustily into the harbor of his courtesan love.

Throughout their correspondence in these years, even as he and Vettori lamented their old age and failing physical abilities, each was anxious to portray himself as a lover and reinforce this aspect of their relationship. Of course, both men were married and enjoyed a traditional Renaissance family life, and Machiavelli, at least, claimed an affectionate relationship with his wife, Marietta. But that was a separate world—a separate consensus reality of family and clan—which simply did not intersect on the level of sex with their friendship and self-portrayal as lovers in an illicit world that was particularly important for their self-portrayals and concepts of self. And Machiavelli, as an acute observer of not just the political scene but also himself and his friends, was well aware of this and played upon it with his usual thoughtful and clever prose. A few lines later in this letter he commented, "Whoever might see our letters, my honored friend [*compare*], and note the range of topics [we discuss] might well be very amazed, because it would seem to him that first we were serious men, totally taken up with great affairs. . . . But then turning the page it would seem to him that we, the same [letter writers], were frivolous, flighty, lascivious and taken up with vain things."[18] These lines are well known because they describe quite accurately and with seeming prescience the impression that many later readers of these letters have had. How could Machiavelli and Vettori, these two mature, critical, and sophisticated analysts of the contemporary political scene, jump so easily from the great questions of state and warfare that dominate their correspondence to discuss the seemingly frivolous passions that they and their friends shared for the illicit sexual pleasures of the day?

Machiavelli, as if reading a query made by many of his future critics, continued immediately with a reply to just that question: "This way of writing, even if it might seem blameworthy to some, to me seems laudable, because we are imitating nature itself, which is changeable, and the person who imitates that cannot be reprimanded."[19] Nature here once again leaps out as the great sustainer of the ideology of illicit sex, a role that it plays across the Renaissance and in many other cultures as well, albeit usually with culturally specific references. Even in the early Renaissance Boccaccio's young lovers, be they adulterers, nuns, or merely unmarried youths, were usually justified by nature— for over and over again Boccaccio appealed to nature and natural desires, even natural sins, to claim his readers' sympathy for formally illicit and often quite outrageous behavior. Boccaccio's happy nuns, who gave in to human nature and put horns on God's head with the aid of their lusty but overworked gardener, Masetto da Lamporecchio, and the would-be Christian Alibech, who discovered paradise in the religious pleasures of putting the Devil back in hell with her desert hermit Rustico, were merely accepting the natural human condition, which leaves us (and presumably a Renaissance audience as well) laughing at their formally quite outrageous and even blasphemous behavior.[20] Suggestively, in this crucial legitimating role played by nature across the Renaissance, that classic (and usually false) dichotomy nature/culture breaks down: for over and over again nature is culturally constructed and hardly natural at all. Yet it served Machiavelli's needs well, for, much as in the case of Boccaccio's tales, it was appealed to in order to disarm those who might criticize the variety of subjects that populate his correspondence cheek by jowl with more "serious" matters, especially the "frivolous" and "lascivious" ones.

Ironically, but not surprisingly, Machiavelli's appeal to nature has failed to convince many later commentators who tend to focus on the "strange mix" of the serious and the frivolous nonetheless. In fact, to preserve Machiavelli's serious and dour reputation some have even suggested that Machiavelli was seduced into writing about these topics by Vettori, who somehow led him away from the serious matters of state to the light world of sex. Unfortunately, for such a thesis Machiavelli had no need for Vettori's lead. He was anxious in his correspondence with his friends to present himself in a sexual light as a man deeply attached to the illicit sexual world of the Renaissance, and with his comedies he playfully alluded to this aspect of his persona in a way that suggests that he believed that a broader audience might appreciate this aspect of his personality as well, as we shall see.

Vettori, in turn, was clearly aware that that was a significant part of their friendship, as he highlights in his own defense of their discussion of such subjects in his earlier letter. Although, as noted above, that letter started out moralizing about the evil mores of the day, it had a strong undercurrent from the first which suggested that those evil mores were practiced not just by others but willingly and with pleasure by Vettori and Machiavelli themselves. In fact, returning to the theme of his old age and its incapacities, Vettori, without directly referring to nature, suggested that it was the norm for old men like the two of them to be melancholy and oppressed by unhappy thoughts that were difficult to escape. "So it is necessary" he concluded, "to focus on thinking about pleasant things and I don't know anything more pleasant to think about or to do than screwing [*fottere*]."[21]

In the end, Machiavelli's and Vettori's sexual exploits and fantasies were a regular and central part of their friendship—a part of the consensus reality of sexual identity that they negotiated in order to maintain their camaraderie and their special relationship with their larger group of male friends. When times were tense between them, when disagreements about politics and the course of events threatened to disturb their relationship, when Vettori's success and Machiavelli's fall from power began to weigh on both men, and perhaps most important, when Vettori could not (or at least did not) deliver as a patron and secure for his friend Niccolò his much desired reentry into politics, both men regularly fell back on those pleasant thoughts of, in Vettori's words, "screwing." But significantly, both men also turned to those discussions without such excuses, perhaps simply for the playful way they could express their friendship in terms of a sexual camaraderie. A particularly fine and rich moment that demonstrates this is the series of letters that Machiavelli and Vettori exchanged beginning late in 1513 and running through the early part of 1515.

By that time it was fairly clear to both men that Machiavelli's fall from power in 1512 was not a momentary setback.[22] The overthrow of the republican regime dominated by Piero Soderini by the Medici had left Machiavelli under a cloud of suspicion with that family, for Machiavelli was closely associated with Soderini and his rule, having served as his secretary of the second chancellery, and was widely perceived as being a client of the fallen leader. These suspicions were reinforced by concerns that Machiavelli had been involved in a 1513 conspiracy against the new Medici regime led by the Capponi and Boscoli families, supporters of a return to a more open republican form of government. Arrested and tortured, he eventually was released to return to his farm, the Albergaccio, in the Tuscan countryside as part of a general amnesty that was proclaimed with the election of Giovanni de' Medici as Pope Leo X on 13 March of that same year. There he was relatively safe from accusations of being involved in any form of organized resistance to the Medici, but he was unable to win their good graces or even their neutrality in his search for some kind of post in the service of his city.

In contrast, his old friend Vettori, who had been a close collaborator during the Soderini period, had weathered that troubled transition to Medici rule much more successfully, apparently because he came from one of the old *ottimati* families that were the base of the renewed Medici power in Florence. In fact, Vettori had managed to secure for himself a post as ambassador to the pope—a particularly appealing sinecure, as it gave him some distance from the initial turmoil and instability of the new Medici regime in Florence and allowed him to cement his relationship with the man who was the real power behind the revival of the Medici not just in Florence but in Italy as well, the new Medici pope Leo X. In this context, Vettori represented for Machiavelli a crucial resource, not just a friend but also as a potential patron given his position in the kind of *ottimati* family that could seemingly promise entrance to the inner circles of power in Florence and, given his own position and contacts, at the Roman court of Leo. From virtually the moment he was released from prison, he and Vettori danced now delicately, now more aggressively around the topic of Machiavelli's reentry into the good graces of the Medici and the halls of power. Sometimes subtly, sometimes directly, Machiavelli asked for Vettori's help, and in an almost perfect reversal sometimes subtly, sometimes directly, Vettori lamented and explained his inability to secure what was clearly one of Machiavelli's greatest desires.

In the better moments when it seemed that Machiavelli might actually be able to win the support of the pope and regain the good graces of the Medici family—the crucial prerequisites for reentering political life—Vettori asked Machiavelli to write letters analyzing the contemporary political and diplomatic scene. It seems that he hoped to use those letters to impress the pope with Machiavelli's political savvy and loyalty to the Medici cause. Unfortunately, it appears that Machiavelli was more interested in being true to his political vision than in winning the pope's support, and unwittingly he seems to have at times backed schemes and visions that went against the pope's own evaluation of events and plans. Vettori's suggestions and criticisms, which may well have been hints at how Machiavelli might make his analysis more satisfactory to the pope (although they might also be read simply as the friendly but no-holds-barred type of discussion that the friends enjoyed), were vigorously refuted by Machiavelli—again in the end not the most appropriate way to win papal support.

As a result, when in late November 1513 Vettori wrote Machiavelli after a several-month hiatus in their letters, it seems that he was anxious to reassert their friendship by taking their correspondence away from the dangerous area of politics, and Machiavelli's lack of success in winning the favor of the pope using Vettori as his patron, to a safer subject that they both shared an interest in, a return to Vettori's preferred pastime for old men like them, "screwing," or to put it less crudely, the pleasures and dangers that sex posed for them. Machiavelli may also have been ready to move their correspondence from politics to sex for a time, for he was preparing a surprise for his friend—he was finishing *The Prince*, a work that in many ways expanded and commented upon the political discussions and disagreements in their correspondence and which it appears Machiavelli hoped to use as his own trump card to play in his return to the active political life. Sex could carry their friendship and correspondence while Machiavelli used *The Prince* as his reentry vehicle into politics and as the first of his formal replies to their ongoing debates on government and diplomacy.

The transition from politics to sex in Vettori's letter of 23 November began with a few wry comments largely at his own expense about the impracticality of trying to rationally anticipate what princes and politicians were going to do, a theme he regularly returned to when their discussions became too intense or when Machiavelli was too strenuously defending opinions that might have gotten him into trouble with powerful potential patrons, like the Medici. In this letter, then, he proposed to let politics and diplomacy move ahead on their own without his analysis and instead to focus on giving Machiavelli a picture of his life in Rome. Tellingly, he opened this account of his Roman days on a sexual note that referred explicitly to Machiavelli's reputation as a lover of courtesans: "And I believe it is useful to let you know first off where I am living, because I have moved. I am not living anymore in that area where there were so many courtesans, where I was this summer."[23] Evidently his earlier house had been notable for both men because of its proximity to a number of courtesans and in turn for the easy access that it provided to their services.

Vettori, however, left that issue for a moment to describe the location of his house near the Janiculum Hill and the Piazza San Pietro hard by a small church and its isolated gardens, where he often strolled. Creating a self-portrait of a lonely ambassador who was being largely ignored and who existed outside the circles of real power in Rome, he continued to note that he got up late in the morning and visited the papal palace only "every second or third day," where at most "every now and then" he exchanged "twenty words with the Pope" and even fewer with the other important Medici and notables there.[24] Then he returned home, normally ate with his staff, and gambled with friends in the afternoon or walked or rode in the countryside. In the evening he read Roman history and wrote the few reports that his position required. After a dinner and now and then talking a bit with friends—exchanging "qualche novelletta"— he went to bed early. In sum, Vettori described for his friend the relatively dull and uninteresting life of an older man at the distant edges of power in Rome; implicitly a life that even Machiavelli, totally exiled from political life, could hardly envy and one that suggested that Vettori was in no position to help his friend regain a position in that world.

Vettori continued to depict his quotidian existence, including a quip that reveals another aspect of Machiavelli's personality which evidently impressed Vettori or perhaps troubled him. "On feast days I hear Mass and unlike you I don't skip them every now and then."[25] In fact, Machiavelli's lack of interest in the forms of religious life of the day is a matter regularly commented upon by his friends in their correspondence with him, along with his lack of enthusiasm for the mendicant orders. From attendance at Mass, however, Vettori jumps immediately to something that he assumes will interest his friend: "If you were to ask me if I have any courtesans, I would tell you that in the beginning [after my move] they came . . . but then as I was worried about the airs of the summer, I held myself back. Still, I had one who regularly came [to visit me] on her own who is quite intelligent and pretty and she is enjoyable to talk with."[26]

Here we have virtually the already traditional representation of an ideal courtesan—exactly the kind of woman who would positively adorn an older man like either Vettori or Machiavelli. Beautiful, intelligent, and a pleasure to talk with, she demonstrated not just their masculinity and virility but also the required intellectual attributes that both men strove so hard to display in their correspondence and life. What more perfect object could one buy to establish one's identity as a man and an intellectual? Actually many others, but this was the object that Vettori chose to display to Machiavelli—without a name, suggestively—and presumably the object that he assumed Machiavelli would appreciate most. Moreover, Vettori's courtesan apparently visited him on her own without being paid, and although this is only implied not clearly stated, it is a telling implication.

Reading between the lines, as perhaps Machiavelli was meant to do, we can see this beautiful and intelligent courtesan choosing to visit Vettori on her own regularly, even when he had stopped keeping and having sexual relations with courtesans out of fear of the summer airs. Would Machiavelli have read that she found the older Vettori so attractive and powerful that she did not care whether she was paid or not, seeking him out to enjoy his own attractive company, manhood, and intellect? Would Machiavelli have read that the older Vettori, no longer burning with the hotter passions of youth, now attracted at least one more intelligent courtesan to chat with him in his isolation there in Rome? Whether or not such was the case, it is a logical narrative and the satisfying self-presentation of the man that can be easily read into his account.

And as long as he was telling Machiavelli about available women, Vettori continued to note that there was also a woman who lived near his new house who would be of interest to Niccolò: "Even if this place is rather isolated, I have also in the neighborhood a woman neighbor who you would not find unattractive. And even if she is of a noble family, she has been known to put out."[27] Without pause Vettori then invited Machiavelli to come join him in Rome to enjoy these attractions: "My dear Niccolò I invite you [to join me] in this life. And if you would come you would make me happy for we would in this way be together again."[28] Evidently the sexual side of their relationship was not merely a diversion from their political debates; it was an important base of their ongoing friendship. Vettori's whole letter, at least on the surface, pointed to this moment when Vettori said to Machiavelli in effect, come live with me in Rome and we will enjoy the simple life of conversation, companionship with a few friends, and easy sex with interesting women.

Of course, behind this apparently simple and warm expression of friendship there may well have lurked the sad admission that Vettori could not bring his friend to Rome to serve the Medici pope or work out a way to make him an official of the Florentine government as Machiavelli desired. But still, for our purposes it is interesting to see how the portrayal of the simple quiet life of older male friends included in Vettori's idyllic evocation a crucial zone of easy, illicit sex. And more tellingly yet, Vettori recognized that this fit with Machiavelli's own vision of himself when he offered him a noble mistress whom Machiavelli "would not find unattractive" in Rome. Vettori closed his letter pointing out that although he had many friends in Rome there were none there to match Machiavelli aside perhaps from Cardinal Bernardo da Bibbiena, an important intellectual and humanist, perhaps best known then, as now, for his rollicking and sexually explicit comedy *La calandra*.[29] What better way to conclude a letter of reconciliation that attempted to delicately slide their relationship once again from the political toward the sexual than to compare Machiavelli to the highly successful cardinal, the only other man comparable to Machiavelli in Rome, noted also for his sexual openness and humor!

Machiavelli replied to Vettori's letter on 10 December, admitting that he had been concerned about the long break in their correspondence. This, perhaps the most famous of Machiavelli's letters, opened both commiserating with Vettori over the quality of his life in Rome and advising him nevertheless to enjoy the tranquility and freedom that Fortune had brought him. He then outlined his own even quieter life at his country villa outside Florence, introducing it with a clearly ironic "and if you judge that you would trade it [my life] for yours, I would be content to trade."[30] In this oft quoted reprise of his own tranquil country life he moves slowly from the quotidian petty squabbles over cutting wood on his woodlands for friends, to the lively squabbles in the local tavern over the small sums wagered in afternoon card games, to the famous account of his evening encounters with the ancients in his study: "[During those evenings] I don't feel any boredom for four hours, forget all my troubles, don't fear poverty and am not dismayed by [the thought of] death: I am totally transported to their world."[31]

This was followed by the even more famous revelation to Vettori that he had written *The Prince* based on those evening conversations with the ancients: "and I have written a little work *De principatibus* where I look as deeply as I can at this subject."[32] This progression from the quotidian to the sublime encounter with the ancients that produced *The Prince* (at least as Machiavelli wished to display it to his friend Vettori) has often been seen as an artful way of redirecting their correspondence to the political issues that really concerned Machiavelli. It is important to note, however, that all this was done in the context of the two friends exchanging pictures of their overly tranquil domestic lives as old men and an invitation from Vettori to Machiavelli to come live with him in Rome for a while, not to reenter the political turmoil of that world but to enjoy the quiet life of pleasurable conversation and illicit sex which Vettori had promised.

This is underlined by the fact that Machiavelli virtually immediately turns to Vettori's invitation to join him in Rome, implicitly to enjoy the sexual pleasures that the city had to offer. "You express the wish, Magnificent Ambassador," he wrote, "that I leave this life and come to enjoy with you yours."[33] Machiavelli admitted that he was tempted by the prospect, but friendship also stood in his way: he pointed out that his old friend Cardinal Francesco Soderini and his former patron Piero Soderini, the fallen *gonfaloniere* and enemy of the Medici, were living in the city and that if he came to Rome, out of friendship he would have to visit them. This, he ruefully concluded, could mean that upon his return to Florence he might well get another chance to visit the Bargello, the city's famous prison. For although the Medici were firmly in power, their rule was still a "suspicious" one, he noted, and his closeness to the Soderini had already played a major role in his own exile from the halls of power and his arrest and torture in 1513; thus, a return to Rome, though attractive for the pleasures that Vettori offered, was dangerous for political implications that perhaps Vettori had not given their due weight from Machiavelli's perspective. Still, he promised his friend that if he could show him a way to overcome this problem, he would join him in Rome—perhaps an unlikely prospect, but a sign that Machiavelli did not want his friend to feel that his offer had been rejected out of hand.

This richly evocative letter has been much scrutinized, but one quietly evoked undertone of Machiavelli's self-portrayal in it has been little noted: a continued preoccupation with his own advancing age. At the time this letter was written Machiavelli was only in his mid-forties, actually only 44, but in the Renaissance this was, demographically speaking, an advanced age. The average life expectancy of a man was actually lower, but this demographic reality must be qualified by the fact that upper-class men like Machiavelli and his friends when they lived into their forties tended to live on considerably longer than the general population. Still, as noted earlier, Machiavelli and his friends began to comment on their advancing years and complain about the physical and mental problems that accompanied them when they reached their forties.[34] This sense of old age provides another significant element of the rather different Renaissance perspective of the life cycle of males; for, as we have seen, upper-class males were youths until their late twenties or early thirties—at certain times and in certain contexts this period could even extend into their forties—but Machiavelli's correspondence with his friends suggests that this brief adulthood slid very quickly into old age after forty.

Perspective was everything here, but even with shifting perspectives that could make a man in his forties at once a youth politically, a mature adult in terms of family affairs and business, and an older man in terms of sex and his body, it is significant to note that a man's prime was relatively short. Adulthood, which is today seen as the longest period of a male's life, was a rather brief period in the Renaissance it appears, with both youth and old age pressing in negatively on its borders. If this vision of the male life cycle is accurate, it almost certainly adds additional weight to the oft depicted generational conflicts between young men and old men seen in literature, law, custom, and everyday life.

Simply put, it appears that most upper-class males in the Renaissance perceived themselves as either youths or old men, and thus the competition was regularly intense between these two groups for power, wealth, and status. The generally shared vision was that youths could offer force, vitality, passion, and potential while old men could offer wisdom, moderation, and calm. Of course, the reverse of such perceptions were also deployed in the war between the young and the old with youth being seen as threatening violence, lack of self-control, and lack of reason and old men being seen as hindered by senility, lack of conviction, and lack of action.

From another perspective, strange as it may seem, one might well argue that the world of adults in the Renaissance was largely inhabited by women, especially at the upper-class level, where a woman could marry and take on an adult role in her mid-teens and live as an adult until she passed her childbearing years in her early forties and began to become old as well; in this age profile upper-class women could be adults for approximately twenty-five years while men might well be adults for a mere ten years or so at best. Perhaps here is another little recognized reason for the misogynistic attacks on women that focused on their nonadult behavior—their childlike foolishness, their tendency to talk too much, their fascination with insignificant things like clothes and jewelry, their lack of constancy—a range of behaviors that seemed to suggest that although they were formally adults in reality very few of them actually lived up to that role. From this perspective all those males who were not yet adults or no longer adults—the vast majority it seems—could feel reassured that women, the long-reigning and perennial adults in their society, were not actually any better than men even as adults.

Be that as it may, Machiavelli's concern with his advancing age quietly suffuses this famed letter. Early on when he describes his tranquil morning reading, he refers to his memories of his loves: "I have a book with me either Dante or Petrarch or one of those minor poets like Tibullus, Ovid and the like: I read about their amorous passions and their loves and, remembering my own, I enjoy such thoughts for a while."[35] Machiavelli, the lover, depicted himself as an older man who in his forced retirement enjoyed reading about the affairs of the ancients and remembering his own. No longer a young man who dreams about future affairs or actually seeks them, Machiavelli portrayed himself as living in reminiscences of past loves that perhaps echoed his reminiscences of his past political exploits. Of course, Machiavelli was not through with a more active pursuit of love, but that actually underlines the point that he was evoking here—a sense of himself as an old man, ignoring his present loves to focus on the topos of an old man reminiscing about his youthful affairs. To Vettori's promise of love in Rome, then, Machiavelli contrasted his quiet reminiscences about past loves, in an artful passage that suggested that he was an ideal old man and upper-class intellectual on the model of the ancients or the great moderns.

His age returned more subtly when he listed the things that his nightly conversations with the ancients in his study helped him to overcome: boredom, troubles, fear of poverty, and fear of death. All were associated with old age in the Renaissance, and although the first three fitted well also with his exile from politics and power, the last shifted the weight of the list, perhaps unconsciously, toward the fears of the aged. Young men might momentarily lose their positions of power, but their dreams and fears seldom turned to death, especially young men like the aggressive and self-assured Machiavelli we see in his early letters. Portraying himself as fearing death, Machiavelli created a powerful image of an isolated *old* man, retiring to his study to return to a better, earlier age and escape the typical fears of old men. Early in the letter Machiavelli made reference also to his need to go to the tavern, gamble, and argue with the locals to keep his mind active and alert, but there he made much clearer his sense that this was necessitated by his bad luck ("di questa mia sorta"), and as a result there is less of a sense that Machiavelli was presenting himself as old. Still wasting his time gambling at midday in the local tavern, Machiavelli fit yet another stereotypical vision of useless old men who whiled away their last years gambling in taverns and arguing loudly over the small sums they wagered.

Finally Machiavelli closed this letter referring directly to his age again and noting that, given how old he was, he was hardly likely to be able to change his nature any longer. He made this point in order to argue that he had always been a loyal and trustworthy servant to those who had employed him and to suggest to Vettori that if the Medici were to take him on they would find that he would serve them in the same way. Of course, Machiavelli frequently referred to the aggressive changeability of young men and the inability of old men to change, but here he reconstructed this negative attribute of the old into a plus—he was trustworthy because he had always been so and was now too old to change. "And as far as my trustworthiness is concerned there ought to be no doubt, because I have always kept my word and I would not be able to learn now to break it. The person who has been faithful and good for 43 years, which is how old I am, is not able to change his nature. And as far as my faithfulness and goodness is concerned my poverty demonstrates both."[36]

Whether Machiavelli was portraying himself as a poor old man who would be a loyal servant to the Medici, a sad character wasting his days playing cards in a local tavern uselessly, a useless old man in his study speaking with the ancients and escaping his fears of poverty and death, or a tired old man reading love poetry and reminiscing about his youthful loves—Machiavelli created in this letter a self that was old and thus both worthy and needful of Vettori's support and continued friendship. And while clearly Machiavelli's portrayal of his sexual self as old was only part of the construction of self presented in this letter, it was a significant part, even in a letter in which sex might at first glance appear to be a minor concern. In fact, this letter shows nicely that sex and politics, friendship and power, pleasure and patronage were not easily separated in the Renaissance. And it reveals how Machiavelli played the interconnections between them and the consensus reality about his identity that they were designed to nourish as a microstrategy of power: a strategy to construct a letter that revealed to his friend a broken old man, still trustworthy and ready to serve, as well as a friend and companion who continued to share his basic interests and desires.

A more aggressive reading of this letter is tempting, however, for it well might be hypothesized that, having finished *The Prince*, Machiavelli would have felt anything but old, tired, and isolated. After all, it is clear that in this period he was enthusiastic about his "little work" and hopeful that it would win him the favor of the Medici and a reentry into the active political life that he so desired. In this context it could be argued that Machiavelli picked up the theme of old age that Vettori had played upon in his previous letter and that both men had regularly referred to in their correspondence with a certain irony because he believed that *The Prince* would demonstrate that he was anything but old and finished as a political player; in fact, the contrast between the political vision and acuity expressed in that work and his self-portrayal in his letter to Vettori would have an even greater impact on his friend Vettori when he read the work. In this light Machiavelli's often self-mocking letters about his sexual foibles or his desire to appear more important than he actually was might be seen as similar ploys;[37] in each case Machiavelli had constructed for himself a personality that allowed him to joke with his close friends and correspondents about such matters. They "knew" he was an important political player and a sexually potent lover; therefore he could laugh with them about the fact that at certain moments that he selected and humorously presented he appeared not to be so, and he knew his correspondents would recognize the "truth" behind his apparently modest self-deprecation.

Nine days later Machiavelli sent Vettori another letter with a quite different tone. From announcing *The Prince* and discussing the lifestyles of the old and forgotten he turned to concerns about patronage: his main concern was to press Vettori to help their common friend Donato del Corno win a place in the service of the Medici. Significantly, however, Donato was a friend who was frequently identified in Machiavelli's correspondence by his sexuality—his enduring attraction to boys as sexual partners and his distaste for women. This made him a regular subject for knowing but gentle jokes about those desires among Machiavelli's group of friends. Tellingly, however, his sexual preference for male youths was clearly not treated by the group of friends as a mere practice or a passing stage on the way to adult sexuality; it was a marking aspect of his personality that was central in how his friends understood him, portrayed him, and enjoyed him. Machiavelli's letter of 19 December to Vettori was primarily concerned with a discussion of strategies they might follow to help Donato win a post. Perhaps to undercut a bit the political patronage tone of the missive, however, Machiavelli turned to sex to close the letter, again stressing the sexual side of their friendship and the importance of such matters among their larger group of friends, as well as Machiavelli's own playful interest in such things.

First, he referred to some verses that Vettori had written about a young male prostitute known as il Riccio in an earlier letter to Donato. Although it is not well known, as discussed in Chapter 4, male prostitution was a regular part of the sexual life of Florence and presumably many other major Renaissance cities as well. And the male prostitute il Riccio seems to have been a well-known denizen of the illicit world at the heart of Florence as well as being well known to Machiavelli's circle of friends for his sexual availability, for he was regularly referred to in their letters. It seems that these verses were another knowing joke at Donato's expense, naming in addition a number of his youthful lovers. But in the end it does not appear that he was much troubled by the exposure of his loves at least among their group of friends, for he apparently shared the verses with his friend Machiavelli. The joke, however, changed direction and grew when in turn Machiavelli and Donato recited this poem to a relative of Machiavelli's, Giovanni Machiavelli, inserting the latter's name for Donato's at appropriately compromising moments.

Machiavelli reported to Vettori that the ploy had worked to perfection: "He [Giovanni Machiavelli] was outraged and said that he did not know where you had found out his affairs [lit. who he touched]."[38] Machiavelli, the clever sexual jokester, reappeared in this letter to replace the tired old Machiavelli of his earlier missive. But significantly, Renaissance sexual identity was at the heart of his joke and this text. At the first level Donato del Corno, il Riccio, and Giovanni Machiavelli (if less willingly so perhaps) had to all be known as men who preferred male youths sexually for the joke to make any sense at all. This is not to deny that the joke referred to their sexual practices, but crucially it re-

ferred to those practices as something that identified them at least among their
group and thus made them available for such humorous play.

Clearly that play fell within the accepted range of behavior in their group
of friends, as all the men involved in this joking remained friends, even if Giovanni Machiavelli was apparently less willing to be portrayed as one who preferred youths even within the group. Still, it seems clear that this joking was a
normal aspect of their friendship. It evoked a comradery in a world of formally
illicit sexual practices where these men moved with ease even if their sexual
desires or objects were not necessarily shared. In sum, in Machiavelli's correspondence and more generally in the Renaissance some men were identified
with their sexual practices, and in Machiavelli's letters that identification was
an important marker of the way they were portrayed and also joked about in a
lighthearted fashion.

Machiavelli, then, seems to have once again shifted registers in his letter,
but in a way that brought him back to his own sexual self-presentation. He reported to Vettori that there was a new preacher in Florence who was attract-
ing a great deal of attention with his apocalyptic predictions, which had everyone in the city whipped into a frenzy. Machiavelli lamented that he found this
continuing gullibility of the Florentines in the face of such fire-and-brimstone
preachers most disconcerting—a clear reference to the earlier and continuing
power of the followers of Savonarola. And he elaborated: "These things upset
me so much yesterday, that although I was supposed to go to visit la Riccia [his
current courtesan paramour] this morning I didn't."

One might almost think that Machiavelli was continuing in the tired old
man tone established in his earlier letters, but here he was portraying himself
as an active lover who visited this well-known courtesan regularly. In fact, his
letters and the letters of his correspondents in this period were full of references to their affair and Machiavelli's active role in it, giving the lie to his earlier self-portrayal as an old man whiling away his days lost in the countryside
and living on his memories. The beauty, of course, of self-portrayal is that although it must be built up with the building blocks of the culturally possible
and accepted, within those parameters one can be at virtually the same time
true to the understanding of old men and true to the understanding of younger
lovers, depending on the self one is trying to present.[39]

And true to his often mocking humor at his own expense, at this point in
the letter Machiavelli took a quick and surprising sexual turn, remarking: "But
I'm not sure at the moment that if I had been supposed to go visit il Riccio, if

I would have let that [the uproar over the preacher's apocalyptic preaching] stop me."[40] Given that Machiavelli had just been writing about humorous verses on il Riccio's availability as a male prostitute, the reversal was perfect. While the uproar over this preacher had soured him on visiting his female courtesan lover, la Riccia, if he had been going to visit the male prostitute, il Riccio, he might well have gone anyway.

Clearly there is a joke here. But what was Vettori supposed to find humorous in Machiavelli's presentation of self? Was Machiavelli with a kind of in-joke reminding his old and close friend Vettori that he was also interested in young men? Most commentators on this letter have quickly dismissed Machiavelli's remark as "facetious."[41] And clearly most of Machiavelli's sexual references to himself in his correspondence present a clear and apparently artfully constructed picture of him as a man very much focused on sex with women, a picture also mirrored back to him by his correspondents, who regularly refer to his strong and enduring interest in women. From that perspective this reference to a potential momentary preference for il Riccio is probably best read as "facetious." But even as a facetious remark it warrants attention, for it says something about attitudes toward male-male sexual relations and about Machiavelli's own vision and presentation of himself sexually.

First, of course, it suggests that although the formal pronouncements and legal strictures against male-male sexual relations remained stern, in Machiavelli's circle, at least, things were considerably more relaxed. A sexual interest in younger men certainly marked and identified a man, especially if it continued after the age when society assumed it was time to move on to a sexual focus on women, as discussed in Chapter 1. A primary identification of Machiavelli's friend Donato del Corno, as we have seen, was that his attraction to young men like il Riccio had endured. But while that attraction for young men might be the occasion for playful joking and remarks, it did not elicit much in the way of moral condemnation or negative evaluation within Machiavelli's circle of friends and correspondents. It was actually fairly interchangeable in terms of moral evaluation within that group with other illicit forms of sex— all formally incorrect forms of behavior that were, however, natural and thus to be expected and at worse quickly forgiven.

Moreover, among men in the know, like Machiavelli's close friends, illicit sex was to be laughed at and gossiped about and, significantly, to be used to construct a sexual persona—a consensus reality of their sexual identity—that marked each of them as in his own way a true man and member of the group.

On a second level, however, as a facetious remark Machiavelli's momentary preference for il Riccio suggests that Machiavelli knew that his reader knew his sexual identity well, that this was a well-settled part of his reputation: that Vettori knew that he was really the lover of women that he presented himself as being in their letters over and over again. For the most likely reading of the remark required that Vettori recognize that Machiavelli was not, in fact, attracted to young men and thus Machiavelli was joking about how upset this fire-breathing preacher in Florence had made him, completely reversing his usual sexual appetites.

That seems clearly to be the most probable reading of Machiavelli's remark. But if we were to take his comment as not quite so facetious and see it as a suggestion that Machiavelli actually at times still sought out young men, what would we make of it? Certainly Machiavelli does not explicitly refer to an interest in young men in the letters we have today. Unfortunately, however, the letters that we have were for the most part those collected and copied in the sixteenth century by Giuliano de' Ricci, Machiavelli's grandson, who admits that he "did not copy" some of the material that dealt with the "loves" and "pleasures" of Machiavelli and his friends and instead focused on copying material that dealt with "states and matters of importance."[42] Thus it could be that the lack of reference to this kind of sexual interest in Machiavelli's letters is a matter of Giuliano's not transcribing this "unimportant" material or even his censorship of this aspect of the letters in a later period when attitudes seem to have hardened into a more negative vision of such sexual practices.

Be that as it may, there is another possible reading of Machiavelli's comment that would fit quite easily with the sexual values and practices of the time already discussed. Machiavelli's joke could be read as a reference to a younger Machiavelli living in Florence at the time of Savonarola who moved easily between younger men and women as sex objects—a phase when many of his male friendships were formed and a comrade like Donato del Corno was not at all unusual for his sexual interests, literally just another of the boys. In that context Machiavelli could well be referring to an earlier time in their lives, a specific earlier time when Savonarola, the prophet, and his supporters ruled Florence—a reference evoked by the current Franciscan preacher sowing turmoil and confusion in the city—an earlier time when Machiavelli and many of his peers and perhaps Vettori as well would have been in their early and mid-twenties and much more likely to be attracted to younger male lovers.[43] In such an admittedly highly problematic reading Machiavelli could have been sug-

gesting that this fire-breathing preacher so took him back to that time that he
wondered if maybe he might find a return to a young male lover, like il Riccio, more in tune with the moment than his current love, la Riccia.

Without going so far as to argue that, it is clear that Machiavelli's ironic sexual tone and the illicit world of male friendship it suggests continue to be a
central theme in the next few letters, laid out first humorously by Vettori and
then replayed by Machiavelli. Old age and sexual desire, friendship and sexual desire, the correct behavior for mature males and sexual desire were all
evoked and played with a series of laughing exchanges that say much about
both men and their sexual relationship. Because he had not yet replied to Machiavelli's letter of the 10th—most noted, it will be remembered, for Machiavelli's revelation that he had written a version of *The Prince*—Vettori began
his reply to the letter of the 19th with an apology: "My dear brother [*compar*],
if I haven't responded to your letter of the 10th, and I don't really reply to it
even now, the reason is Casavecchia and Brancacci who are driving me crazy
everyday trying to make me remember the dignity of the city to which I owe
my office [as ambassador in Rome]. You know that I enjoy women every now
and then, more for a bit of conversation than for other things, given that now
unfortunately I am getting a bit on in years and I am not really able to do much
more than talk."[44]

Vettori evidently was willing to mirror Machiavelli's self-portrayal as an old
lover and went one beyond him with his claim that he was good for little but
talking with women, even if this merely set the stage for a clever and humorous narrative about the way their common friends Filippo Casavecchia and
Giuliano Brancacci were pressuring him to change his ways in order to maintain their vision of his sexual reputation. Within their group Vettori could frequent courtesans and draw upon his sexual exploits or lack thereof to build and
maintain his ties of friendship. But both Casavecchia and Brancacci were worried about the reputation he should maintain for the broader community as
Florentine ambassador to the pope—a broader but crucial consensus reality
for a public figure like the ambassador; thus, both men were pressing him to
modify not so much his sexual behavior as the appearance of his sexual behavior that he displayed to Roman society.

Vettori's problem with their well-meaning concern for his sexual reputation
was straightforward and turned on a perfect Renaissance sexual double bind:
for, as discussed in Chapter 4, Casavecchia was known within their circle as yet
another friend who was not interested in women; and in a nice reversal Brancacci was troubled by sexual relations between males. As a result Vettori re-

ported ironically to Machiavelli that their two friends were "driving him crazy" because Brancacci was pressing him to avoid young men associated with male-male sex and Casavecchia was pressing him to avoid young women associated with male-female sex. This left poor Vettori in his rather ironic telling with no sexual company and very little company at all in the name of presenting a proper face to Roman society.

Vettori's presentation of each man's objections to his presumed sexual choices is revealing. "You know already," he wrote to Machiavelli,

> that Filippo's [Casavecchia] heart is turned against them [courtesans]. Before he came here [to Rome] because my house is rather out of the way, often one courtesan or another came to visit me to see the church here and the garden attached. . . . It never occurred to me when Filippo arrived to alert them that it would not be a good idea for them to visit us. So two days after his arrival right at the dinner hour, one walked into a room where as usual the servants allowed her to enter freely and having entered she took a seat as if she were in her own house. She did this in such a way that I did not know how to send her away or to hide the thing from Filippo, who gave her an amazed and disgusted look [lit., turned on her two amazed and disgusted eyes]. We all sat down at the table and she took his seat. We ate and chatted and after the meal, as was her habit, she went out to walk around in the garden. Filippo and I remained alone and he began to give me a speech in his particular style . . . but I knowing that the speech would be long and what he wanted to say interrupted him and said . . . that I had lived up to the present free and without obligations to anyone and I wanted to live the rest of my life like that.[45]

Clearly this domestic scene had a transgressive aspect even in Vettori's telling: in most Renaissance homes courtesans did not come and go at their pleasure, dining uninvited and taking the seats that they preferred even when they were reserved for more important male guests like Filippo Casavecchia. Such familiarity, virtually domesticity, was unseemly for a host of reasons, but perhaps most notably because it crossed the boundaries between the illicit and domestic realms. For men living on their own without their wives, like Vettori, this was an easier matter to carry off perhaps, but Casavecchia could have made a strong case for the incorrectness of such behavior if Vettori had not cut him off. And significantly, Vettori had softened the negative impact of such behavior by painting it in largely social rather than sexual terms: these courtesans had the run of his house not so much because they were his sexual intimates but because they came to talk with him and enjoy the adjoining garden and church. What actually was the case we cannot know, but, as we shall see, not all was innocent conversation and enjoyment of a garden—nature and intellectual nurture for Roman courtesans provided by the Florentine ambassador to the pope or visa versa.

In turn, their second friend, Brancacci, was upset about a certain well-known Roman "sodomite" known as Sano, who regularly visited Vettori in a way that was causing people to talk.

> I believe you know how great a friend of mine is Jacopo Gianfigliazi [*sic*] and how for many reasons I have cause to not only love him but respect him. When he was ambassador here, he turned over to me certain of his litigations as you know. And perhaps believing that I had more to do than I had, he asked ser Sano to remind me. Sano for this reason virtually every week came to speak with me about these matters and sometimes stayed to eat dinner with me. Giuliano when he had seen him visit once, then two times, and then three, began to say that ser Sano was a notorious man [notorious for his sodomy] and that in the Banchi [an important street of merchant shops in Rome] he was asked by a certain merchant of good name what sort of relationship I had with this Sano. And [he warned me] that I should be careful to avoid such relationships.[46]

Here the broader nature of the evaluation of an individual's sexuality comes to the fore once again. Brancacci's reproach is driven home by what people of good reputation in the merchant shops of Rome were saying about the company he was keeping. Notorious sodomites evidently were not ideal companions for Florentine ambassadors at least as far as the general public was concerned, and significantly there is a negative value judgment here that contrasts with the humorous acceptance of friends who preferred boys to women sexually within the more accepting confines of their circle of friends. Once more the often multiple boundaries between the illicit world and the broader social world of the Renaissance city become more explicit: in the illicit world shared by Vettori, Machiavelli, and their circle of friends sexual choice could and did identify people but without much in the way of a value judgment; in the streets of Rome or Florence in the value judgments of men of substance certain illicit behaviors could cause one to become "notorious" and be the subject of male gossip and reprobation, as Brancacci warned his friend Vettori—different groups once again shared different consensus realities about sexual practice and sexual identity.

Suggestively, in this case, rather than cutting his friend off and telling him that he would live as he lived up to the present without regard for what others said, he reported to Machiavelli, "In order to excuse myself, I was forced to explain to him the whole story about the case involving Jacopo Gianfigliazzi and him [Sano]."[47] It seems clear here that Vettori was more anxious to disassociate himself from sodomy than from sexual relations with courtesans in part because of the public danger of being associated with such activities but also presumably because it was not a part of the sexual portrayal of himself that he was presenting to Machiavelli and their friends. Older, less sexually active, more socially interested in courtesans, he was comfortable with that self-portrayal but not with a self-portrait as an older man sexually interested in male-male sex; thus, his account of his relationship with Sano was all business and not part of a larger set of relationships that brought notorious sodomites to his house. Vettori closed this section of the letter with a query to his comrade in illicit sex with courtesans, Machiavelli, asking him laughingly whose reprimands he should pay attention to, Casavecchia's or Brancacci's, and suggesting that perhaps he should just concentrate on doing what he found most satisfying.

The letter, however, then turned more serious for a time, sliding from sex to politics and strategy for a possible reentry of Machiavelli into political life with the aid of the Medici. First, Vettori acknowledged that he had already heard about the political tract that Machivelli had written, *The Prince*, from Filippo Casavecchia, and cutting to the heart of the matter, he offered to read it, modestly suggesting that his comments about its political contents might not be all that acute but that he would substitute for his lack of critical acumen "his love and faith" in Machiavelli. "And when I have read it," he concluded, "I'll give you my opinion on whether or not you should present it to the magnificent Giuliano [de' Medici]." Although it is still a matter of scholarly debate, it seems evident from these letters that Machiavelli at least for a time hoped to use *The Prince* as a vehicle for regaining Medici favor, perhaps by dedicating it to Giuliano de' Medici, who he hoped might well become a supporter and patron as well.[48]

Patronage, career, and Roman politics continued as the focus, with Vettori evaluating the problems that Machiavelli noted earlier about visiting Cardinal Soderini if he were to visit Vettori in Rome. On the one hand, if Machiavelli did not visit his old friend the cardinal, he would be justly insulted. On the other, if he did visit him, the Medici logically would see this as an reaffirmation of his old ties with the Soderini family, virtually first on their list of enemies. Vettori reassured Machiavelli on this score, noting that the cardinal was well aware of Machiavelli's difficult situation and would understand his reasons for keeping his distance. In passing, Donato del Corno's patronage concerns were dealt with as well, along with a shopping list of other similar issues, and the letter closed by returning to where it opened, the illicit world of sex, noting that a certain el Casa was in his element in Rome. This el Casa, apparently Casavecchia, was enjoying Rome, he reported, because he was able to buy "good things" there—implicitly the male sexual companions he desired—for virtually nothing. And Vettori ended the letter laughingly noting that he had nothing to say about the Franciscan preacher who put Machiavelli off sex with his courtesan mistress, la Riccia, aside from observing that Florence was a strange place where such preachers were listened to willingly.

Machiavelli's reply to this letter ignored the political and patronage issues raised by Vettori to focus on his humorous dilemma with the sexual reprimands of Casavecchia and Brancacci, providing an ironic reprise of Machiavelli's vision of the appropriate sexual conduct for "old" men like themselves. "Magnificent ambassador," he began, "it is certainly striking to consider how blind men are in relation to the areas in which they sin and [at the same time] fierce persecutors of the vices that they don't have."[49] Leaving aside the classic and contemporary examples that he claimed he could cite to prove this point, Machiavelli noted that as far as Casavecchia was concerned he would never be troubled by visits of Brancacci's "notorious" sodomite, Sano: "Actually it would seem to him that you behaved perfectly as an ambassador should; given that such a person must suffer an infinite number of restrictions, it is necessary to have some pleasures and diversions; so this relationship with ser Sano would seem to him perfect and he would have lauded your prudence with every person and praised to the skies that decision."[50]

Behind Machiavelli's irony once again we see clearly that much of the imagined assessment of Vettori's sexual activity here turns on a broader social evaluation of how he handled himself, not on what he actually did. Casavecchia's pronouncements are social evaluations of his behavior that turn more on prudence than on sin or customary morality. Also although it was not stressed, there was an allusion to nature again—what we might label a "natural psychology"—as the poor ambassador, Vettori, limited by an "infinite number of restrictions," needed some "pleasures and diversions," and, of course, for Casavecchia, Sano was the perfect solution to those needs of nature.

"On the other hand," Machiavelli continued, "I imagine that if the whole bordello of Valencia was running around your house, Brancacci would have never found reason to reprove you; actually he would have praised you more highly for this than if he had heard you give a speech before the Pope better than any given by Demosthenes."[51] The humor of the reversal could not have been neater, and Machiavelli's point that every man overlooks his own sins was nicely made. Machiavelli went on to imagine what would happen if Vettori actually took his critics' advice, banishing both Ser Sano and all courtesans from his house, and suggested that after a few days each man would begin to complain in his own way about the lack of the sex objects that interested him. "And to make this clearer for you," Machiavelli added, " if by necessity I, who touch and pay attention to women [*che tocco et attendo a femmine*], had been there and fallen under your austere regime, immediately when I saw how things stood, I would have said, 'Ambassador, you are going to get sick; it doesn't seem to me you have any pleasures whatsoever; here there are no young boys [*garzoni*], here there are no women; what a screwed up house [lit., "what a prick of a house"] is this.'"[52]

Machiavelli then advised his friend to pay little heed to the sexual strictures of his Florentine guests, arguing that there were many people who were quite "crazy" when it came to their opinions about what was correct sexual behavior. As a result Vettori should not bother to attempt to satisfy others on this score, especially as everyone had a different opinion. Moreover he opined, "Such people [who give advice on sexual comportment] don't realize that the man who is held to be wise [for what he does] during the day, will never be held to be crazy [for what he does] during the night. Moreover he who is held to be a good man and who is esteemed, wins honor and not shame and instead of being called a bugger [*buggerone*] or a whoremonger [*puttaniere*], is called broad minded, easy going, or a friendly type."[53] Machiavelli seems to be suggesting, perhaps optimistically, that one's reputation is based more on what one does in a broader social context—"during the day"—than what one does sexually and in a more personal context—"during the night." Suggestively, here in sexual terms we have a distinction that appears to point toward later, harder distinctions between the public and private: what is done in public during the day is what makes reputation, not what is done in private during the night. More pertinent, however, this underlines the point that honor, reputation, and identity were primarily socially determined in the Renaissance, even if it might seem to suggest at first that sexual practices were not all that significant in the broader estimation of these crucial qualities.

Yet in this case context is crucial, for Machiavelli qualified his advice by pointing out that people are "crazy" when it comes to such evaluations and, more important yet, that they hold a wide range of different positions on correct sexual behavior. In that context the person who already has a good reputation and who is able to keep his sexual peccadilloes largely out of the wider public purview, even when they come to light, will be more likely to be forgiven as being merely "broad minded, easy going or a friendly type." Thus the man who is generally respected will find that sexual practices that might otherwise gain him the negative labels of a "bugger" or a "whoremonger" in the broader society instead is viewed as merely human and a pleasant fellow—quite possibly just as Machiavelli hoped to be seen by a broader Florentine society beyond his immediate group of friends. But crucially this all turns on a more subtle evaluation of one's sexual activities in the broader context of one's reputation and honor, and the implied corollary is that men who are not esteemed or as important as Machiavelli or Vettori—men like the notary Sano—will, in fact, be judged to be "buggers" and dishonored by their sexual affairs if they should become widely known. And ultimately all men will be judged on their sexuality: some positively as being good fellows for their sexual peccadilloes, others negatively.

Machiavelli ended his letter with a witty evocation of Vettori's two critics, Giuliano Brancacci and Filippo Casavecchia, which once again returns to a sexual evaluation of their personalities. Laughingly, he noted that Brancacci might appear all prim and proper but when *la civetta* (literally an owl, but commonly used to refer to a woman's genitals) would actually arrive he would be the first to go chasing after it and that Casavecchia was like a vulture who would take any boy he could find and, when he had his fill, he would sit in a tree and make fun of the sexual desire of others for beautiful and fine youths; thus he suggested that Vettori ignore them both and focus on taking care of his own desires as he saw fit.

A little less than two weeks later, on 18 January, Vettori replied to Machiavelli's letter, continuing his saga of the three Florentines' sexual life in Rome. He began with a quick compliment for Machiavelli, noting that he had always had great respect for Machiavelli's judgment in things both great and small and confirming that his evaluation of the situation had proved correct. First, he admitted that because he had been so concerned with what Brancacci and Casavecchia thought he had stopped the visits both of Sano and his courtesans with the result—much as Machiavelli had predicted—that no one visited them except a certain Donato Bossi, a rather austere grammarian of exceptional tediousness. After a few days Brancacci and Casavecchia realized their error, and one evening sitting by the fire Brancacci worried out loud that men who lived without the company of women tended to become savages and suggested that they invite a woman who lived nearby to dinner.

That suggestion, it turned out, had the potential to satisfy all three friends, as Vettori made clear when he described the "condition" of this woman. Not surprisingly, once again, the key to that special condition was sexual. "Near my house there lives a Roman widow of quite good family," he explained, "who has been and is a woman of easy virtue [this may well be the Roman widow to whom Vettori had referred as a possible mistress for Machiavelli in an earlier letter] and even if she is a bit older, she has a daughter of about twenty who is exceedingly beautiful, who has had and has some affairs. In addition she [the widow] has a son of fourteen, pretty and nice, as well as well mannered and honest as is often the case at that age."[54] Two women of loose morals for Brancacci and Vettori and a pretty boy for Casavecchia: Machiavelli's friends in Rome seemed to have found a way to return to their "natural" paths of illicit sex and happiness, much as he had recommended in his earlier letter. Needless to say, in the face of such a promising dinner, both friends changed their tune and pressed Vettori to arrange it.

But Vettori's account of their adventures took a humorous turn for the worse when these promising neighbors came to dinner. First off, they arrived when he was working on his diplomatic correspondence with the Dieci of Florence. Caught off guard, Vettori reported to his friend that he received them as warmly as he could even if he was never very good at such things. In addition, the widow brought along an unexpected brother, who seemed to be a kind of chaperon; thus while Brancacci wooed the daughter and Casavecchia wooed the young boy, Vettori was stuck making conversation with the widow and her brother about a litigation that they were involved in Rome. The picture Vettori painted has the novelistic coloring of a poor victim left with a boring business conversation as his friends ignored his plight to busily pursue their seductions and pleasures.

While talking reluctantly with the older pair, Vettori related, he "could not avoid every now and then overhearing what Giuliano was saying to Costanza [the daughter], . . . and they were the smoothest words you have ever heard, praising her nobility, her beauty, all the things that one can compliment in a woman. Meanwhile Filippo, paying no attention, was cleverly speaking with the young boy, asking him if he was studying, if he had a teacher, and to move toward his goal he began to ask him if he slept with his teacher, so aggressively that the modest young lad lowered his eyes and did not reply."[55] The dinner went smoothly enough in Vettori's recounting of it, with much laughter and conversation. A momentary interruption caused by the unexpected arrival of Pietro del Bene, another friend in Rome, was quickly ended by the threatening looks cast in his direction by the busy suitors Brancacci and Casavecchia.

Pietro got the hint and left immediately, with only some eye contact to indicate his disapproval. And so Vettori concluded: "We spent the evening pleasantly and around midnight our neighbors left and we, left behind, went to bed to sleep."[56]

If finally the three friends seemed to have returned to their normal sexual ways, at least in Vettori's letter, with Brancacci courting this young woman, Casavecchia chatting up this young boy, and the old Vettori looking on enviously, nothing could be further from the truth, or at least the truth as Machiavelli described it in a letter to Vettori from the end of February 1514, already discussed in Chapter 4. It seems that Brancacci and Casavecchia had returned to Florence for carnival, leaving their affairs or hoped-for affairs in Rome behind, and Machiavelli wrote his friend with his own "novella" of Brancacci's humorous sexual metamorphosis there.[57] Given Brancacci's antipathy to male-male sexual relations, his decision one night to go hunting for birds, male phalluses, through the streets of Florence—"andare alla macchia"—should have seemed a particularly unexpected reversal of his sexual practices and his sexual reputation in the group of friends that Machiavelli and Vettori shared.

As the tale unfolded in Machiavelli's letter, after searching through the illicit heart of the city, Brancacci found his "thrush" and with a few "kisses" and "pets" proceeded to have sexual relations with him.[58] It turned out, however, that his thrush was no ordinary bird but rather Michele, the youthful nephew of Consiglio Costi, a most important man in Florence. At that point Brancacci decided to try to trick the youth by convincing him in the dark that he was Filippo Casavecchia, perhaps not particularly hard to do given Casavecchia's reputation or at least not that hard to do in the economy of Machiavelli's tale for their common friend Vettori. As noted earlier, this may well have been the second metamorphosis in Machiavelli's story, for now not only had Brancacci taken Casavecchia's sexual reputation, reversing his own by hunting birds in the heart of the illicit sex district of Florence, but he had taken his name as well, successfully becoming Casavecchia at least for a moment.

But this metamorphosis rapidly unraveled when the real Casavecchia rejected the boy's claims for payment the next day and quickly came to suspect his friend Brancacci as author of the fraud. With the help of a friend a day later young Michele surprised Brancacci and recognized his voice. Discovered, Brancacci fled in shame, and Machiavelli concluded his tale noting that the affair had spawned a new saying in Florence, "Are you Brancacci or are you Casa[vecchia]?" The humorous query was ultimately one of Renaissance sexual reputation and identity—the question was, Was one sexually interested in women or boys? Moreover, this clever tale of metamorphosis was predicated upon Vettori and Machiavelli's shared understanding of Brancacci's and Casavecchia's sexual identity, an understanding that seems to have been shared by their group of friends. Significantly, however, this identity was not shared more widely in the community. Casavecchia, in fact, when faced with Michele's claims and threats, was, as noted earlier, very concerned about his broader reputation in the civic and masculine world of Florence. What was not a problem among friends could well be a problem in the larger world in which these men moved: different consensus realities were again in play. In turn, Brancacci's shame at being discovered suggests a similar concern. A clever joke on a friend in the context of their circle of friends had been turned against him in the broader arena of Florentine society.

In the end this tale was tied directly to the earlier letters of Vettori from Rome and the discussion of his adventures there with Brancacci and Casavecchia, for Machiavelli then closed his letter with a reference to those letters and a question that Vettori had asked there. "In response to your earlier letter I don't have anything else to say to you except let yourself be swept up by love and that pleasure that you will have today, you may not have tomorrow; and if things are as you describe them, I am more envious of you than of the king of England. I beg you to follow your star and not to let go the least little thing . . . for I believe, believed and will always believe that what Boccaccio says is true: that it is better to do it and repent, then to not do it and repent."[59] This love that Machiavelli advises Vettori to let sweep him away was the last strange result of the dinner that Vettori wrote about with his two friends and his neighbors in Rome back on 18 January.

As discussed earlier, in that letter Vettori had with a nice symmetry laid out the attempted seductions of his neighbor's daughter and son by their friends. But his report of the dinner did not end there, for he continued immediately with the problem at the heart of his witty account of the evening: "Still my dear Niccolò I cannot help but lament to you that in trying to make our friends happy I have become virtually the prisoner of this Costanza [the daughter]. Before her there visited now one woman and now another and I enjoyed them very much but without feeling any special affection for them. Now this woman has come into my life and I will insist that you have never seen a more beautiful woman or more courteous. . . . I am so taken with her that I cannot think of anything but her."[60] Vettori had undergone a metamorphosis of his own; from the old, tranquil diplomat whiling away his days in Rome, walking in his garden and occasionally merely chatting with a visiting courtesan, he had suddenly become a passionate lover again, foolishly swept head over heels by a young woman half his age. And for Vettori, at least in his letters to Machiavelli, the question became immediately and insistently how should he respond to his transformation, a transformation that he portrayed as both wonderful and terrible.

Significantly, however, Vettori did not ask this question of his friend in the abstract as one critical thinker to another—for in the realm of passion, Machiavelli had for Vettori a rather different reputation and personality, as he made clear immediately: "And because I have seen you at times in love and understood how much passion you felt, I will resist as much as I can at the beginning. I don't know if I will be strong enough and I doubt that I will, but I will write you about what happens in this case."[61] Vettori seemed to be suggesting that the sexual Machiavelli that he knew was a man who suffered his passions, a man who rather than being the master of love was mastered by it, rather than an active aggressor a passive victim.

As a result the old Vettori, suddenly fallen into the clutches of young love, promised to do his best not to emulate his friend and passively let it sweep him away. In fact, in an earlier letter to Vettori of 4 February also referring to Vettori's suffering in love, Machiavelli had been quite explicit about the passive approach to love, which he recommended. He wrote waxing lyrical: "And because you—remembering what the arrows of love have done to me—are dismayed by my example, I feel compelled to tell you how I have handled myself with him [the god of Love]. In effect I let him do as he pleases and follow him through valleys, woods, cliffs and countryside and I find that he has given me more rewards than if I had tormented him. Let down your defenses, let go the breaks, close your eyes and say, 'Go ahead, O' Love, take me in hand and show me the way: if everything works out well for me, the credit will be yours; if badly yours will be the blame; I am your servant: you can't gain anything more by torturing me; really you stand to lose as you will be torturing [what is] already yours.'"[62]

"Do as he pleases," "follow," "let down your defenses," "let go the breaks," "take me in hand," "I am your servant"—Machiavelli clearly does not seem to be the aggressive, active controller of his fate with love which he suggests one should be with fortune. Suggestively, Love (Amore) for Machiavelli was a male god and Fortune (Fortuna) a female one, and Love's arrows were arguably phallic and penetrating while Fortune's tides were sealike and engulfing, but without probing deeper symbolism or issues of his psyche, Machiavelli seems clearly to be defending a passive approach to love to Vettori, a passive approach that he characterized as his own and which he claimed had worked well for him. In fact, he added almost immediately, "That's the way it is my dear patron, so be happy: don't get all upset, open yourself up to fortune and go along with the things that the heavens, the times, and men put before you and have no doubt that you will break every binding tie and overcome every difficulty. And if you want to serenade her, I offer to come there myself with some good songs to make her fall in love with you."[63] The old Machiavelli caterwauling with Vettori under the windows of a twenty-something young woman in Rome is an intriguing picture, but perhaps no more intriguing than Machiavelli's contention in this letter that one must be passive in love.

It has been noted, of course, that even in the world of politics and diplomacy Machiavelli did not always advocate an aggressive approach. At times the need to adjust to necessity or the times themselves meant that one had to adapt, and, in fact, this is one of the arguments Machiavelli advanced to explain why aggressively successful men not always successful even when their tactics had worked for them in the past. For when the times changed, men had to change with them or those same tactics that had brought them success would bring them failure. But in this case the situation was different, for Machiavelli pictured himself as someone who was totally passive in the face of love, who closed his eyes and followed where love led, and in that abject servitude to love he claimed that he found that things often worked out well for him.

PART II. PERFORMING MACO: THE STAGING OF SEXUAL IDENTITIES

Significantly, it might be argued that Machiavelli did not reserve this self-representation as a passive servant of love solely for his close circle of friends and correspondents but rather seemed curiously willing to playfully allude to it for a broader public, as if testing his claim that his "daytime" reputation would lead people to accept him as a good fellow for such behavior rather than denigrate him for "what he did at night." For when one turns to his literary works, that self-representation seems to be found at the heart of his famous and much admired comedy *La mandragola*. Although there is considerable debate about the exact date of the composition of this comedy, it is clear that it was finished around 1518, which suggests that Machiavelli was working on it at about the same time that he was exchanging these letters and this advice with Vettori or just a bit later and certainly while thoughts of the power of love were still much on his mind.

Machiavelli scholars have repeatedly sought to find Machiavellian themes and Machiavelli alter egos in this clever, quick comedy that turns on the use of a magic fertility potion made from the mandrake root to con a foolish old lawyer, Messer Nicia, into actually putting his young wife, Lucrezia, into bed with a passionate would-be lover, Callimaco. Most notable, they have seen Machiavelli portraying and perhaps caricaturing himself in the cunning and quite Machiavellian parasite Ligurio, who cleverly drives the scam that is at the heart of the plot. Ligurio, conceivably much as Machiavelli thought of himself, was the crafty plotter who worked behind the scenes to make things turn out as they should. As was the case for Machiavelli in his diplomatic and political career, Ligurio was never the hero, never the person at the head of the delegation or the government. Neither the character in the comedy nor the political actor had quite the social standing to function at that level, but Ligurio, much like Machiavelli, was valued for his ability to work behind the scenes to make things happen quietly and effectively. And it might well be argued that just as Ligurio did this largely for the pleasure of making things work and enjoying the complex maneuverings of a clever plot, so too Machiavelli enjoyed the opportunity to use and display his *virtù*—his ability to get things done using analysis and a calculating approach to control the future—virtually as much as the power and authority that had once gone with his position in Soderini's Florentine government before his fall from power. Even without going that far, critics have convincingly argued that Machiavelli represented much that his friends and acquaintances would have recognized as Machiavelli-like in the character of Ligurio.

Others have suggested that the irreverent and wily Fra Timoteo is perhaps even more subtly drawn by Machiavelli to reflect himself. Certainly this friar's very pragmatic approach to religion and his willingness to cleverly twist and manipulate its tenets to secure his own goals seem good examples of what is often labeled a Machiavellian approach to the world. Moreover, as we know from his letters, Machiavelli was not overly enthusiastic about contemporary religious practices and the religious; thus a corrupt friar focused on maximizing his revenues and serving the rich and powerful in their plots might also make a good candidate for a Machiavelli alter ego in the comedy. But perhaps the most significant sign of the friar's Machiavellian nature is to be found in his long speech (act 3, scene 11) in which he tries to convince Lucrezia that sleeping with a young man who has been forced to take the mandrake root potion—a potion that will kill the youth if he has sex with her—and cuckolding her husband (admittedly with his consent) are not serious sins.

To transform murder and adultery into a positive act is certainly a feat worthy of the darkest and most dangerous Machiavelli, and Machiavelli, the comic author, plays the scene with a humor that is classic, giving Fra Timoteo the following lines:

> As far as your conscience is concerned, you need to follow this general rule: where there is a clear good and an indefinite evil, one must never lose that good for fear of that evil. And in this case there is a clear good: you will become pregnant and gain a soul for God Our Father. And the uncertain evil is that the man who lies with you after you have taken the potion may die, but there are those who do not die. Yet, as it is an uncertain thing, it is better that Messer Nicia [her husband] not run that risk. As far the act itself is concerned, don't imagine that it would be a sin. For it is the will that sins, not the body. And the sin in sex comes from not pleasing one's husband or from taking pleasure oneself in the deed, but you will be pleasing him and taking no pleasure. Moreover, one must consider the end of every action: your goal is to fill a seat in paradise and to satisfy your husband.[64]

A speech certainly worthy of Machiavelli and, in its discussion of will and sin, also quite theologically correct. But, of course, the thing that has most attracted critics in this speech is the apparent echo of the famous claim from *The Prince* with which Fra Timoteo ends his argument—that the ends justify the means.[65] All of this seems to make Fra Timoteo another candidate to be a Machiavelli character in the plot.

Our reading of Machiavelli's letters, however, suggests two other possibilities for Machiavelli alter egos in the comedy which have been proposed from time to time also by critics. The name Messer Nicia has often attracted attention to that unlikely character as somehow being related to Machiavelli. At first glance the old lawyer, who is easily tricked into putting his own wife in bed with another man, who is absolutely sure that he knows everything when he actually knows very little, and who is so provincial that he thinks trips to nearby Prato and Pisa have made him a man of the world, seems to have nothing at all to do with Machiavelli. In fact, his evident lack of *virtù* makes him the perfect butt of the joke that is at the center of the comedy and makes him seem an impossible candidate to represent any aspect of the master of *virtù* that Machiavelli regularly represented himself as being. Yet, as a number of scholars have pointed out, his name, Nicia, seems to be a play on *Nic*colò Mach*ia*velli.

Moreover, he does have a speech or two that seem to evoke humorously the more negative side of Machiavelli's condition at the time. Early in the comedy Messer Nicia was convinced by Ligurio that his wife's would-be lover was a doctor who had helped the king of France and the most important princes of his realm to sire children. As that was Nicia's burning desire, he returned home to get a urine sample from his wife to aid the doctor in his diagnosis. As he walked along with the servant Siro, he launched into a complaint that seems in significant ways to mirror Machiavelli's perception of himself as someone unfairly excluded from power in Florence. Referring to the fact that he had been told that the supposed "doctor" planned to return soon to France, Messer Nicia remarked: "And he would do well there [France]. In this land there are only the constipated; no one appreciates ability [*virtù*]. If he remains here no one will give him the time of day."[66]

For Machiavelli, as well, in Florence *virtù* was not recognized or rewarded, and men like himself who had demonstrated that they had it were not even given the time of day for they had been turned out of power and shunned by the Medici. For once Messer Nicia seemed to be saying something intelligent even if his highly critical remark was undercut by a rapid return to his normal foolishness when he continued: "I know what I'm talking about because I've shit bricks to learn some legal jargon, and if I had to live on what I make on that, I'd be out in the cold, I can tell you."[67] The quick return to foolishness might be read as indicating that Machiavelli was not serious about the earlier critique of Florence's lack of support for men of *virtù*, but, of course, Machiavelli was not exactly in favor with the Medici regime of Florence, and open criticism was not likely to improve his situation. Perhaps putting this critique of the status quo in the mouth of his chosen fool in this comedy allowed Messer Nicia to say for Machiavelli what he could not have said openly, much as court fools and jesters could laughingly say the truths that others could not.

And Messer Nicia, perhaps for a moment, as the old truth-telling jester Machiavelli, had yet more to say, pointing out: "In this city, people without status, people like me, can't even find a dog willing to bark at them. And we're only good enough to go to funerals or weddings or pass the day sitting on the pro-consul's bench giggling like young girls."[68] Of course, Machiavelli's situation, subtracting the foolishness of Messer Nicia, was much the same. He could see clearly the success of his old friend Vettori with the Medici regime and compare it with his own failure and feel that not even the dogs of Florence were willing to bark at him. Both he and Vettori had served the fallen Soderini republican regime, but when that regime collapsed and the Medici returned to power supported by the old aristocratic *ottimati* families who had opposed the republican government of Soderini, Vettori, as a scion of one of those aristocratic families, was given the opportunity to prove himself to the new regime as ambassador in Rome. Machiavelli, however, without that crucial status, had a different fate, and while it may not have quite been "go[ing] to funerals or weddings or pass[ing] the day sitting on the proconsul's bench giggling like young girls," the futility of such activities recalls the futility and frustration that Machiavelli evoked in his letter about his life in rural exile arguing in the tavern while gambling and discussing chopping wood with peasants.

Again Messer Nicia was the fool, but there was a bitter truth behind the laughter he evoked. And reinforcing the suggestion that the foolishness of Messer Nicia allowed him to present yet another side of Machiavelli to a broader public—his disappointment with the failure of Florence and its leaders to recognize and utilize his *virtù* as it should have been recognized and used—he finished his complaints to Siro with a suggestive request: "But I wouldn't want anyone to hear that I said this, because I could be stuck with some special tax or, even worse, have the words shoved up my ass in retaliation."[69] Better that Machiavelli told the truth of Florence as the fool Nicia, for as Machiavelli, the fallen politician, knew all too well, the Medici and their regime did not take criticism well. His letters made clear that he remembered well his days in the Bargello of Florence and his torture there and had no desire to repeat the experience.

A less noted and more subtle possible connection between Machiavelli and Messer Nicia draws on what at first might seem an absolute contrast between the character and the man. Whereas Machiavelli traveled widely as an agent of the Florentine government visiting the French and imperial courts, Messer Nicia had barely visited the sites of Tuscany, even if, true to his foolishness, he treated his travels as if they made him a cosmopolitan traveler. When asked if he had seen the sea at Livorno, he replied, "Of course," and continued to describe it by comparing it with the Arno: "Why it's four times . . . more than six times . . . why, more than seven times larger. Actually it's so big I'd have to say that you see nothing but water, water, water."[70] Still, Messer Nicia did correct the clever Ligurio, who was playing off Nicia's foolishness in this scene, for when Ligurio asked him if he had seen the Carrucola of Pisa, he replied quickly, "You mean the Verucola."[71] Actually his correction was not exactly correct either, but what he apparently was referring to was La Verrucca near Pisa, a significant fortification in the southeastern defense perimeter of the city near the sea and the little town of Calci. Suggestively, this wartlike tower (hence the name, which means wart) on the top of a steep hill was a crucial point of resistance in 1503 when Florence retook Pisa. One of the most important leaders in that campaign was none other than our Niccolò Machiavelli, who was quite proud of the military reputation he had gained in the reconquest. Could it be that once again Messer Nicia in correcting Ligurio was evoking his namesake, Machiavelli, and the now all too quickly forgotten (by the Medici at least) services he had performed for his city?

Finally, at a deeper and perhaps unrecognized level Messer Nicia was an old fool, but an old fool with a passion, and that, I would suggest, was something that Machiavelli could both laugh at and empathize with. In a way Messer Nicia might be seen in general as Machiavelli's alter ego reversed or taken to the extreme. Machiavelli prided himself on his wisdom, *virtù*, experience, and reputation as a lover; Nicia prided himself on exactly those same points but was badly mistaken on each count. The humor of this is repeatedly underlined and makes for some of the most comical moments in the comedy. For example, when the conspirators disguised themselves to capture the young man who would be put to bed with Messer Nicia's wife (and die as a result from the poisonous mandrake root potion), Nicia's costume evoked laughter from the others in the group, who were as yet unseen by him. Ligurio quipped, "Who wouldn't laugh? He has on a short little cloak that doesn't even cover his ass. And what the hell is that thing he's got on his head? It looks like one of those fur hoods that church canons wear. And he has a puny little sword sticking out between his legs." But Nicia saw himself in a totally different light, reflecting with pleasure, "Actually, I look rather good in this disguise. Who'd recognize me? I seem taller, younger, thinner, and there's not a woman in Florence who'd charge me to take her to bed."[72] The foolishness of the passions of old men—old men in love like Machiavelli—rings through these lines. Machiavelli and Vettori in their letters, as we have seen, were capable of playing with their own foolishness and laughing at it; perhaps in Messer Nicia Machiavelli, in a more public arena, was laughing at what he might become as an old man, even as, or perhaps because, he was sure that he was not like that, at least not yet.

In this context perhaps the most humorous moment of the play comes when Nicia describes how he put the "victim" to bed with his young wife. Machiavelli, who carefully cultivated a reputation as a pragmatist and a hands-on politician, portrays Nicia as equally pragmatic and literally hands-on in his pursuit of his passionate desire to have a child with his wife. The next morning, describing to Ligurio what happened after the "victim" had been bundled into his house, he reported, "Oh, I have some fine things to tell you! My wife was in bed in the dark. . . . I brought in the guy, and so that nothing remained in doubt, I took him into a little pantry that I have off that room where there was a small lamp that gives off just a little light, so that he couldn't see my face. . . . I made him undress. He protested, but I turned on him like a dog, and he got undressed in a flash and stood there naked. He had an ugly face . . . but you've never seen more handsome flesh—white, soft, comely! And about the rest, don't ask."

Ligurio was content not to hear about the rest but was curious to know why Nicia had to see everything. Machiavelli's serious self-presentation as a pragmatist seems to be reversed for a laugh when Nicia replied, "Are you joking? Since I'd stuck my hands in the stew, I wanted to get to the bottom of the pot. . . . When I saw that he was healthy, I dragged him along behind me, and in the dark I took him into the bedroom and put him to bed. And before I left, I decided I should feel to make sure everything was going as it should. I'm not the type of man who takes fireflies for lanterns!"[73] Nicia would be here the perfect Machiavellian hands-on pragmatist if he were not the perfect fool driven by his passion as an old man to have children.

Machiavelli, of course, had his children, but he also had his own passions that could make him look foolish, and tellingly he had the ability to laugh at those dangerous passions with ironic self-criticism, as his letters reveal repeatedly and as his lesser known comedy *La Clizia* makes perfectly clear, as we shall see. Was, then, Messer Nicia also a Machiavellian alter ego? His foolishness and lack of *virtù* make it hard to sustain that argument in any serious way, but then Machiavelli himself was much less serious than he is often portrayed, and it is at least fun to imagine Messer Nicia as Machiavelli's vision of himself as an old man governed by a blind passion that had changed all his most positive attributes into their negative opposites, which may have been exactly the fun that the character was designed to provide for those in the know.

Aside from the servant Siro, whose minor role does not give him much opportunity to represent any side of Machiavelli, the final candidate for a Machiavelli alter ego is virtually the last male character in the play. But I advance his candidacy reluctantly. Having spent years showing undergraduates that they should not make Callimaco, the young man overwhelmed by his love for Messer Nicia's youthful wife, the hero of the comedy simply because he is a young would-be lover (as so many of them might wish to be), I would feel as if I were betraying them. Yet having ruined their happy positive vision of that character by pointing out how foolish he is, how passive he is, how completely he gives up his *virtù* and reason for his mad and unlikely passion; I now want to argue along with them, and with apologies to them, the apparently absurd position that Callimaco is in fact the most important representation of Machiavelli and the true Machiavellian hero of this comedy.

Once again we are alerted to the possibility of this by his very name, with its "maco" ending that seems to evoke the first syllable of *Ma*chiavelli's name. In fact, if we read the "Calli" that precedes it as a reference to ancient Greek— and Machiavelli loved to play with such references—we can read the character as "the handsome young *Calli Ma*chiavelli."[74] Callimaco/Machiavelli is a handsome young man in love. In a way Callimaco and Nicia might be seen as humorous bookend representations of Machiavelli in love and in the throes of passion with all the dangers and rewards involved in both: one young, passionate, and foolish and the other old, passionate, and even more foolish. The key to this reading of Callimaco harks back to Machiavelli's advice to his friend Vettori in their letters, for in many ways Callimaco fulfills perfectly Machiavelli's injunction to Vettori and his representation of himself as a lover there. Cunning characters like Ligurio and Fra Timoteo notwithstanding, Callimaco is the lover who, penetrated by Love's arrows, allows himself be taken into Love's hands and passively follows along over the roller coaster ride of strong emotions, enduring Love's tortures in the hope of being rewarded in the end. In this more general Renaissance vision, real male lovers who seek pleasure in sex rather than power and domination are often represented as actually passive and feminine, often dangerously or negatively so, and the key to enjoying the pleasure of sex for Machiavelli was being passive, feminine, and open to pleasure.

The song that Machiavelli used to open act 2 of the comedy once again evokes this well, along with the god that both he and Callimaco follow:

Love, the person who doesn't try
Your great power, hopes in vain
Ever to truly witness
What may be Heaven's highest merit.
Nor will such a person know what it means in the same instant
To live and die, to seek evil and flee the good,
To love themselves less than others.
And they'll never know how often
Fear and hope freeze and burn our hearts,
Or understand how both men and gods
Tremble before the arrows with which you're armed.[75]

There is no conquering of love here by a male lover; rather, there is an emphasis on fear and trembling before the arms of Love and the need to bow down passively before such powerful weapons and such a powerful god to truly appreciate the best things that exist and the noblest sentiments one can feel. Almost certainly these are Petrarchian conceits again, but Machiavelli used them to express much the same approach to love for Callimaco as he advocated for Vettori and as he used to describe his own.

And when we look more closely at Callimaco as a lover, we certainly see a lover swept away by love, a young, handsome "Maco" in love:

> Alas, I can't find peace anywhere. Every time I try to get control of myself, my mad passions well up and say to me, "What are you doing? Have you gone mad? Once you've had her, what will you do? You ought to admit your mistake; you'll regret all the effort and worry you've put into this. . . . Face up to fate. Either flee evil or, if you can't, face it like a man. Don't be bowled over by it or laid low like a woman." In this way I lift my spirits, but it only lasts a little while, because from all sides I'm overwhelmed by the desire to be with her just one time—overwhelmed with sighs from my head to my toes and totally shattered. My legs tremble, my insides churn, my heart pounds in my chest, my arms lose their force, my tongue falls mute, my eyes flash, and my head swims.[76]

Callimaco here was a lover humorously portrayed in the style that Machiavelli adopted for his self-portrayal in his letters to Vettori and his other male friends at the time. Yes, for a second he does recall the more familiar Machiavelli of *The Prince* and *The Discourses* when he attempted to discipline his emotions with a call to face up to fate and avoid taking a passive feminine stance like a woman to love, but he was quickly swept away by the stronger emotions of his passionate love. In fact, his self-accusation of being passive and womanlike was affirmed by his quick admission that he was unable to overcome his emotions and the humorous description of the emotions that overwhelmed him which follows. Again those emotions were laughingly reduced to Petrarchian conceits of trembling legs, pounding heart, mute tongue, flashing eyes, and swimming head. Yet even with mocking Petrarchian conceits this character had quite clearly said to Love, "Go ahead, O' Love, take me in hand . . . I am your servant," and had undoubtedly been pierced and deeply wounded by Love's arrows.

Still there is a distinction between the older Machiavelli's self-portrayal in his letters as a lover and young Callimaco. Machiavelli portrayed himself as deciding to give in to love and to accept passivity in the face of its power in order to enjoy it, while Callimaco seemed unable to resist love and not to have a choice. One might argue that with Callimaco Machiavelli was laughing at or playing with the memory of his younger self as a lover, a self that as a more mature, wiser lover he still decided to indulge at times. But admittedly that speculation seems rather thin when it is based largely on reading the name Calli-maco as referring to a young, handsome Machiavelli. Yet when we consider Machiavelli's other well-known comedy *La Clizia*, we will see that there is some reason to take Maco names seriously and to suspect that he did enjoy playing with his Maco characters as representations of humorous aspects of himself on stage. Still, the speculation that Machiavelli was laughing at his self-presentation as a completely out-of-control young lover must remain just that, an interesting speculation.

More telling, I think, is the interesting way that Callimaco wrestled with his emotions and his love, a way that suggests that he was someone who, when he was capable of reasoning at all, thought much like the more familiar Machiavelli: the savvy observer of people and situations who clearly understood how the world worked. Early in the comedy when we first meet Callimaco, he discussed with his servant Siro the reasons he had little hope of winning Lucrezia, and he sounded much like Machiavelli in *The Prince, The Discourses,* or his other more political works—carefully listing alternatives and sorting through the strengths and weaknesses of possible strategies with clever and perceptive reasoning: "First, her very nature blocks my desire, for she's very virtuous and totally against the games of love. Then she has a very rich husband who is completely under her control, and even if he's not young, he's not as old as he looks. Moreover, she doesn't have relatives or neighbors with whom she spends evenings out, and she doesn't go to parties or the other entertainments that young women usually enjoy. No artisans work in her home. There are no women or male servants who aren't afraid of her. All of which means that there's no one to corrupt."[77]

As his Renaissance audience would have appreciated, here Machiavelli had listed the primary ways of corrupting a married women—one can almost imagine the title of this chapter in a short, snappy manual titled "The Adulterer," a sexual counterpart to *The Prince*. To induce a married women to agree to adultery one needed to play on her dissatisfaction with her married state or the fact that her husband mistreated her, but both of these were ruled out with Lucrezia. More important, however, to carry out a seduction one needed the opportunity to make contact with the woman desired and the help of intermediaries. And one by one Callimaco ruled out possible places and intermediaries in a quick, terse prose that seems to reflect Machiavelli's normal, almost scholastic analytical style, and in the process he provided a virtually perfect list of the people who were available to the Renaissance young lover when he sought to make contact with and seduce a married woman. Perhaps here we have a glimpse of a more expected Machiavellian Machiavelli in love.

In a similar fashion he analyzed what he saw as the reasons he might hope for success: "First, there's the stupidity of Messer Nicia, who, even if he is a doctor of law, is the simplest and most foolish man in Florence. Second, there's the longing that he and she share to have children. After being married six years without having any and being extremely rich, they're dying to have them. There's a third point as well: her mother was an easy woman in her day."[78] Again the quick listing of possibilities; and suggestively, as the comedy unfolds, these are exactly the issues that do allow Callimaco to win his desire. Not only does his analysis set up the plot and make its unlikely twists and turns have a logic, but within the logic of the comedy itself it is the perfect Machiavellian analysis of what will happen and does in fact happen.

But perhaps the most Machiavellian moment for Callimaco in this scene occurred when he reflected upon the reliability of his unlikely ally in his plan to win Lucrezia, the parasite Ligurio. When he told Siro that he had asked Ligurio to help with the plot, his servant warned: "Take care that he doesn't make a fool of you—that type of freeloader can't be trusted." Siro was right to be concerned, for the audience had already learned that Ligurio was a marriage broker who had come on hard times and was reduced to "cadging dinners" and borrowing money to survive. The implications were clear: as a parasite and a go-between he was probably not to be trusted or associated with by honorable men who recognized his true character. Callimaco's reply was again nicely Machiavellian, as critics have noted: "You're right. Still when a plan has something in it for an ally, you have to have faith in him from the moment that you involve him. I've promised him that if he succeeds, I'll give him a goodly sum of money, and if he doesn't, he'll receive a few meals and I, at least, won't eat alone."[79]

Our young lover recognized his danger and on the one hand had decided that he was willing to lose what he might lose if things went wrong and on the other understood a deeper truth—the people you bring into your plot, once they are brought in, must be trusted. One might debate whether Machiavelli was right about this, but it definitely has the ring of Machiavelli's thinking on conspiracies and also reflects his concern about why conspiracies often do not work. On the one hand you have to trust your fellow conspirators to plot successfully; on the other hand frequently, especially if you bring too many in on the plot, one of those conspirators will betray you. Of course, as Callimaco pointed out and as Machiavelli knew all too well, "a goodly sum of money" did not hurt in winning the loyalty of a parasite like Ligurio. And once again Callimaco's analysis of the situation was perfect. Ligurio turned out to be the ideal ally and exactly the person capable of using his already established contacts with Messer Nicia—noted earlier by Callimaco—to devise and carry out the clever con of the mandrake potion.

Perhaps, however, Callimaco was most successfully Machiavellian in bed with Lucrezia. We don't actually see this sexual culmination of the plot; it is only reported to us obliquely by other characters and most notably by Callimaco himself in act 5, scene 4. As several characters, including Callimaco, had already noted before the successful bedding, a cloud hung threateningly over Ligurio's scheme: sooner or later Lucrezia, the honest and morally correct wife, would realize that she and her husband had been tricked, that the young man supposedly picked up off the streets to make love to her and die from the poisonous effects of the mandrake potion was actually none other than the false doctor from Paris, Callimaco. Clearly, winning the virtuous Lucrezia at that point would have been no easy task, and the audience might well have expected the worse, especially as her name evoked the virtuous Roman wife Lucrezia who committed suicide rather than live with the dishonor of having been raped.[80] But as Callimaco reported to Ligurio the morning after: "I was uncomfortable [in bed with Lucrezia] until about three in the morning, for even if it was very enjoyable, still it didn't seem right to me. But then I told her who I was and explained to her the love I felt for her and how easily, what with her husband's foolishness, we could continue to enjoy one another without any dishonor and promised her that when God took him to his just reward, I'd marry her."[81]

Here we do not have the full details of Callimaco's arguments, but evidently they were impressive, for Lucrezia up to this point in the comedy had been a hard woman to convince, making life rough for her admittedly foolish husband and her perhaps overly anxious mother but also pushing the clever Fra Timoteo to some of his most Machiavellian arguments to win her over. Of course, Callimaco had certain advantages (whether or not he was the fantasy of Machiavelli as his young, handsome self), as he made clear explaining her capitulation to him in bed: "After considering my arguments and the difference between making love with me and with Nicia, and the difference between the caresses of a young lover and an old husband, she said, after a few sighs, 'Considering that your cleverness, the foolishness of my husband, the simplicity of my mother, and the corruptness of my confessor have led me down this path, which I would never have taken on my own, I feel that this was written in the stars.'"[82] Young love and the caresses of a passionate lover had won her over, but not without Callimaco's effective "arguments" and "cleverness"—crucially, he was not merely Calli (young and handsome), he was Calli-maco (the young, handsome, and cleverly convincing Machiavelli).

It might seem strange that I am arguing here that virtually every male character in this comedy reflects to a degree a self-representation of Machiavelli. But in a way we ourselves (or at least the narratives that we construct about ourselves) are the characters that we perhaps are capable of describing most effectively. And in a society in which the effective presentation of self was so important for success, status, and support—the creation of viable and usable consensus realities of self—it certainly paid to be constantly experimenting with and proofing strategies of self-presentation, as Machiavelli clearly did in his letters. In a period when he was exiled from power and apparently seeking to create new forms of self—as a writer on politics and diplomacy, as a playwright, as a poet, as a correspondent, as an old lover—each of which might help him to win a reentry into politics or at least retain the ties that he had built with his friends before his fall from power, his self-scripting activities may well have been particularly rich, a hypothesis supported by his letters and reinforced, I believe, in his comedies. From this perspective Machiavelli had a well-rehearsed repertoire of selves (and perhaps selves that he worried he might become) that could be drawn on for his comedy: his cunning, politically savvy self as Ligurio or Fra Timoteo; his foolish, old self, overwhelmed by his old man's pretensions and passions as Messer Nicia; and, most notable, his fantasy remembrance of himself as a young lover swept away by passion yet still clever and winning in love as Callimaco.

And, of course, the clearest indication of Machiavelli as a man of *virtù* in the character of Callimaco is the simple fact that his accurate analysis of the situation, his careful use of allies, and his youthful, passive, almost feminine passion brought him success in the end. Much as was the case in Machiavelli's political career, however, recognizing the full extent of that success seems to have been reserved for an inner circle of people in the know who, like Machiavelli and his friends, could see behind the appearances of events to what was actually happening. For, in one of the cleverest endings of a comedy in the Renaissance comedy tradition, *La mandragola* ends with Callimaco's complete success in love. Certainly everyone realizes at the end of the play—aside from the eternally duped Messer Nicia—that Callimaco had won his love Lucrezia and would continue to enjoy her love given the fact that he and Ligurio have been given the free run of Messer Nicia's house and use of his possessions, including from a Renaissance perspective his perhaps most prized possession, his wife.

But even in this there was a clever half-hidden joke for those in the know and capable of seeing it. For at the end of the play when Messer Nicia insisted, "I want to give them [Callimaco and Ligurio] the key to the ground-floor room under the loggia so that they can return there whenever they wish, because without any women in their house, they've been living like beasts," Callimaco replied suggestively, "I accept, and I will make use of it whenever my need arises."[83] "My need," a clever double entendre for his desire for Lucrezia and his phallus, was hidden just below the surface of a seemingly simple exchange of courtesies. But humorously, those in the know would realize as well that Callimaco was telling Messer Nicia to his face that whenever either desire or phallus "arises," he would cuckhold him thanks to the latter's foolish kindness—certainly a moment worthy of Machiavelli's self-representations of the young, beautiful, clever Machiavelli in love.

Yet a still more clever play on Renaissance values and the very genre of comedy itself is hidden in the quick action of this last scene. Comedies, of course, require a happy ending, and Renaissance comedies with their emphasis on young love rewarded, often in the face of adversity and difficult odds, usually ended with a happy wedding or two that seemed to tie up all the lose ends. Evidently, in this comedy the young lovers could not marry, as Lucrezia was already married to Messer Nicia. But I would suggest that in a way there was a cunningly playful marriage in the last scene of this play which did perfect justice to a Machiavellian playwright and his Machiavellian alter ego Callimaco. In the last scene all the characters of the play have gathered on the front steps of the church to speak with Fra Timoteo before entering and going to Mass. Before they enter, however, Messer Nicia turns to Callimaco and says to him, "Doctor, give your hand to my wife." Callimaco replies, "Willingly." Then Messer Nicia turns to his wife and explains, "Lucrezia, this man is the reason we will have a staff to support us in our old age." She replies, "I hold him in the highest regard, and I want him to be our close friend." And when Nicia continues to emphasize that they should live and dine together, she replies, "Absolutely."[84]

In Renaissance Florence wedding ceremonies were often celebrated on the steps of the parish church and followed by a Mass. In fact, before the Council of Trent they were often quite simple, requiring little more than a sincere exchange of consent that implied that a couple wished to be married. Consent was normally expressed verbally with a classic "I do" and confirmed by the gesture of giving one's hand, probably borrowed from the old feudal ceremony of homage. In this case, behind what may be taken as simple pleasantries, Messer Nicia actually might be seen as officiating over a Florentine wedding ceremony on the steps of the church, with Fra Timoteo looking on benignly. When he asked Callimaco to give his wife his hand symbolizing their union and the young lover answered "willingly," a theologically perfect "I do," Lucrezia followed almost immediately with a consent of her own, "absolutely."

Of course, this was not a perfect wedding ceremony even with the exchange of hands and consent, especially because of the minor problem that Lucrezia was already married to Nicia, the man foolishly performing the ceremony. But *in practice*—once again the key to Machiavelli's self-presentation as a political thinker—Messer Nicia actually did not function as a husband, being incapable of satisfying or impregnating his wife, while Callimaco was perfectly capable of doing so and would do so in the future, as we will see in Machiavelli's later comedy *La Clizia;* thus, all the elements were there for a marriage that *in practice* would exist, and this seems just the last clever Machiavellian touch in a comedy of love that is full of Machiavelli and Machiavellis from beginning to end.

If *La mandragola* is largely the happy comedy of a young Machiavelli in love—letting his alter ego Callimaco be swept away by love as he recommended to his friend Vettori—his later comedy *La Clizia* might be seen as a sadder self-presentation, although still laughing and self-reflective. *La Clizia* deals with similar themes but turns on the foolishly mad passion of an old man who has led a life of moderation and *virtù* only to totally lose control of himself in a consuming passion for his young ward, Clizia.[85] Many scholars have noted that this old lover in the comedy, Nicomaco, seems to evoke Machiavelli himself and his love for the young singer and poet Barbara Salutati, with whom he was involved in a well-known and widely commented upon love affair when he wrote the comedy.[86] At the time Machiavelli was in his mid-fifties, as the play was probably written and completed fairly rapidly for performance during carnival in 1525. And once again the name of the old man who is the negative hero of the plot suggests the connection with old Nick. Nicomaco might be read easily as Nico Maco: clearly it has the ring of *Niccolò Machiavelli, but there also seems to be a playful reference once again to the Greek meaning of the name Nicomaco—victor in battle—for to get ahead of the story, Nicomaco is a man who loses in a humiliating way what he is seeking, a young mistress, but wins ultimately the battle of love by retaking control of himself and his life and regaining *virtù*.[87]

Nicomaco, as the play opens, has been reduced to utter foolishness by his mad passion for his young ward, Clizia. Not only has he upset his whole world for this uncontrollable love—alienating his wife and son and demonstrating a total lack of *virtù*—but he seems literally bent on destroying himself and his family for it. Totally out of line with the wisdom expected of old age and against the sage counsels of his wife, Sofronia (again a revealing Greek name), Nicomaco tries to play the lion when he is no longer capable of doing so and even foolishly fails at being the fox, too blinded by love to see what is really happening. Sofronia sums up the situation nicely:

> Anyone who knew Nicomaco a year ago and saw him now would be amazed at how greatly he has changed. He used to be a serious, hard-working, prudent man—spending his days honorably. He would get up early in the morning, hear his Mass, and attend to his work. If he had business in the square, the market or at a magistrate's he took care of it; otherwise, he would converse honorably with fellow citizens or he would go to his study and look to his books. He would lunch happily with his buddies, and then he would talk with his son ... showing him how to understand people and teaching him how to live with a few ancient and modern examples. Then he would go out and pass the rest of the day either in business or in honest and important affairs. When evening came he was always home by sunset: he would sit with us by the fire, if it was winter, then he would go to his study and go over his affairs until at 9:00 we would all happily eat supper together. This order of his life was an example for everyone in the house, and each of us would have been ashamed not to imitate him. And thus everything went smoothly and well.[88]

Although one might be tempted here to draw parallels with Machiavelli's self-presentation in his famous letter to Vettori about his tranquil life as an old man at his country villa outside Florence, written slightly more than a decade earlier, it would almost certainly be pushing the text too far, especially as there are things, such as Nicomaco's regular church attendance and his instruction of his son, which do not square well with that letter. Rather, Sofronia seems to be portraying the perfect old man that Machiavelli knows he should be, Nico-Maco, not Niccolò Machiavelli. Sofronia's characterization of what Nicomaco had once been like evoked the ideal older man, a good husband and father who disciplined his family and set an example for them with his own *virtù* that made everything go "smoothly and well."

Until, that is, he fell in love and began acting like a foolish old man in love. "But as soon as he fell in love with this woman," she continued, "he neglected his affairs, he let his farm lands go to ruin, and his business fall apart. He yells all the time and for no reason; he comes and goes a thousand times a day without knowing what he is doing; he is always late for meals; if you speak to him, either he doesn't answer, or he doesn't make sense. The servants, seeing this, make fun of him, and his son has lost respect for him. Everyone does as he pleases . . . and thus I am afraid that unless God comes to our aid that this poor household will be ruined."[89] Living up to her name, Sofronia wisely describes the problems that the old lover Nicomaco had created for her and their family. His mad passion, his love for Clizia, had literally unmanned him, transforming him from a model of *virtù* into virtually the stock character of a foolish old man in love, a favorite victim of the humor of Renaissance *novellieri* and playwrights. The tensions within the family went deeper, however, for not only was Nicomaco's foolish love for Clizia upsetting the tranquility of the household, but Nicomaco's own son Cleandro was competing with his father for Clizia, whom he had fallen in love with as well. Needless to say, these complications made Nicomaco's plotting complex and Niccolò Machiavelli's plot rich with humorous potential.

Nicomaco, aware that both his wife and his son were working against him, with typically Machiavellian indirection, plotted to marry the young girl to a loyal servant of the family and then secretly enjoy her himself. As Cleandro explained to a friend early in the comedy: "As soon as my father fell in love with her, which would be about a year ago, desiring to fulfill his craving—which continues to torture him—he came to the conclusion that there was no other remedy than to marry her to someone who would then share her with him; because he realized that it would be an evil and impious thing to try to have her before she was married. Not knowing who to pick, he settled on Pirro our servant as the most reliable for this purpose."[90] Again the theme of an old man "tormented" by the passion of love typifies Cleandro's presentation of his father, but that passion was not enough to keep Nicomaco from analyzing the situation fairly effectively. For although Nicomaco was in many ways blinded by his passion for his young ward, he was still capable of working out a complex plot that had the potential to give him what he wanted and keep his misdeeds hidden if his wife and son would agree to turn a blind eye to his schemes.

Of course, they had no intention of doing so; rather, Sofronia, with Cleandro's uneasy consent, proposed the family's steward, Eustachio, as a competitor for Clizia's hand primarily to block Nicomaco's plans. In the face of this threat to his plans, Nicomaco and Machiavelli resurrected the ever crafty Fra Timoteo from *La mandragola* in an attempt to use his corruptible spiritual counsels to save the day in yet another comedy. Nicomaco suggested to Sofronia that they agree to accept the advice of a reputable priest on his marriage plans for Clizia, "If we don't want to go to friends or relatives [to avoid broadcasting our dispute], let's speak to a priest . . . as if we were in confession." Sofronia asked whom they could go to, and Nicomaco replied, "Well we couldn't go to any other than Fra Timoteo who is our family confessor and a virtual saint who has already performed some miracles." Still skeptical, she asked what miracles he had accomplished, and Nicomaco enthused, "Don't you know that due to his prayers *monna* Lucrezia, wife of *messer* Nicia, who was sterile became pregnant?"[91] With this playful reference to his earlier and by now well-known comedy, Machiavelli seems to suggest that we are in a way still in the world of that earlier comedy and perhaps in that same teasingly imaginary world of Machiavelli's self-representations as a lover. Only now the young Callimaco has been replaced by an older Nico-maco, once again the victim of passion and perhaps more clever in his pursuit of it. But in line with the Renaissance vision of old men in love, Nicomaco at his age can no longer be Calli-maco— the handsome, attractive young lover—no matter how much he desires it. At best, even if it is not what he wishes, he might become Nico-maco, winner in the battle for patriarchal *virtù*.

Still, as the patriarch of a Renaissance family, he had real power, and in the service of his mad passion he was prepared to use it even if it destroyed him and his family—in a way he was bent on unfashioning himself as a mature male in control of his passions and his sexual desires and refashioning himself as a lover. This he made perfectly clear to Cleandro when he confronted him about the plot that the youth and his mother had concocted to use Eustachio as a competitor for the hand of Clizia. Cleandro claimed to know nothing about it, but Nicomaco attacked his son's claimed innocence aggressively: "Still you did plot to bring Eustachio to Florence and to disguise him so that I didn't see him and you kept me in the dark so that you could ruin this marriage [with Pirro, his candidate]. But I will have you both thrown into the Stinche [the famous Florentine jail]; and I will give Sofronia back her dowry; and send her packing; because I want to be the Lord [*Signore*] of my house, and all of you had better listen up! I am determined that this marriage will happen this evening or else I will burn the house down."[92] In this threatening speech Nicomaco is a perfect example of patriarchy gone awry; the absolute power of the male head of household hot on the trail of a mad passion threatens to destroy

Cleandro, Sofronia, and Nicomaco himself—but most important it threatens to destroy their family and its reputation in Florence. Young men in love, as we have seen earlier in this volume, had to make a transition to active sexuality to demonstrate a certain sexual aggressiveness; old men in love had to control the same in order to not be distracted from their duties and obligations, as even Machiavelli recognized, albeit reluctantly.

Fortunately, however, for Nicomaco and his family, even if formally all power was in the hands of the male head of household, within the dynamics of the personal relationships that constituted a family and a household there were many opportunities for other microstrategies of power less formally recognized to work—strategies that in the end once again turned on the social recognition of Renaissance sexual identity. In fact, one thing that makes *La Clizia* so attractive as a comedy is seeing the way other members of Nicomaco's family work out strategies to thwart his formally unquestionable authority. And while the countermarriage strategy foundered when Sofronia accepted Nicomaco's suggestion that they leave the marriage decision to chance and fortune—lots were drawn to see who would marry Clizia, and Nicomaco's candidate, Pirro, won—in the end a far more humorous and cleverly theatrical plot ruined Nicomaco's best-laid plans.

The old lover, anxious to consummate his passions, had secured a neighbor's house and arranged that after the wedding he would take Pirro's place with Clizia in the wedding bed unrecognized in the dark—once again a Maco character slipping into someone else's marital bed to enjoy someone else's wife. Unfortunately for this final twist of the plot, his son had overheard him working out the details with Pirro. And Cleandro, together with his mother and some supportive neighbors and servants, devised a counterstrategy to thwart and shame old Nicomaco, a microstrategy to assure once and for all that Nicomaco was not Callimaco and would not become him. Thus in the dark of the bedchamber designated for the consummation of Nicomaco's passion and the plot, they substituted for Clizia a robust male servant of the family. Entering the bed with hope, Nicomaco tried to answer Natalie Davis's famous question for the early modern period, "Who's on Top," in the affirmative for old men like himself and Machiavelli, but he quickly found that the tables had been reversed at his expense.

Later in tears Nicomaco described what followed to the neighbor who had supplied the bedroom: "You know the plan, and I in accordance with it entered the bedroom and silently undressed . . . and in the dark got into bed with the bride. . . . Cuddling up to her like a bridegroom, I tried to put my hand on her breast, but she caught it and wouldn't let go. Then I tried to kiss her, but with her other hand she pushed my face away. Then I tried to jump on top of her, but she gave me a knee that practically broke my ribs." Not exactly getting the response he had been hoping for, Nicomaco switched from his physical approach to try pleading words, but to no avail. "Finally I turned to threats," he admitted, "and started to browbeat her and insist that she do as I said. Well you know what she just coiled up her legs and gave me a couple of kicks that would have sent me flying if I hadn't been wrapped tightly in the covers." Bruised and battered, he decided to let the bride sleep until morning, when perhaps her humor would have changed and he could finally gain his desire. But things did not work out that way, and he explained, "Totally at a loss and bruised and battered, I began to fall asleep. Well all of a sudden I began to feel something long and hard stick me in the tail five or six damned hard thrusts. Half asleep I reached down and found something robust and pointed which scared me so much that I jumped out of bed. . . . And there in the bed totally naked was Siro, my servant who was making obscene gestures and faces at me."[93]

Beaten, and at the least quasi-sodomized by his own servant, this charivari-like shaming forced Nicomaco to regain his senses and literally himself, although a bit the worse for wear. Sofronia put the matter to him bluntly as the comedy moved hurriedly to its close:

I never wanted to make a fool of you, but you are the one who tried to make fools of all of us and in the end of yourself as well! Aren't you ashamed? . . . Did you think you were dealing with blind people or people who did not know how to overturn your dishonest designs? I confess that all the tricks that we played on you were organized by me because there was no other way to recover your senses than to catch you in your crime *with so many witnesses* that you would be shamed and then that shame would make you do what no other thing could make you do. Now this is where we are: if you want to return to the right path *and be that Nicomaco* who you were a year ago, we will all return to your side and what happened will remain a secret.[94]

Nicomaco, finally seeing the truth of his foolish passion, of an old man falling in love with a young woman and literally losing his identity in doing so, gave his wife his word that he would return to his old virtuous ways and thus became Nico-maco—the victorious Maco.

But up to that point the type of mad love that an old man could feel for a young woman had caused Nicomaco to lose his very self—perhaps the ultimate danger of sex for old men and one that Machiavelli knew well from his personal experience with the pleasures and pains of just such a mad passion for the young singer Barbara Salutati. It appears in life off the stage Machiavelli preferred to keep trying to be Callimaco, even as he feared perhaps he was behaving like Nicomaco before he gained mastery of himself and became Nico-Maco. Such a self-parodying in *La Clizia*, if that is what was at play in the comedy, reveals again how attuned Machiavelli was to the complex sexuality of his society and the way narratives of self-presentation could powerfully, and perhaps here more pertinent, playfully evoke one's personality on multiple levels.

Why one might well ask, Would Machiavelli write himself and his passions into these comedies? The question becomes more difficult when one considers that none of these presentations of self was particularly positive. Certainly a young successful and attractive adulterer was a self-image that a man could wear more comfortably in the Renaissance than that of a blind self-destructive victim of passion like Nicomaco. Yet even Callimaco needed all the youthful charm he could muster to overcome his foolish moments that clearly sought laughter from readers and audiences and which were cynically commented upon by his fellow characters, especially that excellent judge of character Ligurio. So the question remains, Why would Machiavelli take the images of himself that he to a great extent played with in his letters with his friends and represent them in the more public arena of the Renaissance theater? Perhaps this is an interesting question that one does not really need to answer when one seeks merely to analyze his self-presentation.

Yet Machiavelli's motivation cries out for a hypothesis, even if, much like most suppositions about motivation in history, it must remain highly problematic. Perhaps it was simply that Machiavelli did not think his more general audiences would be aware of the way his characters lined up with his private passions, that these self-representations were private in-jokes in a more public setting for his more intimate circle of friends. When different understandings of self were negotiated with various groups, it may well have been interesting to play the lack of understanding of one group against the understanding of others, a type of play with shifting realities and what-seemed-to-be which always fascinated Machiavelli—in a way yet another playing with the Devil in which old Nick was the master player. But given the quasi-public nature of his life at least in Florence and the small intimate space of that city along with the clear self-referential nature of these comedies, that may well be too easy an escape. It seems more likely that once again self-presentation and self-fashioning were much more central parts of Renaissance social life than we have appreciated: parts of a process of creating, negotiating, and maintaining a consensus reality of identity with the groups that a person interacted with.

In that context what better place to practice self-presentation, often referred to today metaphorically as a theatrical presentation of self, than in the theater itself. And Machiavelli with his self-presentations of Machiavelli in love, much as with his self-presentations of Machiavelli the politician and the political writer, may well have been deeply involved in trying to re-create himself for close friends, acquaintances, and his fellow Florentines as a passionate lover and a warm comrade, as well as a man of honor and *virtù*—a rather contradictory blend of reason and passion, morality and immorality, playfulness and seriousness, discipline and lack of discipline which created a positive masculine identity in the Renaissance and helped a man win the power and influence that Machiavelli still so clearly wanted. A contradictory blend to be sure, but one that continues to make Machiavelli a fascinating character and his writings so richly difficult to interpret today.

But without attempting to claim all that, I think we can suggest playfully (hopefully following in the footsteps of Machiavelli) that in these two comedies about love we have virtually bookend self-portrayals of Machiavelli in love, even if clearly Machiavelli was far too clever a writer and thinker to merely reduce these comedies to a mockingly humorous self-portrayal. Nonetheless, I would propose that in *La mandragola* we have Machiavelli presenting a younger version of himself in love much as he was presenting himself in his letters to his friends as the impulsive lover Callimaco, who let love take control of him and in the process won out in the end as Love's passive servant rather than as the aggressive male dominator one might expect of the author of *The Prince*. In *La Clizia,* we have Machiavelli seven to ten years older and involved in a disorienting passion for a younger woman, wittily portraying himself as a foolish old man who finally wins in the classic battle of old men in love as Nicomaco by retaking control of himself and giving up on young love.

And in the end it doesn't really matter that it appears that in his life as he lived it, rather than as he portrayed it on stage, Machiavelli seems not to have followed the perhaps wiser course of Nicomaco. For the passions of old men can be every bit as foolish as those of the young, as Machiavelli humorously reveals in his letters and his comedies and most notably in his laughing, cruel, and often deeply perceptive presentations of himself in love.

Death and Resurrection and the Regime of Virtù, or Of Princes, Lovers, and Prickly Pears

I do not know, therefore, if I deserve to be numbered among those who deceive themselves if in these my *Discourses,* I praise excessively ancient Roman times and damn our own. Yet it is true that if the *virtù* which ruled in those times and the vices which rule today did not shine more clearly than the sun, I would not speak so strongly.

[Non so, adunque, se io meriterò d'essere numerato tra quelli che si ingannano, se in questi mia discorsi io lauderò troppo i tempi degli antichi Romani, e biasimerò i nostri. E veramante, se la virtù che allora regnava, ed il vizio che ora regna, non fussino più chiari che il sole, andrei col parlare più rattenuto.]

—Niccolò Machiavelli, *Discorsi sopra la prima Deca di Tito Livio,* bk. II

There was no doubt in the Renaissance that death would be followed by a last judgment. Actually more than one. For while virtually everyone would have agreed that God's Last Judgment was by far the most important and significant, no one would have underestimated the importance and significance of the last judgment of *virtù* carried out by society. In a way death in the Renaissance was like a boulder hurled into the always choppy waters of social evaluation of a person: a boulder that momentarily overwhelmed the chop with a small tidal wave that created an ever widening circle of evaluations by relatives, friends, neighbors, peers, contemporaries, and even at times history itself. In this way, paradoxically the very moment that formally canceled identity mobilized the circles of one's social existence, the most crucial judges of the performance of self in the Renaissance, and provided the ultimate measures of identity—one last series of consensus judgments and realities. Certainly such last judgments considered more than *virtù*, but the significant role played by this crucial term suggests that death in a way helped to give life to the deeper meanings of *virtù* and identity in the Renaissance.

Two Renaissance Tales of *Virtù*-ous Death

Once upon a time—not just any time, however, but rather that most important time of ancient Greece when men were truly noble—one of the most noble kings of Crete, Clearcus, found his kingdom overrun by an invading host. Bottled up in his capital, with his own armies routed and his cities and people being destroyed by a merciless enemy, he decided to appeal to the gods, specifically the oracle of Apollo at Delphi, for advice. When his messengers arrived at Delphi, they found that for once the often slippery oracle's pronouncement was unequivocal, declaring that there was only one way to avoid the conquest and submission of their isle: the king must die. But not just any death would do, for the oracle specified that Clearcus had to be killed by the enemy. If that should happen, the enemy host would withdraw and Crete would be saved. When the messengers returned with the news, there was much lamenting in the city. But Clearcus remained silent, keeping his own counsel for fear of what the citizens might do if they learned of his plans. For rather than considering how he might escape the oracle's decree and save his life, Clearcus planned to die and thus give life to his people—in a way a civic/social death that would resurrect his subjects and his country.

The morning after the news of the oracle's prophecy arrived, Clearcus sneaked out of the city disguised as a common soldier to seek his death. He had no trouble finding it, for almost immediately he came upon a group of enemy soldiers, armed and practicing their military skills. He courageously attacked them, dispatching one quickly, and thus was set upon by the rest and rapidly killed, the enemy soldiers never realizing that they had slain the king. That same morning a number of the most important men of the city came to the palace to discuss with Clearcus what should be done about the oracle. Not finding him there, they questioned several servants, who finally admitted that he had left the city that morning disguised as an ordinary warrior. While it might have been normal for the group of notables to assume that he had fled to save his life, "one of them who was already mature in years and of great intelligence," knowing Clearcus as "a lover of his country [*patria*] and a very just and outstanding prince," convinced the others that he had left the city to fulfill the oracle's prophecy.[1] So a group of armed soldiers was sent out from the city to discover what had happened to their king, and they soon came upon his body "laying all bloody on the ground and pierced by many wounds, dead."[2] A *virtù*-ous death if ever there was one, for true to the oracle's prophecy, upon learning of Clearcus's demise, the enemy army pulled up camp and sailed away, leaving the inhabitants of Crete free to follow their own destiny.

That was the ancient world, however, when men, as Machiavelli noted ruefully in the epigraph to this chapter, were truly full of *virtù*. Still, the "modern" world of the Renaissance was not without its own noble exemplars of *virtù*. In fact, even women could demonstrate most impressively their *virtù*, as the "true" story of a certain humble woman named Giulia da Gazuolo demonstrated. This Giulia lived "not long ago" in Gazuolo, where Lodovico Gonzaga, bishop of Mantua, kept his court. A young woman of "manly spirit" (*virile spirito*), she impressed everyone with her industry, her good manners, and her beauty, which far exceeded what one might have expected of someone of such "base blood."[3] If you should have any doubts on this, you should know that shortly before the main events of this story one day the Marchesa of Gonzaga, seeing this beautiful and elegant young girl walking along with a basket on her head, stopped her coach to ask her who she was. The girl replied in such a mannered and courteous way that the Marchesa had trouble believing that she had not been raised at court. In fact, the Marchesa confided to others that she would have liked to have brought the young girl to court and educated her there. But as our story is a tragedy about death, clearly such a happy ending was not to interfere with its sad course.

That same beauty and courtesy that attracted the Marchesa attracted less savory characters and their attentions, however, specifically the dangerous passion of a servant of the bishop who fell madly in love with Giulia at one of the dances thrown by the youths of the area. He tried to win Giulia's favors in the standard ways of young Renaissance lovers with longing looks, sighs, entreaties, declarations of love and suffering, gifts, promises; all were rejected in the name of her strong commitment to chaste ways and her virginity. When all else failed, he turned to a corrupt old woman to serve as an intermediary to press his suit, a fairly standard Renaissance ploy given the limited opportunity for contact between youths of opposite sex and the ideal of respect for elders. But all the old woman's enticements only served to harden Giulia in her resolve. Finally the young man decided to force the issue by taking advantage of the fact that she often had to go back and forth alone to the fields where she worked. With the help of a groom of the Duke he trapped Giulia in an isolated spot and took by force what he could not win by courtship.

Giulia freed, returned home, and finding only her little sister there, she dressed in her finest clothes, all white except for a pair of red shoes and a yellow scarf. Trailed by her sister, she then went to the house of a sick neighbor woman, where she explained what had happened and concluded: "In God's name I do not want to continue living because I have lost the honor that was the reason for my very life. There will not be a future when people will point a finger at me or give me a look and say, 'There is that poor girl who became a whore and shamed her family. If she had any intelligence she ought to hide herself.' I don't want anyone to ever throw up to me that I willingly gave myself up to the servant. My end will demonstrate to the whole world and give clear proof that even if my body was violated by force, my spirit remained always free."[4] With her uncomprehending little sister still trailing along, she left the neighbor's house and went straight to the Oglio River, which passed nearby, and dived headfirst into the current. Her sister's cries quickly attracted a crowd, but to no avail, "as Giulia willingly had thrown herself into the stream to drown and she immediately abandoned herself [to the water] and drowned."[5]

Giulia's noble death was lauded by everyone and honored by the tears of all the women of the place "and even the men." And although her body could not be buried in consecrated ground (because her death was a suicide), the bishop placed her body in a bronze sepulcher on a column in the main square of the town. "And truly in my judgment . . . this our [modern] Giulia deserves no less praise than the Roman Lucrezia and perhaps if one considers the whole case, she should be given first place. One can fault only nature who did not give a more noble birth to such a magnanimous and generous spirit as Giulia had. But the person who puts honor before everything else and is a friend of *virtù* is held to be quite noble indeed."[6] And so *virtù*-ously ends the story of Giulia da Gazuolo.

Two deaths in the name of *virtù*. Two deaths that lived on in the imagination of the time in large part because they heroically marked out that important component of the consensus reality of identity that made one person better than another—*virtù*. Both tales were written down by Renaissance *novellieri:* Giulia's was retold by Matteo Bandello, Clearcus's by Sebastiano Erizzo. Both were writers of the mid-sixteenth century who focused on the tragic and the moral in tune with the reforming and perhaps tragic spirit of the times. But be that as it may, for both, as for Machiavelli, *virtù* was a crucial evaluative term, and for them a *virtù*-ous death gave honor and meaning to a person's life. Apparently our *novellieri*'s vision of *virtù* was more moral than Machiavelli's (although it might be noted that in both tales *virtù*-ous deeds led to what was essentially suicide in the case of Clearcus and clearly suicide for Giulia, mortal sins in formal theology), but nonetheless, as for Machiavelli, *virtù* stressed positive active/aggressive behavior that confirmed the honor and nobility of even a non-noble woman of humble origin. In a society with a strict sense of social hierarchy and in tales told by essentially conservative defenders of that hierarchy like Bandello and Erizzo, the power of this way of behaving and identifying people comes through clearly—both tales end with literally telling deaths, deaths that speak to an individual's superiority and *virtù*.

To make his moral evaluation absolutely clear, Erizzo was quite willing to interrupt the action of his plot to sermonize on *virtù*, breaking the action-oriented tradition of the novella genre. In Clearcus's tale he virtually doubles the length of the story by reporting a long funerary speech in honor of the fallen prince given by Trasinoo, "one of the first citizens of the city, who was of great age."[7] Trasinoo's laudatory evaluation of Clearcus turned on the *virtù* of the fallen leader, not surprisingly, because the third day of tales in Erizzo's collection of tales, *Le sei giornate*, was dedicated to accounts of the *virtù* of princes. But it was also not surprising because the story as retold by Erizzo was first and foremost a morality tale about the *virtù* of Clearcus. As a result Trasinoo begins with the tears and laments of the crowd gathered to hear his speech, noting that such expressions of loss were the just way to honor the *virtù* of their lost prince—a community expression, a consensus reality of his identity as an ideal prince. He then continues with a paean to the *virtù* of Clearcus's progenitors and a warning that it will be difficult for his successors to match his *virtù*. Next, in a manner that has echoes of Machiavelli, he points out that their deceased prince's *virtù* in ruling will allow those who follow to rule successfully even if they cannot fully live up to his fame: "After his rule even if there is a successor who does not have the *virtù* that he had, [the new prince] should be able to still maintain his rule solely because of the *virtù* of he who ruled before him [i.e., Clearcus]."[8]

The leitmotif of Trasinoo's praise was that Clearcus ruled with *virtù* and it was the key to his success as a prince. Again the echoes of Machiavelli are clear in his speech. He asserts, "But our king was a mirror of every type of *virtù*. . . . In him the justice, the religion, the piety, the liberality, the magnanimity, the strength, the humanity, the temperance, the courtesy, the seriousness [of a prince] were so notable, that his gentle spirit, ornamented with all those divine *virtù*, was never blemished with a lack of same."[9] In fact, this virtual overflowing of *virtù* meant that even as a stern prince he was loved by his people. Trasinoo continues, "He was so loved and at the same time feared, that he never . . . was hated by his people; rather for the love and reverence which they had for him there ceased all crime and evil behavior among those he ruled. And as a most just prince he always abstained from taking the goods of his citizens or injuring them . . . avoiding always being denigrated for base ways or hated for using cruelty."[10] In sum, with the death and subsequent evaluation of the life of Clearcus we learn a deep lesson about the man and his rule—a deep lesson about the social performance of self as a ruler. He was a man of *virtù*, and that made him not only a good man, but also a great prince whose memory was worth "eternal sanctification" by his subjects.[11]

Yet even more important, as his exemplary death made clear, through him *virtù* ruled Crete, and because of that, "as a valorous, understanding, and wise prince with that honored scepter that Heaven gave him, in the form of a pastor he corrected the wayward members of his flock and with his honest examples he recalled his citizens to justice."[12] Significantly, in this rule of *virtù* we find many of the attributes of a form of a civic morality. Just governance is ultimately about not simply providing justice or an effective rule; at its very heart it is about creating a moral society, a "flock" that under a just pastor—in the original double sense of the term as one who guides a flock and one who leads a Christian community—follows the path of *virtù*. And, of course, this "just pastor" is not a cleric, not even a Christian in this case, but the prince, as Clearcus reveals with his life-giving death that ultimately may be seen as consciously or unconsciously recalling the life-giving death of Christ himself. Here we have the central mystery and message of Christianity, once again being incorporated into the ideology of the state. Civic life, to be successful and perhaps ultimately to be worthwhile, in this vision needs to satisfy this moral dimension of living together in a community, and that requires princes/pastors who lead their flocks with love and fear but, most crucial, with *virtù*.

Tellingly, in the context of a Renaissance tale, this evaluation of the death of Clearcus is pronounced by Trasinoo, the wise and elderly citizen of note. It is easy to overlook that, while many could and did evaluate a person, certain evaluations were more valued by society than others, especially at death. In the everyday world of the Renaissance the pointed fingers of children in the street or even the looks of other women feared by Giulia da Gazuolo (and by Grasso in Chapter 4) could have great weight—they were highly significant measures of the social performance of self, significant enough in Giulia's case to warrant suicide—but the best judges were those who themselves stood at the top of the hierarchies identified by *virtù:* those of the right class—the aristocrat or noble; those of the right age—the mature in years and experience; those of the right intelligence—the wise with passions under control; and, of course, those of the right gender—male (true Nico-macos rather than Calli-macos or Messer Nicias).

This may seem less clear in the tale of Giulia da Gazuolo, but it is there as well. First, Giulia gives us her rationale for suicide in the context of neighborhood womanly networks when she explains her motives to her sick neighbor—perhaps suggesting the power of women's evaluations of *virtù* and even gossip. Then, we witness her death through the uncomprehending eyes of her young sister—perhaps allowing us to experience the pure, unreflected emotional pathos of the moment. Thus, as might be expected, family and neighbors are the first circles of evaluation for this more humble young woman in Bandello's tale. Yet when it comes to more telling evaluations of the event, the narrative reaches for a different register; those local intimate circles of consensus reality are no longer adequate for this morality tale.

Once again all the women of the town cry at her heroic death, but suggestively "also some of the men." Women, of course, were expected to cry at such emotional moments, being dominated by the passions and more likely to respond to *virtù* in an emotional, irrational way, but that some men joined in the tears suggests the strength of the feelings that Giulia's heroic act engendered. As was the case with Clearcus, great *virtù* was recognized by pure emotions like grief and mourning, but more measured and rational confirmations were required for truly exceptional *virtù*-ous deaths. To meet this higher evaluative need—moving beyond family, neighbors, and community—the Marchesa returned to the tale to order (along with the bishop) that Giulia's body be recovered from the river and at a deeper level to remind the reader that a person of true nobility had not only recognized Giulia's *virtù* early on but had not forgotten it and was more than ever ready to recognize it in her tragic death. The Marchesa's gender handicap as a woman was, of course, largely mitigated by the immense social gap that separated her from Giulia. That such a person would respond to Giulia's death at all from her social heights said worlds about how the young woman's *virtù*-ous deed had confirmed her earlier reputation and ennobled her.

Still the Marchesa remained a woman, and thus the final assessment of this young woman's *virtù* is placed in the hands of *virtù*-ous men, the tale ending as it should for the Renaissance with male evaluations of her death. First, the bishop ordered that Giulia's body be interred in a bronze casket on a pillar in the central square of the town: a symbolism that could hardly be more perfect, for her *virtù* was thus enshrined at the heart of the central civic space of the community—the main square of the town. Her lonely self-sacrifice there became public performance and a civic monument to her womanly *virtù*. It might seem strange at first that a bishop would mold civic space to commemorate what might appear to be a moment of personal *virtù*, but, as has been argued, the distances between the holy, the public, and the personal were not clearly separated out in the Renaissance. And tellingly, Giulia's deed was not as personal or private as it might at first appear, for the chastity and sexual honor that she held in such high esteem were deemed to be crucial for marriage and the regime of sexual reproduction that was seen as the centerpiece of Renaissance social order and society. But there was more yet in the civic perspective on Giulia's heroic suicide because she was a woman who demonstrated *virtù* well beyond her chastity and virginity: as the Marchesa made perfectly clear early in the tale, her courtesy, her manners, her beauty all marked her out as a young woman worthy of living at court. In sum, her *virtù* marked her out as someone special and exemplary, an understanding underlined and demonstrated by her heroic death. As Clearcus's *virtù* especially in death made him virtually the patron saint of Crete, so too Giulia's *virtù* again confirmed at death made her virtually the patron saint of the women of Gazuolo.

Perhaps the apparent incongruity of placing Giulia's bronze casket on top of a pillar also carries a deeper meaning. Pillars, especially in civic or religious spaces, breaking the horizontal plane of the cityscape to reach toward the heavens, often expressed a special connection between the divine and the mundane. They were the place where the divine entered the mundane social world of humans and vice versa; thus they were often placed in central civic spaces to establish the necessary connections between the civic world and the divine order of things. It might be suggested, then, that the bishop, by placing Giulia's body on the top of a pillar in the central square of this small town, was confirming her spiritual *virtù* as well. Even though her suicide was a mortal sin (and thus she could not be buried in sacred ground), the bishop understood that her *virtù* merited a very special place in society—a place at the heart of the civic space of her community where the divine and the social intersected.

But there was one last male evaluation of Giulia's death, perhaps the most telling of all: Matteo Bandello, the *novelliere* himself, concludes the story by giving his own judgment of Giulia's death. First he evaluated her death in comparison to the more famous classical example of the ancient Roman noble wife Lucretia who committed suicide after being raped, arguing that not only did Giulia's case match the ancient precedent but that it in fact surpassed it. Here the Renaissance topos of the competition between the ancients and the modern takes an anomalous turn with the modern proving superior to the ancient, and a modern peasant girl at that. Bandello's vision seems to turn on social rank, for although he does not make clear his reasoning, he does suggest that the Roman Lucrezia as a noble would have found it easier to act with such *virtù*—it was a natural attribute of her nobility. Giulia, as a common woman by birth, had no such natural *virtù*; rather, her *virtù* was a product of her love of *virtù*, which led her to chose a *virtù*-ous death over dishonor. That love and that ongoing difficult choice for a woman of "too lowly blood" ennobled her and made her superior to her more famous Roman counterpart in death—and nicely in afterlife as well in the tale told by Bandello, where she was resurrected metaphorically and literally (in her burial she was uplifted from the ground of normal burial to her central place in the community) to serve as a model for chaste young women in civil society.[13]

A Prickly Pear and *Virtù*, Part I: A Lack of Discipline and Respect

In a way, then, both our stories tell their tales of *virtù* in terms of death and resurrection, not surprising when one considers that the central religious myth of Renaissance society turned on the death and resurrection of a most *virtù*-ous man/God who much like Clearcus accepted his foretold death to save his people. But perhaps the most suggestive Renaissance tale of death and resurrection that turns on *virtù*, even if the term is never used in the story, is told by the fifteenth-century Sienese *novelliere* Gentile Sermini: the tale of Scopone, the epitome of the Renaissance nasty and untrustworthy male peasant—the virtual antithesis of Giulia. Lauro Martines has recently provided an insightful reading of this novella in his *An Italian Renaissance Sextet: Six Tales in Historical Context*, a reading that reveals the deeper social and cultural contexts of this engaging tale.[14] Almost as an aside he notes that the tale takes place at Easter and that the character nicknamed Scopone (literally Prickly Pear) is metaphorically crucified—actually destroyed economically and socially—by his lord and master Buonsignori only to be resurrected after three days as a new and better person and renicknamed Salice (literally Pliant Willow) in honor of his newfound and correct identity. At the heart of this resurrection is the rebirth of the once unmannerly, grasping, and undisciplined peasant Scopone, who totally lacked *virtù*, as the good Salice, a truly *virtù*-ous peasant.

But we are getting ahead of the story, which merits a closer examination for its rich evocation of the complexities of Renaissance social life and masculine identity. Sermini's tale turns on a series of contrasts between city life and country life, good lords and evil peasants, loyal friends and untrustworthy clients, courtesy and boorishness, civility and villainy, young and old, and good lords and not so good lords. The central conflict, however, is between the Sienese gentleman Bartolomeo Buonsignori and one of his rural peasant clients, nicknamed Scopone. Perfectly representing the Renaissance stereotypical identity of the clever, cheating peasant, this Scopone regularly took advantage of his young patron's largesse and kindness, appropriating/stealing as much as he could from him while treating him without the respect and honor due to his lord—behaving, in sum, as a "prickly pear." Name, identity, and behavior overlapped virtually perfectly.

Yet his young lord, Buonsignori ("of the good lords"), for all his attractive qualities—he was labeled handsome, aristocratic, well mannered, and civil— was not quite ready to live up to his name. For rather than performing with the *virtù* required of a good lord, taking in hand his peasant and disciplining his incorrect behavior, he too manifested a stereotypical defect of young nobles. In accordance with a general concern of the times about aristocratic youths, he was more interested in enjoying his *gioventù* and indulging his passions than in disciplining his rural peasants. Thus he too needed to reform himself to fulfill his name, and in those needed changes for Buonsignori and Scopone lay Sermini's tale.

Sermini sets Buonsignori's problem immediately as the story opens, telling us that, "left fatherless at the age of twenty-five, Bartolomeo delighted greatly in hunting, falcony and fishing" at his country home not far from Siena.[15] As we have seen, 25 was a telling age in the Renaissance; at that point in life an upper-class male was at the cusp of that most difficult transition of all, from *gioventù* to adulthood. Marriage and full adult male responsibility and sexuality lurked just around the corner, but for most aristocratic men their late twenties offered the last freedom and pleasures of youth. Actually with the death of his father and at that age, Bartolomeo was in the enviable position of many youths portrayed in Renaissance *novelle* and comedies, for he could follow his youthful desires without the constraints placed on most young men outside literature by disciplining fathers anxious to protect the family patrimony from youthful excess. And Sermini makes perfectly clear that Bartolomeo was ready to take full advantage of the situation, not yet willing to take up the heavy mantle of adulthood. Rather, he notes that the young man wished to enjoy himself and his newly inherited wealth, entertaining his youthful friends from Siena ("le compagnie de' giovani") on his country estate, "and [that] he resolved to live in this manner as long as he was young [*giovane*]."[16]

In this context, like many a *giovane* more concerned with his own youthful passions and pleasures, he overlooked Scopone's disrespectful and uncivil behavior, apparently hoping that his boorish peasant would see the error of his ways. Of course, Bartolomeo was bound to be disappointed in that hope. Sermini's morality tale could not let such a lack of the mature *virtù* required of a full adult male head of household, and even more required of a true Buonsignori, be ignored for long. For *virtù* at its very deepest level required an active commitment and forceful deeds from an adult aristocrat—that was virtually the central performance of an aristocratic self. Thus there was little space for passivity—waiting for Scopone to change his ways—in the face of the action that needed to be taken. The discipline and control of those in power, as Machiavelli loved to point out, required deeds, performance, often violent male action; otherwise the unreliable whims of that most fickle of females and the nemesis of *virtù*, Fortuna, would have her way. Lovers might be passive and forgiven by a kinder, gentler Fortuna who smiled on the pure passion of youthful love at times, but lords who sought to rule could not rely on her fickle favor and thus could not afford to be passive.

Yet Bartolomeo might be forgiven his youthful passivity in the face of the disrespect and misbehavior of Scopone, not just because of his age and inexperience but also because there was a deep organizing discipline interwoven in the very fabric of the hierarchical world of Renaissance client-patron relationships which should have righted things—and once again it was based on *virtù*. That same *virtù* that required that Bartolomeo leave his youthful ways behind and act as a Buonsignori also played a role in the way Scopone should have related to his young lord. For he too was required to perform *virtù*, even if, rather than aristocratic/lordly *virtù*, it was the *virtù* appropriate to peasants and clients. In the course of everyday life without government, without undue violence, *virtù* promised that eventually even Scopone should find the correct path and treat his patron as a *virtù*-ous peasant should.

At the simplest level rewards and kindness from above were given in return for service and respect from below; when that unwritten rule and its many corollaries were respected, such relationships worked with a smooth discipline, and *virtù* was served. When those rules were broken, disorder and the Scopones of the world reigned, as Machiavelli feared was the case in his own time in the text that opens this essay. But fortunately for Bartolomeo, he lived in the imaginary world of a positive novella where true to the everyday hopes of the time young aristocrats matured quickly and with minimal problems into Buonsignori, where *virtù* won in the end as it always should, and where the undisciplined prickly pears of the world were forced to accept the correct order of things; thus he could afford to enjoy his youth for a while.

But not for long. One day those deep wheels of Renaissance order and discipline began to role toward the inevitable victory of *virtù*, and Bartolomeo was forced to take on the mantle of all Buonsignori, to perform his role as an adult male aristocrat. The transition began in the most prosaic of manners when the young lord asked Scopone to sell him some fish to serve to a group of friends from Siena who were coming to visit him at his country home. Like a good patron, he offered to pay Scopone well for the small favor. But the latter, rustic villain that he was, ignoring the respect and service due to his patron, decided to sell his catch instead at the nearby baths in Bagno a Petriuolo. Moreover, when he arrived at the baths laden with his rich catch, he continued his un-*virtù*-ous behavior—demanding unjust prices for the fish and refusing to treat others with the common courtesies required in everyday social intercourse—living up (or actually down) to his name.

For a Renaissance aristocrat who read or heard Sermini's tale, what was wrong with Scopone then was clear: he lacked *virtù* (the correct set of behaviors expected of an honorable man; not necessarily virtuous or moral, but deemed socially correct and honorable for one's social station), and this lack upset the carefully calculated and preserved order of social life. His social performance of self fitted his name perfectly, as was often the case in Renaissance moralistic literature: he was a prickly pear, and everyone judged him to be one—his consensus reality was his name. Machiavelli, ever the sensitive observer, true to his Renaissance vision, saw the shortcomings of his day in terms of a similar lack of *virtù* and opined in the quotation that opened this chapter that "the *virtù* which ruled in those times" made ancient republican Rome a well-ordered and disciplined society. For when *virtù* ruled in ancient Rome according to Machiavelli—that is, when society lived under what we might label a regime of *virtù*—people were disciplined in large part by their desire to perform *virtù* and be adjudged by society *virtù*-ous.

Virtù and Tragedy in Boccaccio:
An Interlude and a Historical Perspective

Machiavelli's vision of how *virtù* should rule, although often referring to classical precedents found especially in Aristotle, Cicero, and Livy, was ultimately a Renaissance one; as noted in Chapter 4, *virtù* was a crucial disciplining concept across the Renaissance even as its meaning changed gradually as the society and social uses it engendered and reflected changed over time.[17] For the early Renaissance the term had virtually revolutionary potential, as it was used regularly to distinguish the social values of a newer elite, the *popolo grosso*, from the traditional values of an older nobility. Merchants, bankers, lawyers, and a smattering of rich, powerful artisan masters of the most important guilds who by the fourteenth century had already captured political power in many of the major cities of northern Italy found in *virtù* a potentially rich ordering principle and ideology. Whether it was consciously pursued or merely the outcome of proselytizing for and defending group values, when the vision of *virtù* that *popolo grosso* saw as reflecting their values came to dominate over a more traditional and perhaps more European noble vision of *virtù*, that new elite's dominance was built into the very cultural underpinnings of society, virtually into the genetic structure of its social organization.

It should come as no surprise, then, given the authoritative status of the ancient world, that the search for classical roots for contemporary visions of *virtù* should have attracted the attention of early humanists and the support and patronage of early Renaissance governments and elites or that a form of civic *virtù* emerged at the heart of civic humanism and the self-presentation of early Renaissance governments, especially republican ones dominated by the *popolo grosso*. Significantly, this vision of civic *virtù* had a long life, living on in republican ideology, as one can see clearly in Machiavelli and early modern republican thinkers more generally.[18] It was so strong, in fact, that it can even be seen gaining a place in some more aristocratic and courtly contexts later in the period, as is argued below in the context of Castiglione and that key codification of aristocratic values his *The Book of the Courtier*.

But clearly for the urban elites of northern Italy, *virtù* was a crucial and contested term especially in the early Renaissance. In Boccaccio it was a virtual leitmotif, with the fascination, power, and hence the popularity of many of his *novelle* in the *Decameron* turning on the workings of *virtù* and its challenge to older values. One of the most tragic tales that he tells which opens the stories told on day four—a day dedicated to stories of love that have sad endings—illustrates this well. Like many other tales retold by Boccaccio, this novella relates a story of illicit love, in this case between a young widow, Ghismonda, and a young man of lower-class origins named Guiscardo, who served her father, Tancredi, the prince of Salerno. Tancredi, with a possessiveness that seems to cry out for a modern psychoanalytical reading, had kept his young, vivacious daughter virtually locked away after the death of her first husband, refusing all offers for her remarriage, apparently content to enjoy his own close relationship with her. But as Boccaccio pointed out, Ghismonda, "living with her doting father . . . and realizing that because of his love he showed little interest in marrying her again, not having the courage to ask him to do the honest thing [and marry her], . . . decided to secretly find a worthy lover if possible."[19] Young love against the power of old men—a classic literary conflict and a very familiar one in the everyday life of the Renaissance as well, as we have seen.

As one might expect in a novella about young love, even tragic love, Ghismonda had no trouble finding a suitable lover, even if her choice might seem rather off the mark for the daughter of a prince: the man she decided upon, Guiscardo, was a mere page of her father. Here, I would suggest, Boccaccio found himself in a bit of a bind—or to be more accurate, the story he was retelling had put him in a bit of a bind—for given the formal values of his Renaissance audience, Ghismonda was striking out in directions decidedly dangerous and unlikely to win a reader's sympathy. In deciding to love Guiscardo, she was going against the wishes of her father (but, of course, fathers were supposed to rule in the Renaissance);[20] she was entering a sexual relationship outside marriage (a form of sex condemned by the church); she was indulging her own desires and sexual appetites (a feared proclivity of widows, especially young ones, which contributed to their being viewed with apprehension in the period); and one could go on. But worst of all she was ignoring and breaking across class barriers for this love.

In sum, she was breaking a host of the most traditional and deeply held values of early Renaissance society. At this point one might well expect that a contemporary would have found an ending that punished these lovers a positive one and, rather than tears, expect cheers from patriarchal readers. It may well be that Boccaccio, faced with this situation, would have appreciated the postmodern death of the author, for he would have been spared a difficult problem in telling the tale of Ghismonda's love: how to retain the sympathy of his readers, winning their hearts for her, her lower-class lover, and their highly problematic sexual relationship.

Enter *virtù*—the magic key that in the Renaissance opened all doors and hearts. Boccaccio early on played the *virtù* card when he described this young noblewoman's decision to take a lower-class lover: "And observing all the men who were at her father's court, both noble and non-noble . . . and considering their manners and behavior . . . among them there was one, a young [*giovane*] page of her father called Guiscardo of very humble family, but still she found him attractive more than anything else because of his noble manners and *virtù*."[21] Simply put, his *virtù* made Guiscardo a superior man and a suitable choice for Ghismonda's illicit love. Luckily for Ghismonda—as if luck were needed in literary love affairs—Guiscardo returned her love, and all that was required was the means to bring the young lovers together. With the cleverness and cunning that often typified early Renaissance *virtù* and the behavior of youths inspired by love in Boccaccio's tales, Ghismonda closely watched her lover and, when the moment was right, passed him a note that explained to him how they could meet secretly in her room. In turn, Guiscardo carried out her instructions perfectly and also used considerable ingenuity and prowess— again *virtù*—to overcome the numerous physical obstacles that made using the secret entrance to her bedroom possible. Once more we find formally questionable behavior elevated to a higher level by young love and *virtù*.

Regrettably, as in all of the tales of the fourth day of the *Decameron,* young love, even if it endured for many happy days and nights, was not to have a happy end, as Boccaccio noted, switching the tone of his tale from the sweet pleasures of love to tragedy: "But *Fortuna,* jealous of such long and great pleasure with sad deeds changed the happiness of the two lovers into sad tears."[22] One day, unnoticed by Ghismonda or her servants, her father came to her room to chat with her as he often did, but not finding her there, he lay down to wait for her in a little hidden nook at the foot of her bed and fell asleep. Ghismonda, unfortunately, had arranged to have her lover visit her that very afternoon, and thus as the young couple in bed "*played and enjoyed*" themselves as usual, Tancredi woke up and heard and saw what Guiscardo and his daughter were doing. Overwhelmed by pain, at first he wanted to cry out, but then he realized it was better to keep quiet and keep hidden if he could contain himself so that he could do what he had already made up his mind to do with the minimum of shame ("vergogna") for himself."[23] The next night he had Guiscardo secretly arrested and brought before him. And when he saw the youth "almost crying he said: 'Guiscardo, my kindness to you doesn't merit the offense and the shame [*vergogna*] you have given me."[24] As one might expect of a lover full of *virtù*, Guiscardo was not the least bit passive in the face of Tancredi's anger and as a youthful lover based his defense on young love: "Love is capable of much more than either you or I."[25] But, of course, young love was not capable of overcoming Tancredi's rage and desire for vengeance, and he left the valiant youth locked away while he considered what to do with the lovers.

The next day he went to Ghismonda's room, and locking himself in with her, with tears (again) in his eyes, he reproached her for her affair. Not surprisingly his reproaches began by calling upon her *virtù:* "Ghismonda, I thought I knew your *virtù* and your chastity; thus, I would have never thought . . . if I had not seen it with my own eyes that you would give yourself to any man who was not your husband."[26] Tancredi, however, quickly moved on to what upset him even more than her sexual relations with a man she was not married to, for although Christian morality and the ideal of marriage were obviously important to him, Ghismonda's affair with Guiscardo was upsetting for a deeper and more significant reason: "And in God's name I wish that if you had to lose your chastity in this way that you would have taken a man more in line with your nobility. But among all the men of my court, you picked out Guiscardo, a youth of the most vile birth."[27] Low birth abasing nobility—an old story told tragically in many societies—but Boccaccio, now well into building sympathy for his lovers, had a trick up his sleeve to turn the tables on the righteously indignant Tancredi and his audience, who should have felt sympathy with this wronged father's plight. What upper-class man or women for that matter would feel sympathy for a noble daughter who had broken across class lines to satisfy her illicit sexual desires! Even young, natural love and sexual attraction could hardly defend such literally revolutionary desires and deeds—in fact, such passions were feared precisely because they could lead to revolution in the form of such misalliances overthrowing the very family structure that was seen as the basis of a divinely ordered hierarchical society.

As noted earlier, in the tradition of the Italian novella, in which action and plot line are virtually everything, the action is usually quick and tight with minimal concern for describing the characters' thoughts or the background to their deeds.[28] As a result, when the fast pace of a novella slows and characters begin long, set speeches, a reader does well to pay attention because usually the author is taking the time to explain something not only important but so necessary to say that it warrants breaking the conventions of the genre. Thus when Boccaccio is faced with defending his young lovers against Tancredi's telling accusations, his tale slams to a halt to play the trump card that he had alluded to all through the earlier action—*virtù.* Although he did not use the term immediately, he presented a Ghismonda full of *virtù* in the face of her father's accusations. She did not break down before his harsh accusations; the ubiquitous literary Renaissance feminine emotions and tears are totally absent. Rather, she remained calm and cool. And clearly she understood her situation under fire, knowing exactly what her fate would be and what she had to do. It may be that her love for Guiscardo had given her these strengths and the ability to face without fear the tragedy that was upon her, but her actions were a perfect example of fourteenth-century *virtù*, and with her cool, calm, reasoned understanding she had already begun to win the sympathy not just of modern feminists but of an early Renaissance audience as well.

In fact, the contrast with her father is instructive, for his righteous indignation and suffering were undermined by his own emotional behavior which clearly lacked that same *virtù* that his daughter displayed so effectively. As noted above, Tancredi began his recriminations with tears in his eyes, and although what he said was quite reasonable, his tearful lack of self-control was telling and would be crucial for the tale. As Tancredi finished his reproaches, Boccaccio took a moment to describe the patriarch: "Having said this he hung his head crying as hard as a well-beaten child."[29] The contrast is striking: the *virtù*-ous Ghismonda in control of her emotions and dealing impressively with a difficult situation and the un-*virtù*-ous Tancredi, the victim of his emotions, totally out of control and crying like a "well-beaten child." It does not take a great leap of empathy to imagine who a Renaissance audience would have sympathized with at that moment.

If anyone had missed the contrast, with perfect timing the action of the novella stops for one of those rare long explanatory speeches: a truly revolutionary speech by Ghismonda that turns on a crucial aspect of the early Renaissance reign of *virtù*. She began: 'Tancredi, I have no desire to deny [anything] or beg for [mercy]. . . . But rather to confess the truth, first in order *to defend my reputation* with honest reasons and then *with deeds to be most strongly true to the greatness of my soul.*" No wilting woman, but steeled by a *virtù* that fortified her very soul, Ghismonda could hardly demonstrate a more attractive alternative to her sobbing and vengeful father. "It's true," she continued, "that I have loved and love Guiscardo and as long as I live—which will not be for long—I will love him. This, however, is not a result of my feminine weakness but rather your lack of desire to marry me and *Guiscardo's virtù.*"[30]

Although Ghismonda had played the *virtù* card, she let it lay on the table for a moment to defend another theme central to Boccaccio's tales, the imperatives of young love that he championed throughout the *Decameron:* love and sex as natural human passions that young people follow as the law of youth, against the dictates of formal morality and even at times against the dictates of *virtù*. "It ought to be clear to you, Tancredi, as you are made of flesh that you fathered a daughter made of flesh and not of stone or iron; thus, even if you are now old, you should have and should still remember how powerful the laws of youth [*le leggi della giovanezza*] are.... I remain as you fathered me, of the flesh ... and still young [*giovane*] and for both reasons I am full of sexual desire, whose most wonderful powers I have already enjoyed as I was once married.... Certainly against this [desire] I used all my power [*virtù*] because as much as I could, I didn't want the attractions of this *natural sin* to bring shame [*vergogna*] on you or me."[31] The sins of the flesh were sins certainly, but for young people in love they were "natural sins" hard to avoid and best handled with understanding for what they were: very human and rather mild faults in and of themselves, even if their potential social danger was great in terms of shame, lost honor, and, more telling, disruptions in the marriage alliance plans of families and clans.

Suggestively, Ghismonda concluded this section of her discourse with the explanation that aided by love and fortune she found a way to keep the affair secret so that that social danger was minimized and no one's pubic reputation compromised. But now that the affair had been discovered by her father, she confessed freely what she had done. Her hiding of the affair, then, was not dishonesty so much as a thoughtful and clever strategy, *virtù* once again—the wise mastery of events that controlled them for the best. Once that wise secret no longer served its purpose of protecting honor and reputation, she freely admitted what she had done. In fact, throughout the *Decameron* the secret "natural sins" of young love were not a problem as long as they remained secret, in other words not performed in a social setting that would have made them the grist for a broader community evaluation. With sins and faults kept hidden *virtù* still ruled, for it was essentially a demonstrated force, an outward quality evaluated by others, and when unnoted by others, un-*virtù*-ous deeds virtually did not exist. Simply put, no consensus reality could be built about an individual's *virtù* or broader identity for that matter based upon what was unknown.

Leaving the laws of youth and natural sins behind, however, Ghismonda returned to the real heart of her father's despair—her love for and sexual relations with a lower-class man, a mere page. "I did not take Guiscardo, as many women do, for some minor attraction, but rather with deliberate consideration I chose him over all the others and with careful thought I introduced myself to him and both he and I with wise perseverance have long enjoyed the fulfillment of my desires."[32] Again Ghismonda was asserting the *virtù* at the heart of her choosing Guiscardo: she relied on reason, not emotion, and the relations went ahead with "careful thought" and "wise perseverance." Still, she realized that the question of her *virtù* as far as her father was concerned turned on that deeper issue in her choice of Guiscardo, his lack of nobility, and she began her counterattack by pointing out that this was not so much caused by some lack of his as by fortune, which often placed the most worthy at lower social levels and raised the unworthy to the heights. A troubling idea for a Renaissance reader at first sight, but Boccaccio's Ghismonda pressed ahead to express a crucial argument: status, she claimed, should not be based on the traditional standards of nobility (noble birth and blood given by fortune) but on newer behavioral models that turned on reason, manners, and the ability to get things done—in sum, the central attributes of *virtù* for the *popolo grosso*.

"But let's move on [from the question of fortune]," Ghismonda lectured her father and Boccaccio's audience,

> to consider a bit the origins of this situation. You will note that we are all made from the same flesh and created by the same Creator with souls of equal strength and potential and equal *virtù*. *Virtù* was what first created distinctions among us, who all were born and are born equal; and those who had the most *virtù and demonstrated it the most were named nobles* and the rest non-nobles. And even if later contrary practices have hidden this law, it has not been eliminated, or overturned by nature or good manners; for this reason the person who *demonstrates virtù* reveals to all his nobility and those who call him otherwise are in the wrong. . . . Look carefully at all your nobles and examine their lives, their manners, and their ways, then consider Guiscardo in the same way. *If you judge them honestly you will admit that he is most noble and that all your nobles are peasants.*[33]

Virtù makes commoners noble and nobles peasants. Here nakedly stated by a young woman in love and about to die was the ultimate power of *virtù:* the person who displayed *virtù* was superior, superior to the merely noble in name, to the merely rich in wealth, to the merely powerful in terms of position. Now, of course, no one would have denied that noble title, great wealth, or powerful positions could and did regularly overwhelm *virtù* in the Renaissance. In fact, the tragedy of the love of Ghismonda and Guiscardo was that the power of Tancredi as a prince, patriarch, and noble seemed to win easily over their *virtù*, for natural youthful passions and these young lovers were swept aside and destroyed by the torrent of his vengeful wrath.

Still, one of the most satisfying things about literature is that in that imaginary, but no less real for that, realm of life, often what is true and beautiful wins out—what regularly does happen in everyday life is replaced by what should happen. And aside from all the significant things that that ability to replace the "does happen" with the "should happen" implies, for scholars it means literature often offers a fascinating insight on how people thought things should be. So Tancredi in his un-*virtù*-ous rage—not so much immoral but unreasonable and blinded by emotions—that very night had the two men who were guarding Guiscardo strangle him and cut out his heart. The next day he had the heart secretly delivered to Ghismonda in a golden chalice with the words "Your father sends you this to console you with the thing that you love the most, just as you have consoled him with that which he most loved."[34]

Ghismonda, when she was shown the golden cup and heard her father's words, once again with true *virtù* turned his cruel deeds and words immediately on their head—making of his tragedy of vengeance her triumph of love—and once more won a Renaissance reader's approval and sympathy. "There is no more fitting tomb," she responded sagely, "than gold for a heart of the quality of this one: in this at least my father has acted with good judgment."[35] And again the contrast was clear, especially with Ghismonda's last ironic comment that at least in placing her lover's heart in a golden chalice her father had shown some *virtù;* for throughout he had been blinded by his pride and rage while the lovers had lived up to and suffered true to their *virtù.* Now, sadly, it was Ghismonda's turn to meet her tragic fate, and with perfect symmetry she mixed with her lover's heart in the chalice a poison that she had brewed herself as she pronounced yet another soliloquy on love and the noble qualities of that heart. Then she drank it down and lay down "modestly," recomposing herself on her bed to await death and the reuniting of her heart and soul with her lover.

Yet even poison conspired with *virtù* and Boccaccio's literary hand to reinforce her paean to *virtù,* for Ghismonda lived on long enough to confront her father's emotions and lack of *virtù* one last time. Called by her servants, who realized too late what was happening, Tancredi arrived in tears, and Ghismonda chastised him: "Tancredi, save those tears for a less desired fortune than this, and don't waste them on me as I don't want them. Who has ever heard of anyone aside from you, who cried when he got what he wanted."[36] This prince was brought down by his uncontrolled emotions and lost because of his lack of *virtù* what was most dear to him, his beloved daughter—in this Boccaccio prefigures the warnings of Machiavelli about the fate of princes who lack *virtù.* Tancredi is the anti-Clearcus and the anti-Machiavellian prince because, dominated by emotions, outdated notions of personal honor and violence that reflected more traditional noble values, he destroyed his daughter and his life. Violence and tears over *virtù* and reason, a Renaissance recipe for tragedy.

Ghismonda capped her father's fall, however, with a crucial final request that revealed one last time her own *virtù:* "But if there still is alive in you any of that love which you once felt for me, as a last gift—even if you were unhappy with the fact that I lived *secretly and quietly* with Guiscardo—grant me that my body be buried with his where you have thrown it *in such a way that all may know* [of our love]."[37] Here in the virtually eternal romantic topos of tragic lovers buried together it is easy to miss a crucial added detail: Ghismonda wanted their hidden love in death to be publicly acknowledged. What had been hidden she asked to become known by all—to become the lovers' last consensus reality, their last identity as truly *virtù*-ous lovers—through a public ceremony of burial. Hidden *virtù*—which was hardly *virtù* at all in a world where *virtù* and self were performative and social—before the whole community would finally gain its due recognition. With his tearful consent and a public burial the lovers' tragedy was turned to triumph: "So the love of Ghismonda and Guiscardo ended in tragedy as you have heard. Repenting his cruelty when it was too late and after many tears, that Tancredi, with the widespread mourning of the people of Salerno, had the two buried together in one tomb, *honorably*."[38] Beyond death, beyond the power of fathers, patriarchs, and princes, *virtù* ruled, and when it did, even tragedy became a triumph—at least in the imaginative world of the Renaissance.

The honorable burial of the *virtù*-ous lovers suggests a deeper reading of this story, for it might be suggested that throughout there is a conflict between the disciplining dynamic of honor/shame and the regime of *virtù*. Tancredi was clearly driven by a vision of honor and shame which at the time was regularly associated negatively with a traditional and violent nobility that the governments of early Renaissance city-states like Florence and Venice were anxious to limit or eliminate. In that context his vengeance on those who shamed him was to be expected and virtually required by his noble status. Ghismonda and Guiscardo, however, followed the imperatives of a dramatically different regime of *virtù*—imperatives that at least in the *Decameron* Boccaccio seemed to celebrate over and over again. As this tale illustrates nicely, the honor/shame dynamic could unleash dangerously destructive passions both socially and personally even as it was used to discipline society. Forced to decide between the two, Boccaccio may well have seen the regime of *virtù* as the better choice for civil society, as Machiavelli later did. Of course, in the best of Renaissance worlds honor sheared of its negative violent passions and *virtù* could overlap, reinforcing each other to create not tragedies but the best of all possible societies. And in the fictional world of Boccaccio, Ghismonda's tale ends with the young lovers' honorable burial—in the end finally honor and *virtù* did work together.

What makes this hard to parse is that honor often was closely interwoven with *virtù* in the Renaissance: both were terms used to evaluate behavior and social position; both were largely evaluated by a broader community; both were frequently performative; and both were crucial for the disciplining of society, as we have seen. Moreover, often the terms were even used interchangeably. But I would suggest that honor was generally a narrower concept more focused on social station and the virtually ontological status of a person—what a person was at a deep level—whereas *virtù*, while also profoundly concerned with status, was more concerned with what a person did and thus focused on an evaluation of one's abilities, prowess, and comportment in general. Also in part because *virtù* was a term closely associated with the power or the active nature of things, when the term was applied to evaluating people, it tended to stress the active force of a person, the ability to accomplish things, more than honor did. Herbs healed by *virtù* of their healing powers; stones fell toward the center of the earth by *virtù* of their nature; prayers worked by *virtù* of God's grace. In this context virtually everything had its *virtù*, its active principle, and thus it was relatively easy and logical to use the term with this strong sense of action when evaluating a person. It may be as well that the association of the active and action with the superior male and the passive with the less positive aspects of the female also strengthened the positive valence of the term.

Be that as it may, a crucial aspect of this active principle of *virtù* in the Renaissance was that one could accomplish something with *virtù* that was not necessarily honorable or morally correct but nonetheless socially or politically positive. This aspect is something that has troubled modern commentators on Machiavelli but which can be seen more generally in representations of *virtù* across the Renaissance. Our young lovers' affair provides a perfect example: as noted earlier, it was not honorable at many levels—not so much because it was hidden but because it crossed class lines in ways that caused loss of honor; yet as related by Boccaccio, it was essentially a parable of *virtù*, and in terms of *virtù* it was a positive affair that demonstrated the best of both characters. In turn, people could be honorable without necessarily demonstrating *virtù*, as Tancredi poignantly reveals. Killing Guiscardo and having his heart torn out and presented to his daughter certainly could be seen as having redressed his lost honor and subsequent shame—a legitimate and even necessary vendetta in the face of the dishonoring affair that his daughter had had with a commoner.

In a more traditional telling of this tragic tale Tancredi could well have been presented as the hero/victim, an epitome of honor, regretfully exacting a just and rather poetically brutal vengeance on the dishonoring behavior of a wayward daughter and a disloyal servant—dishonoring shame giving way to a symbolic retribution that reestablished the correct balance of honor with shame in the community and in the relationships of the protagonists. Ghismonda dishonored and shamed—symbolically underlined by the brutal but perfect gesture of being given her lover's heart in a golden chalice—ideally balanced the dishonor and shame of her father, and she might well have been shipped off to a convent to leave Tancredi to live honorably ever after, respected by his subjects (and Boccaccio's readers) for his stern but just management of his own family.

In fact, to a large extent, the real tragedy of this tale turns on a classic ethical double bind created by these systems of discipline that did not overlap perfectly. Across the early Renaissance, as the everyday conception of *virtù* shifted from values of an older aristocracy based on blood, warfare, and rural ideals to those of a newer urban elite (the *popolo grosso*) whose vision of *virtù* tended to stress reason, self-control, and a planning, even cunning mastery of the future, a potentially difficult disjunction developed between the disciplining drive of a more traditional honor/shame dynamic and the newer values of the regime of *virtù*. Although honor and *virtù* could often work effectively together to discipline society, when one or the other was taken to its logical conclusion, things worked less well, as honor was a discipline that turned ultimately on righteous anger and violence, often dangerous emotions from the perspective of this newer vision of *virtù*. From this perspective Tancredi reflected the older values of a traditional honor/vengeance dynamic while Ghismonda and Guiscardo represented the values of the newer discipline of *virtù*, and it is clear in this story, as it is clear throughout the *Decameron*, where Boccaccio's sympathy fell.

If Tancredi had followed the dictates of *virtù* as outlined by his daughter, he would have recognized Guiscardo's *virtù*-induced nobility publicly and married her to her lover with no mention of their affair. With no one aware of his dishonor (as honor was also socially evaluated) it simply would not have existed, and all three would have lived happily ever after: a *virtù*-ous daughter, a *virtù*-ous son-in-law, and a *virtù*-ous prince. But the tragedy in all of this was that Tancredi was following a disciplining system that still worked, one that was still believed in and which even Boccaccio could see the value of (when it worked in conjunction with *virtù*). As a result, the ultimate disjunction between honor and *virtù* at the heart of the tale resulted in tragedy, the tragic death of the young, attractive, *virtù*-ous lovers. But nicely, whether consciously or not, that tragic disjuncture was overcome at the end of the tale, for at the last Tancredi repented and allowed his daughter and her lover to be buried together publicly as she had requested. Thus, as noted earlier, the lovers' *virtù* was recognized by the broader community and granted an honorable status with an "honorable" burial as the tale concludes. In the end the tragic conflict between honor and *virtù* was overcome at least in Boccaccio's fiction.

The Positive Equivocality of *Virtù*

In cultures like that of Renaissance Italy where there was a strong sense of absolute social and moral values, where relativity was shunned or virtually unrecognized, the polysemous nature of disciplining terms such as *virtù* was highly useful and to a great extent absolutely necessary. Perhaps in philosophical or theological discourses there was the possibility for a stronger and unequivocal use of such terms, but in the discursive economy of everyday life— in what I have called elsewhere the poetics of the everyday—such terms had to be polyvalent to be meaningful and useful.[39] In this way the flexibility and relativity of everyday disciplining discourses, absolutely required for social functioning and even the survival of society itself, were reintroduced covertly (and largely unrecognized) behind a facade of moral certainty. In fact, it was in large part this crucial slipperiness in Renaissance evaluative and disciplining terms such as *honorable, natural, good, customary, mannerly, courteous, honest,* and, of course, *virtù-ous* which has created and continues to create serious problems for writing a tightly argued account of the significance of such terms or the regime of *virtù* in the everyday practice of the Renaissance.

Yet that same lack of precision that frustrates our desire to have a clear, precise definition of *virtù* in the Renaissance is precisely what reveals the term's range of powers and effectiveness—*virtù*, because of its polysemous nature, could be tailored to different classes, genders, groups, and situations, and people with very different values could still embrace its evaluative power. In sum, the equivocal nature of *virtù* was not as negative as the modern usage of the term *equivocal* would suggest but rather merely a widely adopted way to make it flexible enough to work in a culture that eschewed relativity and insisted on absolute values. Of course, people could still disagree and did disagree about the parameters of *virtù* regularly, even vehemently, but the key was that they consistently believed that they should live by its dictates and insisted that others do the same, and they regularly felt comfortable that they were dealing with an absolute social value, not a relative one.

Machiavelli's much discussed use of *virtù*, I would argue, provides a good example of *virtù*'s positive polysemous nature: the equivocality and flexibility that made it a powerful force in the poetics of the everyday. Scholars who have labored mightily and brilliantly to force Machiavelli's usage into one precise definition have seen him using the term in every sense from the amoral or immoral to the moral, from an ancient Roman vision of masculinity to a surprisingly modern vision of purpose and pragmatism, from a pagan sense to a Christian one, from an aggressively masculine sense of it to a dangerously passive feminine one. And some have finally given up and argued that his lack of a single usage of the term demonstrates that he was not a systematic thinker at all. But one might well make the case that, like his Renaissance contemporaries, Machiavelli used the term equivocally, in a range of ways that, given its everyday flexibility, it was particularly suited for. To put it simply, he used it like a skillful rhetorician with the assurance that its usage would lead his readers to agree with his arguments in much the same way that a modern writer might use the term *natural* in several different ways and contexts but with the faith that readers would be predisposed to accept arguments that promised that the imperative of the "natural" would be met.

This, of course, is not the place to review Machiavelli's many uses of the term or the vast scholarship on the subject, especially as of late the discussion has been complicated by modern conservative commentators who have tried to co-opt his use of *virtù* for what is ultimately an alien and anachronistic political agenda. Still, I would like to suggest briefly that he used the term regularly in a rather traditional sense that seems to echo the republican values and usage of the early Renaissance: *virtù* as that ability/prowess to get things done via reasoned calculation of the future and understanding of the past which often went beyond calculation and cleverness to more questionable attributes in terms of honor and morality, such as cunning and craftiness. Ghismonda's reasoning in Boccaccio's tale would not have been that alien to him even though a great deal had changed in the century and a half between her lectures to her prince and Machiavelli's essaying of *virtù* in *The Prince*.

More pertinent perhaps, in the political realm Cesare Borgia, the immoral but prescient and cunning prince, is a fine example of this type of *virtù*, and in the literary realm of Machiavelli's comedy *La mandragola*, Ligurio, the crafty sycophant who directs the plot, is another, perhaps even more effective example. In this early Renaissance way of seeing it, *virtù* also stands up well to Machiavelli's great nemesis, Fortuna. For it is just such prescient and careful planning that can limit the damage of Fortuna, the raging, flooding torrent that is channeled with careful planning and forethought via canals and dikes safely away from ordered society, minimizing her destructive powers. And, of course, it is just such bold prowess with more of an emphasis on the *vir* in *virtù* which allows the aggressive young male to grab Fortuna by the hair and bend her to his will. At such moments *virtù* is at its most active and has a tendency to leave morality and even honor behind.

One might well ask if older men mastered Fortuna in ways more appropriate to their years, with less aggression and more of the wisdom of a more mature *virtù*. This at least was one way that old Nick portrayed himself in his later letters, as we have seen—a man whose *virtù* was measured by his understanding and ability to calculate the ins and outs of the complex political and diplomatic maneuvers of the times. The slide in meaning in that context worked nicely to encompass Machiavelli's vision of gender, and perhaps age, while still using *virtù* to underline his faith in reason, cleverness, and practical planning. But suggestively, Machiavelli was not adverse to using *virtù* in a more moral sense at times. In *The Discourses,* in which the republican ideals of ancient Rome are held up as a model for reestablishing a modern republic of *virtù* in the lands of Italy torn by foreign invasion and local corruption, the corruption/*virtù* contrast seems to require a more moral reading. Machiavelli seems to be using *virtù* often in that work to refer to the manly virtues of ancient Rome that included, along with reason and self-control, masculine values such as courage and discipline, as well as more moral/civil values like loyalty, honesty, and living within the constraints of law and a religion. Still, this more moral/ancient Roman/manly vision often morphs quickly into a vision that Machiavelli seems to find more comfortable: a vision of *virtù* as action, prowess, reason, and cunning—a vision much closer perhaps to the civic *virtù* espoused by the scribal and civic culture of the fourteenth century, especially in republics like Florence and Venice, and the civic humanists of the early fifteenth century.

Even in *The Prince*, Machiavelli's apparent paean to the amoral *virtù* of tyrants, there is a notable and often noted moralistic aside on *virtù*. Discussing in chapter 8 the Greek tyrant Agathocles as an example of a ruler who used evil means to gain and maintain his rule, Machiavelli first stressed the tyrant's *virtù* while admitting his total lack of morality and evil life, apparently once again using the term amorally. He noted that Agathocles led an "infamous life; but nonetheless he accompanied his infamy with such *virtù* of soul and body" that he became the military leader of Syracuse. Note that the reference to soul and body seems to imply that this is a deep form of *virtù* that virtually reveals the essence of the man, not merely an external socially judged attribute. There followed a rapid sketch of the tyrant's ruthless rule and broader success, which Machiavelli pointed out could not be attributed to the help of others or fortune but rather to his strong will and his willingness to ruthlessly overcome the dangers he faced—apparently *virtù* again, although the term is not used.

Suddenly, however, Machiavelli does a startling about-face; evaluating Agathocles, he opines: "Still one cannot call it *virtù* to kill one's subjects, betray one's friends, to be unfaithful, without pity, without religion. Such practices can win rule, but not glory."[40] Here Machiavelli seems to have jumped to a more moralistic evaluation of *virtù;* a morality that turns still on glory and reflects his concerns with the correct use of the power of the state and the judgment of history perhaps but which nonetheless retains a strongly moral tone. It may well be that Machiavelli had allowed his usage of the term to take a more moral perspective because he wanted to have his cake and eat it too and the flexible usage of *virtù* in everyday speech allowed him to do so: he could use *virtù* to commend the immoral actions of a Cesare Borgia or an Agathocles yet still opt in the best of worlds for a leader and a state that were ultimately moral and good, a reflection of civic morality—*virtù*-ous and virtuous.

However, as some have suggested, it might be that virtù had for Machiavelli a deeper and relatively unequivocal underpinning of moral virtue; in fact, an argument can be made that his understanding of *virtù* turns on his very republican sense of civic morality: a moral system based on a vision of an orderly and just society controlled by *virtù* itself, defended by a government of law that supports and is made possible by a *virtù*-ous citizenry. Crucially, however, to defend such a state of affairs and such a state from the evil ways of the un-*virtù*-ous—and Machiavelli accepts without question the ultimately Christian tenet that people are inherently evil and thus constantly in danger of sliding away from *virtù*—the state must defend *virtù* when necessary even with amoral and dishonorable means. He makes this perfectly clear when he points out that if people were all *virtù*-ous and good, a leader could act in good faith and morally at all times, but given that people are "triste" (not so much sad as unreliable and sinners), a leader cannot always act within the constraints of honor, honesty, and traditional morality but rather must do what needs to be done to maintain law and the state. In other words, act with *virtù*, even if that means without honor and immorally.

If this reading is correct, it is not simply, as has often been argued, that for Machiavelli the state's morality overrules all other moralities. I would suggest rather that his deepest claim is that there is no morality in the modern, every-day world of civic life ultimately without the regime of *virtù*, and without the civic morality of the state that regime cannot long survive. In essence *virtù* always requires a social group to evaluate and discipline individuals, to mold the correct Renaissance social identity: to evaluate and maintain via consensus reality a society of *virtù*-ous individuals, Machiavelli's ideal citizenry in his ideal republic. In the end, without that evaluation *virtù* does not meaningfully exist as a disciplining social reality, and significantly Machiavelli elected the state and its laws as the ultimate defenders of such judgments, over other possible judging groups such as family, neighbors, guilds, fellow citizens, or other solidarities. In fact, this emphasis on the state may help to explain Machiavelli's curious lack of interest in the family as a significant building block of social and political order, a vision of the family that was central for most other Renaissance political thinkers.[41]

Ultimately the best judgments were made by republican states, but at times when *virtù* was particularly lacking (as he deemed was the case when he wrote *The Prince*), a *virtù*-ous prince was the best option to redirect a state and its people to the path of *virtù*. If I am right, for Machiavelli, then, without the state there was no real enduring morality, no meaningful measure or disciplining of *virtù*. Certainly many other groups could and did judge *virtù*. Even individuals could judge it, as he did in the case of Agathocles. But in the best of possible worlds and the best of possible states the civic morality of truly a *virtù*-ous republic regulated by *virtù*-ous laws and a *virtù*-ous citizenry was the best judge. It offered true morality, a civic morality that preserved a civic *virtù*. In less perfect states *virtù*-ous princes or *virtù*-ous laws or, better yet, a combination of both could point society in the right direction, ultimately giving birth to moral republics.

Perhaps in a true regime of *virtù*, in which all demonstrated *virtù*, cunning could become reason, self-control could become self-fulfillment, self-presentation would match a true moral self, prowess could become art. All the aspects of *virtù* that had a tendency to slide toward the amoral and the negative could in a better world (as in the Roman republic imagined by Machiavelli) slide back toward their more positive and moral poles, and *virtù* would become simply virtue. The term that in the corrupt present had to be equivocal would regain in that regime the univocal nature it had in the Garden of Eden before the Fall and sin, when Adam confidently named things with their true and absolute names. But this is probably claiming too much for Machiavelli and forcing him to be a more systematic and a more Christian thinker than he cared to be. It might be wiser to leave him as an accomplished writer, rhetorician, and political activist with an agenda that turned on his own return to power, who cleverly used the everyday evaluative term *virtù* in its several Renaissance senses to make his points and win his arguments, although it is always tempting to make him more.

Suffice it to say that there seems to be a strong case to be made for the fact that Machiavelli, like his contemporaries, saw "*virtù*" as a crucial term and that he used it in several different ways that swung from the apparently immoral to the moral, from what he perceived as ancient to modern usages, from "manly" strengths to more "feminine" wiles—all crucially, however, positive and benchmarks against which a life of glory, honor, and true power could be measured. Simply put, for Machiavelli, as for most people in the Renaissance, *virtù* ruled even with its many faces and equivocal nature.

Virtù and the Perfect Courtier

In many ways the early decades of the sixteenth century in Italy might be seen as the age of *virtù* or at least of its intense discussion in the prescriptive literature of the time. Given the turmoil that engulfed the peninsula as once proud city-states one by one fell to the superior military power of European nation-states, it is not surprising that commentators on Italy's travails would focus on the loss of an earlier *virtù* as an explanation and on schemes for recovering it as a means of regaining lost glories. Machiavelli is the most well known of those commentators perhaps, but his hopes for *virtù* as the key to solving Italy's demise were widely shared, even by those who might seem furthest from his political and social vision.

On the surface Baldassare Castiglione's *The Book of the Courtier*, one of the most important and popular books on aristocratic and courtly comportment of the premodern period written, like Machiavelli's most important works, in the second decade of the sixteenth century, might seem light years away from his vision.[42] Castiglione's world of mannered courtiers with their elaborate attention to etiquette and courtship at first seems to have virtually nothing in common with Machiavelli's aggressive and hard-driving princes or his stout neoclassical republican citizens or even his apparently more personal ideas about love, passion, and self-presentation discussed in the previous chapter. But both writers shared a deep affinity because both shared a deep faith in *virtù*, and interestingly for both love and passion were not minor concerns but intimately connected with the way *virtù* ideally should be played out in social life.

For both, then, *virtù* was the key to reconstructing Renaissance social and political order, even if their vision of that order seems at first glance dramatically different. And for Castiglione, as for Machiavelli, *virtù* was highly polyvalent. Not surprisingly, in Castiglione's work, written as a dialogue, the equivocal nature of the term is more easily seen, as various participants in the dialogue express quite different visions of what *virtù* entails, even as they all agree that *virtù* should rule at court, in governance, and in society. Most important, as one might expect, *virtù* played a central role in the discussion of the ideal courtier, the primary focus of the first two books of the four-book work. And, in fact, in that discussion, although there is considerable disagreement on what the perfect courtier should be and how he should behave, it was *virtù* that made the perfect courtier perfect. Noble birth, honor, masculine ways (as opposed to feminine or soft, passive ways), courtly manners, grace, *sprezzatura*, quick wit, playful spirit, military prowess, musical ability, artistic taste, ability as a lover, and, crucially, the ability to advise the prince all require *virtù*, and when they are displayed in a social setting all are regularly labeled by their diverse advocates *virtù*.[43]

Significantly, however, *virtù* is a central theme not just for the perfect courtier but for the perfect lady of court as well. In book III, where the ideal court lady is discussed, once again behind all the disagreements all the discussants concur that it is *virtù* or its lack that makes one woman better than another and makes or unmakes the lady of court. In this discussion, however, the misogynistic perspective of some of the discussants suggests that not everyone in the Renaissance actually believed women could have *virtù*. Yet even in denying that women could display *virtù*, the naysayers reveal the crucial connection between the concept and correct behavior, status, and ultimately identity in the Renaissance.

Finally, to get ahead of our story a bit, in the last book of the work, book IV, often viewed as a paean to Platonic love in the context of court, *virtù* also plays a deep and perhaps underappreciated role: first, in the discussion of the relationship between the courtier and the prince in the context of an ideal of perfect rule; second, in the context of the ideal of courtly love itself, in which sex, identity, age, and love come together in a rich theoretical mix that turns on a more philosophical vision of Renaissance *virtù* reworked in a Platonic frame.

Turning for a moment to the discussion of womanly *virtù* in book III, suggestively, Giulia da Gazuolo, the dying and risen acolyte of the regime of *virtù* discussed earlier, appears there in an earlier telling of the tale to serve as a contemporary example of female *virtù* even though she was a peasant and not a court lady. And once again she is held up as an exemplar that compares favorably with ancient women. Earlier, at the end of book II, an antiwomen group of discussants led by Gasparo Pallavicino and Ottaviano Fregoso broach the issue of whether women could exhibit *virtù* in the context of a wide-ranging discussion of the double standard that required a greater chastity for women than for men. When Gasparo attacked the claim that men should not joke or gossip about a woman's sexual honesty and chastity, arguing that women did this regularly at the expense of men and equal treatment required that women be open to the same joking as men, Bernardo Dovizi countered that there was not a true equality in this area and thus one could not subject women to such jokes about their sexual reputation. The reason for that lack of equality, Dovizi argued, was the following: "We men have ourselves made a law that a dissolute life is not considered a vice or a fault or infamous, but for women the same life is considered so shameful and worthy of great opprobrium that whether what is said about her is true or false ... a woman is forever disgraced."[44] This inequality in the evaluation of the sexual behavior of women meant for their defenders that one could not question or even joke about their sexual reputation or chastity.

In this context Ottaviano defended this Renaissance double standard and attacked women, claiming to speak for Gasparo: "[It is] perhaps not as unreasonable as it seems to you. For given that women are very imperfect animals and of little or no dignity in comparison with men, by necessity they are not capable of any *virtù*-ous deeds"—and thus they needed shame and fear to be kept chaste.[45] This claim that women could not act with *virtù* was quickly challenged, but in the end it led to a call for the discussion in book III in which the *virtù* of the court lady became the center of debate. There the more traditionalist male discussants continuously raised doubts about the ability of women to display *virtù*, while those who were portrayed as defenders of women defended their *virtù* and provided an ongoing set of mini-narratives about exemplary women—again underlining the centrality of the regime of *virtù*. Eventually losing ground, the traditionalists got to the point where they began to stake out a fallback position in the face of the many historical examples of *virtù*-ous women advanced by the defenders of women. They argued that although some women in the past were capable of displaying *virtù*, such women were no longer to be found in the present. This opened the door in the economy of the discussion for a new series of stories about contemporary *virtù*-ous women and the story of Giulia da Gazuolo.

Her story, then, was triggered by Gasparo's claim that *virtù*-ous women to match those of the ancient world (just discussed) were not to be found in the present. "Such [women]," he argued, "I believe do not exist in the world today."[46] Cesare Gonzaga immediately took up the challenge first with a brief nod at the story of a young woman who escaped the clutches of the French soldiers who were sacking Capua. While she was being led off as a captive, as they passed near the river that traversed the city, she gained a moment of freedom by pretending to kneel down to tie her shoe. In that instant she threw herself into the river and thus saved her "*virtù*." This example of *virtù* saved by drowning called to mind immediately the story of the young peasant woman of Gazuolo, which occurred "just a few months ago." In Cesare's brief narration of the tale of this young unnamed girl,[47] the story was much less developed. Unlike in Bandello's later account, her manners and *virtù* were not evaluated by the Marchesa before her rape; there was no mention of dances where she demonstrated her manners or her beauty; she was raped not by a servant who had fallen in love with her but rather by another peasant who lived in a hut near the fields where she worked with her sister; there was no scene with her neighbor to allow her to state her noble motives for suicide.

Yet there were at least two interesting different details in the tale in Cesare's briefer account. First, he stressed that after she threw herself into the river her sister tried to save her by throwing her a rope. Even though the rope was easily graspable, the young girl refused to grab hold, instead pushing herself out away from the bank to her death. This led him to conclude, "She was moved to do this not because of her nobility of blood, nor out of fear of a cruel death or infamy, but only because of the sadness she felt for her lost virginity. Now from this we can understand how many other women do things most worthy of memory about whom we know nothing because . . . just a few days after she made such a great testimonial to her *virtù* no one speaks of her [anymore], nor do we even know her name."[48] Second, he lamented, "But if the Bishop of Mantua had not died at that time . . . the bank of the river Oglio where she jumped in would now be ornamented with a sepulcher in honor of such a glorious soul."[49]

In this telling of the tale Giulia had not yet won her honorable burial in the central square of the town and her renown—the civic frame and fame of Bandello's account. In sum, she still had not gained her broader civic *virtù*-ousness and was depicted only as a cruelly victimized woman who, losing her virginity, gave up her life as well. And, we might add, she also lacked that telling attribute of identity that was probably not of interest to Cesare's courtly listeners given her peasant status, her name. But none of this detracted from Cesare's purpose in telling the story, which was to suggest that there were many more stories of *virtù*-ous contemporary women that could be told if they had not been quickly forgotten and lost to history. At a deeper level he implied that in Giulia's case this was in part because of her humble birth—a theme that was stressed in both stories and made her *virtù* more impressive yet for both storytellers—and in part because the things that marked the *virtù* of a woman were less the stuff of memory and history than the *virtù*-ous deeds of princes and noble men.

Court ladies, of course, were a much more memorable and serious matter for the discussants, not just because of their status but also because in theory at least they were the officially recognized group that disciplined and recognized the identity of male courtiers as true courtiers and lovers. To accomplish this critical task they too, then, needed to display *virtù* as well as recognize it, at least for the courtiers who held that they were capable of doing so. As a result, the way the male courtiers of the dialogue used women to think *virtù* in gendered terms becomes especially revealing about how Castiglione envisioned *virtù* as central in forming identity and an ordered society at court and more broadly. Thus, although the chastity displayed by Giulia remained crucial, the court lady also was expected to demonstrate a much wider range of *virtù*-ous attributes, including courtly manners, grace, *sprezzatura*, musical and artistic sensibilities, and ultimately the discernment to pick the best courtiers as true lovers.

Early in book III Giuliano de' Medici claimed, "I hold that many of the *virtù* of the soul that are necessary for a woman [of court] are much the same as for a man [of court]: the same nobility, the same avoiding of affectation, the same natural grace in all deeds, the same good manners, the same wit, the same prudence, avoiding pride, avoiding envy, avoiding insults, avoiding vanity, avoiding conflict, avoiding foolishness."[50] At first glance, as Giuliano suggested, many of these *virtù* seem to be the same as those of the courtier, which might seem to indicate that Castiglione envisioned a much greater range of positive behaviors for women than most Renaissance writers, who focused pri-

marily on chastity and modesty as the measures of a woman. Certainly Giuliano's emphasis on such things as courtly manners, grace, and wit which went
normally with court life significantly enlarged the more traditional vision of
the areas in which more humble women could display *virtù.* But even in the
list provided by Giuliano the positive nature of the court woman's *virtù* seems
to slide away from his claim of gender parity as he tacked on a group of things
to be avoided—pride, envy, insults, vanity, conflict, and foolishness—which
seem more in line with traditional attacks on women than the opposites of the
normal attributes of a male courtier. The courtier certainly would want to
avoid these vices, but, significantly, doing so was hardly mentioned when the
ideal male courtier was being considered in the first two books.

The limits to parity are made clearer yet as Giuliano concluded by insisting
that the court woman "should execute with skill and grace" the deeds that
were "correct" for a woman: "It seems to me that it is more necessary that she
be beautiful than is the case for the courtier, because to tell the truth a woman
is most wanting who lacks beauty. She must also be very cautious and take special care to not to do anything that would cause others to speak badly of her.
She must act in such a way that she is not stained by misdeeds or even suspected
of them, because a woman is not capable of defending herself against false accusation as is a man."[51] Here we have returned to the double standard and the
physical issues concerned with the control of birth and women's bodies which
opened the discussion of the *virtù* of women and undermined any real gender
parity. Even for Castiglione's defenders of women the female body allowed
concerns about chastity and modesty to reenter through the back door, as it
were, and to limit what at first might appear to be a much broader range of
positive behaviors in which a woman could display *virtù.*[52] Still, even with this
necessary qualification, the discussion of the *virtù*-ous court lady in Castiglione
ranges far beyond sexual discipline and control and serves as a useful reminder
that chastity after marriage and virginity before it were not the only measures
of a woman's *virtù* in the Renaissance.

Yet the court lady had an even more telling lack of parity. For although she
might advise her lady, the wife of the prince, unlike the courtier, she was not
called upon to advise the prince himself even by her most stout defenders. This
comes out as Giuliano continued his paean to the court lady, even allowing her
a bit of freedom and *virtù* in her style of dress[53] to function more effectively
in the social world of court: "And because Signor Gasparo asks again what are
these many things about which the court lady needs to be aware . . . and if her
virtù [in these things] should serve a social function [in the life of court], I say

that she must have the same understanding of these things as the others lords here have required of the courtier."[54] Giuliano, however, once again qualified this apparent gender parity immediately, noting that for certain things that women could not do, such as fighting on horseback, they needed only to understand what was involved so that they could appreciate and judge the merits of the males who did these deeds. Still, most of the social *virtù* necessary for a successful court lady were the same as for the courtier: "And to answer [Gasparo] . . . I want these women to be familiar with literature, music, painting, and to know how to dance and celebrate with that same discreet modesty and ability to make a good impression . . . as was required of the courtier. . . . And in the same way in conversation, laughter, playing, and verbal play, in sum, in everything to demonstrate the greatest grace."[55]

But then Giuliano moved away from the social world of court and the more performative *virtù* required in that environment to speak of what might appear more internal/personal *virtù*: "And although continence, magnanimity, temperance, strength of spirit, prudence and the other *virtù* may not seem to be important for social life [at court], I want [the court lady] to be adorned with all these [*virtù*] not so much for social life as in order to be *virtù*-ous and so that these *virtù* make her a person that is worthy of honor and everything that she does is filled with it."[56]

No small claim and the misogynistic Gasparo rose immediately to the bait: "'I am surprised,' Signor Gasparo said laughing, 'that now that you have given to women literature, and continence and magnanimity and temperance, that you do not want them to govern cities, make laws, and lead armies.'"[57] Giuliano replied with a laugh of his own, "Maybe in fact this would not be that bad." He continued to point out that Plato, "who was no friend of women," nonetheless called for them to rule cities and lead armies just like men. But he then quickly deflected this difficult (for the Renaissance) idea: "I have not given them these responsibilities, however, because I am describing the lady of court not a queen."[58] Still, by upping the ante for the court lady's political potential Gasparo had cleverly attempted to undercut Giuliano's claims of a deeper gender parity, and he continued with a famous all-out attack on women that ended by arguing on the authority of Aristotle that a woman "is a defect or error of nature" even if she should not be despised for this but rather merely accepted for what she was, in his opinion, "a manifest error."[59]

All these misogynistic fireworks, however, mask a crucial point. If Gasparo had meant to argue fairly against women, he should have claimed for them the real parallel that gender parity between the courtier and the court lady would have implied for politics. Not rule, for no one was arguing that the courtier should or could rule, but rather that the court lady, like the courtier, should advise the prince on how to rule by ultimately showing him the path of *virtù*. Clearly Gasparo was making a rhetorical point, a point that would have been less dramatic if he had suggested that women merely advise the ruler on the ways of *virtù*. Yet if he had made that more modest point, Giuliano could not have escaped the real issue with his laughing quip that he was describing the court lady and not a queen. Why, we might well ask, did Giuliano take the easy way out instead of countering Gasparo's attacks with a call for the court lady to advise the prince just as the courtier was supposed to do? If she had the same *virtù* of the spirit as male courtiers and was only somewhat handicapped by her female body in more deed-oriented *virtù*, why was her potential advisory role ignored? It is hard to argue about the absence of an argument in a discussion, but it may well be that the answer lies again in a shared vision of the female body and its sexual dangers. For in these areas often what is not said is as important as what is said, and this was as true in the Renaissance as it is today.[60]

Here the unspoken may well be that the court lady could not advise the prince, even though she had the *virtù* to do so, because there was always the danger at court that the court lady would become the prince's mistress or at the least arouse dangerous passions in him. It might be argued in the abstract that becoming his mistress would not be at all bad if she was a *virtù*-ous court lady and thus truly deserving of the prince's love. For if what the prince loved in her was *virtù*, surely she would have been in an ideal position to teach it to him and keep him on the correct path. But what negated all this, it appears, was the fears of the sexual powers of a woman and her body. Suggestively, although *virtù* is a feminine noun and, as we have seen, regularly associated with power, even amoral power, it was rarely used in the context of the sexual power of a woman's body—for male lust for that body was normally deemed much more capable of leading men and princes away from *virtù* than back to it, as Machiavelli's Nicomaco learned forcefully in *La Clizia*. Yet one could imagine, instead of the series of tales about *virtù*-ous deeds and deaths of chaste/virginal women which followed Gasparo's attack on women as rulers and as humans, a series of tales about how the mistresses of great rulers taught them *virtù*. Another eloquent silence: for clearly that would have required a virtually impossible flight of fantasy for the masculine vision of the early sixteenth century.

In fact, this rather dangerous reading of silences in *The Courtier* is reinforced to a degree by several moments in the discussion of how the courtier should advise the prince where it was recommended that he should encourage the prince to avoid sensual and immoral activities. In everyday life as well the prince's illicit sexual activities were often viewed as the source of disruption and disaffection among the people he ruled, as Machiavelli frequently argued. Thus it is not surprising to find that the mistresses of Renaissance princes were usually portrayed in a negative light and were often held to be responsible for their bad decisions, usually representing, then, the exact reverse of the *virtù*-ous woman. Here too the potential moral dimension of *virtù* almost certainly played a role. Morality might be downplayed when the moment required strong action or when reason and cunning triumphed over foolishness, even moral foolishness. But the sexual negatives of a prince's mistress and her feared power over his passions and ultimately his rule far outweighed any abstract potential for *virtù* that she might have.

If this reading is correct, it also suggests that we might take another look at the silences surrounding the call for the courtier to not be overly feminine, or *molle*. Most scholars have aptly seen these injunctions for a strongly masculine courtier as reflecting the misogynistic assumptions and fears of the times. But when we look more closely at what is not said or barely said, it is interesting to note that these comments are largely aimed at young courtiers who found dangerously attractive the new foppish styles of court. As we have seen, youths in their late teens and early twenties were passing through what was viewed at the time as a dangerous period of transition from passive to active in their sexual lives and more generally as well. Clothing that seemed to accentuate the feminine and the passive, then, would have seemed particularly inappropriate. This may well have been felt more strongly at court, where newer manners and ways of social interaction were at least in part aimed at limiting the more direct confrontations and violence that were a significant part of an aristocratic adult male's expression of the required masculine active/aggressive demeanor. That positive goal, however, limited to some extent the signs of traditional masculinity and emphasized a more passive, flexible male behavior that could easily be seen as dangerously feminine.

But at a yet deeper level all this concern with appropriately masculine appearance may also have intersected with fears that the feminine appearance of young males at court could attract inappropriate lusts from the older males there and, more dangerously, from the prince himself. We have already seen how the prince could joke about such attractions in Aretino's irreverent comedy *Il marescalco*, but many found the situation considerably less humorous. In Renaissance Venice, for example, the government was extremely worried about the potential impact of male groups of sodomites functioning as sexual factions with political agendas; so concerned, in fact, that they were willing not only to torture young nobles to find out the extent of such feared dangers but also to execute young men of the best families who seemed to be involved in such cliques.[61] The dangerously feminine body of the young male courtier, from that perspective, needed to be "masculinized," and given the significant power clothing had in demonstrating sexual identity, dressing that body in a manner that signified an active, mature masculinity went a long way toward accomplishing the deed.

In that way, if this reading is correct, the same masculine aggressiveness of the prince that could be a *virtù* if correctly expressed would not be led astray by the feminine looks and wiles of the young male courtier. Ultimately, in terms of sex the young male courtier presented the danger of being a virtual echo of the court lady. Both had the potential *virtù* to advise the prince, but that potential *virtù* was overwhelmed by the dangers of their bodies and the passions those bodies might well engender. As a result, at court young males (*giovani*) were not to be feminine, and they and young women were not even to be imagined as being capable of advising the prince by any of the discussants in Castiglione's dialogue—if this hypothesis is accurate, these were eloquent silences about the role of sex, identity, and *virtù* at court.

Whether such conjectures are accurate or not, one thing is clear: the mature courtier's role as adviser to the prince was the key to what made all his other *virtù*-ous qualities more than a mere social game and in the end truly *virtù*-ous and moral. This is what kept Castiglione's ideal court from becoming an aristocratic Land of Cockaigne or a Cloud-Cuckoo Land—a pre-Versailles— where nobles wasted their time in pointless courtesies as the prince overrode aristocratic prerogatives to rule absolutely in the real world that mattered beyond court. As in Machiavelli's *The Prince*, for Castiglione's *The Book of the Courtier* the ultimate goal was a prince who acted with *virtù*. Thus the crucial role of the courtier for Castiglione was to lead the prince down the correct path of *virtù* and in this way assure that his rule would be good and just. In book IV Ottaviano Fregoso opened this discussion by pointing out that many of the positive attributes of the courtier discussed to that point actually might be considered merely "frivolous and vain." Boldly he argued that he did not think it was worth the effort if the courtier sought only to make himself "noble, graceful and pleasant as well as expert in many bodily exercises [*esercizii*]" without producing "other fruits." In a fashion that echoed Aristotle and also suggested

Machiavelli's reasoning again, he argued that real *virtù* must be measured not by personal accomplishments but by the ends that it allowed one to reach.[62]

With the wrong ends—that is, mere self-aggrandizement via courtly skills—the dangers Ottaviano feared were well known and much the same as those discussed above. "Often these skills," he worried, "merely make the spirits of men effeminate [*effeminare gli animi*], corrupt youth [*gioventù*], and reduce [the courtier] to a most lascivious life." Once again those familiar dangers of sex, gender uncertainty, and corrupt youths which so deeply threatened the underlying sense of order in the Renaissance are invoked, and Ottaviano concluded that it was these negative ends of court life that had led to the fact that the name of Italy was "distained."[63] Significantly, these vices were actually the incorrect ends of a courtier's potential for *virtù*. He held that, correctly applied, *virtù* should have a rather different goal, a political goal—ultimately a virtually Machiavellian end/goal.

"The end/goal, therefore, of the perfect courtier," Ottaviano argued, "I hold to be to win the grace and the heart of the prince he serves." As he continued, however, building ends upon ends, it was the end of this end/goal that was crucial because personal advancement was not the ultimate reason the courtier sought to win the heart of his prince; rather, the goal was to advise him and make sure that his rule was a *virtù*-ous one. Once again *virtù* was the key and a *virtù*-ous prince the goal: "In this way [the courtier] is able to tell him [the prince] and always say to him the truth of every thing that he should know without fear or danger of displeasing him. And when [the courtier] sees that [the prince] is inclined toward something that is unwise he has the courage to contradict him thanks to the grace he has gained with those good qualities [of the perfect courtier discussed in the earlier books]. In this way [the courtier] leads [his prince] away from every evil intentions and *onto the path of virtù*."[64]

The true goal of the *virtù* of the courtier, then, is not courtly games of love or prowess, graceful manners, playful wit or *sprezzatura*, or even individual noble self-fashioning; it is virtually the same goal as for Machiavelli: establishing the regime of *virtù* by winning the influence and political power to lead the prince onto the path of *virtù*. Thus the perfect courtiers of a court form the inner group that makes the prince's *virtù* real—in advising the prince they negotiate and confirm his *virtù*, the ultimate social *virtù* in a princely state. And they are capable of creating and maintaining this consensus reality of the prince's identity as a *virtù*-ous ruler and using it to make him actually function as same because all their *virtù* makes them capable of doing so—perfect courtiers.

"Because the courtier has in himself the fullness [of *virtù*] as described by these lords . . . he will know in every situation how to smoothly make his prince see how much honor and utility he and his supporters can gain from justice, generosity, magnanimity, gentleness and the other *virtù* which are required of good princes and in contrast how much infamy and damage are the result of the vices which contradict them."[65] The end, then, of the courtier is the just state ruled by a just prince—once again we return to the goal of a *virtù*-ous state, based on a *virtù*-ous prince advised and pressed to *virtù* by a *virtù*-ous courtier. In what I would argue is Castiglione's moral vision of the court and the courtier expressed by Ottaviano, once again *virtù* rules: the regime of *virtù* is fully reified. Clearly this is a utopian vision and one that ignores many of the other opinions expressed in *The Book of the Courtier* as well as a great deal of the impact that Castiglione's work had on early modern society and courtly life. But for our discussion of the regime of *virtù*, what matters is the explanatory power and central role that *virtù* had in this admittedly utopian vision of a *virtù*-ous state.

A deep historical irony, however, may underlie this political vision of a moral state that could uphold and guarantee *virtù* and ultimately virtue as well in Castiglione and Machiavelli. For if we look behind their state-oriented theories, the regime of *virtù* really came before the states that their utopian dreams envisioned. Yet unlike those utopian visions, the regime of *virtù*, in fact, already ruled. It worked—not always well or in a positive way—but it worked nonetheless in the context of multiple groups within society and often most effectively at a local level well below the level of government. Actually, in many ways it might be understood as a deeper social discipline with which the emerging state was in competition and whose power the state often attempted to co-opt. In the end, however, if people lived in accordance with what *virtù* required and in social groups ordered in terms of the performance of *virtù*, there was really little need for more formal laws or rule at least as those were envisioned by Machiavelli and Castiglione. In fact, at the time both law and government could seem inflexible and heavy handed by comparison. Essentially social order in a *virtù*-ous populace would be the product of individually repeated performances of *virtù* and the social pressures to display the same in this Renaissance form of social discipline. The irony, then, is that the state as envisioned by Machiavelli or Castiglione could not exist without the regime of *virtù*, but *virtù* could well and did exist at many levels without the state.[66]

But to return to Castiglione's courtier, there seems to be a crucial disjunction between the high moral purpose of leading the prince on the path to *virtù* and the games of courtly love that the first three books spent so much time preparing the courtier and court lady to play. How could one make a vision of so high a moral/political purpose meld with the play and display of court, even if that play was accomplished with artful grace and *sprezzatura?* That, of course, was the last big question to be faced in Castiglione's work, and, as is well known, the highly Platonic answer was provided by the famous sixteenth-century poet of love and future cardinal of the church Pietro Bembo. His powerful and poetic evocation of the higher mysteries of love that lead to truth, beauty, and ultimately God himself created an ennobling identity for the courtier as a perfect mix of aristocrat, philosopher, Christian, and lover which seemed to transcend the mundane world of daily life and politics. Yet along the way he dealt with some less poetic issues: issues that nonetheless tied *virtù*, politics, and love into a powerful and relative seamless whole of great ideological power and weight and thus worth briefly reconsidering here from the perspective of *virtù.*

Gasparo, ever the counterfigure, following the discussion of the political goal that made the courtier truly *virtù*-ous, posed a significant reservation that turned on the age distinctions discussed earlier and which opened the door to Bembo's famous disquisition. "Reviewing what has been said to this point," he began, "one may draw one conclusion: that the courtier who leads the prince to *virtù* with his authority and courage must almost necessarily be old."[67] Certainly, as we have seen, from a Renaissance perspective the young were too dominated by passions to play the careful and balanced political role envisioned for the courtier as adviser to the prince. But, of course, at the same time and apparently contradicting this need for the mature wisdom of age and the mature control of passions, the courtier also was supposed to be a successful lover. Compounding this problem, however, virtually all the discussants had already agreed on at least one thing when it came to love—that old men in love were at best foolish and at worse distasteful, shades of Machiavelli's alter ego Nicomaco in *La Clizia.*

With more than a touch of irony, then, to make his point Gasparo returned to an earlier discussion of ancient examples of courtiers/advisers in which Aristotle's role as adviser to Alexander the Great was held up as a perfect example of the ideal courtier: "If your old courtier Aristotle were in love and were to do the things that we see some young lovers [*giovani inamorati*] do today, I doubt that he would find the correct harmony to teach his prince and it may well be that children would run after him insulting him [*baia*] and women would delight in making fun of him."[68] Bembo rose to the challenge, countering that a true courtier, "even if he is old," could love and enjoy "those loves that are sweet without sadness" and do so without being insulted or gossiped about. "Loving, the [older] courtier could love in a way that not only would not bring him any censure but rather much praise and the highest felicity ... something that the young [*giovani*] seldom find; and as a result he would not have to give up on advising the prince."[69]

Bembo's love that is without censure and without sadness, of course, turned upon his vision of Platonic love—a love that leaves sensual and physical beauty behind to seek the true spiritual beauty and perfection that literally in-form all the beautiful things and thus allows one to find true spiritual love.[70] Although in his own love life, even as an older man and a cardinal, Bembo, like Machiavelli, kept a mistress and seems to have been willing to accept the dangers of considerably less Platonic liaisons,[71] what matters for our discussion is that Bembo in his defense of Platonic love linked that love directly to the essential political role of the courtier and *virtù*. When a courtier loved with this true love, not only could he be older, but—in order to have that control over his emotions and sexual appetites and the deeper understanding that *virtù* and such love required—he had to be older, a mature lover in full control of his passions. And crucially that same maturity and self-control driven by those very same *virtù* that made him a successful true lover made him capable of guiding the prince on the true path of *virtù*. "In this way our no longer young courtier [*non giovane*]," he opined, "will find himself beyond all the heartache and disgrace which the young [*giovani*] almost always encounter such as jealousy, suspicion, distain, rage, desperation."[72]

Bembo followed this with a by now familiar litany of the dangers of youthful love which focused on the dishonors, disgraces, and violence that often accompanied it, all stemming ultimately from passions and appetites not yet successfully limited by a more mature *virtù*. The mature courtier/lover escaped all these dangers and negative attributes of love because "he has enclosed in his heart always with him his precious treasure," his love of true beauty beyond the mere physical beauty of this world of emotions and appetites.[73] This precious treasure was enjoyed by the mature courtier obviously not through physical love—although spiritual kisses were allowed—but by turning inward and using "the eyes of the mind" (*occhi della mente*) in contrast to "our clouded eyes" (*nostri tenebrosi occhi*) of everyday life to discover the true beauty always safely there. Young lovers, then, were attracted to "corrupt bodies" that were little else but "dreams and weak shadows of beauty." In contrast, the perfect mature courtier turned inward to discover "the sweet flame," "the gracious fire" "of divine beauty."[74] And in doing so, crucially, he became not only a true lover and a true courtier but truly *virtù*-ous, that is, capable of truly controlling his emotions and appetites, truly acting with grace and manners, truly noble, and truly advising his prince on the path of *virtù*.

Bembo's closing vision of *virtù* in the service of love and rule in Castiglione's *Courtier* could hardly seem more distant from the apparently pragmatic and this-worldly vision of political thinkers like Machiavelli. His seamless metaphysics, metapolitics, and meta-erotics enfolded a universe of secure beauty and truth that might seem at first to be infinitely distant from the everyday world of Renaissance politics, society, and life and our modern world for that matter. Yet his understanding of *virtù* and the courtier's ultimate goal / end of advising the prince reveals the basic common ground that the regime of *virtù* created for people across the social and intellectual divides of Renaissance society and culture and successfully closes *The Book of the Courtier* where it began, with *virtù* as the truly ultimate goal of the courtier.[75]

A Prickly Pear and *Virtù*, Part II:
One Last Death and Resurrection

Few, however, would have the opportunity to encounter *virtù* at the level envisioned by Bembo at court or beyond; for that matter even Machiavelli's vision of the state disciplined and ordered by *virtù* was doomed to remain a utopian ideal, as noted earlier, lost in an imagined past and unrealized in any future. Still, in everyday life the regime of *virtù* was anything but an abstract or utopian concept, as is revealed in the imaginary (but no less real for that) world of Renaissance literature again and again. Returning to the tale of Scopone (the Prickly Pear), at the simplest level those who did not live under that regime were neither Buonsignori (good lords) nor good clients but rather prickly pears (*scoponi*) or ineffective youthful masters who had to be reigned in and learn to live with *virtù*. Thus in Sermini's novella, as noted earlier, we encounter a social morality tale that turned on the regime of *virtù* and how it underlay the everyday, practical discipline of Renaissance society, and as such it warrants a last closing look.

When we interrupted Scopone's tale to briefly sample the centrality of *virtù* in Boccaccio and Castiglione, he had defied the wishes of his young lord and taken the fish that the latter had wanted to buy from him to sell instead at the local market. There he demonstrated to all that he lacked *virtù*, asking unfair prices, misrepresenting his lord, and treating others in a rude and unseemly manner; his performance of un-*virtù* marked him out as a true villain and an uncivil lout, identities that were not appreciated by anyone at the market or by his lord and patron when he learned of his behavior. But the regime of *virtù* that inexorably drove the action of his novella was about to swing into action bringing him pain, suffering, and metaphorical death, followed by one last literary resurrection in the name of *virtù.*

"Since everyone saw what a churl he [Scopone] was, two men went to the Lord of the Baths (for it was customary to choose one during holiday times [carnival]), a fun-loving young man from the Malavolti family, and accused Scopone of having come with fish to starve the company of folk who were staying at Bagno a Petriuolo."[76] Suddenly Scopone found himself arrested, tried, and convicted by this young Lord of the Baths, leader of a merry band of youths who during carnival ruled for a time, playfully turning the world on its head. And when the Lord of the Baths' secretary, Ugo, read out Scopone's sentence with a laugh that rings true to Alice's dealings with the Queen of Hearts, laughter became discipline and shared community ideals of correct behavior, and an everyday moral economy became concrete reality.

"All the bathing crowd were in the square, where they watched Ugo ceremoniously read the man's punishment . . . rul[ing] that Scopone was to wear a fool's cap and be beaten [*scopato*] with brooms throughout the town."[77] Ugo then listed the crimes that had earned Scopone these punishments, concluding that he was neither their *compagno* nor a good client, for he "had placed more value on fish" than the honor of his lord or his own correct social behavior.[78] Once again implied group judgment was central, as both the community of people at the market (Ugo's *compagni*) and the client group that served Scopone's lord Buonsignori had been treated incorrectly. "And now Ugo willingly went from being a secretary to a public executioner. He took the heavy brooms . . . and began to strike Scopone . . . and he carried out the sentence so well that everyone was laughing hilariously."[79]

Clearly, Scopone was the victim of a charivari, frequently called a *mattinata* or *baia* in northern Italy, administered by a group of upper-class youths. Such disciplining moments, as Natalie Zemon Davis and others have shown, were a part of community life during carnival and beyond that helped to enforce community ideals of correct behavior. Entrusted to the young males of the community, such group displays of power and often violence at the expense of those who were perceived as offending the values and traditions of the community were seen as helping to redirect the frequently irresponsible and violent enthusiasms of youth at least for a moment to socially useful ends.[80] But, crucially, at the hands of Ugo and his young friends, Scopone was the victim of a passion play based on the regime of *virtù*, for his *mattinata* violently and humorously crucified him socially for his lack of *virtù*, and this community response demonstrated to all how shame and pain returned to those who were identified as having overstepped the boundaries established by that regime. In this tale honor, shame, and *virtù* worked together as they should in an ideal society, reinforcing each other (unlike the tragedy of Ghismonda and Guiscardo), and thus the tale had a happy ending, as we will see. Such moments were public spectacle at its most telling—the disciplining gaze of a community was literally focused and acted out in a way that transformed shared ideals of behavior into action and which allowed *virtù* to rule.

Suggestively, this literary *mattinata*, like many others actually carried out in daily life, was performed borrowing the forms of government itself. Ugo was labeled first chancellor (a government official usually concerned with keeping and reading out the records of government) when he was presenting the case against Scopone in the mock trial and then labeled *manigoldo* (executioner) when he switched roles to carry out the mock sentence, which also echoed the spectacle of many executions.[81] In fact, one of the most articulated aspects of Renaissance government was the complex of law, courts, bureaucracy, and policing functionaries which attempted to limit disorder and violence, especially in the urban centers of the time.[82] And although this apparatus was less developed and effective in smaller towns and the countryside, Sermini's tale suggests how deeply this vision of governance was embedded in the consciousness of the day. Indeed, it has become a commonplace that one of the primary goals of Renaissance government was to create more peaceful and disciplined urban spaces, limiting the violent prepotency of old nobilities and maintaining an environment more conducive to activities like banking, trade, and artisan production.

Yet it would be unwise to overestimate the effectiveness of government in this area. Renaissance cities remained violent and dangerous places with a seething underbelly of tensions that turned quickly to fisticuffs and stabbings over minor slights and subtle questions of honor at every social level. Behind both the desire for a more peaceful urban environment and fears about the violent tenor of daily life in Renaissance cities lay the hard fact that governments of the day simply did not have the numbers or the technologies of rule capable of disciplining society effectively—policing bodies, courts and magistracies, laws, punishment, and even periodic dramatic repression were incapable of actually controlling the urban spaces of the period, never mind the countryside beyond the city walls. Of course, even supposedly "modern" bureaucracies with "professional" staffs and much more effective systems of record keeping and repression are inadequate to the task.

Considering this, one begins to wonder whether we are not the captives of a governmental delusion (much like Machiavelli and Castiglione) that overrates the importance of the state and misses the way in which social discipline—via socially imposed cultural norms such as *virtù*—is actually built deeply into the cultural matrix of society, as anthropologists have long suggested. Still little studied from a historical perspective, these cultural matrixes of discipline made sustained community order possible without relying on the often corrupt and regularly inefficient and ineffectual bureaucracies of governmental control. Not surprisingly from this perspective, governmental forms that were aimed at disciplining society often reflected and articulated these deeper cultural discourses, consciously or unconsciously evoking them to gain power and legitimacy. And at times the tables could be reversed with governmental forms being reintroduced into cultural forms that discipline—with a nice reinforcing circularity—as Scopone's trial and punishment at the baths reveals.

But to return to Scopone, while that prickly pear suffered the discipline of the regime of *virtù* in the form of a judicial-style *mattinata* during carnival carried out by a youthful merry band, his final reform struck a deeper cord. Much deeper. For when Buonsignori learned of Scopone's crimes against his peers and against himself, he realized that he too must change. He had to give up his easy-handed youthful ways (in contrast to Aretino's Marescalco, who refused to do so). With his disloyal and dishonorable peasant he had to finally step up to be what his name promised that he would be, that is, a Buonsignori, a good lord. His youthful pleasures and passions had to be left behind and mature responsibilities faced rationally and with *virtù*, which meant taking Scopone in hand and changing his identity from that of a stereotypical rustic villain—recognized in the consensus realities of diverse social groups by this point—to a mannered and correctly respectable and respectful rural client.

Thus this young lord took up his lordly status, calling his steward to ask him how much Scopone owed him; a goodly sum of some 102 florins it turned out, reflecting his own earlier youthful open-handed way of treating his peasant. He then brought together a group of his men to witness his own performance of lordly *virtù* and had Scopone brought before him. With all present he began the process of creating a new consensus reality of his client's identity, in-

forming Scopone that he had decided to forgive him 2 florins of his debt but
intended to collect the rest immediately. Realizing that he was being destroyed
financially, Scopone tried to cleverly talk his master out of his resolve, but true
to what was required of a good lord, Buonsignori remained firm in the face of
these "prickly-pearish blandishments" (*scoponesche lusinghe*). This performance of true lordship demonstrated to all that things had changed and that
Bartolomeo Buonsignori had taken up his adult patriarchal responsibilities at
least as far as being lord of his estates was concerned, and even Scopone quickly
understood that he would have to change not only his ways but his "very nature" (*natura sua*).

Here it seems that we have moved from simple performance to something
deeper, Scopone's nature itself. The text is suggestive and worth reproducing
in full: "Seeing exactly where his own best interests lay, Scopone at once took
a decision, and insofar as his own character allowed, he suddenly altered *his
own nature*. For he determined to be the very opposite of what he had been,
and thus he continued always."[83] When Scopone realized after a night of reflection that what he had been was the reason for his destruction by his lord—
a virtual economic and social death—and of course that his lord had the power
to do this to him, the reality of the situation forced him to see that he had to
change his nature itself, not just his behavior, not just his performance of self.
Thus he decided to become just the opposite of what he had been before. As
the text comments, "it was a miraculous thing" because Scopone did just that.
He rushed off to his lord and in tears, dropping to his knees and placing his
arms in front of him in the form of a cross, he admitted his misdeeds and the
justness of his punishment and promised to become "a new man" in the future.

It may be that Bartolomeo believed the deep change that Scopone promised,
but his response to his man's tears and promises revealed that now as a good
lord he was determined to make sure that his man's future performance would
match his claims of a transformed nature. For the change that really mattered
for him and the Renaissance was still ultimately measured in terms of deeds.
Thus he sent Scopone home for the night, asking him to come back the next
day, when he would respond to his plea. Neither tears nor private words about
a "new" man were enough to move him. The next morning he called four of
his most important men supposedly on other business but, in fact, so that they
would be there when his man returned "in order to make Scopone's case an example not only to himself but also to others."[84]

When Scopone arrived and saw the important men there, he withdrew a bit, preferring, Sermini states, to have his judgment be private. But Buonsignori called him forward and asked him in front of the group if he was still determined to change his nature, and Scopone responded "yes," dropping to his knees. Bartolomeo asked him to stand and then began a long recitation of all the un-*virtù*-ous deeds he had done against his lord. Again a trial-like moment, but here I would argue it reflects the fact that Renaissance trials were in many ways a formalized form of an ideal complaint in the regime of *virtù*, which this moment more properly was—a lord listing out his complaints against one of his men in front of the community of his most important men to create a new consensus reality and ultimately a new identity for his peasant. Be that as it may, once again, this time in front of others, Scopone admitted his guilt and proclaimed his commitment to changing his nature and his ways, "his *sco-ponesca condizione*."[85]

Buonsignori took total and final control of the situation, ordering, "I want to change your name, as you have changed your demeanor [*condizione*]. And seeing you become so humble, since you were called Scopone before because you would never bow down to anything, so now that you are bending like the willow, I wish henceforth to call you Salcione [Willow]."[86] So shortly after Easter, exactly three days after his master had destroyed him by literally putting him on the kind of cross the Renaissance *popolo grosso* would have appreciated (the cross of his debts), Scopone was reborn—a final resurrection at the hands of his own good lord—as Salcione, a *virtù*-ous client/peasant of a now *virtù*-ous good lord. And although there is more than a hint of a sense of deeper identity in this tale of miraculously changing nature and renaming, the quasi-public performance of the creation and evaluation of identity and self is never overlooked. In fact, the re-creation of a new consensus reality orchestrated by the now truly Buonsignori seems to be in the end the primary measure of self and identity, as we would expect, even when it required stopping the action of the tale for a night so that the good lord could call together his men to witness the transformation of Scopone into Salcione.

And although it was Scopone's personal decision to change, it was a decision driven by group actions against him: first his *mattinata* at the baths; then his economic and social destruction by his lord; and finally his renaming and rebirth before the important men of his lord. Ultimately, of course, although Scopone decided, it was not his decision that really mattered, nor that of his lord, who in renaming him in front of his best men performed before that group his resurrection; rather, it was the deeds of both and the social negotiation of self that were crucial. If any doubts on that remain, the evaluation of the reborn Salcione ends with a listing of his new positive performances of peasant/client *virtù:* it is reported that he "lived" ever after as a willow and not a prickly pear, having become "humble, courteous, ready to serve, loving, amiable, grateful, and tactful with everyone, and above all with Bartolomeo," finally his Buonsignori.[87]

Clearly in fiction, at least, the regime of *virtù* worked exactly as it should, with honor, *virtù,* and Christian morality all successfully interwoven to produce a disciplined, peaceful society in which the Scopones of the Renaissance resurrected as Salciones allowed all to live happily ever after in a disciplined civil society. In that world Castiglione and Bembo's perfect courtier would have been perfect indeed, Ghismonda and Guiscardo recognized and honored, and Giulia da Gazuolo and Clearcus truly revered as saints of *virtù.* And in the end Machiavelli would have found the salvation that he sought for his besieged and failing city-states of Italy. With *virtù* his modern Italy could return to a glorious future following in the footsteps of the ancient Roman Republic, and perhaps he would be able to leave his own aged *virtù*-ous persona behind for a moment to secretly enjoy the pleasures of his la Riccia or Barbara Salutati as Callimaco. Surely we can imagine him doing so to be resurrected one last time as Machiavelli in love.

How Machiavelli Put the Devil Back in Hell

Although Machiavelli in his letters and his comedies often revealed the touch of a *novelliere* and Bandello remarked that he was well known as a person who loved to spin out clever tales in company, only one freestanding novella of note of his has survived: the tale of the devil who took a wife, *Belfagor*.[1] If it is possible to write a wonderfully misogynistic work, this would qualify as a prime candidate, even if in many ways in a Renaissance context its attack on women would have been somewhat masked by its more canonical attack on marriage. Aretino's Marescalco, if he could have escaped his comedy, would have agreed heartily with that attack on women and marriage; Rustico, after his adventures and failures with Alibech, might have nodded, a sadder, wiser desert hermit; Captain Fear perhaps would have even felt a bit of fear himself remembering his Amazons; Abbot Ruis would certainly have recognized the sharp-tongued danger of the devil's human wife in the aggressive counterattack of his former concubine and her mother; the antiwoman faction of the *Book of the Courtier* would have enthusiastically concurred with Belfagor's negative judgment of women; and, of course, Nicomaco and presumably old Nick himself—although they had undoubtedly appropriated the story from earlier sources—would have seen it as a clever tale that aptly summed up the stereotypical negative vision of women, wives, and marriage of the time.

The story line of this fast-moving novella is as simple as it is clever. The devils of hell had become concerned because so many of the men who fell into their hands tried to soften the fiendish punishments of their tormentors by blaming their sins on the miseries that their wives had inflicted on them. These virtually universal complaints had led the Devil and his closest henchmen, even as fallen angels, to wonder about the justice of their cruel tortures. They decided, therefore, that an experiment was in order to determine the truth of those claims, and one poor archdevil, our Belfagor, was volunteered to take human form and a wife. As a handsome man of marriageable age (30), then, he gallantly entered Florence as Roderigo di Castiglia with everything a man might need to create the right consensus reality of identity as a young man marriageable in the best circles there—a handsome fortune, good manners, and a magnanimous open-handed way that quickly made him the most attractive catch in the city. In sum, he appeared to be a model of upper-class male *virtù*. And, of course for *virtù* as for consensus reality about sexual identity, what mattered most was appearance; thus, with the correct appearance even though he was really a devil, in short order he was caught and married to a beautiful and promising young woman.

Unfortunately for Belfagor as Roderigo, however, not only had he been forced to take a human body, but he had also been forced to take up what went hand in hand with a body, a body's passions and emotions. In this way the devils of hell planned that he would be able to report back accurately on the human pain and suffering he experienced being married to a woman. And the plan worked perfectly. Like many a young man of 30 who had still not fully mastered the mature *virtù* necessary to control his emotions and desires, he soon fell madly in love with his young wife and was unable to resist her slightest desire. This, along with his pride and pleasure at being a popular young aristocrat accepted into the Florentine upper classes, meant that he quickly ran through his money aided by poor investments in his wife's family and their unlucky business schemes. Suggestively, in this downfall, although his wife and her family were major factors, as fitted the misogynistic/antimarriage theme of the novella, Belfagor's male human desires and emotions (and actual lack of *virtù*) also played a significant role.

When it became clear that Belfagor had run up major debts to continue his lifestyle and would be unable to pay them off, the streets and masculine spaces of Florence turned mean for him, as they had for Grasso. And although little children and women hardly had a chance to laugh and point at him in those familiar streets, his creditors and their thugs chased him through them as he fled the city. Escaping Florence but with his creditors still in hot pursuit and fearing that he would have the unpleasant opportunity to experience human justice or worse, he begged a peasant he came upon in his flight, one Gianmatteo, to hide him and promised him riches and happiness in return. Suitably the peasant hid him under his manure heap, and the devil escaped his human judgment day. As a reward to his savior, Belfagor offered a perfectly devilish plan. He would possess a young woman or two, creating a furor much like that suffered by Suor Mansueta with her devil; then Gianmatteo would show up and do a little mumbo jumbo and Belfagor would free his victim, allowing the peasant to collect handsome rewards for his fake exorcism. The devil kept his word, twice allowing his rescuer to become rich as promised, but true to his devilish ways, as he left his last victim, Belfagor warned Gianmatteo that he felt that he had kept his bargain and that in the future the neo-exorcist should enjoy his wealth and not presume to interfere with his possession of young women again.

That, of course, was the crunch, for Belfagor, being an evil devil at heart ("suo essere"), had escaped his wife and his Florentine/human consensus reality of identity to return to his true nature. And true to that nature, he possessed the daughter of the king of France, knowing full well that Gianmatteo would eventually be called to exorcise her and that would give Belfagor his chance to take away what he had given and cause the peasant's own fall. And thus it happened that, against all his efforts to avoid it, Gianmatteo was forced to go to the French court and ordered under threat of death to exorcise the king's daughter. Gianmatteo now realized what it really meant to play with the devil and how cruel his games could be, for when he whispered in the ear of the king's daughter, pleading with Belfagor to help him just one more time, Belfagor refused with the righteous indignation of a true devil. The game was over and apparently lost.

Facing death, Gianmatteo decided on a desperate strategy. He asked the king to set up an altar in the main square, call all his nobility and people together, and bring his daughter for a final attempt at exorcism. But he asked for one last rather strange measure. He requested that the king order that a crowd of musicians be waiting at the edge of the square and that at a sign from him they should enter the square loudly playing their instruments. And so it was ordered. As Gianmatteo performed his desperate last exorcisms, the devil laughed at his futile attempts at impressing him with the crowd and the nobles of France and confirmed his death sentence. With no other hope Gianmatteo signaled the musicians to enter the square, and they did so, setting up a great clamor. Befagor "perked up his ears" and asked as innocently as Rustico's devil what was up with all the noise. Gianmatteo, a clever but good peasant, never a Scopone (or a Salcione for that matter), replied without missing a beat that it was Belfagor's wife come to Paris to reclaim him. At that truly awful thought the devil fled back to hell. Thus all the devils of hell learned from the devil/husband/victim Belfagor that the complaints of the men that came to suffer at their hands had a great deal of merit. And, nicely, one more time the devil was put back in hell thanks to the *virtù*-ous trickery of another clever man.

Misogynistic, antimarriage, and heavy handed, Machiavelli's cruelly clever sense of humor once again forces a wry smile, and in a way it also highlights something that surprises me as I reflect on this book and the way this novella reflects its main themes. For it is literally full of devils, little devils and big ones; funny ones, sad ones, and dark ones; devils that are fun to think and devils that are trying and difficult to think as well. The beastly Marescalco and the unmanned husbands of Renaissance Venice cured by Fra Gabriele all suffered from a heavy dose of the Devil at least from the perspective of the theology of the time; Rustico's theology and devil were rather different but equally telling; Suor Mansueta's devil was as dark and dangerous and, unhappily for her, disturbingly evil as real devils should be; Brunelleschi's masterpiece of *virtù* was as devilish a *beffa* at the expense of Grasso's sense of self as could be imagined; Cecilia's magic (real or imagined) was feared because it seemed to draw on the Devil's powers; Captain Fear, of course, was a buddy of the Devil (sending many of his slain foes directly to hell) when he was not sleeping with Death herself; the *virtù*-ous deaths of Clearcus and Giulia da Gazuolo, as well as Guiscardo and Ghismonda, not only cheated the Devil of his due but showed the true path of Renaissance *virtù;* and finally Machiavelli, or old Nick, was literally the Devil for the English Renaissance and for many as the author of *The Prince,* even as I hope he has lost some of his Devil-ness as a political thinker here, if not as a lover.

But beyond these devils, hopefully readers will have found a more playful sinning (although not necessary less dangerous) in the approach that I have taken to Renaissance texts both literary and archival which are at the heart of this book and my suggestions about Renaissance identity, sex, and society. To sin and play well I have attempted to be serious about treating Renaissance texts with the respect that they deserve and with what technical skills a career as a Renaissance historian has honed. But my awe before great writers like Machiavelli, Boccaccio, Castiglione, and Aretino and the suffering and pleasures of lives lived by Renaissance people like Suor Mansueta, Cecilia Padovana and her mother, Grasso and Giulia da Gazuolo (if perhaps they were more than a figment of Renaissance dreams of *virtù*), and Machiavelli himself has tempered my play and also has moved me to attempt to play fruitfully—to open their stories and their lives to new meanings rather than to close their lives and works with final answers.

From that perspective not just any opening would do, not just any new meaning, not just any reading. As readers will note, in this book I have *suggested* that some readings are better than others and occasionally, *gently,* that some readings are not powerful enough to play with at all. Normally, however, in my interpretative scheme some readings have been privileged as better (or more powerful) based on three straightforward and simple-sounding criteria—readings should stay close to the internal demands of the text; they should stay close to the context; and they should find meanings that are interesting openings to critical thinking and new pleasurable ways of encountering a text.[2] When I have come close to meeting these straightforward but ultimately impossible goals, I think my readings have been both playful and devilish at their best, although I am perfectly willing to concede that from other perspectives or with other criteria of evaluation they may well seem empty play or devilish in quite a different sense.

Each chapter, then, has offered a more or less aggressive rereading of at least one literary text in relation to the ongoing discussion of Renaissance sexual identity and how it was formed, maintained, and negotiated in the context of consensus realities. "Of Birds, Figs, and Sexual Identity in the Renaissance, or The Marescalco's Boy Bride" reread Aretino's *Il marescalco* placing a heavier emphasis on the role a Renaissance sense of sexual development and identity played in the economy of the comedy and the representation of sodomy as a way of life and pleasure that was an alternative to matrimony and family. In the process the character of Giannicco, the Marescalco's young servant and lover, emerged as more central than has normally been recognized, and the Marescalco's beastly ways and lack of sympathy for court were melded with the suggested pro-sodomy theme of the comedy to propose more of a truth-sayer role for the Marescalco in the context not just of court life but of more general sexual practice as well.

These readings turned on a closer look at what the stages of life looked like in the Renaissance from the perspective of sex. Women, it was argued, were virtually always sexually defined across their life cycle, starting out as asexual girls until they reached puberty, when suddenly they became sexually adult and quickly through marriage and childbirth became fully adult; thus upper-class women were adults from their mid-teens (lower-class women were allowed to mature a little later, usually in their late teens). For males sexual maturation was much more complex. They too started out as relatively asexual boys, it was hypothesized, but as they neared puberty, their youthful looks began to attract sexual attention in large part because they were usually seen as feminine and passive sexually and socially. As they matured, however, and be-

gan to develop a beard and a heavier, more muscled body, it was expected that
these *giovani* would undergo a transition to a more active approach to life and
sex. In terms of sex, their once passive desires were expected to become active
and focus on either younger boys or women, a particularly difficult transition
illustrated positively by Giannicco in Aretino's comedy and negatively by
Simeone before the Venetian Council of Ten.

Significantly, whether with younger boys or women, this sex was almost always formally illicit, and in that context sex with younger males could actually seem less dangerous socially than sex with unmarried women or prostitutes. Finally, in their late twenties and early thirties these youths would lose
their youthful ways, *gioventudini* (unlike the Marescalco, who refused to give
them up), and move on to full adult status with marriage and taking on the
role of the head of a family. These developments for both males and females
were closely monitored by Renaissance society and, especially for males, required careful negotiation and self-presentation to assure that the consensus
realities shared within the various groups with which an individual lived,
worked, and played—groups such as family, neighbors, friends, social peers,
fellow workers, fellow worshipers, fellow members of a community—were
positive and reflected the correct identity required at any moment in life. This
broad sketch of how consensus realities worked within the ideal of sexual development not only provided the context for rereading Aretino's comedy but
also set the stage for the readings of the relationships between sex, self, and society discussed throughout the volume.

In Chapter 2, "Playing with the Devil: The Pleasures of Sex and Play," Boccaccio's oft considered and highly playful tale of Rustico and Alibech (the last
story of the third day of the *Decameron*) provided the opportunity to examine
more closely the temptations and pleasures of sex from an early Renaissance
perspective, humorously highlighting stereotypes of male and female desire.
But the laughing blasphemy of the text with its "resurrection of the flesh" and
its "putting the Devil back in hell" led me to suggest a series of readings that
slid from the highly possible to the admittedly unlikely—allowing the aes-
thetic pleasure of the reading to take precedent over a stricter reading of text
and context perhaps. At the same time I tried to return to the tale the humor
and warmth that it seems to require both on the face of it and in the context
of its placement in the *Decameron* itself, without trying to make Boccaccio a
protofeminist or ultimately denying his Renaissance male vision of sex and
gender.

With the necessary signposts of warning along the way, however, the interpretation moved on to progressively more devilish readings of the tale, ending with a claim that perhaps its apparently innocent blasphemy was the key to seeing that Alibech's sexual service to God reversed the biblical Fall, made the desert bloom as a new Garden of Eden, and even promised the arrival of the long-awaited third and last age of man inaugurated by none other than that innocent servant of God. Certainly it is amusing to think that Boccaccio might have seen Rustico's resurrection of the flesh and Alibech's pleasure putting the Devil back in hell as a prophecy of a new age of natural sexual pleasure that served God, even if in the end no one will accept the idea and, perhaps more telling, that age never arrived. In turn, Suor Mansueta's play with the Devil outside literature (but perhaps not outside a literary style of imagination) was equally rich and certainly more dark to consider with its revealing insights on the ultimate evils of play, sex, and life. But in these virtual bookend encounters with ultimate play—playing with the Devil—from the start and the end of the Renaissance we discovered broadly sketched the evolving perceptions of the danger of play itself and the way sex and sexual pleasure defined both positively and negatively the ultimate good and evil of a woman's identity in the Renaissance.

"The Abbot's Concubine: Renaissance Lies, Literature, and Power" in many ways had the least to say about rereading literary texts, simply because Captain Fear's adventures as a character in the late Renaissance tradition of the commedia dell'arte have not garnered the readings that they perhaps deserve and thus there was little rereading to do. As a fascinating send-up of the male sexual stereotypes of the period, these plot sketches are revealing, fun, and worth reading, even if they are also unfortunately too brief (and too punningly clever in their written form) to provide a clear idea of how they were actually performed on stage or received at the time. As a result, Captain Fear's demise as the male concubine of the Amazons served mainly as a foil for Abbot Ruis's claimed unmanning and demise at the hand of his concubine, Cecilia Padovana, and a brief advertisement for this largely forgotten but lively and engaging late Renaissance text.

More important, both texts demonstrated how central sexual performance and its consensus reality were for male identity in the Renaissance. Of course, the humor of Captain Fear's character left no room for doubts about his sexual performance until, tellingly, his fearfully demanding Amazons undid him, a testament to how scary truly powerful women could be at the time. In contrast, Abbot Ruis's fall was so impressive that it could lend credence to his claim that he was a victim of hammering love magic, and more centrally it was crucial in his fall from power and prestige in the little rural community where he once was a man to be reckoned with. His lack of control of his passions—demonstrated forcefully to his community, friends, and neighbors—also played a central role in his loss of power and identity. But crucially in the tales of both men's demise, aggressive, powerful women, evil manipulative women, lustful unmanning women, these stereotypical misogynistic visions take on a deeper resonance as once again it becomes clear how important sexual performance was for male identity and the consensus reality of self in the Renaissance.

Chapter 4, "Brunelleschi's First Masterpiece, or Mean Streets, Familiar Streets, Masculine Spaces, and Identity in Renaissance Florence," provided perhaps one of the less dangerous rereadings of the book because it followed in the footsteps of Lauro Martines's excellent recent historical reading of "The Fat Woodcarver," a novella written by Antonio Manetti, who claimed it was based on a true story. Still, Grasso's loss and rediscovery of himself literally in the streets and spaces of Florence at the hands of his friends' (and especially Brunelleschi's) ability to *virtù*-ously re-form his consensus reality and convince poor Grasso that he was no longer himself added hopefully greater depth and nuance to Martines's reading, to a fascinating novella, and to our discussion of identity in the Renaissance. The city, friendship, and identity were also at the heart of a briefly discussed exchange of letters between Francesco Vettori and Niccolò Machiavelli which turned on the metamorphosis of Giuliano Brancacci from a man who disliked sodomites (and even the hint of sodomy) to a man who went hunting sexual encounters with young boys in the illicit heart of Florence; an exchange of letters that, although claiming to be a true account of events in Florence and Rome, clearly had an element of the novella. The melding of these letters with the novella offered the opportunity to propose a more hypothetical reading about the deeper sexual dimensions of the male friendship between Grasso and Brunelleschi which may have originally set in motion the cruel *beffa* at the heart of Manetti's tale and the story that circulated earlier in oral form. But more important, in both tales we saw once again how central sexual identity was in thinking about who a person was and the important role friendship, place, and urban space played in forming consensus realities and unforming them.

In the central chapter of the book, "Machiavelli in Love: The Self-Presentation of an Aging Lover," all these themes came together with a rereading of Machiavelli that proposed a rather different man: a laughing Machiavelli who was constantly negotiating and demonstrating a complex and rather surprising sexual self with his friends and acquaintances and perhaps a broader Florentine public as well—as a lover, and a passive one at that, who was swept along by his mad passions for younger women and who both celebrated and mocked this behavior. First, Machiavelli's letters were reread with an eye to drawing out the meaning of the sexual banter and discussions that play such a significant role in them, especially in his correspondence with Francesco Vettori. Although that aspect of his correspondence has often been dismissed (just as Machiavelli presciently predicted) or reinterpreted in terms of the political and patronage issues that are also central to this correspondence, I have tried to take it seriously (and humorously as well) by looking at it once again as a way of negotiating identity and in this case writing it out and honing it in response to his friends' letters—a rare opportunity to try a bit of literary response theory in the Renaissance. Suggestively, Machiavelli presented himself as decidedly not Machiavellian in love and clearly believed that that made him more attractive to his circle of friends. Rather than aggressive, cunning, and controlling, he wrote himself in his letters as passive and helpless before the arrows of Love and as a perennial lover of younger women even in "old age." What that might mean for the better-known political Machiavelli was suggested only in passing, but hopefully a more complex, anxious, humorous, and human man was highlighted here, helping to make the Machiavellian Machiavelli what it probably should be: a teleological stereotype that obscures more than it reveals about the man and his thought.

In turn, in rereading Machiavelli's two most important Renaissance comedies, *La mandragola* and *La Clizia,* this passive vision of Machiavelli in love seemed to be reaffirmed in the young Callimaco in the first and the old Nicomaco in the second. Callimaco, it was conjectured, was the alter ego of a young, handsome Machiavelli in love and was literally swept along by love and more traditionally Machiavellian characters such as Ligurio and Fra Timoteo (and in a cruel, self-mocking way even by Messer Nicia) to triumph in the bed of Messer Nicia with his truly *virtù*-ous wife, a thoroughly modern Lucretia. It was also suggested that the comedy ends with a playful nod to the requirements of genre by staging a perfectly Machiavellian wedding between the young lovers. In *La Clizia,* Nicomaco, the alter ego of the older and eventually wiser Machiavelli, fared less well at the hands of Love and his aptly named wife, Sofronia, but still echoed the sexual themes of his letters and to a degree Machiavelli's late affair with Barbara Salutati. In the end old Nicomaco, like virtually all old men in Renaissance comedies, failed in his quest to bed his young love—and found himself virtually sodomized by a servant in the process—but he did gain the "happy" ending required by the genre, regaining literally himself and his *virtù.* Hopefully in these rereadings Machiavelli's comedies and letters have also regained some of the humor and sense of self-mocking playfulness that seem to have been at the center of his self-presentation to his friends and perhaps a larger Florentine community as well. And perhaps some new complications have been added to our understanding of this rich, complex thinker.

In the last chapter, "Death and Resurrection and the Regime of *Virtù,* or Of Princes, Lovers, and Prickly Pears," the discussion wove through a series of literary texts to rethink the role of that crucial concept *virtù* in Machiavelli, proposing that to understand Machiavelli and, more important, the Renaissance itself and the way self and passions were disciplined at the time one must look more closely at what I have labeled the regime of *virtù* that ruled then. The goal was not to provide a traditional intellectual history of *virtù* across the Renaissance but rather to offer some suggestions about how the term was used in practice to conceptualize identity and social order. Starting with the little-discussed tales of two virtual saints of *virtù,* Clearicus and Giulia da Gazuolo, and the way their deaths (and death in general) spawned a crucial reflection on identity via *virtù,* the discussion of the chapter is framed by a morality tale about the figurative death and resurrection of the stereotypical evil and corrupt peasant Scopone at the hands of his equally stereotypical good lord Buonsignori—a tale that turns on un-*virtù* virtually crucified first by the Renaissance passion play of a charivari/*mattinata,* then by a good lord only to be resurrected as true *virtù* after the required biblical three days by that same good lord.

But within that frame story rereadings of Boccaccio, Machiavelli, and Castiglione provided windows onto the complex world of Renaissance *virtù* and its close relationship to concepts of identity, order, and love and sex. Boccaccio's tragic tale of the love between Ghismonda and Guiscardo and their death at the hands of her father, Tancredi, the prince of Salerno, was read as a morality tale about the way *virtù* ennobles both lovers and love itself, even illicit love. In a way the prince of the tale, Tancredi, seems to prefigure Machiavelli's *The Prince* and could be read as an antiprince. And this is not merely by chance, as it was suggested that in Machiavelli's apparently equivocal use of the term *virtù* the usage he seemed most comfortable with turned on an earlier Renaissance understanding, similar to that expressed by Boccaccio and many of the civic humanists, whereby *virtù* was a set of behaviors involving reason, control of emotions, and an ability to see and mold the future via reason (often sliding into cunning) which marked one person as superior to another. Crucially, it was suggested, this similarity was not so much because Machiavelli and these writers were sharing a high cultural tradition as because they were reflecting more everyday usages, taking them up from the poetics of the everyday and giving them a high-culture polish and logic. And although the chapter looks at several ways of rereading Machiavelli's use of the term, only a few suggestions for doing so are advanced, as in the end I am not sure a clear-cut definition of Machiavelli's use of the term is possible. Rather, in what is probably the least adventuresome rereading of the book, I have done a rapid review of Castiglione's *Book of the Courtier* from the perspective of *virtù* to draw out some interesting parallels with Machiavelli, stress once again the widespread importance of the term, and hopefully show the way it was used via Pietro Bembo's closing paean to love to help pull together at the level of high culture love, order, government, and courtly ways into a virtually perfect Renaissance dream of *virtù* and male identity.

That dream returned the discussion to a more mundane but more significant Renaissance dream and the frame story, where Scopone was resurrected with *virtù* as Salice, a pliant willow. In that vision of reformulated identity, sex and society worked as perhaps Machiavelli also dreamed they would in the best of possible worlds, with true *virtù* assuring that not only would men seem to be good but—in a good state, with good laws and with good rulers—they actually would be good again, as they had been in the glorious days of the ancient Roman Republic. In sum, *virtù* would finally become virtue again, a Renaissance dream perhaps still worth dreaming—for although *Machiavelli in Love* ends here, hopefully the play of its ideas and rereadings will continue and perhaps help to put a few devils at least back in hell.

Introduction

1. Filippo de' Nerli to Francesco del Nero, 1 March 1525 (from Modena), quoted in Machiavelli, *Opere di Niccolò Machiavelli* (ed. Gaeta), 3:541 n. 8.

2. Ibid.

3. Filippo de' Nerli to Niccolò Machiavelli, 22 February 1525, in Machiavelli, *Opere di Niccolò Machiavelli* (ed. Gaeta), 3:540. This performance was richly staged with the sets designed by Bastiano da San Gallo, known as Aristotle, and music composed by Philippe Deslonges to celebrate the lifting of the bans against Filippo Falconnetti, called il Fornaciaio, a rich businessman who had been a powerful member of the Signoria of Florence before he was banned for five years to his estates just outside the gate of San Frediano. Nerli's compliments about Machiavelli's widespread fame for the performance thus also included Falconnetti, who apparently financed it as part of this celebration.

4. Niccolò Machiavelli to Francesco Guicciardini, 3 January 1526, in Machiavelli, *Opere di Niccolò Machiavelli* (ed. Gaeta), 3:573. This and other references to her sharing her favors more widely have led some to claim that she was a courtesan as well as a singer and poet.

5. *La mandragola*, in Giannetti and Ruggiero, *Five Comedies*, p. 81.

6. Ibid., p. 109.

7. Ruggiero, "Sexual Criminality in the Early Renaissance."

8. Ruggiero, *Boundaries of Eros.*

9. Ruggiero, *Binding Passions.*

10. Giannetti and Ruggiero, *Five Comedies.* Over the same period I have also published a number of articles and coedited a series of books, Studies in the History of Sexuality, for Oxford University Press on the subject.

11. The article was published with the title "Marriage, Love, Sex, and Renaissance Civic Morality" in Turner, *Sexuality and Gender in Early Modern Europe.* Sarah Maza presents an interesting discussion of some of the most critical historical issues involved in such interdisciplinarity with special attention to the New Historicism in her "Stephen Greenblatt, New Historicism, and Cultural History"; for the New Historicism and its apparently antitheoretical claims, see Gallagher and Greenblatt, *Practicing New Histori-*

cism. As will become clear, although I have been influenced by the New Historicism—especially its reluctance to lose sight of Renaissance texts and history by privileging theoretical debates over close analysis of texts—in the end my approach has been more eclectic. See the bibliography for some examples of the broader range of works that have influenced this study.

Chapter 1 • Of Birds, Figs, and Sexual Identity in the Renaissance,
or The Marescalco's Boy Bride

1. Garzoni includes in a long list of popular games "del dar beccare all'uccello." Garzoni (da Bagnacavallo), *La piazza universale di tutte le professioni del mondo,* p. 244v. A more detailed description of how the game was played is provided by Girolamo Bargagli, from which the above quote was drawn; see Bargagli, *Dialogo de'giuochi che nella vegghie sanese si usano di fare,* p. 47. According to George W. McClure, Bargagli's book, written in Siena in 1563 by a member of the city's Academy of the Intronati, attempted to give a higher tone to his collection of 130 games, although *eros* was a primary theme. Bargagli's work, he argues, "reflects the efforts of his fun-loving academy to devise a better cut of games (than those 'base and vile' ones of their youth)," and, needless to say, this was not one of those deemed a better cut. McClure, *Culture of Profession,* p. 52, and for a more extended discussion of Bargagli and other works on games in the period, see pp. 51–66.

2. I use the term *heterosexuality* reluctantly, as it may seem to entail a whole modern discourse of "correct" sexuality. Here and throughout it is used simply in the sense of sexual intercourse between a male and a female and with the understanding that in the Renaissance such intercourse was part of a rather different series of discourses whose complexity we are just beginning to appreciate. Significantly, however, there was no space in this game for birds pecking at other birds, and no figs were left to rot on their trees when the season was over—this was a game in which all play and all were identified as being attracted to the opposite sex. I use the term *phallus* in the same way with apologies to those Lacanians who hold that the term is no longer appropriate to denote a penis.

3. I have long argued that although this vision of Foucault's has been "widely held" it misrepresents his position—first, because his hypotheses about premodern sex and identity were exactly that, hypotheses, often playful hypotheses, designed to deconstruct modern certainties and open up our understanding of sex to new perspectives not dominated by modern disciplines; and second, because he realized that his hypotheses were limited by the fact that his analysis of premodern Europe was based largely on a limited range of prescriptive literature. David Halperin, one of the most noted followers of Foucault, has recently made much the same argument in "Forgetting Foucault." Foucault perhaps most clearly states his position as follows: "Let us put forward *a general working hypothesis.* The society that emerged in the nineteenth century . . . put into operation an entire machinery for producing true discourses concerning [sex] . . . it also set out to formulate the uniform truth of sex. As if it suspected sex of harboring a fundamental secret" (italics mine). Foucault's *hypothesis,* then, was that the resonance of knowledge,

truth, and power in the modern discourse of sex was central in the construction of *the modern* sense of self and individuality. Foucault, *History of Sexuality,* 1:69–70.

4. Perhaps the best example of this approach applied to the Italian Renaissance is Rocke, *Forbidden Friendships.* One of the most important and influential exponents of this position has been David Halperin, especially in his *One Hundred Years of Homosexuality and Other Essays on Greek Love* and his aptly titled volume *Before Sexuality,* coedited with John Winkler and Froma Zeitlin. Lately he has begun to modify his views, however; for this, see his important article cited above in note 3, "Forgetting Foucault," and his more recent *How to Do the History of Homosexuality,* which reprints that article as the first chapter. The area that has produced the most works influenced by this perspective is Renaissance and early modern England; among the voluminous literature see Bray, *Homosexuality in Renaissance England* and *The Friend;* Goldberg, *Sodometries* and his edited volume, *Queering the Renaissance;* and Trumbach, *Sex and Gender Revolution,* vol. 1, *Heterosexuality and the Third Gender in Enlightenment England.* See also Gerard and Hekma, *In Pursuit of Sodomy,* which was published in the *Journal of Homosexuality* 16 (1988) as well, a journal that has also been heavily influenced by and influential in the widespread acceptance of this paradigm.

5. Over the past few decades there has been a growing literature and debate on the nature of Renaissance and early modern identity. Without attempting to review the vast literature on Renaissance identity here, let me just note a few of the most important titles, starting with the seminal work of Natalie Davis and Stephen Greenblatt on the subject, particularly Davis, "Boundaries and the Sense of Self in Sixteenth-Century France," and Greenblatt, *Renaissance Self-Fashioning from More to Shakespeare.* A very interesting review and promising rethinking of the debate with a stronger Italian perspective can be found in the recent works of John Martin, particularly his *Myths of Individualism;* see also "Inventing Sincerity, Refashioning Prudence" and "Myth of Renaissance Individualism." See also Weissman, "Importance of Being Ambiguous"; Freccero, "Acts, Identities, and Sexuality's (Pre)Modern Regimes," and the general discussion in the same issue of the *Journal of Women's History;* and again Halperin, "Forgetting Foucault." See also the additional titles listed in the bibliography, but note that this study with its focus on the Italian Renaissance is not intended to be a comment on the theoretical debates on modern concepts of self and the individual.

6. It needs to be stressed that the distinction between public and private often associated with modern societies was less well defined in the Renaissance, and this was especially true when dealing with matters sexual. As will become clear, things that might today seem private often had a significant social dimension as well—in part because the need to construct consensus realities about sexual identity meant that a wider range of practices had to be known in order to form a consensus about who a person was. Thus, the seemingly private often seeped into the public, and the seemingly public often penetrated the private, as we shall see.

7. Joanne Ferraro in her important study of marriage in Renaissance Venice, *Marriage Wars in Late Renaissance Venice,* points out that freshly washed bed sheets the morning after newlyweds first slept together were an important sign for neighbors (and eccle-

siastical courts as well) which demonstrated that a marriage had been sexually consummated; see pp. 73, 80, 102.

8. Aretino, *Sei giornate*, p. 50; all translations are mine. See also the excellent translation of Raymond Rosenthal: Aretino, *Aretino's Dialogues*, p. 60.

9. Aretino, *Sei giornate*, p. 51; Aretino, *Aretino's Dialogues*, p. 61.

10. Aretino, *Sei giornate*. Here *pane unto*, literally bread soaked in oil or grease, is translated as "hot joint" to maintain the food metaphor and give it a more understandable English reading; bread soaked in oil or grease was a much appreciated form of Renaissance food and remains so in certain circles today in Italy.

11. For an important discussion of Renaissance individualism that stresses the importance of an internal dimension of the same in the Renaissance, see Martin, *Myths of Individualism*, pp. 17–19, 46–48, 97–98.

12. Ruggiero, *Binding Passions*, see esp. chaps. 3 and 4.

13. Ibid. One remembers as well the story of Martin Guerre, who in another place and social context but in much the same time frame failed in his marital duties and blamed his failure on witchcraft as well. His failure also was widely discussed in his community and became an important part of his community's consensus about his identity. Davis, *Return of Martin Guerre*. Even San Bernardino complained about such fears, noting that people often attempted to avoid being made impotent by enemies by initiating sexual intercourse before the contract of marriage was made public to avoid "spells and enchantments." Reported by Gentilcore, *From Bishop to Witch*, p. 217; he also documents the persistence of such fears in the south of Italy, pp. 215–17.

14. Archivio di Stato, Venice (hereafter cited as ASV), Sant'Uffizio (hereafter cited as S. Uffizio), busta 62, Case of Fra Gabriele Garofolo, 11 August 1588, unfoliated. Moreover, before using this cure to help the bound, he made it clear that he had gotten the approval of his superior, the prior of the Augustinian monastery of the city, who had reassured him that this was "not a superstition" but a useful cure for a serious problem.

15. Ferraro in *Marriage Wars in Late Renaissance Venice* provides a number of fascinating examples of how this theological position played out before the Patriarchal Court of Venice; see especially the chapter "Bedtime Stories," pp. 69–103.

16. As I have argued elsewhere, family was a crucial measure of sex in the Renaissance: it disciplined, organized, and ultimately sanctioned sex. Certainly the family's prerogatives in this area were reinforced by a wide range of other Renaissance players—including but not limited to government, the church, local religious organizations, neighbors—as well as disciplining discourses such as those revolving around honor, *virtù*, tradition, and morality/sin. But even in this very broadly sketched picture the central discourse of licit sex was dominated by family and marriage, whether it was articulated by church, government, or intellectuals. See my *Boundaries of Eros* and "Marriage, Love, Sex, and Renaissance Civic Morality," pp. 10–30.

17. Originally from *zita* or *cita* and meaning a female child but applied to an adult woman who in her asexuality was perceived as childlike in her identity.

18. And a woman who transgressed her placement in those areas sexually threatened identity at the most basic level—threatening to give her husband a bastard or, if unmarried, transform herself from an important piece in a family's strategy of alliance and

honor into a dishonored and dishonoring stain on both her natal and marital families. In the case of illegitimate children this was especially true when one recalls that in the Renaissance view of sex the male seed was widely believed to provide the form of a child while the female was held to contribute merely the matter. Thus, for women, rather than a largely nonexistent concomitant of a social system of Alliance, Renaissance sex was the very heart of that system and a crucial measure of their identity and honor, as I have argued in *Binding Passions*, especially in the discussions of Andriana Savorgnan (chap. 1, pp. 24–56) and Elena Cumano (chap. 2, pp.57–87). Suggestively, a woman's sexual identity was virtually always also "heterosexual." Still, there were areas of potential ambiguity, and as a result a small but significant space in the discourse of the time was given to the sexual dangers of widows and nuns, and a considerably larger space was carved out for the dangers of adulterous wives and prostitutes. But significantly, a wife, nun, or bride-to-be who accepted her role as such was literally correctly embedded in a system not only of Alliance but of sexual identity which ensured the correct order of Renaissance society.

19. For example, in Venice when Vicenzo Capello was made commander of a Venetian fleet, he was labeled by detractors "a *zovene* of 43 years," and similar concerns were raised a few years later when Girolamo Pesaro was elected captain of Padua at the same age. For this and a discussion of the Venetian suspicion of *giovani* in governmental office, see Finlay, *Politics in Renaissance Venice*, pp. 131–41; specific examples are on p. 132. For a more general discussion of age distinctions and gender in fifteenth-century Venice, see Chojnacki, "Measuring Adulthood: Adolescence and Gender," in his *Women and Men in Renaissance Venice*, pp. 185–205 and esp. pp. 193–95; this article originally appeared in a slightly different form as "Measuring Adulthood: Adolescence and Gender in Renaissance Venice" in the *Journal of Family History*. While Chojnacki suggests that the marriage break for women might be somewhat softened by practice and cites other important political signs of approaching maturity for noble males, he agrees with my earlier findings that marriage "completed the passage to adulthood" for men and provides statistics that show that average marriage ages for noble males moved into the thirties after the 1430s in Venice. In other cities old age for political participation may have been less significant, but adulthood was not reached for the upper classes until the late twenties or early thirties, and marriage was usually associated with that transition. For Florence, see Herlihy and Klapisch-Zuber, *Tuscans and Their Families*, esp. pp. 86–88. For a discussion of similar issues from the perspective of Renaissance theater, see Giannetti, "When Male Characters Pass as Women." For a legal perspective on adulthood in Florence, see the important work of Thomas Kuehn, especially his *Emancipation in Late Medieval Florence*. For a general overview, see Eisenbichler, *Premodern Teenager*, and the two volumes edited by Levi and Schmitt, *History of Young People*, vol. 1, *Ancient and Medieval Rites of Passage*, and vol. 2, *Stormy Evolution to Modern Times*.

20. James C. Grubb in his *Provincial Families of the Renaissance* notes a considerably shorter range of *gioventù* in the more provincial towns of Verona and Padua, which may mark a significant distinction between more provincial towns and larger, more cosmopolitan cities like Venice and Florence. For his distinction based on age of marriage, see pp. 4–6 and table 1, p. 221. Given, however, that the sample from which Grubb draws these

figures is rather small and from a more heterogeneous social pool, the distinction may not be as great between provincial and major cities as his data seem to suggest. This is especially the case when one considers that artisanal and lower-class women often married at a later age and men in those social categories often married earlier. As statistically these social groups were larger, presumably they would skew the figures, producing results much like those reported by Grubb. Similar figures are reported for rural Tuscany by Herlihy and Klapisch-Zuber in *Tuscans and Their Families,* p. 87. For figures that reflect a specifically noble/upper-class practice in Venice, see Chojnacki, "Measuring Adulthood," in his *Women and Men in Renaissance Venice,* p. 195, table 11.

21. A codpiece (or *braghetta,* as it was called in Italian) of one of the sons of Cosimo I de' Medici from 1562, conserved at the Pitti Palace in Florence, was described recently as follows: "The front closes with a velvet cod-piece, made like a folded pouch, decorated with couched gold cord and cut to reveal the crimson satin lining which pads it out. The cod-piece measures 20.6 cm ($8\frac{1}{2}$ inches) over the curve from the top to the base," quoted in Arnold, *Patterns of Fashion,* pp. 53–54. See also for this fashion Simons, "Alert and Erect," and Eisenbichler, "Bronzino's Portrait of Guidobaldo II Della Rovere." See also the more general article by Persels, "Bragueta Humanistica, or Humanism's Codpiece."

22. These were crucial public moments of evaluation of status which turned on gender, social position, and sexual identity, but not solely, as men ideally were to leave their *giovanili* passions and pursuits behind with marriage, as we shall see. Still, it seems highly likely that they did not have to literally become what their social position required them to be but merely meet the requirements of appearances for the sake of maintaining the correct consensus reality for the groups in which they moved. For a broader review of the literature, especially the prescriptive literature, see now Finucci, *Manly Masquerade.*

23. See Rocke, *Forbidden Friendships.*

24. They were not burned alive—the law had recently been mitigated in response to complaints about its brutality; instead they were decapitated between the Columns of Justice and then their remains burned. For a brief description of this case, see Ruggiero, *Boundaries of Eros,* pp. 121–22, and for a more general discussion of sodomy, pp. 109–68. For a more recent study that also covers a later period, see Davidson, "Sodomy in Early Modern Venice."

25. This loss of beauty—a penalty associated normally with women—seems to imply that the penalty was aimed at making him less attractive as a passive partner.

26. For a suggestive reading of the comedy from a Mantuan perspective, see Shemek, "Aretino's *Marescalco.*" Aretino moved to Venice in 1526 after the death of his protector, Giovanni delle Bande Nere. *Il marescalco* was completed there in the late 1520s and published in 1533. For a brief introduction to the comedy, see Giannetti and Ruggiero, *Five Comedies,* pp. xi–xlii, esp. xv–xvi and xxxvii–xxxix; all texts from *Il marescalco* are taken from this translation, pp. 117–204.

27. Although the term is often translated as "nurse," a *balia* was actually the woman who breast-fed and brought up a child in Renaissance Italy—the modern term might be *wet nurse.* But even that term is somewhat misleading, as the relationship between the *balia* and the person she nursed was often a long-term one, creating a special bond that lasted into adulthood, as is the case in this comedy. In fact, the *balia* was a regular char-

acter in Renaissance comedies, often playing the affectionate, protective role that in other cultures is usually associated with a child's mother. Indeed, shortly after her initial appearance in the comedy the Balia refers to the Marescalco as "my little son." From this perspective the Balia might be seen as representing the consensus reality evaluation of the Marescalco's sexual practices by a member of his broader family. *Il marescalco*, in Giannetti and Ruggiero, *Five Comedies*, p. 128. For a more extended discussion of this, see Klapisch-Zuber, "Blood Parents and Milk Parents."

28. *Il marescalco*. in Giannetti and Ruggiero, *Five Comedies*, p. 129.

29. Ibid., p. 130. Clearly here the Balia is stressing a widely shared ideal that it was time to change his sexual practices and identity—to move from chasing after youthful pleasures to marrying the bride offered by the Duke and settling down to continue the family line. It is suggestive to note here that in this world of social evaluation of sexual identity via sexual practices the modern distinction between practice and identity tends to collapse. In the end, practices are what provide the raw material for forming consensus realities about identity.

30. Ibid.

31. Ibid.

32. Ibid., p. 131.

33. Ibid., p. 134.

34. Ibid., p. 131.

35. Ibid., p. 132.

36. Ibid., p. 124. Messer Jacopo opens the scene greeting the Marescalco amicably: "I always find you here with your young sweetheart" (Sempre ti trovo in conclavo col tuo pivo). As the couple had been arguing, the Marescalco replies rather irately, "May God punish him." But he made no attempt to deny that his boy, Giannicco, was his *pivo*, that is, his passive sexual partner. *Pivo* literally means "flute."

37. Ibid., p. 129.

38. Ibid.

39. Ibid., p. 151. In the Italian original what is translated here as "hen" is actually a *civetta*, an owl. Once again this term had a double sexual meaning, connoting a coquettish young woman who attracts men.

40. It should be noted that this is not classical pederasty, for in this Renaissance ideal the younger partner is a willing sexual participant taking pleasure from the relationship as well as pride in his own beauty; the older male is not an adult but an older youth—in the case of the Marescalco, on the cusp of adulthood. Education and politics are not stressed; in fact, the latter is downplayed, if not feared, while the former tends to be limited to an association with clerics and tutors. More important, perhaps, it is not classical pederasty because it was fully incorporated in a quite different Renaissance sexual world.

41. *Il marescalco*, in Giannetti and Ruggiero, *Five Comedies*, p. 193. For a general overview of such "miraculous" transformations in Italian Renaissance theater, see Giannetti, "When Male Characters Pass as Women."

42. Ibid., pp. 198–201.

43. Ibid., p. 200. The Latin reads, "In the beginning God created heaven and earth. Shortly thereafter . . . fishes for the water, and to the thrushes, among birds, and to rab-

bits, among four-legged creatures, went first glory. . . . [During the Renaissance, rabbits were associated with males who were attracted sexually to males.] Later, in his own image . . . after which . . . that is . . . without . . . until . . . above all . . . lions and dragons . . . solely . . . and that is."

44. Ibid., p. 201.

45. Ibid., p. 202.

46. Ibid.

47. Perhaps only the Balia is truly disappointed by the truth, and even she, responding to the Marescalco's pleasure, comments grudgingly, "He's in seventh heaven, the big rogue [*rubaldone*] isn't he," and concludes, "You can never pull the frog from his mud," perhaps her final disapproving nod at the Marescalco's sexual preferences. But the reversal of the comedy is a laughing one, and a sympathetic friend of the Marescalco's returns the last line of the scene to that emotion, remarking gaily to his friend, "You are not complaining now Marescalco!" Ibid.

Chapter 2 • *Playing with the Devil*

1. Grazzini (Il Lasca), *Le cene*. This opening scene, briefly summarized here, can be found on pp. 47–50.

2. This is not to deny the importance of politics and power for the history of sex and gender; certainly both are crucial in any consideration of these issues in the Renaissance, as I hope my own studies have helped to demonstrate. The point is merely that both sex and gender are deeply intertwined with a broader range of cultural factors in the Renaissance which also warrant study. For a discussion of the need to look more closely at pleasure in history and literature without eschewing politics and power, as I am suggesting here, see Eagleton, *Literary Theory*, pp. 191–93, 202.

3. Huizinga, *Homo Ludens*. The definition also includes the rather more culturally specific: "It promotes the formation of social groupings which tend to surround themselves with secrecy and to stress their difference from the common world by disguise or other means" (p. 13).

4. "If we stick to the formal and functional characteristics of play as summed up earlier it is evident that few of them are really illustrative of the sexual act. . . . None of these functions can be called play in the strict sense. . . . Caresses as such do not bear the character of play, though they may do on occasion; but it would be erroneous to incorporate the sexual act itself, as love-play in the play category." Ibid., p. 43.

5. Yet to be fair to Huizinga, much has changed since 1944 both in the writing of history and in the sexual customs of Western society. With or without a sexual revolution; effective, easily available birth control; a more open discussion of sex in the context of pleasure and play for both women and men; and an information revolution—these are only the most obvious factors that have made it possible to see sex in a decidedly different light as far as play is concerned. Clearly making reproduction an optional component of sex with readily available birth control has allowed more room for other considerations, such as play, to come to the fore. But there is, of course, a warning as well in this realization of the distance that separates contemporary society from Huizinga and his

classic work; for just as he may have been blinded by his time and place not to see at least some sex as a form of play, we may be dangerously emboldened to find this combination in the past given our own values and perceptions.

6. The work of Laura Giannetti has been most influential for me on this topic; see "I discorsi del gioco nella commedia rinascimentale italiana"; "On the Deceptions of the *Deceived*"; "*Feminae ludentes* nella commedia rinascimentale italiana"; and her book in progress "For Play: An Analysis of the Ludic Worlds and Strategies of Italian Renaissance Comedy."

7. Bargagli, *Dialogo de'giuochi che nelle vegghie sanese si usano di fare*; but see also from the period Ringhieri, *Cento giuochi liberali, et di ingegno*. Bargagli's book, written by a member of Siena's well-known Academy of the Intronati, clearly attempted to give a higher tone to his collection of 130 games. George W. McClure in a recent study concludes that Bargagli's collection of games "reflects the efforts of his fun-loving academy to devise a better cut of games (than those 'base and vile' ones of their youth)." McClure, *Culture of Profession*, p. 52, and for a more extended discussion of Bargagli and other works on games in the period, see pp. 51–66. For all the idealization of more aristocratic forms of gaming and play, needless to say, even aristocrats could still be attracted to the rough-and-tumble world of more "popular" games. Attraction, after all, is regularly the bedfellow of proscription. A good example of this is provided by Robert Davis's fascinating study of the battles of the fists in early modern Venice, *War of the Fists*. Suggestively, however, Davis notes that Venetian aristocrats preferred to remain spectators and patrons of the violence he describes, leaving the common fisticuffs to lower-class heroes.

8. From this perspective it might be suggested that virtually all the Renaissance collections of novelle would qualify as *giochi* and were perhaps intended to be viewed in this light. For Bargagli verbal games had three essential components: the proposal of a topic for consideration, the agonistic discussion or narration of that topic, and a judgment of that narration or discussion. Normally in the novella tradition the "frame" story provided the first and last of these components, with the narrative or discussion providing the central aspect of the play/game. In this light the repetitive brief comments, smiles, and occasional mild recriminations provided by the listeners in frame stories after the main narrative are the necessary evaluations of a society that saw such storytelling as not simply storytelling but also as an agon that turned on the demonstration of wit, wisdom, and verbal virtuosity.

9. This conversation is found in book II, chapter 3. Federico makes explicit his concerns about maintaining status distinctions when he states, "and the gentleman should be virtually certain that he will win or not become involved, because it would be too incorrect, too ugly, and too lacking in dignity to see a gentleman (*gentilomo*) lose to a peasant (*villano*) and especially in wrestling." Castiglione, *Il libro del cortegiano*, 1:111–12 (II:3.14). The closely related issues of play, correct courtly behavior, and *virtù* are discussed more fully in Chapter 6.

10. This clearly was another consensus reality that was extremely important for Renaissance society and which could appear quite different from the perspective of different groups in society, even if virtually all groups agreed that some sort of hierarchy was natural and a given of social life; in other words, such distinctions were seen as real and

ultimately not a matter of opinion or mere power. Although it might seem to be a controversial claim, it is worth considering that many of the protoencyclopedic works of the period had a similar program of separation and distinction in the name of classification. Dress was divided into socially appropriate categories; professions were analyzed to reveal the appropriateness of social divisions and the place of various *arti* within the social hierarchy; manners were analyzed to discriminate social levels. While none of these distinctions were particularly new, the drive to clarify distinctions and categorize them more aggressively and more systematically seems to have accelerated from the middle of the fifteenth century through the sixteenth. And here in the context of games and play, of course, we find play and pleasure returning us to power; see note 2 above.

11. "Honesty" (*onestà*) was a term with a strong social labeling context in the Renaissance. Often it was a term that had less to do with truth than with social correctness and status, and that was especially true when the term was used to describe games or the behavior of those claiming a certain status.

12. Elias, *Civilizing Process,* vol. 1, *History of Manners,* first published in German in 1939. The term *process* should be underlined, as Elias did not see this "civilizing" as a progress, as is at times mistakenly assumed. Simply put, in his eyes civilization was not a progress, as the history of the twentieth century made abundantly clear; rather, it was a process that was concerned with the disciplining (if we borrow the term from Foucault and the sixteenth century, when *disciplina* was another key term) of the body and its practices. From this perspective what typifies the modern might be seen as disciplined bodies in disciplined spaces and times that are perceived as controlled by the state (following Elias) or by the disciplines (following Foucault). Perhaps, however, it might be argued that both Elias and Foucault were overinfluenced by the topics they studied so perceptively and that neither the state nor the disciplines are as key as they believed in what should probably be considered a more general cultural-social process of internalization of much older concepts of discipline and self-control. For this, see Chapter 6.

13. Garzoni (da Bagnacavallo), *La piazza universale di tutte le professioni del mondo,* p. 903; italics mine. This chapter (pp. 903–910) begins with a review of ancient theories of play and games plus examples (pp. 903–8), followed by a brief discussion of "our modern games," which are divided into two categories—those for youths and those for adults; those for adults are in turn divided into those for *veglie* (evening gatherings), those for taverns, card games, and games played with balls (pp. 908–9). The chapter concludes with a brief discussion of the games that Bargagli collected in his *Dialogo de'giuochi che nella vegghie sanese si usano di fare* (pp. 909–10). For an extended discussion of Garzoni's work, see McClure, *Culture of Profession,* pp. 70–140.

14. This vision from prescriptive literature in many ways is reflected in Foucault's vision of Alliance discussed in Chapter 1, not surprisingly, for his analysis was based primarily upon prescriptive literature and the work of others who had studied Renaissance sex from the perspective of prescriptive literature; for a similar analysis more closely attuned to the complexities of the Italian Renaissance, see my "Marriage, Love, Sex, and Renaissance Civic Morality."

15. One also finds reference to sex as play in the rather atypical sixteenth-century Venetian comedy *La venexiana* (*The Venetian Comedy*). Its prologue promises: "Today

you will come to understand this clearly, O spectators, when you hear of the boundless love that a fellow noblewoman of yours felt for a foreign youth. And you will hear of her boldness and her determination to have him, and then the happy play and pleasure [*il gioco e il gaudio*] that she enjoyed with him." *La venexiana*, in Giannetti and Ruggiero, *Five Comedies*, p. 286. The promise is kept with several playful scenes that are surprisingly explicit even in the context of sixteenth-century comedies; for more on this, see the brief discussion below.

16. Renaissance literary texts did tend to associate pleasurable sex with play and playful sex with pleasure, which might seem to support this concern. But significantly these texts were not limited to classical examples and were often set in otherwise carefully contextualized contemporary settings.

17. For a more complete discussion of these issues, see Muir and Ruggiero, *History from Crime*, esp. pp. vii–xviii and 226–36.

18. Two examples: (1) a law of 1460 taken from a general summary of the laws on prostitution provides a clear association of prostitution and play: "Moreover it is ordained that no one should dare or presume to play [*ludere*] nor organize any games [*ludi*] where money is wagered with any prostitute or whore [*meretrice vel peccatrice*]," ASV, Collegio, Notatorio, 1460–67, fol. 10r; (2) a part of the complaint to the Sant'Uffizio against the famous courtesan Veronica Franco by Ridolfo Vannitelli from 1580: "Moreover she [Veronica] holds gatherings with prohibited games [*giuochi prohibiti*], that is card games . . . and she knows how to do many evil things with every type of game [*giuochi*]," ASV, S. Uffizio, busta 46, Veronica Franco, October 1580, unfoliated.

19. A good example of such concerns is provided by a *parte* passed by the Ten in 1455 which associated age mixing in the homes of pastry cooks, games (*ludi*), and sodomy: "As this council has become aware that in the homes of many pastry cooks in this our city, many youths and others of diverse ages and conditions come together both during the day and at night and there they hold games [*ludi*] and drinking fests and commit many dishonesties and much sodomy. . . . Therefore it is ruled that . . . from now on no pastry cooks may accept in his house anyone of any condition or age either during the day or at night for playing games [*tenendo ludos*] or drinking or any other dishonest activity"; ASV, Consiglio dei Dieci, Deliberazioni Misti, reg. 15, fol. 80r, 13 September 1455. Another interesting example is found in a *parte* passed by the Ten in 1512 which associated age mixing, ball games (*ludi ad ballam parvam*) in private places, and the evil life of youths: "For some time it has become the [evil] custom of youths . . . that in certain places in this city . . . certain private schools or gatherings places have been built to play small ball [*a ludendo ad ballam parvam*]; therefore it is ruled by this council . . . that such [private] schools and gatherings places are absolutely prohibited and anyone who keeps such places must immediately destroy them and they may not construct or have such places in any part of this city or any vacant building, but only in open spaces or public places [*locis publicis*]"; ASV, Consiglio dei Dieci, Deliberazationi Misti, reg. 35, fol. 93v, 28 September 1512.

20. What this meant for elite illicit sex in an increasingly aristocratic society, in which for the upper classes certain forms of play were seen as confirming status, could well be the subject for another essay. Suffice it to say here that aristocrats played on with courte-

sans, even as for the lower classes their play with common prostitutes was being increasingly frowned upon as illicit and restricted.

21. ASV, Avogadori di Comun, Raspe, reg. 3655, fol. 132v.

22. Ibid.

23. Ibid. Once again it might be noted that the concept of consensus reality fits well here: the vision that with prostitution a male was merely renting a woman's body was a fiction difficult to maintain given the complex issues involved, but it was stoutly maintained by many groups in society nonetheless and was no less "real" for its fictitious nature. For a more complete discussion of this case, see my *Boundaries of Eros,* pp. 33–35.

24. *La venexiana,* in Giannetti and Ruggiero, *Five Comedies,* p. 305. There is also a fascinating scene of sexual play in bed between Angela and her servant Nena at the end of act 1, scene 3 (pp. 290–92) and another between Angela and Giulio, act 3, scene 2 (pp. 304–9).

25. Ibid., p. 305. Although this give-and-take may seem rather overblown and stilted to modern eyes, in many ways it is a fine example of the type of witty and courteous aristocratic conversation that was called for at the end of the second book of Castiglione's *Book of the Courtier.*

26. Boccaccio, *Decameron,* pp. 265–66.

27. Ibid., p. 266.

28. Ibid.

29. Ibid.

30. Ibid., p. 267.

31. Ibid.

32. Ibid., p. 268.

33. Ibid.; italics mine.

34. Ibid.; italics mine.

35. For a brief overview of the literature on the Venetian Holy Office, see Chapter 3, n. 14. The significant gap in time between these narratives, along with the fact that one was constructed for imaginative purposes and one apparently at least for judicial purposes, makes a close comparison impossible, but as an exercise in thinking outside the normal disciplinary boundaries of history and literary criticism, comparing the narratives offers interesting possibilities, as I hope will become clear below, especially when one is more interested in thinking with history than arguing the truth of the past. As far as Suor Mansueta's case was concerned, it was not actually a trial before the Holy Office in a formal sense; rather, it was officially an investigation of her claims of sexual intercourse with the Devil. Although such investigations regularly developed into formal trials, in this case it seems that charges were never formulated, and the Holy Office eventually decided that exorcism was the correct response to her claims.

36. A good overview of the literature and the problems involved can be found in Romeo, *Inquisitori, esorcisti e streghe nell'Italia della Controriforma.* But see also the study by Stephens, *Demon Lovers.* Both works offer a rich bibliography on the subject—as might be expected, Stephens from a more literary perspective, Romeo from a more archival one, although both share a perspective that privileges prescriptive texts over prac-

tice. Carlo Ginzburg's imaginative study of the origins of witchcraft provides an introduction to some of the historical traditions that prefigured Renaissance concerns with sexual intercourse with the Devil: Ginzburg, *Storia notturna*. For a brief rethinking of the sexual dimensions of Renaissance witchcraft which attempts to balance everyday practice with prescriptive literature, see also my "Witchcraft and Magic," pp. 475–90.

37. For a rich and revealing discussion of the forced nature of the monachization of young women in sixteenth- and seventeenth-century Venice and the nature of convent life there in general, see Sperling, *Convents and the Body Politic in Late Renaissance Venice*, esp. pp. 18–71; for an earlier and slightly less official view, see my *Boundaries of Eros*, pp. 70–88, which examines the sexual climate of fourteenth- and fifteenth-century Venetian convents.

38. ASV, S. Uffizio, busta 38, fol. 3r. A large portion of this case was published by Marisa Milani, who discusses the case briefly from a modern perspective, seeing Suor Mansueta as essentially a hysterical woman troubled by erotic fantasies induced by confinement in a convent against her wishes. While such a modern reading may have an element of truth to it, it ignores a number of other possible modern readings (e.g., that Mansueta was just pushing a lie that she thought would result in her being banished from the convent or which would gain her attention), and, more important, it misses much of the sixteenth-century nuance and complexity of the case. Needless to say, my reading, focusing as it does on Suor Mansueta's playing with the Devil, cannot do full justice to her complexity, either. Milani, "L'ossessione secolare di Suor Mansueta." pp. 129–52.

39. ASV, S. Uffizio, busta 38, fol. 3r. For a similar prayer and offer to the Devil, see the case of Andrea Meri heard by the Holy Office of Venice in 1590 and discussed in Ruggiero, *Binding Passions*, pp. 88–90.

40. ASV, S. Uffizio, busta 38, fol. 3r.

41. Ibid.; italics mine.

42. A particularly good example of this can be found in the deposition of Gostanza ("donna già di un certo Francesco di Vernia") before the inquisitor of Florence taken in San Miniato on 19 November 1594. "Asked: 'Explain if this charged person had the same pleasure in similar affairs with the devil [*il demonio*], having sexual relations with him, as she had with her husband.' [She responded:] 'I was young and it seemed to me that I had the same pleasure with the devil that I had with my husband, but because the devil caressed me more than my husband and because it seemed to me that really I had greater pleasure in intercourse with the devil than my husband because he gave me more caresses and fooled around more and made things more exciting [*più forcche et baie intorno*]. . . . Those caresses were that he embraced me, he kissed me, he touched me in all the ways [of sexual pleasure], he mounted me, he touched my breast, and in sum he touched me all over and it seemed to me that I had such delight and pleasure that it seemed to me that I was at a great party where he laughed and played [*cicalava*] with me." Published in Cardini, *Gostanza, la strega di San Miniato*, pp. 173–77.

43. ASV, S. Uffizio, busta 37, fol. 3r.

44. Peter Burke provided an overview of this vision in *Popular Culture in Early Modern Europe*, pp. 205–86; for a more aggressive reading, see the pioneering work of Robert

Muchembled, especially his *Culture populaire et culture des èlites dans la France Moderne.* I use the term *weekend* here to refer to the varying lengths of time that separate work-weeks in modern societies.

45. For sex crimes that were perceived as victimizing God, see Ruggiero, *Boundaries of Eros,* chap. 4, "Sex Crimes against God," pp. 70–88 and esp. pp. 72–84 for nuns as brides of Christ.

46. ASV, S. Uffizio, busta 37, fol. 3r.

47. Boccaccio, *Decameron,* p. 270. Dioneo laughingly relates that Alibech innocently confessed that she had served God by putting the Devil back in hell to the women who were preparing her for marriage after she returned to Gafsa. When they understood from her gestures what that service entailed, the phrase quickly became popular and spread rapidly from city to city, and Dioneo points out that "the said way of speaking passed over the sea and is still used here [in Florence] today."

48. Ibid., p. 269.

49. Ibid. That male failure to perform rather than pregnancy was the problem that disrupted their happy play, Valeria Finucci has suggested, is another reflection of the fact that the tale is written from a male perspective.

50. Ibid., p. 268.

51. Ibid.

52. Ibid., p. 270.

53. With this suggestion, however, I do not want to minimize the male-centered phallic orientation of Boccaccio's vision of sex or his often negative stereotypes of female desire and ways of behaving. Given the period, it would be hard to expect much else of him. Yet in the context of the fourteenth century, for all his misogyny, in the *Decameron* at least he seems to often demonstrate a deeper sympathy for and awareness of the realities of a woman's existence than most of his male contemporaries.

54. And, in fact, it has continued to be regularly cut up through the present; suggestively, it has recently been revealed that even the "transgressive" Italian poet, writer, and filmmaker Pier Paolo Pasolini cut and destroyed the prints of his version of the tale originally filmed for his noted 1971 cinematic version of the *Decameron.*

55. ASV, S. Uffizio, busta 38, unfoliated in this section.

56. This observation and disciplining of the body in a way parallels the observation and disciplining of the courtier's body which was stressed by virtually all the discussants in Castiglione's *The Book of the Courtier;* see the discussion of this in Chapter 6. The signs of the body were crucial for evaluating identity and forming a consensus reality about who one is—thus, the body had to be disciplined and closely watched whether one was reforming a nun or forming a perfect courtier.

57. It would be interesting to speculate how often ultimate battles have been fought out in the Western tradition over women's bodies and pleasures, ranging from Eve (and perhaps Alibech) or Helen of Troy up through modern conflicts about birth control and abortion. But this brief essay is not the place to take up these issues.

58. ASV, S. Uffizio, busta 38, unfoliated; italics mine.

59. Ibid.; italics mine.

60. Ibid.

61. Ibid; italics mine. I have attempted to capture in my translation the scribe's slid-ing sense of Suor Mansueta's body: sometimes it is an impersonal body—"it"; sometimes it seems to be masculine in the power of the spirit that has captured it—"he"; sometimes it is the feminine body of Mansueta—"she"; but often it seems to be all three at once.

62. Ibid.

Chapter 3 • The Abbot's Concubine

An earlier version of this chapter was published as "The Abbot's Concubine: Lies, Lit-erature and Power at the End of the Renaissance" in Kittell and Madden, *Medieval and Renaissance Venice.*

1. Andrieni. *Le bravure del Capitano Spavento,* p. 117v.

2. Ibid., pp. 117v–118r.

3. Ibid., p. 12v.

4. Actually Captain Fear found Death a particularly attractive mistress, explaining: "Ah Death she is a good piece of work if you know how to handle her: she's a piece to not leave for money, she gets right to it and does not make one wait for her like some women little experienced in the profession who take forever to finish." Ibid., p. 17v.

5. Ibid., p. 118r. Captain Fear's fearful fecundity is noteworthy throughout his brag-ging accounts of his exploits. Significantly, what counted most in his sex seemed to be his reproductive capacity rather than his sexual exploits or conquests, contrary to what one might expect from a late Renaissance rake. Was this because his humor stressed a God-like power and thus creative and destructive deeds rather than more mundane Casanova-like qualities?

6. The Italian term *nature* used in this passage and translated as "natures" has a telling double sense, meaning both nature and female genitals. In light of the earlier claim that a woman's identity in the Renaissance always had a strong sexual labeling com-ponent, it is interesting that the Italian word *natura* could mean nature, female genitals, or a woman's nature or identity all at the same time. Ibid., p. 118v.

7. Ibid.

8. In many ways characters in fiction may provide a better measure of how a partic-ular society sees identity, as characters in fiction, especially on the stage, must establish their identity for an audience quickly and effectively. Misperceptions at that level can quickly derail a performance, and that is especially true in comedy, where an audience had to be able to quickly read what was to be taken seriously in a character and what not. Captain Fear obviously was a character built upon earlier stereotypes and clearly was played for humorous effect, but it is exactly those stereotypes and that humor that are telling for Renaissance concepts of self and identity. Perhaps the most accessible account of this famous troop and its wanderings is provided in the brief biography of Isabella An-drieni, wife of Francesco, published by de'Angelis, *La divina Isabella,* pp. 9–62. At the moment of Abbot Ruis's complaints about his concubine, the company, already well known, was probably in France or on the way there to play for the king. But in the later 1570s they would be back in Italy, using Padua as their base and performing often in Venice and the Veneto.

9. Di Simplicio, "Le Perpetue." For a more developed study of concubinage in sixteenth- and seventeenth-century Venice, see Byars, "Concubines and Concubinage in Early Modern Venice."

10. A particularly complex and revealing example of such self-presentation and self-negotiation can be found in the tale of Elena Cumano's attempt to reclaim her lost husband/lover and her reputation at the end of the sixteenth century; see my "'More Dear to Me Than Life Itself.'"

11. See Ruggiero, *Binding Passions.*

12. The abbot ruled over an ancient Benedictine establishment that no longer had monks; his position seems to have been basically a revenue-producing sinecure. Ruis actually had previously been a merchant in Venice, a place he still regularly frequented, and had had a rather checkered past there. He had also been married and widowed, and his appointment as abbot apparently had more to do with family connections than any spiritual commitment. Sumaga, in turn, was described in a general survey of Friuli in 1548 as follows: "Sumaga is a monastic town on the other side of the Tagliamento river between Sesto and Portuguaro toward Ponente and twenty-six miles from Udine.... One finds there 164 useful inhabitants and 442 not useful." In 1557 the population was reported to have dropped to 494. ASV, Collegio, Relazioni Ambasciatori, Rettori ed Altre Cariche, busta 41, unfoliated.

13. The literature on the Venetian Holy Office is large and growing rapidly. For an excellent discussion of its organization and operation, see Pullan, *Jews of Europe and the Inquisition of Venice,* pp. 3–142. Paul Grendler has also published several important works that draw heavily on documents from the Holy Office and provide a careful analysis of it as an institution, especially his *Roman Inquisition and the Venetian Press.* Perhaps the institution has been most studied, as one might expect, from the perspective of how it dealt with heresy; for this, see Martin, *Venice's Hidden Enemies,* which provides a significant overview and a thorough review of previous scholarship. Finally, for an important overview of its creation, relationship with the Roman Inquisition, and early activities in Venice and its territories, see Del Col, "Organizzazione, composizione e giurisdizione." For examples of other cases handled by the Holy Office in the countryside, see my *Binding Passions,* chaps. 2 and 4.

14. ASV, S. Uffizio, busta 35, testimony of Alessandro Ruis, 18 December 1573, fol. 4r.

15. Ibid., fol. 4r–v.

16. The extensive use of holy oil for love magic is discussed in detail in my *Binding Passions.* Even the use of the words of the consecration of the host was frequently reported in Venice and the Veneto, although seldom so explicitly in the Boccaccio-esque manner here implied, which conjures up images of Rustico and Alibech's repeated experiments with the "resurrection of the flesh" in the *Decameron* discussed in Chapter 2.

17. ASV, S. Uffizio, busta 35, Alesandro Ruis, fol. 4v.

18. Ibid. In the margin by this text the scribe added in Latin, "The beginning of the case," a clarification that seems hardly necessary!

19. Ibid., fols. 4v–5r.

20. Ibid., fol. 5r. For women using holy oil to heal, see Ruggiero, "Strange Death of

Margarita Marcellini," and for its use in love magic, *Binding Passions*, pp. 89–129, esp. pp. 94–96 and 120–24.

21. Asked if he thought that perhaps the priest of Morsana had given the holy oil to his servant, Ruis replied, "This was not said to me and if it had been I would not have believed it, because I know and I understand the priest Domenigo Borgana [of Morsana]; he is a good man [*un homo da bene*] and he would not have done it or consented to any similar evil deeds." ASV, S. Uffizio, busta 35, Alesandro Ruis, fol. 5v.

22. Ibid., fol. 7r–v.

23. Ibid., fol. 7v.

24. Ibid., fol. 7r. Note that this means that Lucia had given birth to Cecilia when she was about 16.

25. Ibid., fols. 6v–7r. Again, if we trust Ruis's memory, Cecilia returned to live with him at 15.

26. Ibid., testimony of Domenigo Borgana, 18 December 1573, fol. 9v. Note that by Domenigo's estimate of the couple being together about fourteen years, if Ruis's claim that she was then 32 is correct, the relationship would have started when Cecilia was 18, not 15. Tellingly, no one was particularly scandalized by either age; young women in their mid-teens were ready to embark on careers as prostitutes and concubines in the eyes of late Renaissance society.

27. Ibid., testimony of Lucia, 24 December 1573, fol. 10v; italics mine. Lucia's colorful language is interesting for its borrowing from the world of love magic to express the emotions and animosities that Cecilia's abandonment of the abbot had aroused in him. His rage is coupled with his being "hammered"—something suggested as well by other witnesses who referred to him suffering greatly the loss of his mistress—and his blackmail attempt is also described as a "hammer." A "hammer" (*martello*) was a form of magic that punished a victim physically and psychologically until he or she gave in to the desires of the person employing the magic. The term was also used at times to metaphorically describe the emotional travails of one suffering from jealousy, which also might fit well in this case.

28. Ibid.

29. Ibid., testimony of Cecilia, 1 January 1574, fols. 11v–12r.

30. Ibid., fol. 12v.

31. Ibid.

Chapter 4 • Brunelleschi's First Masterpiece, or Mean Streets, Familiar Streets, Masculine Spaces, and Identity in Renaissance Florence

This chapter was published in an earlier form as "Mean Streets, Familiar Streets, or The Fat Woodcarver and the Masculine Spaces of Florence" in Crum and Paoletti, *Renaissance Florence.*

1. Quoted in Trexler, "La prostitution florentine," 988–89. Given the dedication of this work to Cosimo de' Medici, it is interesting to note that it seems that its author, Panormita, has placed this whorehouse on the east side of the Mercato along the axis that runs

from just to the west of the Baptistery following Via della Macciana and eventually becoming Calimala. If that is the case, the visitor would pass through two warrenlike blocks of buildings dominated by Medici palaces and find it lying near the Church of San Tommaso, a church where the Medici had had sole patronage rights from at least the late 1340s and which was their main church until the completion of San Lorenzo in the 1460s. Medici palaces were ubiquitous in the area; thus, in a way, in celebrating this place of masculine pleasure at the heart of Florence, Panormita was celebrating also a place intimately associated with Cosimo and one of the city's most powerful families. I would like to thank John Paoletti for this suggestion and him along with Roger Crum for their thoughtful reading and comments on this chapter.

2. On this, see Martines, *Power and Imagination.* For a suggestive discussion of how one encounters a city, see de Certeau, *Practice of Everyday Life,* esp. pp. 91–130.

3. Which is perhaps just another way of restating Joan Kelly's negative response to her question, Did women have a Renaissance? in her essay "Did Women Have a Renaissance?"

4. A fuller discussion of the regime of *virtù* is provided in Chapter 6. For an interesting look at similar issues from the perspective of artistic representations, see Simons, "Alert and Erect," pp. 163–75. In this chapter I use the term *regime* as a premodern substitute for Foucault's noun *discipline.* A regime is a group of discourses coupled with signs, gestures, and other nonverbal indicators such as the spaces of a city which serves to order, control, and discipline (in the narrow sense of the term) people. From this perspective, the term seems more appropriate for the premodern era than *discipline* because a regime does not have the formal rules, methodology, or practitioners of modern disciplines; nor does it work in the same way—there is a modern discipline of psychology, but there was no formal premodern discipline of prince-ology. I would suggest that there were a number of regimes in the premodern world beyond the obvious political ones which ordered, controlled, and disciplined the lives of people without formally existing as a discipline—one of the most significant of which was the Renaissance regime of *virtù.*

5. Significantly, although the root word was the Latin *vir, virtù* is a feminine noun, *la virtù,* a seeming contradiction that is echoed by the fact that it was such a crucial evaluative term in the Renaissance that even the often quite gender-specific *virtù* of women was closely monitored and controlled, as will become clear in Chapter 6.

6. Martines, *Italian Renaissance Sextet,* pp. 171–241; the translation of the novella is on pp. 171–212, Martines's analysis on pp. 213–41. Given Martines's perceptive analysis and knowledge of Renaissance Florence, much of what follows is indebted to him: at best this chapter uses his original insights and reading as the key to an exploration of the masculine culture and masculine spaces of Florence.

7. Manetti, *Life of Brunelleschi.* This edition also reprints the original Italian. Interestingly, the manuscript of the life begins in the autograph manuscript immediately after the novella about the fat woodcarver and seems a direct continuation of the former; the biography of Brunelleschi opens: "Girolamo [Benevieni], you wish to know who that Filippo was who played the practical joke you admire so much on il Grasso, the true account of which I related to you" (p. 34).

8. Manetti refers to this growth emphasizing the superiority of his account and how

the story had been passed down among some of the most important artists of the fifteenth century, a group he actually lists apparently to stress the artistic ambience of the tale. For the English translation I am following Martines, *Italian Renaissance Sextet,* pp. 171–241; see p. 212 for the list. For the Italian text I have used Manetti, "La novella del Grasso Legnaiuolo."

9. Martines, *Italian Renaissance Sextet,* pp. 172–73.

10. See Martines's social analysis of the group in ibid., pp. 220–23.

11. This ongoing lack of a clear distinction between public and private space in the Renaissance is a significant reason why Bourdeau's suggestive analysis of the impact of public and private spheres on later societies does not work well for Renaissance cities. For an interesting discussion of similar issues, see Martines, "Séduction," pp. 266–69.

12. Martines, *Italian Renaissance Sextet,* p. 172.

13. Ibid.

14. This discourse of male friendship, then, ranged widely and included a host of masculine relationships central to the political and social world of Florence. Included was a spectrum of relationships that swung from the sexual, with both sodomy and the illicit world of prostitution often being organized around male friendship, on to male sociability and everyday support networks, on to work relationships, and to patronage; thus in the masculine world of Renaissance Florence it is not unusual to find a patronage component in friendship, just as it is not unusual to find a sexual one.

15. I am not suggesting here that this *beffa* created a scapegoat that bound together the group. That might seem to be the case, but such a reading is a modern one that misses the nuanced way in which Renaissance men used the *beffa* to discipline their social lives. As will become clear, here the *beffa* is much more a part of a complex *virtù*-honor-shame dynamic; in this interpretation I am largely following Martines. The fascination with the *beffa* in Renaissance novelle, and especially Florentine novelle, is a testament not only to the cleverness that Florentine masculine culture appreciated so much (closely associated with concepts of masculine *virtù*) but also to a powerful social strategy that men used to discipline their relationships. On the *beffa,* see Rochon, *Formes et significations de la "Beffa."*

16. Martines, *Italian Renaissance Sextet,* p. 173. It is interesting to note that at the time this form of the tale was written down Brunelleschi had become one of the heroes of a generation of great artists in Florence, but at the time it supposedly occurred, in 1409, he was merely a promising young craftsman, primarily a goldsmith/sculptor, and actually at what might be seen as a low point in his career, having just failed to win the commission for the Baptistery doors. In fact, as Manetti notes in his biography, during this period Brunelleschi spent most of his time in Rome with his friend Donatello studying antiquities to better equip himself for his ongoing rivalry with Ghiberti. On this, see Manetti, *Life of Brunelleschi,* p. 62. And tellingly, when Manetti later relates Brunelleschi's cunning feat of building the dome for the cathedral—stressing his cleverness and ability to manipulate the officials overseeing the project and tricking his opponents as well—he once again seems emblematic of the regime of *virtù.*

17. On this intimate nature of the city, see Herlihy and Klapisch-Zuber, who estimate the population in 1427 as 37,144 and see population as never much exceeding 40,000 across

the century, in *Tuscans and Their Families*, p. 74, table 3.5. Actually, such numbers overstate the size of the male population that mattered. A large proportion of the urban population was made up of day laborers in the cloth industry who did not really count in the eyes of Brunelleschi, Grasso, and their friends. If we consider the "meaningful" people they would actually be encountering in the shops and streets of their city, we would be hard pressed to reach a total of more than a few thousand men, if that. For this, see p. 126, table 4.6.

18. Rocke, *Forbidden Friendships*, pp. 186–87. Perhaps one of the most remarkable representations of this erotic context of the shop is the painting by Vasari now in the Uffizi which represents an older nude male working in his shop surrounded by nude apprentices, a painting whose fascinating mix of male power, sensuality, and eroticism might be seen as emblematic. It has been suggested that this painting represents Benevenuto Cellini and his workshop; as Cellini was actually prosecuted for a long-term sexual relationship with one of his shop assistants, the erotic context would be yet stronger if this was the case.

19. Martines, *Italian Renaissance Sextet*, p. 175.

20. Ibid., p. 176. In 1409 Donatello was a good friend of Brunelleschi's, in fact, sharing with him both a deep animosity toward Ghiberti and a good deal of time in Rome studying antiquities, as noted earlier. Donatello had just finished his marble David and would work together with Brunelleschi on a failed project for a sculpture for the cathedral in 1412 involving an innovative use of lead sheathing over marble.

21. Ibid. Here I do not mean to suggest that the piazze of Florence were strictly masculine spaces. Clearly women, especially lower-class women, did not have the economic resources to be locked up at home as the ideal of feminine chastity recommended for upper-class women and thus had to frequent these spaces as well. Nonetheless, they were viewed by men as largely extraneous to the masculine culture that Grasso was attempting to use to find himself, as is suggested by the fact that women virtually are invisible in the Florentine streets of this tale. On this see also Martines, "Séduction," esp. pp. 266–75.

22. Martines, *Italian Renaissance Sextet*, p. 178; italics mine.

23. Ibid., p. 179; italics mine.

24. See my *Binding Passions*, esp. pp. 57–87.

25. Exact translations are difficult because, like many of the slang terms used in the illicit world of the Renaissance, these terms could be quite flexible depending on their contexts. On this, see Toscan, *Le carnaval du langage*.

26. On this, see Brucker, *Society of Renaissance Florence,*pp. 183–204; Trexler, "La prostitution florentine"; Rocke, *Forbidden Friendships*, pp. 151–61; and especially Mazzi, *Prostituzione,* who gives a good account of this area and its vicissitudes across the fifteenth century (pp. 249–92). Interestingly given our tale, the palaces of the Brunelleschi family were also located nearby at the northwest corner of the Mercato Vecchio.

27. Of course Grasso frequented this area of the city and probably daily: his home and shop were hard by it, and as it was alive with shops, churches, guild halls, and the economic life of the city center, both he and Matteo must have been there frequently.

28. A favorite theme of Renaissance comedies was the intrigues of *giovani* often aided

by clever servants to gain money from their fathers to pay for their illicit adventures; a theme that reflects the financial difficulties of not gaining a patrimony until *gioventù* had passed. For a more legalistic discussion of this, see Kuehn, *Emancipation in Late Medieval Florence.* For the artistic representation of this relationship, see Simons, "Alert and Erect," pp. 165–69.

29. Mazzi, *Prostituzione*, pp. 268–92, gives a detailed picture of these developments in Florence. For a more theoretical overview of these changes from a Venetian perspective see my *Binding Passions*, pp. 29–56.

30. Rocke, *Forbidden Friendships,* pp. 95–97. While Rocke's statistics have been questioned, he presents compelling evidence that sodomy was perceived in Florence as a relatively normal practice for youths. I discussed similar patterns with much the same age distinctions for males in Venice in my earlier book *The Boundaries of Eros;* for a comparison, see there pp. 121–25 and 160–63. See also the discussion of these issues in Chapter 1.

31. Machiavelli to Vettori, 25 February 1514, in Machiavelli, *Opere* (ed. Vivanti), 2:313–16; all subsequent citations of "Machiavelli, *Opere,*" refer to the edition edited by Vivanti. For a fascinating but slightly different analysis of this letter that downplays the sexual to suggest a deeper argument about "the illusion of using language as an instrument of power and domination," see Najemy, *Between Friends*, pp. 271–76.

32. Machiavelli to Vettori, 25 February 1514, in Machiavelli, *Opere*, 2:314.

33. Ibid., p. 315.

34. Ibid.

35. For more on this group of Machiavelli's friends and their sharing of sexual exploits, see Chapter 5.

36. Machiavelli to Vettori, 25 February 1514, in Machiavelli, *Opere*, 2:315.

37. This refers to the scene in which Vulcan captured Mars in a net while committing adultery with his wife, Venus, and then showed the couple to the other gods. See Ovid, *Metamorphosis,* IV, verses 188–89.

38. Machiavelli to Vettori, 25 February 1514, in Machiavelli, *Opere*, 2:316. If Machiavelli had entirely made up the story, it seems unlikely that he would apologize about the possibility that Vettori had already heard it. Moreover, his claim that everyone in Florence was going around asking jokingly if one was Brancacci or Casavecchia would be an unnecessary and unlikely touch. In fact, without mentioning such things, Machiavelli had the perfect conclusion if his story was a total fiction in his classical reference to Ovid's tale.

39. According to Rocke, in the period 1478–1502 accusations of sodomy concentrated on four main categories of place: public streets or open areas (28%), private homes (36%), workshops (15%), and taverns (15%). Rocke, *Forbidden Friendships*, p. 153, and for the above, see pp. 154–61.

40. Curiously Rocke, after laying out all the details of a complex and rich subculture of sodomy in the city, argues that it did not exist in any way distinct from the more general illicit world of Florence (for his position, see *Forbidden Friendships*, pp. 149–51 and 191; for evidence to the contrary, however, see in the same work pp. 64–68, 74–75, 126–47, 162, and 279 n. 190).

41. Martines, *Italian Renaissance Sextet*, p. 218.

42. For a fuller discussion of these age distinctions, see Chapter 1. In this context it is suggestive to reread the brief description of Brunelleschi's involvement with Grasso when the tale provides his age: "Now Filippo, who at that time was about thirty-two years old, was *very familiar with Grasso* and had taken his measure and *sometimes discreetly amused himself at Grasso's expense.*" Martines, *Italian Renaissance Sextet,* p. 173; the Italian original is equally suggestive, if not more so: "Costui dunque, che in quel tempo era d'età d'anni trentadue in circa, e che per *lo essere molto uso col Grasso,* l'aveva carattato a nuoto, e *qualche volta cautamente ne pigliava piacere.*" Varese, *Prosatori,* p. 770; italics mine. Clearly this text does not prove that anything more is being implied in their relationship, but both the "*molto uso col Grasso*" and the "*cautamente ne pigliava piacere*" could be read as suggesting something more than a simple friendship.

43. Martines, *Italian Renaissance Sextet,* p. 186.

44. Ibid., p. 192.

45. Ibid., p. 193.

46. Ibid., pp. 193–94.

47. Ibid., p. 207.

48. If we opt for the sexual reading suggested above, we might argue that the offer of dinner signaled the successful breaking of sexual intimacy, which now would be replaced by an adult friendship. Brunelleschi had proved himself an adult in the regime of *virtù,* dishonored his old friend, and now could reaccept him in a more mature relationship. In this admittedly hypothetical reading the story becomes even more emblematic for the process of becoming an adult in Renaissance Florence.

49. Martines, *Italian Renaissance Sextet,* p. 209. The fear of being laughed at in the streets and treated as a madman ironically is echoed in Manetti's life of Brunelleschi with Filippo himself being the victim. Manetti's life relates that in the early stages of Brunelleschi's attempts to win the commission to build the dome of the Duomo his plan was rejected as mad and that Brunelleschi reported "he was ashamed to go about Florence. He had the feeling that behind his back they [the people in the streets] were saying: look at that mad man who utters such nonsense." Manetti, *Life of Brunelleschi,* p. 68.

50. Martines, *Italian Renaissance Sextet,* p. 212.

Chapter 5 • *Machiavelli in Love*

1. On Machiavelli's correspondence, see for a masterful analysis as well as an overview of the literature Najemy, *Between Friends,* pp. 82–276. My reading of these letters has been greatly enriched by Najemy's thoughtful study. For Machiavelli's life in general, see the classic study of Ridolfi, *Vita di Niccolò Machiavelli.* A recent study that briefly considers his sexual life in the context of his literary and political accomplishments is Dotti, *Machiavelli rivoluzionario.* A more popular study, but with many interesting insights, which looks more closely at Machiavelli's love life, sexual exploits, and humor is Viroli, *Il sorriso di Niccolò.*

2. Vettori to Machiavelli, 16 January 1515, in Machiavelli, *Opere,* 2:347.

3. Ibid.

4. Ibid.

5. Ibid.

6. Ibid.; italics mine. This letter has been read as suggesting that both Machiavelli and Vettori were also interested in male youths sexually. Mario Martelli, the noted editor of Machiavelli, in a difficult-to-find article, "Machiavelli politico amante poeta," closely rereads a number of their letters and concludes that they refer in a coded way (using the jargon of sodomy) to their own desires and practices. Not only is the article hard to find, but the argument is as well. It actually begins only after fourteen pages of close philological analysis of a short poem that may have been written by Machiavelli as part of a plan to write a holy play on the Pisan saint San Torpe (pp. 211–25). Those hearty souls who read on will find a clever, if at times a bit forced, argument that claims Machiavelli remained a sodomite even as an adult. For our purposes the issue, however, is not what Machiavelli's desires and sexual practices actually were but how he presented both in a way that helped form and maintain a series of consensus realities about his sexual identity.

7. Vettori to Machiavelli, 16 January 1515, in Machiavelli, *Opere,* 2:347; Vergil, *Ecologues,* II, line 69. Martelli reads this, however, as a direct reference to Machiavelli's sexual interest in males; see Martelli, "Machiavelli politico amante poeta," p. 227.

8. Vettori to Machiavelli, 16 January 1515, in Machiavelli, *Opere,* 2:347. In this passage Vettori uses the term *foia,* which stresses the force of lust, its unreasonable, animal-like character, rather than *lussuria;* in a way one decided on *lussuria* and was carried away by *foia.* The overlap between love and this form of lust was not perfect obviously, even when love was a mad passion. Still, the two were perceived as much closer in the Renaissance, when love, especially young love, tended to be viewed as a wild force, a mad passion.

9. Machiavelli to Vettori, 31 January 1515, in Machiavelli, *Opere,* 2:348–49. Martelli, "Machiavelli politico amante poeta," pp. 248–52, reads this poem with its expression of male passivity and penetrating arrows as another indication of Machiavelli's interest in sodomy.

10. Needless to say, with Machiavelli's comedies we cannot be sure that the audience actually did laugh where Machiavelli's text seemed to call for laughter. We do know, however, that the comedies were well received, especially *La mandragola,* and at a deeper level it appears that Machiavelli reworked the comedies for publication, which would have allowed him to make his humor more effective. Unfortunately for such an analysis, however, it must be admitted that he may have made his humor more literary in reworking the comedies for publication as well. In sum, we can assume that he had the possibility to respond to his audience when he revised his comedies, but one would not want to push the assumption too far. For Machiavelli's three major comedies, see Machiavelli, *Tutte le opere: Andrea,* pp. 847–67; *La mandragola,* pp. 868–90; *Clizia,* pp. 891–913.

11. See Ruggiero, *Binding Passions,* esp. the chapter "That Old Black Magic Called Love," pp. 88–129.

12. Machiavelli to Vettori, 31 January 1515, in Machiavelli, *Opere,* 2:348.

13. Ibid.

14. Ibid.

15. Ibid.

16. Ibid.

17. As *legno* also meant "wood," it was a particularly apt metaphor for phallic word-play. Note that when Machiavelli refers directly to the object of his sexual desires he invariably refers to women, as here—aside from one humorous reference to the male prostitute il Riccio discussed later in this chapter. This seems to be the most serious problem for Martelli's thesis that Machiavelli continued to practice sodomy with male youths.

18. Machiavelli to Vettori, 31 January 1515, in Machiavelli, *Opere,* 2:349. The term *compare* was used to denote close friendship, even though it formally referred to someone who was a relative through god-parentage. In fact, Machiavelli, like many other Renaissance upper-class males, used god-parentage relationships to cement ties of patronage and friendship, and Vettori may well have stood as godparent for one of his children. It should be noted, however, that Machiavelli and his correspondents, much in the manner of the times, often used the terminology of family to express close friendship, referring to each other as *compar,* as well as brother, father, and so on. On this, see Klapisch-Zuber, "Compèrage et clientèlisme à Florence (1360–1520)," and more generally Weissman, *Ritual Brotherhood in Renaissance Florence.*

19. Ibid.

20. For Rustico and Alibech's blasphemous adventures, see Chapter 2. These tales bookend the third day of stories in the *Decameron* about much-sought-after things that are gained or recovered through hard work, with Masetto's adventures opening the day and Alibech's service to God closing it.

21. Vettori to Machiavelli, 16 January 1515, in Machiavelli, *Opere,* 2:348.

22. See the excellent analysis of this in Najemy, *Between Friends,* pp. 82–276.

23. Vettori to Machiavelli, 23 November 1513, in Machiavelli, *Opere,* 2:291.

24. Ibid., p. 292.

25. Ibid., pp. 292–93.

26. Ibid., p. 293. The reference to summer airs probably refers to a contemporary fear that syphilis and other diseases were somehow spread or caused by the airs of summer and sexual relations with prostitutes.

27. Ibid.; "*fa qualche faccenda*" implies that she occasionally had sexual relationships with men; Vettori will use this same phrase again in his letter to Machiavelli of 18 January, when he more explicitly labels her as sexually available.

28. Ibid. Once again throughout this letter Vettori assumes that Machiavelli's preferred objects of sexual desire are women, pace Martelli.

29. For this comedy, see *La calandra,* in Giannetti and Ruggiero, *Five Comedies,* pp. 1–70.

30. Machiavelli to Vettori, 10 December 1513, in Machiavelli, *Opere,* 2:294.

31. Ibid., p. 296. It is interesting to note how closely Machiavelli's account of his country life parallels Vettori's self-presentation in his earlier letter.

32. Ibid.

33. Ibid.

34. For an interesting discussion of similar visions of aging among Renaissance artists, see Campbell, "Art of Aging Gracefully." The literature on concepts of old age and aging in general has grown rapidly over the past few years, perhaps as a result of the gen-

eral aging of the populations in the West. Leaders in such studies have been the *Journal of Social History* and the journal's editor, Peter Stearns, in the United States and Peter Laslett and his group (more interested in demographic issues) in England. For Italy work has been more limited, but David Herlihy from a demographic perspective and Richard Trexler from a more cultural perspective have produced pioneering work. For a general overview, see, for example, Stearns, *Old Age in Preindustrial Society*; Stearns, *Old Age in European Society*; Kertzer and Laslett, *Aging in the Past*; Kertzer and Schaie, *Age Structuring in Comparative Perspective*; Thane, "Social Histories of Old Age and Aging," who provides a recent review of the literature; Minois, *History of Old Age*, who provides a classic overview; Shepard, *Meanings of Manhood in Early Modern England*, esp. pp. 38–46, 214–45; Thomas, "Age and Authority in Early Modern England"; and Roebuck, "When Does 'Old Age' Begin?" For briefer discussions of the situation in Renaissance Italy, see Chojnacki, "Political Adulthood"; Herlihy and Klapisch-Zuber, *Tuscans and Their Families*, but also the longer original version published in French, *Les Tuscans et leurs familles*; Gilbert, "When Did a Man in the Renaissance Grow Old?"; Groves, "Gabrina the Whore"; Terreaux-Scotto, "'Vous êtes des enfants de cent ans'"; Martin, "Old People, Alcohol and Identity in Europe"; and Finlayson, "Of Leeks and Old Men."

35. Machiavelli to Vettori, 10 December 1513, in Machiavelli, *Opere*, 2:295.

36. Ibid., p. 297. There is some debate about the age Machiavelli claims in this letter. As he was born in May 1469, he was actually 44 at the time he wrote it. By the reckoning of the time this meant that he was 44 going on 45; thus it has been suggested that this letter was mistranscribed and that he actually wrote that he was 45. It may be, however, that Machiavelli was trying to suggest that he was not all that old an old man, as here he has returned to angling for a post with the Medici. From that perspective 43 would still be old and thus allow Machiavelli to argue that he would not change because of his age, but nonetheless it would be at the younger edge of old age with plenty of service left in him. In the end, however, whether he was claiming he was 43 or 45 here, he was evoking his old age once again.

37. Most notable perhaps with regard to his sexual foibles is his famous letter to Luigi Guicciardini about his encounter with a Veronese prostitute in the dark in which he presents himself as so foolishly driven by his sexual needs that he inadvertently has sexual intercourse with a diseased old crone. Machiavelli to Luigi Guicciardini, 8 December 1509, in Machiavelli, *Opere*, 2:205–6.

A particularly fine example of such self-mockery with respect to his own importance can be found in Machiavelli's side of a series of letters exchanged with Francesco Guicciardini in 1521 in which he laughs at how the arrival of Guicciardini's letters by a courier made him appear more important than he was with the Franciscans with whom he was dealing at the time and laughingly conspires with his friend to keep up the sham. See the exchange between the two that went from 17 May 1521 to 19 May 1521, in Machiavelli, *Opere*, 2:371–79.

38. Machiavelli to Vettori, 19 December 1513, in Machiavelli, *Opere*, 2:299. But see on this Martelli, "Machiavelli politico amante poeta," p. 243, as a reference to Machiavelli's own sodomitic desires. It is unclear in this brief account whether Donato and Machiavelli recited these verses to Giovanni or whether a not further identified Filippo and

Machiavelli did so. Machiavelli uses the "we" form ("dicemmo a mente") immediately after referring to the fact that Donato had received the verses in a letter from Vettori. Several lines later he suddenly refers to a Filippo who enjoyed this joke with him, which might imply that his earlier "we" refers to him and Filippo. The context seems to call for Donato, however.

39. In fact, it may be that the very shortness of the period of adulthood and the way that youth encroached on it from one side and old age from another allowed a man like Machiavelli in his mid-forties more play in his self-portrayal than one would have in other cultural settings. Close enough to being old, he could assume that self and be accepted while still presenting himself sexually as an adult and, as we shall see, perhaps also occasionally as a young man.

40. Machiavelli to Vettori, 19 December 1513, in Machiavelli, *Opere*, 2:299.

41. See, for example, the particularly perceptive reading of Najemy on this in his *Between Friends*, p. 243. A few, however, have held that the comment should be taken at face value, and, in fact, Martelli has argued that in this letter when Machiavelli refers to himself as one who "tocco e attendo a femmine," which is usually translated "touches and enjoys women," *tocco* actually refers specifically to sexual relations with young men and thus the line should be read as one who "has sexual relations with young men and enjoys women." For this, see Martelli, "Machiavelli politico amante poeta," pp. 238–42, esp. p. 238. Tellingly, he provides a number of other texts in which Machiavelli may be using *toccare* in this sense, which lends weight to his reading, even if Machiavelli presents himself (at least openly) in his letters as precisely a man who "touches and enjoys women."

42. Cited in Machiavelli, *Opere*, 2:1587 n. 1. Given the amount of sexual material that survives in the correspondence that Giuliano copied, one wonders what the original corpus looked like and rues the loss. Although Martelli does not develop it, this could also provide an argument for why the only references to Machiavelli's sexual interest in males which he believes he found in his letters are oblique and coded in the jargon of the time.

43. Perhaps this would be a way to incorporate Martelli's provocative vision of Machiavelli as a "homosexual" into a more Renaissance vision of the sexual stages of a male's life and display of sexual identity. From this perspective it is interesting to note that later in life, in 1523, Vettori wrote to a Machiavelli worried about an affair of his own son, Lodovico, with a younger boy, recommending that he not fret about it and advising him to remember his own youth: "Since we are verging on old age, we might be severe and overly scrupulous, and we do not remember what we do as adolescents. So Lodovico has a boy with him, with whom he amuses himself [*cum illo ludit*], jests, takes walks, growls in his ear, goes to bed together. What then? Even in these things perhaps there is nothing bad." Quoted in Rocke, *Forbidden Friendships*, p. 114. Note also that, as suggested in Chapter 2, once again sexual pleasure is associated with play ("cum illo ludit").

44. Vettori to Machiavelli, 19 December 1513, in Machiavelli, *Opere*, 2:300; it should be noted that Vettori was actually a bit younger than Machiavelli and mentions in a letter of 9 February 1514 that he is 40 years old (p. 311).

45. Ibid., pp. 300–301.

46. Ibid., p. 301.

47. Ibid.

48. Ibid. It seems that Machiavelli considered Giuliano de' Medici an old friend whose support might be regained by a dedication. The whole issue of the dedication of *The Prince* has been long and hotly debated; for an overview of the issues involved which suggests that the true addressee of the work was Vettori himself, see Najemy, *Between Friends*, pp. 176–214.

49. Machivelli to Vettori, 5 January 1514, in Machiavelli, *Opere*, 2:303.

50. Ibid.

51. Ibid., pp. 303–4. As far as the reference to Valencia is concerned, the city was a famous port in the sixteenth century noted for its sinful ways; thus Machiavelli's reference to the bordello seems to imply humorously that these whores would be really sinful and reprehensible in contrast presumably to Vettori's "intellectual" courtesans.

52. Ibid., p. 304. But for another reading of this text, see the discussion in n. 41 above.

53. Ibid.

54. Vettori to Machiavelli, 18 January 1514, in Machiavelli, *Opere*, 2:306.

55. Ibid., p. 307. Note that here the assumption is that tutors did, in fact, at times sleep with their charges, as seemed to be implied in Vettori's earlier letter about lust and the way the young were encouraged to learn bad habits and the way he and Machiavelli had learned them.

56. Ibid.

57. Machiavelli to Vettori, 25 February 1514, in Machiavelli, *Opere*, 2:313–16.

58. Ibid., p. 314.

59. Ibid. On this quote from Boccaccio, see Boccaccio, *Decameron* III, 5. Obviously this is a sexual reference in Boccaccio: for this is what the wife of Francesco de'Vergellesi says when she decides to go ahead and take a lover, "It is better to have done it and repent, than to not and repent." Boccaccio, Decameron, pp. 219–20.

60. Vettori to Machiavelli, 18 January 1514, in Machiavelli, *Opere*, 2:307–8.

61. Ibid., p. 308.

62. Machiavelli to Vettori, 4 February 1514, in Machiavelli, *Opere*, 2:310.

63. Ibid. Maurizio Viroli in his recent, excellent overview of Machiavelli's thought stressed a similar understanding of Machiavelli's vision of love, although he does not refer to a passive/active dichotomy; see his *Machiavelli*, pp. 28–35, esp. pp. 28–29. He argues: "Dependence and abandonment to the love of a woman are for Machiavelli one of the best conditions of men's life. As his own life amply illustrates, he was always more than happy to trade autonomy for love" (p. 29).

64. *La mandrgola*, in Giannetti and Ruggiero, *Five Comedies*, p. 97.

65. It should be noted here that in *The Prince*, as a number of recent critics have pointed out, Machiavelli does not really say that the ends justify the means; he says more moderately that the means must also be judged in terms of the goals one is seeking—a considerably more complex claim. Here the statement appears to be stronger than in *The Prince*, but it still is not an unqualified claim that the ends justify the means.

66. *La mandragola*, in Giannetti and Ruggiero, *Five Comedies*, p. 84.

67. Ibid.

68. Ibid.

69. Ibid.

70. Ibid., pp. 78–79.

71. Ibid., p. 78. Although no such place exists, Carrucola evokes the Italian verb *car-rucolare*, to make a fool of someone, and that is clearly what Ligurio is doing here. There is another way, however, to read *carrucola* which is less laughable and more self-referential—if we see Nicia as representing Machiavelli as a foolish and self-delusional old failure. For a *carrucola* was also the technical name for the pulley that was used in the torture of the *strappado*, in which a person was hoisted with a rope that went through this pulley and then dropped only to be jerked up short just before the person's feet touched the ground, dislocating the shoulders. In fact, Machiavelli had recently had a chance to see the *carrucola* of Florence, at least much more closely than he would have wished, when he was tortured by the Medici with six drops in early 1513 for his supposed role in a conspiracy against the new regime.

72. Ibid., pp. 106–7.

73. Ibid., p. 111. Martelli reads this scene with its frequent use of the verb *toccare* (see n. 41 above) as a direct reference to the "practices" and "passions" of sodomy, implying once again Machiavelli's close familiarity with both; see Martelli, "Machiavelli politico amante poeta," pp. 238–42. For a different reading of the character of Messer Nicia as a Machiavelli alter ego and the comedy itself which stresses a biological, reproductive sexual interpretation, see Finucci, *Manly Masquerade*, pp. 79–117, esp. pp. 90–92.

74. Callimaco has also been read as meaning in Greek "he who battles well," but the problem with that reading is that Callimaco does not battle well aside, perhaps, from his amatory battle in bed with Lucrezia; in fact, he hardly battles at all otherwise, passively being led to success by Ligurio. In the end he is much more a pretty boy, in the full Renaissance sense of *pretty* and *boy,* than a successful warrior.

75. *La mandragola*, in Giannetti and Ruggiero, *Five Comedies*, p. 81. In fact, the songs between acts in *La mandragola* apparently were written at a later date with the help of Barbara Salutati, who was a noted singer in Florence and Machiavelli's mistress at the time. For this, see Machiavelli to Francesco Guicciardini, 16–20 October 1525, in Machiavelli, *Opere*, 2:408.

76. *La mandragola*, in Giannetti and Ruggiero, *Five Comedies*, pp. 99–100. In the sentence translated here as "Face up to fate," Machiavelli uses *sorte* (fate) instead of *fortuna* (fortune), but the sense is similar to the vision of fortune expressed in *The Prince*. There, as is well known, he argues that one must be a man with the feminine Fortuna and take her by force.

77. Ibid., p. 76.

78. Ibid.

79. Ibid., p. 77.

80. The apparent parallel with the legendary classical figure Lucrezia, who after being raped by Sextus, the son of Tarquinius Superbus, revealed all to her husband and promptly committed suicide, has spawned a host of interesting commentaries on the deeper meanings of Lucrezia's character in this comedy. Many interpretations that attempt to read this laughing and cynical comedy as moral and perhaps even ultimately containing a deeper Christian message use the supposed connections between the classical and the modern Lucrezia as a key to their reading. It may well be, however, that her

name, instead of hiding deeper meanings, was a much simpler type of reversal humor very popular in the Renaissance. This clever, honest, and finally sexually awakened Renaissance Lucrezia responded to her violation in a way that was exactly the opposite of the classic Lucrezia's response, and a Renaissance audience could laugh ruefully at the contrast. In fact, in such a reading there is room for a lighter moral reading as well, as Machiavelli could well have been laughingly suggesting that the times and the morality of women had changed for the better—women with *virtù* no longer committed suicide in such situations; they evaluated the moment, the pleasure, and the dangers for their honor and decided, if they were truly clever and *virtù*-ous in the Renaissance sense of the term, in favor of pleasure when possible. In this, even Lucrezia would have had her Machiavellian dimension. More telling for the name, however, may have been the simple fact that in 1510 Machiavelli was accused anonymously of having committed sodomy with one Lucrezia, called la Riccia, the courtesan who would continue to be widely known as his mistress for almost a decade—exactly the period when Machiavelli wrote *La mandragola;* for the accusation see Trexler, "La prostitution florentine," p. 995 and n. 79. What better name for the mistress of the young, handsome lover Calli-maco, a Machiavelli alter ego, than that of Machiavelli's actual courtesan mistress at the time—presumably Machiavelli could have imagined many responses of his Lucrezia to sexual intercourse with a younger, handsomer version of himself, but suicide was hardly likely to be one of them!

81. *La mandragola*, in Giannetti and Ruggiero, *Five Comedies*, p. 113.

82. Ibid.

83. Ibid., p. 115.

84. Ibid.

85. The plot of this play is taken from Plautus's ancient Roman comedy *Casina;* Plautus in turn had borrowed the plot from a lost Greek comedy by Diphilus of Sinope, *Cleroumenie* (The Lot Throwers). Although Machiavelli follows the mechanical aspects of the plot fairly closely, his characters are much more developed, and the sexual desires that drive the plot in Plautus's version are made more complex in Machiavelli's reelaboration by a strong interest in the emotion of love and its impact on the lead characters. Tellingly, Nicomaco, although he seems at first a foolish old lover in the Roman tradition, is a much more nuanced character, at once more sympathetic and in a way almost tragic, as many commentators have noted.

86. A letter from Filippo de' Nerli to Francesco del Nero, a relative of Machiavelli's, of 1 March 1525 associated the comedy and Machiavelli's new love directly. As discussed briefly in the Introduction, Filippo wrote that during carnival season Machiavelli was completely caught up with Barbara and would have been the talk of the town if it weren't for the recent battle of Pavia, which had shut down the normal gossip mills for a bit. Machiavelli, *Opere*, 2:1617–18 n. 7.

87. This Greek reading of the name Nicomaco has been often suggested, but I am particularly influenced here by Ronald L. Martinez's important article "Benefit of Absence," esp. p. 132. Although our readings might be seen as almost diametrically opposed—he sees the play as virtually a tragedy because of its unhappy ending (featuring Nicomaco's beating and failure to have Clizia), and I read it as a classic comedy with Nico-

maco winning out in the end because he regains *virtù* when he gives up on his foolish love for Clizia—Martinez's reading has merit. In fact, the play could be read both ways. The key to the difference in our readings seems to turn largely on the understanding of *virtù*. For Martinez it is a concept that has endured from antiquity through the Renaissance in Mediterranean culture (see p. 136), whereas I see it as a term that evolved and changed in the Renaissance (see Chapters 4 and 6); thus he sees Nicomaco's inability to have Clizia as a failure for the latter's sense of his own *virtù* (where *virtù* is the enduring concept of male power and dominance), while I see Nicomaco's failure to have what he wants as less important than his rediscovering and returning to *virtù* (i.e., the moderation and control of self and emotions that, combined with an active approach to life, is the key to Machiavelli's vision of political action and a correctly ordered society).

88. *La Clizia,* in Machiavelli, *Tutte le Opere,* 898. Also used for the text of the comedy was Machiavelli, *Niccolò Machiavelli, Teatro.*

89. *La Clizia,* in Machiavelli, *Tutte le Opere,* 898.

90. Ibid., p. 894.

91. Ibid., p. 898. Sofronia's reply warrants quoting: "Some miracle, a friar who makes a woman become pregnant. If a nun impregnated her, now that would be a miracle." Still it is nice to learn here that the Machiavelli fantasy of self as Callimaco has lived up to his promise in *La mandragola.* Clearly he has impregnated Lucrezia, and perhaps even their love has gone on as the ending of the earlier comedy implied it would. Romantics might even wish that Machiavelli would have reported that Messer Nicia had passed on, allowing the young lovers to actually marry and live happily after, but Machiavelli does not provide that happy post ending, ending, perhaps because he was too cynical and ironic in his humor to see that as an interesting further clarification.

92. Ibid., p. 900.

93. Ibid., pp. 909–10 for this whole speech. Suggestively, the faces and gestures that Siro made seem to suggest the kind of insults made to men reputed to be involved as passive partners in sexual relationships at the time: "mi faceva bocchi ... e manichetto dietro." It is also interesting to note that Nicomaco's servant was named Siro just as Callimaco's was—yet another continuity between the two comedies and Maco characters.

94. Ibid., p. 911; italics mine.

Chapter 6 • Death and Resurrection and the Regime of Virtù, or Of Princes, Lovers, and Prickly Pears

Epigraph: Machiavelli, *Opere,* 1:326–27. The translations are mine throughout unless otherwise stated.

1. Erizzo, *Le sei giornate,* p. 151 (Day 3 Avenimento 16).

2. Ibid.

3. Bandello, "Giulia da Gazuolo," p. 212.

4. Ibid., p. 218.

5. Ibid., p. 219.

6. Ibid. The contrast with Machiavelli's modern Lucrezia in *La mandragola* is stark, but Matteo Bandello was a Dominican with a sterner moral streak and thus a very differ-

ent storyteller than Machiavelli. In fact, his tales are well known for their dark and often violently cruel vision; they also tend to reinforce a much more negative vision of the dangers of sex and passion as well as a strict sexual morality especially for women.

7. Erizzo, *Le sei giornate*, p. 152. The speech goes from p. 152 to p. 156; the action of the story goes from the end of p. 148 to the beginning of p. 152.

8. Ibid., p. 153. In his notes to the text, Renzo Bragantini points to the famous section in *The Discourses* (in bk. I:19) where Machiavelli makes the same point. It is interesting to compare the two texts. Trasinoo states: "Doppo il quale, ancora che venisse un altro successore non di tanta virtù quanto egli, potria nondimeno mantenere lo stato per la sola virtù di chi l'ha retto per innanzi." Machiavelli's words are virtually the same: "Uno successore, non di tanta virtù quanto il primo, può mantenere uno stato per la virtù di colui che lo ha retto innanzi." It seems clear that Erizzo had read his Machiavelli.

9. Ibid., p. 154. Perhaps this list of attributes stresses a more moral and religious tone than one finds in Machiavelli, but most of these traits can also be found in *The Prince* and *The Discourses,* especially when Machiavelli speaks about ideal traits of a ruler.

10. Ibid., pp. 154–55. Again the parallels with Machiavelli are evident. Here is an answer similar to Machiavelli's in *The Prince* (chap. 17) as to whether the prince should be loved or hated, although it should be noted that Erizzo's prince is both loved and feared at the same time. But like Machiavelli's ideal prince he keeps the faith of his subjects by avoiding threatening their property and unnecessarily threatening the things they value.

11. Ibid., p. 155.

12. Ibid.

13. Bandello, "Giulia da Gazuolo"; for Bandello's evaluation of Giulia as having "too lowly blood," p. 211; for his concluding evaluation, p. 219. Evidently this was a male's evaluation and a quite conservative cleric's evaluation at that (see n. 6 above). Women writers could provide quite a different vision of womanly *virtù*. Perhaps the best example of this is to be found in Moderata Fonte's late sixteenth-century treatise *Il merito delle donne.* In this dialogue Corinna argues throughout that the problems of the present day are caused by a male lack of *virtù* (echoing Machiavelli in this) and holds that women are the true repository of *virtù.* "We have already proven that on all counts in *virtù,* in dignity and in a thousand other ways we [women] are their [men's] superiors," she opines, "and it is clear that they are full of errors which are totally absent in women who are rather graced with every beautiful *virtù* . . . in women you find instead of rage, calm and prudence; instead of gluttony, temperance; instead of overweening pride, modesty; instead of unrestrained desire, continence; instead of discord, peace; instead of hate, love; in sum, every type of *virtù.*" Fonte, *Il merito delle donne,* p. 61.

14. Martines, *Italian Renaissance Sextet.* In my discussion of this novella, once again I have been much influenced by Martines's analysis. In the text quoted here I use the translation of the tale by Murtha Baca from this edition unless otherwise noted. For the Italian edition I have used Sermini, "Scopone."

15. Martines, *Italian Renaissance Sextet,* p. 39; Sermini, "Scopone," p. 750.

16. Martines, *Italian Renaissance Sextet,* p. 40; Sermini, "Scopone," p. 750.

17. As should be self-evident by now in this chapter, I am primarily concerned with how the concept of *virtù* was used in the Renaissance and its contemporary implications

and much less with what the classical precedents were which may or may not have contributed to that usage. Needless to say, those classical precedents have been closely studied by intellectual historians and historians of humanism and with great erudition. My goal is a more humble one here, merely to suggest how this complex concept worked and how it was perceived and lived in the Renaissance. It might be noted in this context that the search for the origins of ideas can often cause problems for the project of understanding contemporary usage, as there is a tendency to assume that the original usage translated perfectly across time and social and cultural settings. That, perhaps, was more possible for works that were highly theoretical but much less likely, I would argue, for works that attempted to comment upon and have an impact on contemporary society.

18. Again the literature on this is immense, but the classic works remain Pocock, *Machiavellian Moment;* Bouwsma, *Venice and the Defense of Republican Liberty;* Gilbert, *Machiavelli and Guiccardini;* and Skinner, *Foundations of Modern Political Thought.*

19. Boccaccio, *Decameron,* p. 283.

20. As noted earlier, Bartolomeo Buonsignori was more fortunate from this perspective; with his father dead he was free to follow his youthful passions and pleasure without the interference of mature authority.

21. Boccaccio, *Decameron,* p. 283.

22. Ibid., p. 285. *Virtù,* of course, was frequently depicted as the one power that could overcome fortune in the Renaissance, but often in a typical Renaissance reversal fortune was seen as the nemesis of *virtù.*

23. Ibid.; italics mine. Again *vergogna,* or shame, was a term closely related to *virtù;* people who publicly acted without *virtù* were often seen as having acted shamefully. What made the *virtù*/shame dichotomy different from the honor/shame dichotomy was in large part due to the fact that in the Renaissance the shame that accompanied the loss of *virtù* required reasoned, controlled action whereas the shame that followed upon dishonor regularly required violence and vendetta. Note also in light of the discussion in Chapter 2 on the close association of play and pleasure in sex that the young lovers are described as playing and enjoying themselves in bed.

24. Ibid., p. 286. Actually Tancredi says, "given to my things [*cose*]," but here "my things" refers to his world and his life.

25. Ibid.

26. Ibid.

27. Ibid.

28. See the crucial discussion of the form of this genre and its relationship to historical analysis in Martines, *Italian Renaissance Sextet,* pp. 11–14 and throughout.

29. Boccaccio, *Decameron,* p. 287.

30. Ibid.; italics mine. Here *virtù* has tellingly both a social dimension and an internal dimension. Ghismonda wants to defend both her reputation and the greatness of her soul.

31. Ibid., pp. 287–88. For this, see also, in Chapter 2, the discussion of Alibech and Rustico's natural sexual attraction and the way their pleasures made the desert bloom and made their service to the Christian God a true pleasure.

32. Ibid., p. 288.

33. Ibid., pp. 288–89; italics mine. Suggestively, Moderata Fonte expresses similar sentiments in a long poem that effectively concludes *Il merito delle donne,* arguing that when love ruled young lovers did not consider "either dowry, parents or inequality of social position" (p. 175). Unfortunately, that golden age of love was lost, and "the noble *virtù* . . . have left the world, leaving it blind and sad" (p. 180).

34. Boccaccio, *Decameron,* p. 290.

35. Ibid.

36. Ibid., p. 292.

37. Ibid.; italics mine. She closes her last request to her weeping father with a crucial description of how the burial should be done: "palese stea," in other words, "so that it will be known by all," in clear contrast with the secrecy of the lovers' affair, which had been carefully kept hidden. It may be that the interpolation of "of our love" overstates what is implied, but the more neutral "our affair" or "our case" seems to undercut the clearly intended tragic yet heroic ending of the lovers.

38. Ibid.; italics mine.

39. See Ruggiero, *Binding Passions,* esp. pp. 223–28, and for less theoretical examples pp. 156–63, 172–74.

40. Machiavelli, *Tutte le opere, Il principe,* p. 269.

41. On this I would like to thank my graduate student John Visconti—our long discussions of the lack of a significant role for the family in Machiavelli's political thought were crucial for my thinking here.

42. The work was written between 1513 and 1518 and revised thereafter until it was finally published in 1528. In what follows, I have used Castiglione, *Il libro del cortegiano,* ed. Amedeo Quondam; volume 1 provides the text (all citations unless otherwise noted are to volume 1) and volume 2 a review (without notes, however) of the extensive interpretative scholarship on the work. An excellent English edition with a small group of essays by leading scholars and a brief bibliography of the most important scholarship has been edited for Norton by Daniel Javitch, *Book of the Courtier.* For the work's impact, see Burke, *Fortunes of the Courtier.*

43. Castiglione, *Il libro del cortegiano.* These qualities are discussed primarily in bks. I and II. For nobility and grace, see esp. pp. 30–52 (I:4); for bodily comportment and self-control, pp. 72–75, 104–21 (I:6, II:2, 3); for arms and learning, pp. 75–83 (I:7); for music and the arts, pp. 83–93 (I:8); for wit and conversation, pp. 120–32, 154–216 (II:4, 7–11); for dress, pp. 133–37 (II:5); for friendship, pp. 137–55 (II:6).

44. Ibid., p. 210 (II:11.3). Bernardo Dovizi became a cardinal in 1514 and was better known thereafter as Cardinal Bibbiena.

45. Ibid., pp. 210–11 (II:11.5). For a woman's perspective on these arguments that stressed the importance of female *virtù* and the male lack of same, see Fonte, *Il merito delle donne,* and n. 13 above.

46. Castiglione, *Il libro del cortigiano,* p. 278 (III:5.79).

47. Ibid., pp. 278–79 (III:5.81–89). The account of events that appears in Castiglione was probably written well before Bandello's account and certainly published before it. Apparently in earlier manuscripts of Castiglione's work her name was given as Maddalena Biga, but as Cesare wanted to make the point that her name had already been forgotten

in order to claim that such *virtù*-ous acts by women, although relatively common, were not well known because they were quickly forgotten, the name was dropped from the final published version.

48. Ibid., p. 279 (III:5.88).

49. Ibid. (III:5.89). It should be noted that Bandello in his introductory letter to his telling of the tale reiterates this theme—such deeds are quickly forgotten—and makes explicit the role that lack of social status plays in this lack of historical memory, even if ironically he resurrects the tale and the young peasant woman and develops a much more *virtù*-rich account. Bandello, "Giulia da Gazuola," p. 211.

50. Castiglione, *Il libro del cortigiano*, p. 227 (III:2.22–23).

51. Ibid. (III:2.23–25).

52. That a woman's body is the key issue here is made clear as Giuliano begins his discussion of a woman's *virtù*; ibid., p. 226 (III:2.20). In fact, he posits a clear distinction between the *virtù* of the soul ("virtù dell'animo") and the practices of the body ("esecizii del corpo"); as far as the latter are concerned, he argues, "Above all it seems to me that a woman must be very different from a man in her ways, manners, words, gestures and comportment." The body/soul contrast is clear: qua soul a woman could demonstrate the same *virtù* as a man, but qua body she was more limited and in many areas could not.

53. Ibid., pp. 232–33 (III:2.55–58). More normally in the Renaissance prescriptive literature called for the strict disciplining of women in this area, concerned with women's frivolous and expensive dress and also their use of makeup. Both were often lamented as wasting money, masking or even destroying a woman's natural beauty, and hiding her true nature. Giuliano's concession in this area, even hemmed in with his many reservations, was thus unusual and interesting: "But because it is licit and necessary for women to pay more attention to their looks than for men . . . this lady [the court lady] should be able to judge which clothes increase her grace and select them in accordance with the activities that she intends to do at the moment. . . . And if she sees herself a certain gentle and happy beauty, she should augment it with [graceful] comportment, words and clothes. . . . In the same way another woman who realizes that she has a style more reserved and grave should accompany that style with deeds of a sort that increase that natural gift. In the same way those who are more heavy or thinner than they should be, or more white or dark, can help themselves with their dress, but they must hide this as much as possible. And keeping themselves delicate and happy, they must always demonstrate that they are doing this without any art or effort."

54. Ibid., p. 233 (III:2.59).

55. Ibid. (III:2.61–62).

56. Ibid. (III:2.63). Here we have another indication that although *virtù* was largely performative and social, it also had a more internal dimension. Suggestively, however, Giuliano's internal *virtù* seem to circle back to honor and external evaluations of a court lady's deeds. And tellingly, once again the ideal is that honor and *virtù* should overlap and reinforce each other, even if in practice that was not always the case.

57. Ibid., p. 234 (III:3.1). Gasparo concludes his derisive speech with an even more damning "and leave the men in the kitchen and to do the sewing."

58. Ibid. (III:3.2).

59. Ibid., p. 235 (III:3.10–12). This vision turned ultimately on the one sex model in which a woman was essentially an imperfect male; for an overview of this concept in Renaissance medical theory, see Laqueur, *Making Sex*.

60. One of the weaker points in Foucault's analysis of the history of sex is his tendency to devalue the significance of what is not said about it. It has long been clear, however, that in the realm of sex what is not said (especially in the prescriptive and legal literature that Foucault studied most carefully) is often extremely important, and that is yet another reason it is so difficult to study its history using such sources alone. In fact, his claim that for the modern world the primary problem with sex is not the silence that has surrounded it but rather the opposite, that too much has been said, is a clever reversal that would have won the heart of Renaissance intellectuals enamored with clever reversals of received wisdom. For Foucault this meant that this explosion of discussion of sex, and the modern discourses on sex, were really what created sex in the modern world. This is not the place to take on this large and richly suggestive thesis, but suffice it to say that the discourses that he sees as dominating modern sexuality have done so (to the degree that they have dominated) because they filled the apparent silences in everyday discourses on the subject, silences that may well have been more apparent than real. More generally speaking, early modern science and material culture had to overcome powerful competing discourses that were deeply ingrained in everyday culture and religion; the nineteenth-century disciplinary discourses of sex that he discusses more fully may have had a much easier time because they overwhelmed what appeared to be largely a silence. Thus to understand the actual level of dominance of these discourses and the historical processes involved in winning that dominance in the modern world, I would suggest that it is crucial to study the silences and the unexpressed or underexpressed ways of understanding things.

61. Ruggiero, *Boundaries of Eros*, pp. 127–40. See also Chapter 1.

62. Castiglione, *Il libro del cortigiano*, p. 319 (IV:2.10). His argument is actually slightly more complex and thus worth reporting more fully. He argued that some things, such as temperance, strength, and health, are good in themselves but others, "like the law, liberty, riches and similar things," are good "for the ends which they lead to." And he concluded more forcefully that "the perfect courtier described by Count Lodovico and Messer Federico may be truly good and worthy of praise, not simply for himself in his own right, but in respect to the ends which he leads to."

63. Ibid., p. 320 (IV:2.12). Again it might be noted that although Machiavelli does not speak of these things in terms of court life, he does identify similar forms of corruption as being among the primary reasons for Italy's political demise and a direct result of a lack of *virtù* in contemporary society.

64. Ibid. (IV:2.15–16); italics mine. This metaphor "the path of *virtù*" (*cammin della virtù*) onto which the courtier should guide princes becomes a virtual topos of book IV.

65. Ibid., pp. 320–21 (IV:2.17).

66. Still, as discussed earlier, both writers sought to overcome this problem by making government the ultimate of arbiter of true *virtù* and thus morality as well. Both argued that individual *virtù* was not necessarily moral or positive in and of itself. A highly *virtù*-ous courtier in his refined manners, military prowess, and courtly loving might commit a host of misdeeds and be a negative factor at court and in society. In the same way a

prince with all the *virtù* to hold on to power and rule with fear and violence might not be judged to be truly *virtù*-ous if his rule was destructive and unjust or the state he created immoral and unstable. What transformed these *virtù* into vices for both writers was that they did not have as their end or goal the *virtù*-ous state that, in their view, was the only entity capable of judging and maintaining *virtù*. This mix of an ontology based on ends or goals and the Renaissance ideals of civic morality and a moral state made the state crucial. In the face of such a vision of the state the question becomes, however, whether such moral and *virtù*-ous states ever could exist. And whether this vision of the state continues to underlie the modern conception of the state—no small question.

67. Castiglione, *Il libro del cortigiano*, p. 371 (IV:6.1).

68. Ibid. (IV:6.3). In this text the ubiquitously feared social control of children with their mocking *baie* and women with their laughing *burle* once again suggests the ease with which *virtù* could be and was enforced without recourse to government or laws.

69. Ibid., p. 372 (IV:6.6–7).

70. See ibid., pp. 373–75 (IV:6.15–21), where Bembo explicitly discusses this ascent in terms of *virtù*, explaining in a traditional manner that our souls have three ways of knowing: the senses, reason, and intellect. The senses give rise to appetites such as the desire for beautiful things; reason, which is particular to humans, allows reasoning; and the intellect, which allows humans to communicate with angels, gives us the will/desire for things that are intelligible, such as the underlying spiritual form of beauty. Thus humans have the ability to desire things that are in the realm of appetites, but they can also desire them and have them in the much more real spiritual realm of the intellect. And this is especially true of beauty, which can be found in nature but found in a much more enduring and literally real way in the spiritual realm opened by the *virtù* of the intellect.

71. See Ruggiero, *Binding Passions*, pp. 178, 212–17.

72. Castiglione, *Il libro del cortigiano*, p. 391 (IV:6.110).

73. Ibid. (IV:6.112). Suggestively, Moderata Fonte stressed the importance of love without Bembo's full Platonic trappings in her *Il merito delle donne* and also associated it with *virtù* throughout the dialogue. For example, one interlocutor, responding to a poem on love's power recited by Corinna, wistfully remarked, "If things were that way [today] . . . love would be if not the father of *virtù*, at least the teacher of good manners, inventor of happiness and donor of all graces" (p. 45).

74. Castiglione, *Il libro del cortigiano*, pp. 392–94 (IV:6.119–27). It is interesting to note that here Bembo uses the same language, "the eyes of the mind," to see the ultimate spiritual beauty which Suor Mansueta used to describe the way she saw the ultimate negative temptation, her devil lover (see Chapter 2).

75. Perhaps in the way that we seem to see the regime of *virtù* in the Renaissance working across all levels of society and thought from the highest to the most everyday there is a suggestion about a rethinking of intellectual history more generally: a rethinking that goes beyond the tradition of the great chains of ideas or the newer social history of ideas to look at how crucial ideas are deeply embedded in a culture and society at every level and how they interact not in a neat structural way but in the messy complex way of a range of discussions or dialogues or even nondialogues and silences—in a process that I have called the poetics of the everyday.

76. Martines, *Italian Renaissance Sextet*, p. 43; Sermini, "Scopone," p. 752.

77. Martines, *Italian Renaissance Sextet*, p. 43; Sermini, "Scopone," p. 752. Here, perhaps, Scopone's name suggests a deeper meaning, for although the theme of the novella privileges the reading "prickly pear," the perfect epitaph for this difficult peasant, it also can be read as "ugly large broom," and fittingly his evil behavior is now swept out (again the verb used here, *scopare* = to sweep, is closely related to Scopone) of the community. Brooms and their sweeping motion also suggested in the Renaissance, as they do today, the motion of sexual intercourse, and thus the pejorative ending "*one*" of Scopone could also suggest a negative label something on the order of "evil screwer or fucker," a fitting label as well, although the final transformation of Scopone into Salice (a pliant willow) privileges the tree metaphor.

78. Martines, *Italian Renaissance Sextet*, p. 44; Sermini, "Scopone," p. 753.

79. Martines, *Italian Renaissance Sextet*, p. 44; Sermini, "Scopone," p. 753.

80. For a good overview of this now, see Muir, *Ritual in Early Modern Europe*, pp. 98–108; see also Cashmere, "Social Uses of Violence in Ritual"; Davis, "Charivari, Honor, and Community in Seventeenth Century Lyon and Geneva," as well as her classic "Reasons of Misrule"; and Klapisch-Zuber, "'*Mattinata*' in Medieval Italy."

81. See Ruggiero, "Deconstructing the Body, Constructing the Body Politic," and Edgerton, *Pictures and Punishment.*

82. For an overview of the extensive literature on this in the early Renaissance, see Zorzi, "Giustizia criminale e criminalità nell'Italia del tardo medioevo," and for specific cities, see Cohn, "Criminality and the State in Renaissance Florence"; Brackett, *Criminal Justice and Crime in Late Renaissance Florence;* Romani, "Criminalità e giustizia nel Ducato di Mantova alla fine del Cinquecento"; Ruggiero, *Violence in Early Renaissance Venice;* Astarita, *Village Justice;* Chambers and Dean, *Clean Hands and Rough Justice;* and Dean and Lowe, *Crime, Society, and the Law in Renaissance Italy.*

83. Martines, *Italian Renaissance Sextet*, p. 49; Sermini, "Scopone," p. 757; italics mine. "[Scopone] veduto il suo vantaggio, di subito prese partito, in forma che, quello che la natura li concedeva, tanto forte si fece, che di colpo, preso partito, snaturò, deliberato essere, e così fu sempre, di contraria condizione alla prima natura sua."

84. Martines, *Italian Renaissance Sextet*, p. 50; Sermini, "Scopone," p. 758.

85. Martines, *Italian Renaissance Sextet*, p. 51; Sermini, "Scopone," p. 759.

86. Martines, *Italian Renaissance Sextet*, p. 52; Sermini, "Scopone," p. 760. It might be noted that this renaming/resurrection has a rich biblical precedent as well which draws out the deeper double sense of Buonsignori as a good lord (once he took up the mantle of adult male responsibility), for in the Bible the ultimate Good Lord often renames significant characters after they have experienced dramatic transformations at his behest. Abram was renamed Abraham, Jacob was renamed Israel, and Saul became Paul; moreover, regularly their new names had a deeper meaning, as for example when Jacob, whose original name meant "deceiver," was renamed Israel, essentially foretelling what his future would bring. I would like to thank Hope J. Myers, a member of my Spring 2005 seminar on literature and history, for pointing this out to me.

87. Martines, *Italian Renaissance Sextet*, p. 53; Sermini, "Scopone," p. 760.

Afterword • How Machiavelli Put the Devil Back in Hell

1. For this novella, see Machiavelli, *Tutte le opere*, pp. 919–23; an English translation can be found in Machiavelli, *Portable Machiavelli*, pp. 419–29.

2. Although these three criteria may seem simple, meeting them within the disciplinary constraints of literary theory (text), history (context), and aesthetics (critical ideas that are interesting to think) significantly reduces the range of possible readings and ultimately is no easy task. "Simply" fitting readings into, for example, a Foucauldian, Freudian, or Marxist frame makes the sinning somewhat easier but also, I would suggest, often less interesting and less rich as well.

Archival Sources

Archivio di Stato, Florence
    Filze Medici
    Onestà
        Practica Secreti
        Suppliche
Archivio di Stato, Venice
    Avogadori di Comun
        Libro d'Oro, Nascite
        Miscellanea Civile
        Miscellanea Penale
        Raspe, reg. 3673/33–3691/51
    Collegio
        Relazioni Ambasciatori
        Relazioni dei Rettori
        Notatorio
    Consiglio dei Dieci
        Deliberazioni Miste
        Capi, Lettere dei Rettori
        Parti Criminale
        Parti Secreti
    Esecutori conto la Bestemmia
        Processi
    Quarantia Criminal
    Provveditore sopra Monasteri
    Sant'Uffizio, buste 9–70

Published Works

Accati, Luisa. "The Spirit of Fornication: Virtue of the Soul and Virtue of the Body in Friuli, 1600–1800." In *Sex and Gender in Historical Perspective: Selections from*

Quaderni Storici, edited by Edward Muir and Guido Ruggiero, pp. 110–40. Baltimore: Johns Hopkins University Press, 1990.

Alberti, Leon Battista. *I libri della famiglia*, ed. Cecil Grayson. In *Opere volgare*, vol. 1. Rome: Laterza, 1960.

Amelang, James. *The Flight of Icarus: Artisan Autobiography in Early Modern Europe.* Stanford, CA: Stanford University Press, 1998.

Anderson, Benedict. *Imagined Communities: Reflections on the Origin and Spread of Nationalism.* London: Verso, 1983.

Andrieni, Francesco. *Le bravure del Capitano Spavento; Divisi in molti ragionamenti in forma dialogo.* Venice: Giacomo Antonio Somasco, 1609.

Aretino, Pietro. *Aretino's Dialogues.* Translated by Raymond Rosenthal. New York: Marsilio, 1994.

———. *Sei giornate.* Edited by Giovanni Aquilecchia. Rome: Laterza, 1980.

Arnold, Janet. *Patterns of Fashion: The Cut and Construction of Clothes for Men and Women c. 1560–1620.* New York: Drama Book, 1985.

Ascoli, Albert Russell. *Ariosto's Bitter Harmony: Crisis and Evasion in the Italian Renaissance.* Princeton, NJ: Princeton University Press, 1987.

Ascoli, Albert Russell, and Victoria Kahn, eds. *Machiavelli and the Discourse of Literature.* Ithaca, NY: Cornell University Press, 1993.

Astarita, Tommaso. *Village Justice: Community, Family, and Popular Culture in Early Modern Italy.* Baltimore: Johns Hopkins University Press, 1999.

Bakhtin, Mikhail. *Rabelais and His World.* Translated by Hélène Iswolsky. Bloomington: Indiana University Press, 1984.

Bandello, Matteo. "Giulia da Gazuola" (Tale I:8). In *Novelle Italiane: Il Cinquecento*, edited by Marcello Ciccuto, pp. 209–18. Milan: Garzanti, 1982.

———. *Le quattro parti de le Novelle del Bandello.* 4 vols. Edited by Gustavo Balsamo-Crivelli. Turin: Unione Tipografico-Editrice Torinese, 1924.

Bargagli, Girolamo. *Dialogo de'giuochi che nella vegghie sanese si usano di fare* (1572). Edited by P. D'Incalci Ermini. Siena: Academia Sienese degli Intronati, 1982.

Bembo, Pietro. *Bembo. Opere in volgare.* Edited by Mario Marti. Florence: Sansoni, 1961.

———. *Gli Asolani.* Translated by Rudolf Gottfried. Freeport, NY: Books for Libraries Press, 1971.

Ben-Amos, Ilana Krausman. *Adolescence and Youth in Early Modern England.* New Haven, CT: Yale University Press, 1994.

Bernard, John. "Writing and the Paradox of the Self: Machiavelli's Literary Vocation." *Renaissance Quarterly* 59:1 (2006): 59–89.

Boccaccio, Giovanni. *Decameron.* In *Decameron, Filocolo, Ameto, Fiammetta*, edited by Enrico Bianchi, Carlo Salinari, and Natalino Sapegno in *La letteratura italiana: Storia e testi*, vol. 8. Milan: Riccardo Ricciardi Editori, 1952.

Boerio, Giuseppe. *Dizionario del dialetto veneziano.* Venice: Tipografia di Giovanni Cecchini, 1856.

Bornstein, Daniel, and Roberto Rusconi, eds. *Women and Religion in Medieval and Renaissance Italy.* Chicago: University of Chicago Press, 1996.

Bossy, John. *Christianity in the West, 1400–1700.* Oxford: Oxford University Press, 1985.

————. "The Counter-Reformation and the People of Catholic Europe." *Past and Present* 47 (1970): 51–71.

Boswell, John. *Christianity, Social Tolerance and Homosexuality.* Chicago: University of Chicago Press, 1980.

Bourdieu, Pierre. *Outline of a Theory of Practice.* Translated by Richard Nice. Cambridge: Cambridge University Press, 1977.

Bouwsma, William J. *Venice and the Defense of Republican Liberty: Renaissance Values in the Age of the Counter Reformation.* Berkeley: University of California Press, 1968.

Brackett, John K. *Criminal Justice and Crime in Late Renaissance Florence, 1537–1609.* Cambridge: Cambridge University Press, 1992.

Bray, Alan. *The Friend.* Chicago: University of Chicago Press, 2003.

————. *Homosexuality in Renaissance England.* New York: Columbia University Press, 1995.

Brown, Judith C. *Immodest Acts: The Life of a Lesbian Nun in Renaissance Italy.* New York: Oxford University Press, 1986.

Brown, Judith C., and Robert C. Davis, eds. *Gender and Society in Renaissance Italy.* London: Longman, 1998.

Brown, Peter. *The Body in Society: Men, Women, and Sexual Renunciation in Early Christian Society.* New York: Columbia University Press, 1988.

Brownlee, Kevin, and Valeria Finucci, eds. *Generation and Degeneration: Tropes of Reproduction in Literature and History from Antiquity to Early Modern Europe.* Durham, NC: Duke University Press, 2001.

Brucker, Gene. *Giovanni and Lusanna, Love and Marriage in Renaissance Florence.* Berkeley: University of California Press, 1986.

————, ed. *The Society of Renaissance Florence: A Documentary Study.* New York: Harper and Row, 1971.

Burke, Peter. *The Fortunes of the Courtier.* University Park: Pennsylvania State Press, 1995.

————. *The Historical Anthropology of Early Modern Italy.* Cambridge: Cambridge University Press, 1987.

————. *Popular Culture in Early Modern Europe.* New York: Harper and Row, 1978.

————. "The Renaissance, Individualism, and the Portrait." *History of European Ideas* 21 (1995): 393–400.

————. "Representations of the Self from Petrarch to Descartes." In *Rewriting the Self: Histories from the Renaissance to the Present*, edited by Roy Porter, pp. 17–28. London: Routledge, 1997.

Byars, Jana. "Concubines and Concubinage in Early Modern Venice." Ph.D. diss., Pennsylvania State University, 2006.

Campbell, Erin J. "The Art of Aging Gracefully: The Elderly Artist as Courtier in Early Modern Art Theory and Criticism." *Sixteenth Century Journal* 33 (2002): 321–31.

Camporesi, Piero. *Il pane salvaggio.* Bologna: Il Mulino, 1980. Translated by David Gentilcore as *Bread of Dreams* (Chicago: University of Chicago Press, 1989).

————. *La carne impassibile.* Milan: Il Saggiatore, 1983. Translated by Tania Murray as

The Incorruptible Flesh: Bodily Mutilation and Mortification in Religion and Folklore (Cambridge: Cambridge University Press, 1988).

Cardini, Franco, ed. *Gostanza, la strega di San Miniato.* Rome: Laterza, 1989.

Carroll, Linda. *Angelo Beolco (Il Ruzante).* Boston: Twayne, 1990.

————. "Carnival Rites as Vehicles of Protest in Renaissance Venice." *Sixteenth Century Journal* 16 (1985): 487–502.

————. "Who's on Top? Gender as Societal Power Configuration in Italian Renaissance Painting and Drama." *Sixteenth Century Journal* 20 (1989): 531–58.

Cashmere, John. "The Social Uses of Violence in Ritual: Charivari or Religious Persecution." *European History Quarterly* 21 (1991): 291–319.

Castiglione, Baldassare. *Il libro del cortegiano.* 2 vols. Edited by Amedeo Quondam. Milan: Mondadori, 2002.

Cavallo, Sandra, and Simona Cerutti. "Female Honor and the Social Control of Reproduction in Piedmont between 1600 and 1800." In *Sex and Gender in Historical Perspective: Selections from Quaderni Storici,* edited by Edward Muir and Guido Ruggiero, pp. 73–109. Baltimore: Johns Hopkins University Press, 1990.

Cellini, Benvenuto. *The Autobiography.* Translated by George Bull. New York: Penguin, 1985.

————. *Vita.* Edited by Ettore Camesasca. Milan: Rizzoli, 1985.

Chambers, David, and Trevor Dean. *Clean Hands and Rough Justice: An Investigating Magistrate in Renaissance Italy.* Ann Arbor: University of Michigan Press, 1997.

Chartier, Roger. *Cultural History: Between Practices and Representations.* Ithaca, NY: Cornell University Press, 1988.

Chojnacki, Stanley. "Measuring Adulthood: Adolescence and Gender." In Chojnacki, *Women and Men in Renaissance Venice,* pp. 185–205. Baltimore: Johns Hopkins University Press, 2000.

————. "Measuring Adulthood: Adolescence and Gender in Renaissance Venice." *Journal of Family History* 17 (1992): 371–95.

————. "Political Adulthood." In Chojnacki, *Women and Men in Renaissance Venice,* pp. 227–43. Baltimore: Johns Hopkins University Press, 2000.

————. *Women and Men in Renaissance Venice.* Baltimore: Johns Hopkins University Press, 2000.

Cohen, Thomas V. "Three Forms of Jeopardy: Honor, Pain, and Truth-Telling in a Sixteenth-Century Italian Courtroom." *Sixteenth Century Journal* 29 (1998): 975–98.

Cohen, Thomas V., and Elizabeth Cohen. *Words and Deeds in Renaissance Rome: Trials before the Papal Magistrates.* Toronto: University of Toronto Press, 1993.

Cohn, Samuel. "Criminality and the State in Renaissance Florence, 1344–1466." *Journal of Social History* 14 (1980): 211–33.

Connell, William J., and Andrea Zorzi, eds. *Florentine Tuscany: Structures and Practices of Power.* Cambridge: Cambridge University Press, 2000.

Cottino-Jones, Marga. "Desire and the Fantastic in the *Decameron:* The Third Day." *Italica* 70 (1993): 1–18.

Cozzi, Gaetano. "Padri, figli e matrimoni clandestini (metà sec. XVI–metà sec. XVIII)." *La Cultura* 15 (1976): 169–212.

————, ed. *Stato, società e giustizia nella Repubblica Veneta (sec. 15–18)*. Rome: Jouvance, 1980.

Cressy, David. *Birth, Marriage, and Death: Ritual, Religion, and the Life-Cycle in Tudor and Stuart England*. New York: Oxford University Press, 1997.

Crum, Roger J., and John T. Paoletti, eds. *Renaissance Florence: A Social History*. Cambridge: Cambridge University Press, 2006.

da Rif, Bianca Maria, ed. *La Bulesca*. In *La letteratura "alla Bulesca": Testi rinascimentali veneti*. Padua: Antenore, 1984.

Darnton, Robert. *The Great Cat Massacre and Other Episodes in French Cultural History*. New York: Random House, Vintage, 1985.

Davidson, Nicholas S. "Sodomy in Early Modern Venice." In *Sodomy in Early Modern Europe*, edited by Tom Betteridge, pp. 65–81. Manchester, England: Manchester University Press, 2002.

Davis, Natalie Zemon. "Boundaries and the Sense of Self in Sixteenth-Century France." In *Reconstructing Individualism: Autonomy, Individuality, and Self in Western Thought*, edited by Thomas C. Heller, Morton Sosna, and David E. Wellbery, pp. 53–63. Stanford, CA: Stanford University Press, 1986.

————. "Charivari, Honor, and Community in Seventeenth Century Lyon and Geneva." In *Rite, Drama, Festival Spectacle: Rehearsals toward a Theory of Cultural Performance*, edited by John J. MacAloon, pp. 42–57. Philadelphia: Institute for the Study of Human Issues, 1984.

————. *Fiction in the Archives: Pardon Tales and Their Tellers in Sixteenth-Century France*. Stanford, CA: Stanford University Press, 1987.

————. "The Reasons of Misrule." In *Society and Culture in Early Modern France*, pp. 97–123. Stanford, CA: Stanford University Press, 1975).

————. *The Return of Martin Guerre*. Cambridge, MA: Harvard University Press, 1983.

————. "The Sacred and the Body Social in Sixteenth-Century Lyon." *Past and Present* 90 (1980): 40–70.

————. *Society and Culture in Early Modern France*. Stanford, CA: Stanford University Press, 1975.

Davis, Robert. *The War of the Fists: Popular Culture and Public Violence in Late Renaissance Venice*. New York: Oxford University Press, 1994.

Dean, Trevor, and K. J. P. Lowe, eds. *Crime, Society, and Law in Renaissance Italy*. Cambridge: Cambridge University Press, 1994.

de'Angelis, Francesca Romana. *La divina Isabella: Vita stroardinaria di una donna del Cinquecento*. Florence: Sansoni, 1991.

de Certeau, Michel. *The Practice of Everyday Life*. Translated by Steven F. Randall. Berkeley: University of California Press, 1984.

Del Col, Andrea. "Organizzazione, composizione e giurisdizione dei tribunali dell'Inquisizione romana nella Repubblica di Venezia (1500–1550)." *Critica Storica / Bollettino A.S.E.* 25:2 (1988): 244–94.

de Lorenzi, Giovanni Battista, ed. *Leggi e memorie venete sulla prostituzione*. Venice: published privately by the Count of Orford, 1870–72.

Delumeau, Jean. *Le Catholicisme entre Luther et Voltaire.* Paris: Presses Universitaires de France, 1971.

————. *Le péché, et la peur: La culpabilisation en Occident (XIIIe–XVIIIe siècle).* Paris: Fayard, 1983. Translated by Eric Nicholson as *Sin and Fear: The Emergence of a Western Guilt Culture, 13th–18th Centuries* (New York: St. Martin's Press, 1990).

Diefendorf, Barbara. "Family Culture, Renaissance Culture." *Renaissance Quarterly* 40 (1987): 661–81.

Diefendorf, Barbara, and Carla Hesse, eds. *Culture and Identity in Early Modern Europe: Essays in Honor of Natalie Zemon Davis.* Ann Arbor: University of Michigan Press, 1993.

Dionisotti, Carlo, ed. *Maria Savorgnan-Pietro Bembo, Carteggio d'amore (1500–1501).* Florence: Felice le Monnier, 1950.

Di Simplicio, Oscar. "Le Perpetue (Stato Senese, 1600–1800)." *Quaderni Storici* 68 (1988): 381–409. Translated by Corrada Biazzo Curry, Margaret A. Gallucci, and Mary M. Gallucci as "Perpetuas: The Women Who Kept Priests," in *History from Crime: Selections from Quaderni Storici,* edited by Edward Muir and Guido Ruggiero, pp. 32–64 (Baltimore: Johns Hopkins University Press, 1994).

————. *Peccato, penitenza, perdono: Siena 1575–1800. La formazione della coscienza dell'Italia moderna.* Milan: Franco Angeli Storia, 1994.

Dotti, Ugo. *Machavelli rivoluzionario: Vita e opera.* Rome: Carocci Editore, 2003.

Eagleton, Terry. *Literary Theory: An Introduction.* Minneapolis: University of Minnesota Press, 1983.

Eamon, William. *Science and the Secrets of Nature: Books of Secrets in Medieval and Early Modern Culture.* Princeton, NJ: Princeton University Press, 1994.

Edgerton, Samuel Y., Jr. *Pictures and Punishment: Art and Criminal Prosecution during the Florentine Renaissance.* Ithaca, NY: Cornell University Press, 1985.

Eisenbichler, Konrad. "Bronzino's Portrait of Guidobaldo II Della Rovere." *Renaissance and Reformation* 13 (1988): 13–20.

————, ed., *The Premodern Teenager: Youth and Society, 1150–1650.* Toronto: Center for Reformation and Renaissance Studies, 2002.

Elias, Norbert. *The Civilizing Process.* Vol. 1, *The History of Manners;* vol 2, *State Formation and Civilization.* Translated by Edmund Jephcott. Oxford: Blackwell, 1994.

Erizzo, Sebastiano. *Le sei giornate.* Edited by Renzo Bragantini. Rome: Salerno Editrice, 1977.

Farr, James R. *Authority and Sexuality in Early Modern Burgundy (1500–1700).* New York: Oxford University Press, 1995.

————. "Crimine nel vicinato: Ingiurie, matrimonio e onore nella Digione del XVI e XVII secolo." *Quaderni Storici* 66 (1987): 839–54.

Ferguson, Margaret, Maureen Quilligan, and Nancy Vickers, eds. *Rewriting the Renaissance: The Discourses of Sexual Difference in Early Modern Europe.* Chicago: University of Chicago Press, 1986.

Ferrante, Lucia. "Honor Regained: Women in the Casa del Soccorso di San Paolo in Sixteenth-Century Bologna." In *Sex and Gender in Historical Perspective: Selections from Quaderni Storici,* edited by Edward Muir and Guido Ruggiero, pp. 46–72. Baltimore: Johns Hopkins University Press, 1990.

Ferraro, Joanne. *Marriage Wars in Late Renaissance Venice.* New York: Oxford University Press, 2001.

Finlay, Robert. *Politics in Renaissance Venice.* New Brunswick, NJ: Rutgers University Press, 1980.

Finlayson, John. "Of Leeks and Old Men: Chaucer and Boccaccio." *Studia Neophilologica: A Journal of Germanic and Romance Literature* 70 (1998): 35–39.

Finucci, Valeria. *The Lady Vanishes: Subjectivity and Representation in Castiglione and Ariosto.* Stanford, CA: Stanford University Press, 1992.

———. *The Manly Masquerade: Masculinity, Paternity, and Castration in the Italian Renaissance.* Durham, NC: Duke University Press, 2003.

Flandrin, Jean-Louis. *Families in Former Times: Kinship, Household and Sexuality in Early Modern France.* Translated by Richard W. Southern. Cambridge: Cambridge University Press, 1979.

Fonte, Moderata (Modesta Pozzo). *Il merito delle donne ove chiaramente si scuopre quanto siano elle degne e più perfetto de gli uomini.* Edited by Adriana Chemello. Mirano/Venice: Editrice Eidos, 1988. Translated by Virginia Cox as *The Worth of Women: Wherein Is Clearly Revealed Their Nobility and Their Superiority to Men,* edited by Virginia Cox, in the series entitled The Other Voice in Early Modern Europe, edited by Margaret L. King and Albert Rabil Jr. Chicago: University of Chicago Press, 1997.

Foucault, Michel. *The History of Sexuality.* Vol. 1, *An Introduction,* translated by Robert Hurley. New York: Random House, Vintage, 1980.

———. *The Order of Things: An Archaeology of the Human Sciences.* New York: Random House, Vintage, 1973.

Fradenberg, Louise, and Carla Freccero, eds. *Premodern Sexualities.* New York: Routledge, 1996.

Freccero, Carla. "Acts, Identities, and Sexuality's (Pre) Modern Regimes." *Journal of Women's History* 11 (1999): 186–92.

———. "Bodies and Pleasures: Early Modern Interrogations." *Romanic Review* 86 (1995): 379–90.

Gallagher, Catherine, and Stephen Greenblatt. *Practicing New Historicism.* Chicago: University of Chicago Press, 2000.

Gallucci, Margaret A. *Benvenuto Cellini: Sexuality, Masculinity, and Artistic Identity in Renaissance Italy.* New York: Palgrave, 2003.

Garzoni (da Bagnacavallo), Tomaso. *La piazza universale di tutte le professioni del mondo.* Edited by Paolo Cherchi and Beatrice Collina. 1584. Turin: Einaudi, 1966.

Geertz, Clifford. *The Interpretation of Cultures: Selected Essays.* New York: Basic Books, 1973.

———. *Local Knowledge: Further Essays in Interpretative Anthropology.* New York: Basic Books, 1983.

Gentilcore, David. *From Bishop to Witch: The System of the Sacred in Early Modern Terra d'Otranto.* Manchester, England: Manchester University Press, 1992.

Gerard, Kent, and Gert Hekma, eds. *In Pursuit of Sodomy: Male Homosexuality in Renaissance and Enlightenment Europe.* New York: Haworth Press, 1988.

Ghinassi, Ghino. "Fasi dell'elaborazione del *Cortegiano.*" *Studi di Filologia Italiana* 25 (1967): 155–96.

Giannetti, Laura. "*Feminae ludentes* nella commedia rinascimentale italiana: Gli esempi di *Calandra e Veniexiana.*" *Italian Culture* 18:2 (2000): 47–71.

———. "I discorsi del gioco nella commedia rinascimentale italiana." Ph.D. diss., University of Connecticut, 1998.

———. "On the Deceptions of the *Deceived:* Lelia and the Pleasures of Play." *Modern Language Notes* 116 (2001): 54–73.

———. "When Male Characters Pass as Women: Theatrical Play and Social Practice in the Italian Renaissance." *Sixteenth Century Journal* 36:3 (2005): 743–60.

Giannetti, Laura, and Guido Ruggiero, eds. and trans. *Five Comedies from the Italian Renaissance.* Baltimore: Johns Hopkins University Press, 2003.

Gilbert, Creighton. "When Did a Man in the Renaissance Grow Old?" *Studies in the Renaissance* 14 (1967): 7–32.

Gilbert, Felix. *Machiavelli and Guiccardini: Politics and History in Sixteenth-Century Florence.* Princeton, NJ: Princeton University Press, 1965.

Ginsberg, Elaine, ed. *Passing and the Fictions of Identity.* Durham, NC: Duke University Press, 1996.

Ginzburg, Carlo. *I Benandanti, Stregoneria e culti agrari tra Cinquecento e Seicento.* Turin: Einaudi, 1966. Translated by John Tedeschi and Anne Tedeschi as *The Night Battles: Witchcraft and Agrarian Cults in the Sixteenth and Seventeenth Centuries* (Baltimore: Johns Hopkins University Press, 1983).

———. *Il formaggio e i vermi: Il cosmo di un mugnaio del'500.* Turin: Einaudi, 1976. Translated by John Tedeschi and Anne Tedeschi as *The Cheese and the Worms: The Cosmos of a Sixteenth-Century Miller* (Baltimore: Johns Hopkins University Press, 1980).

———. *Miti, emblemi, spie: Morfologia e storia.* Turin: Einaudi, 1986. Translated by John Tedeschi and Anne Tedeschi as *Clues, Myths and the Historical Method* (Baltimore: Johns Hopkins University Press, 1989).

———. *Storia notturna: Una decifrazione del sabba.* Turin: Einaudi, 1989. Translated by Raymond Rosenthal as *Ecstasies: Deciphering the Witches' Sabbath* (New York: Pantheon, 1991).

Goffman, Erving. *Interaction Ritual.* Garden City, NJ: Anchor Books, 1967.

Goldberg, Jonathan, ed. *Queering the Renaissance.* Durham, NC: Duke University Press, 1994.

———. *Sodometries: Renaissance Texts, Modern Sexualities.* Stanford, CA: Stanford University Press, 1992.

Goody, Jack. *The European Family: An Historico-Anthropological Essay.* Oxford: Blackwell, 2000.

Grazzini, Anton Francesco (Il Lasca). *Le cene.* Edited by Ettore Mazzali. Milan: Rizzoli, 1989.

————. *Le rime burlesche edite e inedite.* Edited by Carlo Veronese. Florence: Sansoni, 1882.

Greenblatt, Stephen. *Learning to Curse: Essays in Early Modern Culture.* New York: Routledge, 1990.

————. *Marvelous Possessions: The Wonder of the New World.* Chicago: University of Chicago Press, 1991.

————. *Renaissance Self-Fashioning from More to Shakespeare.* Chicago: University of Chicago Press, 1980.

————. "What Is the History of Literature?" *Critical Inquiry* 23 (1997): 460–81.

Grendler, Paul. *Critics of the Italian World, 1530–1560: Anton Doni, Nicolò Franco and Ortensio Lando.* Madison: University of Wisconsin Press, 1969.

————. *The Roman Inquisition and the Venetian Press, 1540–1605.* Princeton, NJ: Princeton University Press, 1977.

————. "The Tre Savii Sopra Eresia 1547–1605: A Prosopographical Study." *Studi Veneziani,* n.s. 3 (1979): 283–340.

Groves, David. "Gabrina the Whore: Art and Nature in the Body of the Text." *Rivista d'Italianistica* 14 (1999): 5–22.

Grubb, James C. "Memory and Identity: Why Venetians Did Not Keep *Recordanze.*" *Renaissance Studies* 8 (1994): 375–87.

————. *Provincial Families of the Renaissance: Private and Public Life in the Veneto.* Baltimore: Johns Hopkins University Press, 1996.

Guidi, José. "De l'amour courtois à l'amour sacrè: La condition de la femme dans l'oeuvre de Baldassar Castiglione." In *Images de la femme dans la literature italienne de la Renaissance: Prèjugès misogynes et aspirations nouvelles,* edited by André Rochon, pp. 9–80. Paris: Université de la Sorbonne Nouvelle, 1980.

————. "Reformulations de l'idéologie aristocratique au XVIe siècle: Les différentes rédactions et la fortune du *Curtisan.*" In *Réécritures,* vol. 1, edited by Jean Toscan et al., pp. 121–84. Paris: Université de la Sorbonne Nouvelle, 1983.

Halperin, David M. "Forgetting Foucault: Acts, Identities and the History of Sexuality." *Representations* 69 (1998): 93–120.

————. *How to Do the History of Homosexuality.* Chicago: University of Chicago Press, 2002.

————. *One Hundred Years of Homosexuality and Other Esays on Greek Love.* New York: Routledge, 1990.

Halperin, David M., John Winkler, and Froma Zeitlin, eds. *Before Sexuality: The Construction of Erotic Experience in the Ancient Greek World.* Princeton, NJ: Princeton University Press, 1990.

Hampton, Timothy. *Writing from History: The Rhetoric of Exemplarity in Renaissance Literature.* Ithaca, NY: Cornell University Press, 1990.

Hanning, Robert, and David Rosand, eds. *Castiglione: The Ideal and the Real in Renaissance Culture.* New Haven, CT: Yale University Press, 1983.

Herlihy, David, and Christiane Klapisch-Zuber. *Tuscans and Their Families: A Study of the Florentine Catasto of 1427.* New Haven, CT: Yale University Press, 1985.

————. *Les Tuscans et leurs familles: Une etude du Catasto florentin de 1427.* 3 vols. Paris: Editions de L'Ecole des Hautes Etudes en Sciences Sociale, 1978.

Hsia, R. Po-chia, ed. *A Companion to the Reformation World.* Oxford: Blackwell, 2003.

————. *Social Discipline in the Reformation: Central Europe, 1550–1750.* London: Routledge, 1989.

Huizinga, Johan. *Homo Ludens: A Study of the Play Element in Culture.* Boston: Beacon Press, 1955.

Hunt, Lynn, ed. *The New Cultural History.* Berkeley: University of California Press, 1989.

Il gioco dell'amore: Le cortigiane di Venezia dal Trecento al Settecento. Milan: Berenice, 1990.

Il potere e lo spazio: La scena del principe. Florence: Electra, 1980.

Javitch, Daniel, ed. *The Book of the Courtier.* Translated by Charles S. Singleton. New York: Norton, 2002.

Jed, Stephanie H. *Chaste Thinking: The Rape of Lucretia and the Birth of Humanism.* Bloomington: Indiana University Press, 1989.

Johnson, Geraldine A., and Sara F. Mathews, eds. *Picturing Women in Renaissance and Baroque Italy.* Cambridge: Cambridge University Press, 1997.

Jones, Ann Rosaline. *The Currency of Love: Women's Love Lyric in Europe, 1540–1620.* Bloomington: Indiana University Press, 1990.

Karras, Ruth Mazzo. "Prostitution and the Question of Sexual Identity in Medieval Europe." *Journal of Women's History* 11 (1999): 159–77.

————. "Response: Identity, Sexuality and History." *Journal of Women's History* 11 (1999): 193–98.

Kelly, Joan. "Did Women Have a Renaissance?" In Kelly, *Women, History and Theory: The Essays of Joan Kelly,* pp. 19–50. Chicago: University of Chicago Press, 1984.

————. *Women, History and Theory: The Essays of Joan Kelly.* Chicago: University of Chicago Press, 1984.

Kertzer, David, and Peter Laslett, eds. *Aging in the Past: Demography, Society and Old Age.* Berkeley: University of California Press, 1995.

Kertzer, David, and K. Warner Schaie, eds. *Age Structuring in Comparative Perspective.* Hillsdale, NJ: Lawrence Erlbaum, 1989.

King, Margaret L. *Venetian Humanism in an Age of Patrician Dominance.* Princeton, NJ: Princeton University Press, 1986.

Kirkham, Victoria. "Love's Labors Rewarded and Paradise Lost." *Romanic Review* 72 (1981): 79–98.

Kittell, Ellen E., and Thomas F. Madden, eds. *Medieval and Renaissance Florence.* Champagne: University of Illinois Press, 1999.

Klapisch-Zuber, Christiane. "Blood Parents and Milk Parents: Wet Nursing in Florence, 1300–1530." In Klapisch-Zuber, *Women, Family, and Ritual in Renaissance Italy,* translated by Lydia G. Cochrane, pp. 132–64. Chicago: University of Chicago Press, 1985.

————. "Compèrage et clientèlisme à Florence (1360–1520)." *Ricerche Storiche* 15 (1985): 61–76.

————. "The '*Mattinata*' in Medieval Italy." In Klapisch-Zuber, *Women, Family, and Ritual in Renaissance Italy*, translated by Lydia G. Cochrane, pp. 261–82. Chicago: University of Chicago Press, 1985.

————. *Women, Family, and Ritual in Renaissance Italy.* Translated by Lydia G. Cochrane. Chicago: University of Chicago Press, 1985.

Krekíc, B. "Abominandum Crimen: Punishment of Homosexuals in Renaissance Dubrovnik." *Viator: Medieval and Renaissance Studies* 18 (1987): 337–45.

Kuehn, Thomas. *Emancipation in Late Medieval Florence.* New Brunswick, NJ: Rutgers University Press, 1982.

————. *Law, Family, and Women: Towards a Legal Anthropology of Renaissance Italy.* Chicago: University of Chicago Press, 1991.

Labalme, Patricia. "Sodomy and Venetian Justice in the Renaissance." *Legal History Review* 52 (1984): 217–54.

Laqueur, Thomas. *Making Sex, Body and Gender from the Greeks to Freud.* Cambridge, MA: Harvard University Press, 1990.

Larivaille, Paul. *La vie quotidienne des courtesanes en Italie au temps de la renaissance.* Paris: Hachette, 1975.

Lavrin, Asunción, ed. *Sexuality and Marriage in Colonial Latin America.* Lincoln: University of Nebraska Press, 1989.

Levi, Giovanni, and Jean-Claude Schmitt. *A History of Young People.* Vol. 1, *Ancient and Medieval Rites of Passage*, translated by Camille Nashe. Cambridge, MA: Harvard University Press, 1997.

————. *A History of Young People.* Vol. 2, *Stormy Evolution to Modern Times*, translated by Carol Volk. Cambridge, MA: Harvard University Press, 1997.

Macfarlane, Alan. *The Origin of English Individualism: The Family, Property and Social Transition.* Cambridge: Cambridge University Press, 1978.

Machiavelli, Niccolò. *Niccolò Machiavelli, Teatro: Andria, Mandragola, Clizia.* Edited by Guido Davico Bonino. Turin: Einaudi, 2001.

————. *Opere.* Vols. 1 and 2, edited by Corrado Vivanti. Turin: Einaudi, 1997, 1999.

————. *Opere di Niccolò Machiavelli.* Edited by Franco Gaeta. Vol. 3, *Lettere.* Turin: UTET, 1984.

————. *The Portable Machiavelli.* Edited and translated by Peter Bondanella and Mark Musa. New York: Penguin, 1979.

————. *Tutte le opere.* Edited by Mario Martelli. Florence: Sansoni, 1971.

Maclean, Ian. *The Renaissance Notion of Woman: A Study in the Fortunes of Scholasticism and Medical Science in European Intellectual Life.* Cambridge: Cambridge University Press, 1980.

Manetti, Antonio di Tuccio. *The Life of Brunelleschi by Antonio di Tuccio Manetti.* Edited by Howard Saalman, translated by Catherine Enggass. University Park: Pennsylvania State University Press, 1970.

————. "La novella del Grasso Legnaiuolo." In *Prosatori volgari del Quattrocento*, edited by Claudio Varesi, pp. 769–802. Milan: Riccardo Riccardi, 1955.

Marchini, Nelli Elena Vanzan. "L'altra faccia dell'amore ovvero i rischi dell'esercizio del piacere." In *Il gioco dell'amore: Le cortigiane di Venezia dal Trecento al Settecento*, pp. 47–56. Milan: Berenice, 1990.

Martelli, Mario. "Machiavelli politico amante poeta." *Interpres: Rivista di Studi Quattrocenteschi* 17 (1998): 211–56.

Martin, John J. "Inventing Sincerity, Refashioning Prudence: The Discovery of the Individual in Renaissance Europe." *American Historical Review* 102 (1997): 1309–42.

———. "The Myth of Renaissance Individualism." In *A Companion to the Worlds of the Renaissance*, edited by Guido Ruggiero, pp. 208–24. Oxford: Blackwell, 2002.

———. *Myths of Individualism.* New York: Palgrave, Macmillan, 2004.

———. *Venice's Hidden Enemies: Italian Heretics in a Renaissance City.* Berkeley: University of California Press, 1993.

Martin, Lynn A. "Old People, Alcohol and Identity in Europe, 1300–1700." In *Food, Drink and Identity: Cooking, Eating and Drinking in Europe since the Middle Ages*, edited by Peter Scholliers, pp. 119–37. Oxford: Berg, 2001.

Martines, Lauro. *An Italian Renaissance Sextet: Six Tales in Historical Context.* With translations by Murtha Baca. New York: Marsilio, 1994.

———. *Power and Imagination: City States in Renaissance Italy.* New York: Knopf, 1979.

———. "Séduction, espace familial et autorité dans la Renaissance italienne." *Annales: HSS* 53 (1998): 255–90.

———. *Strong Words: Writing and Social Strain in the Italian Renaissance.* Baltimore: Johns Hopkins University Press, 2001.

Martinez, Ronald L. "Benefit of Absence: Machiavellian Valediction in Clizia." In *Machiavelli and the Discourse of Literature*, edited by Albert Russell Ascoli and Victoria Kahn, pp. 117–44. Ithaca, NY: Cornell University Press, 1993.

Masten, Jeff. *Textual Intercourse: Collaboration, Authorship and Sexualities in Renaissance Drama.* New York: Cambridge University Press, 1997.

Mayer, Thomas, and D. R. Woolf, eds. *The Rhetoric of Life-Writing in Early Modern Europe.* Ann Arbor: University of Michigan Press, 1995.

Maza, Sarah. "Stephen Greenblatt, New Historicism, and Cultural History, or, What We Talk about When We Talk about Interdisciplinarity." *Modern Intellectual History* 1:2 (2004): 249–65.

Mazzi, Maria Serena. *Prostituzione e lenoni nella Firenze del Quattrocento.* Milan: Saggiatore, 1991.

McClure, George W. *The Culture of Profession in Late Renaissance Italy.* Toronto: University of Toronto Press, 2004.

Milani, Marisa. "L''Incanto' di Veronica Franco." *Giornale Storico della Letteratura Italiana* 162 (1985): 250–63.

———. "L'ossessione secolare di Suor Mansueta: Un esorcismo a Venezia nel 1574." *Quaderni Veneti* 7 (1988): 129–52.

Minois, Georges. *History of Old Age: From Antiquity to the Renaissance.* Translated by Sara Hanbury-Tenison. Chicago: University of Chicago Press, 1989.

Molmenti, Pompeo. *La storia di Venezia nella vita private.* 3 vols. Trieste: Lint, 1973.

Montaigne, Michel de. *The Complete Essays.* Stanford, CA: Stanford University Press, 1958.

Mormorando, Franco. *The Preacher's Demons: Bernardino of Siena and the Social Under-world of Early Renaissance Italy.* Chicago: University of Chicago Press, 1999.

Moulton, Ian Frederick. *Before Pornography: Erotic Writing in Early Modern England.* New York: Oxford University Press, 2000.

Muchembled, Robert. *Culture populaire et culture des èlites dans la France Moderne (XVe–XVIIIe siècle): Essai.* Paris: Flammarion, 1978. Translated by Lydia Cochrane as *Popular Culture and Elite Culture in France, 1400–1750* (Baton Rouge: Louisiana State University Press, 1985).

———. *La société policiée: Politique et politesse en France du XVIe au XXe siècle.* Paris: Seuil, 1998.

———. *L'invention del l'homme moderne: Culture et sensibilities en France du XVe au XVIIIe siècle.* Paris: Hachette, 1994.

Muir, Edward. *Civic Ritual in Renaissance Venice.* Princeton, NJ: Princeton University Press, 1981.

———. *Mad Blood Stirring: Vendetta and Factions in Friuli during the Renaissance.* Baltimore: Johns Hopkins University Press, 1993.

———. *Ritual in Early Modern Europe.* Cambridge: Cambridge University Press, 1997.

———. "The Sources of Civil Society in Italy." *Journal of Interdisciplinary History* 29 (1999): 379–406.

———. "The Virgin on the Street Corner: The Place of the Sacred in Italian Cities." In *Religion and Culture in the Renaissance and Reformation,* edited by Steven Ozment, pp. 25–40. Kirksville, MO: Sixteenth Century Studies Journal Publications, 1989.

Muir, Edward, and Guido Ruggiero, eds. *History from Crime: Selections from Quaderni Storici.* Translated by Corrada Biazzo Curry, Margaret A. Gallucci, and Mary M. Gallucci. Baltimore: Johns Hopkins University Press, 1994.

———, eds. *Microhistory and the Lost Peoples of Europe: Selections from Quaderni Storici.* Translated by Eren Branch. Baltimore: Johns Hopkins University Press, 1991.

———, eds. *Sex and Gender in Historical Perspective: Selections from Quaderni Storici.* Translated by Margaret A. Gallucci with Mary M. Gallucci and Carole C. Gallucci. Baltimore: Johns Hopkins University Press, 1990.

Muir, Edward, and Ronald F. E. Weissman. "Social and Symbolic Places in Renaissance Venice and Florence." In *The Power of Place: Bringing Together Geographical and Sociological Imaginations,* edited by John Agnew and James S. Duncan, pp. 81–103. Boston: Unwin Hyman, 1989.

Najemy, John. *Between Friends: Discourses of Power and Desire in the Machiavelli-Vettori Letters of 1513–1515.* Princeton, NJ: Princeton University Press, 1993.

Neill, Michael. *Issues of Death, Mortality and Identity in English Renaissance Tragedy.* Oxford: Clarendon Press, 1997.

Niccoli, Ottavia. "'Menstruum quasi monstruum': Monstrous Births and Menstrual Taboo in the Sixteenth Century." In *Sex and Gender in Historical Perspective: Selections from Quaderni Storici,* edited by Edward Muir and Guido Ruggiero, pp. 1–25. Baltimore: Johns Hopkins University Press, 1990.

Nye, Robert A., and Katherine Park. "Destiny Is Anatomy." *New Republic,* 18 February 1991, pp. 53–57.

Orgel, Stephen. *Impersonations: The Performance of Gender in Shakespeare's England.* Cambridge: Cambridge University Press, 1997.

Padoan, Giorgio. "Il mondo delle cortigiane nella letteratura rinascimentale." In *Il gioco dell'amore: Le cortigiane di Venezia dal Trecento al Settecento,* pp. 63–71. Milan: Berenice, 1990.

Parker, Patricia, and David Quint, eds. *Literary Theory / Renaissance Texts.* Baltimore: Johns Hopkins University Press, 1986.

Perry, Mary E. *Gender and Disorder in Early Modern Seville.* Princeton, NJ: Princeton University Press, 1990.

Persels, Jeffrey C. "Bragueta Humanistica, or Humanism's Codpiece." *Sixteenth Century Journal* 28 (1997): 79–99.

Pitkin, Hanna Fenichel. *Fortune Is a Woman.* Berkeley: University of California Press, 1984.

Pocock, John G. A. *The Machiavellian Moment: Florentine Political Thought and the Atlantic Republican Tradition.* Princeton, NJ: Princeton University Press, 1968.

Porter, Roy, ed. *Rewriting the Self: Histories from the Renaissance to the Present.* London: Routledge, 1997.

Pullan, Brian. *The Jews of Europe and the Inquisition of Venice, 1550–1670.* Totowa, NJ: Barnes and Noble, 1983.

Ridolfi, Roberto. *Studi sulle commedie del Machiavelli.* Pisa: Nistri-Lischi, 1968.

———. *Vita di Niccolò Machiavelli.* 7th rev. ed. Florence: Sansoni, 1978.

Ringhieri, Innocentio. *Cento giuochi liberali, et di ingegno.* Bologna: Giaccarelli, 1551.

Rocke, Michael J. *Forbidden Friendships: Homosexuality and Male Culture in Renaissance Florence.* New York: Oxford University Press, 1996.

Rochon, André, ed. *Formes et significations de la "Beffa" dans la littérature Italienne de la Renaissance.* Paris: Université de la Sorbonne Nouvelle, 1972.

Roebuck, Janet. "When Does 'Old Age' Begin? The Evolution of the English Definition." *Journal of Social History* 12 (1979): 416–28.

Romani, Marzio. "Criminalità e giustizia nel Ducato di Mantova alla fine del Cinquecento." *Rivista Storica Italiana* 92 (1980): 680–99.

Romano, Dennis. "Gender and the Urban Geography of Renaissance Venice." *Journal of Social History* 23 (1989): 339–53.

———. *Housecraft and Statecraft: Domestic Service in Renaissance Venice, 1400–1600.* Baltimore: Johns Hopkins University Press, 1996.

———. *Patricians and Popolani: The Social Foundations of the Venetian Republic.* Baltimore: Johns Hopkins University Press, 1987.

Romeo, Giovanni. *Inquisitori, esorcisti e streghe nell'Italia della Controriforma.* Florence: Sansoni, 1990.

Roper, Lyndal. *Oedipus and the Devil: Witchcraft, Sexuality and Religion in Early Modern Europe.* London: Routledge, 1994.

Rosenthal, Margaret F. *The Honest Courtesan: Veronica Franco, Citizen and Writer in Sixteenth-Century Venice.* Chicago: University of Chicago Press, 1992.

Ruggiero, Guido. "The Abbot's Concubine: Lies, Literature and Power at the End of the

Renaissance." In *Medieval and Renaissance Florence*, edited by Ellen E. Kittell and Thomas F. Madden, pp. 166–80. Champagne: University of Illinois Press, 1999.

———. *Binding Passions: Tales of Magic, Marriage and Power from the End of the Renaissance*. New York: Oxford University Press, 1993.

———. *The Boundaries of Eros: Sex Crime and Sexuality in Renaissance Venice*. New York: Oxford University Press, 1985.

———, ed. *A Companion to the Worlds of the Renaissance*. Oxford: Blackwell, 2002.

———. "Deconstructing the Body, Constructing the Body Politic: Ritual Execution in the Renaissance." In *Riti e rituali nelle società medievali*, edited by Jacques Chiffolueau, Lauro Martines, and Agostino Paravicini Bagliani, pp. 175–90. Spoleto: Centro Italiano di Studi sull' Alto Medioevo, 1994.

———. "Marriage, Love, Sex and Renaissance Civic Morality." In *Sexuality and Gender in Early Modern Europe: Institutions, Texts, Images*, edited by James Grantham Turner, pp. 10–30. New York: Cambridge University Press, 1993.

———. "Mean Streets, Familiar Streets, or The Fat Woodcarver and the Masculine Spaces of Florence." In *Renaissance Florence: A Social History*, edited by Roger J. Crum and John T. Paoletti, pp. 295–310. Cambridge: Cambridge University Press, 2006.

———. "'More Dear to Me Than Life Itself': Marriage, Honor, and a Woman's Reputation in the Renaissance." In Ruggiero, *Binding Passions: Tales of Magic, Marriage and Power at the End of the Renaissance*, pp. 57–87. New York: Oxford University Press, 1993.

———. "Sexual Criminality in the Early Renaissance." *Journal of Social History* 8 (1975): 18–37. Reprinted in *Reflections on World Civilization, a Reader*, edited by Ronald H. Fritz, James S. Olson, and Randy W. Roberts, 1:208–18. New York: HarperCollins, 1993.

———. "The Strange Death of Margarita Marcellini: '*Male*,' Signs and the Everyday World of Premodern Medicine." *American Historical Review* 106:4 (2001): 1141–58.

———. *Violence in Early Renaissance Venice*. New Brunswick, NJ: Rutgers University Press, 1980.

Ruzante [Angelo Beolco]. *Teatro*. Edited and translated into Italian by Ludovico Zorzi. Turin: Einaudi, 1967.

Santore, Kathy. "Julia Lombardo, '*Somtuosa Meretrize*': A Portrait by Property." *Renaissance Quarterly* 41 (1988): 44–83.

Sanuto, Marino. *I diarii di Marino Sanuto*. 58 vols. Edited by Rinaldo Fulin et al. Venice: Deputazione R. Veneta di Storia Patria, 1897–1903.

Saslow, James M. *Ganymede in the Renaissance: Homosexuality in Art and Society*. New Haven, CT: Yale University Press, 1986.

Scarabello, Giovanni. "Devianza sessuali ed interventi di giustizia a Venezia nella prima metà del XVI secolo." In *Tiziano e Venezia, Convegno Internazionale di Studi*, pp. 75–84. Venice: Neri Pozza Editore, 1976.

———. "Le 'signore' della repubblica." In *Il gioco dell'amore: Le cortigiane di Venezia dal Trecento al Settecento*, pp. 11–35. Milan: Berenice, 1990.

Scott, Joan W. "The Evidence of Experience." *Critical Inquiry* 17 (1991): 773–97.

―――. *Gender and the Politics of History.* New York: Columbia University Press, 1998.

Sermini, Gentile. "Scopone." In *Prosatori volgari del Quattrocento,* edited by Claudio Varesi, pp. 750–61. Milan: Riccardo Riccardi, 1955.

Shemek, Deanna. "Aretino's *Marescalco:* Marriage Woes and the Duke of Mantua." *Renaissance Studies* 16 (2002): 366–80.

―――. *Ladies Errant: Wayward Women and Social Order in Early Modern Italy.* Durham, NC: Duke University Press, 1998.

Shepard, Alexandra. *Meanings of Manhood in Early Modern England.* Oxford: Oxford University Press, 2003.

Sherberg, Michael. "Il potere e il piacere: La sodomia del *Marescalco.*" In *La rappresentazione dell'altro nei testi Rinascimento,* edited by Sergio Zatti, pp. 96–112. Lucca: Pacini Fazzi, 1998.

Simons, Patricia. "Alert and Erect: Masculinity in Some Italian Renaissance Portraits of Fathers and Sons." In *Gender Rhetorics: Postures of Dominance and Submission in History,* edited by Richard C. Trexler, pp. 162–86. Binghamton, NY: MRTS, 1994.

―――. "Portraiture, Portrayal, and Idealization: Ambiguous Individualism in Representations of Renaissance Women." In *Language and Images of Renaissance Italy,* edited by A. Brown, pp. 271–85. Oxford: Clarendon Press, 1995.

Skinner, Quentin. *The Foundations of Modern Political Thought.* 2 vols. Cambridge: Cambridge University Press, 1978.

―――. *Visions of Politics.* Vol. 2, *Renaissance Virtues.* Cambridge: Cambridge University Press, 2002.

Sperling, Jutta. *Convents and the Body Politic in Late Renaissance Venice.* Chicago: University of Chicago Press, 1999.

Spiegel, Gabrielle. "History, Historicisms and the Social Logic of the Text in the Middle Ages." *Speculum* 69 (1990): 59–86.

Stallybrass, Peter, and Allon White. *The Politics and Poetics of Transgression.* Ithaca, NY: Cornell University Press, 1989.

Stearns, Peter. *Old Age in European Society: The Case of France.* New York: Holmes and Meier, 1977.

―――, ed. *Old Age in Preindustrial Society.* New York: Holmes and Meier, 1982.

Stephens, Walter. *Demon Lovers: Witchcraft, Sex, and the Crisis of Belief.* Chicago: University of Chicago Press, 2002.

Stone, Lawrence. *Family, Sex and Marriage in England.* New York: Harper and Row, 1979.

Storey, Harry Wayne. "Parodic Structure in 'Alibech and Rustico': Antecedents and Traditions." *Canadian Journal of Italian Studies* 5 (1982): 163–76.

Talvacchia, Bette. *Taking Positions: On the Erotic in Renaissance Culture.* Princeton, NJ: Princeton University Press, 1999.

Terreaux-Scotto, Cécile. "'Vous êtes des enfants de cent ans': Age reel et âge mètaphorique dans les sermons de Savonarole." *Rivista di Storia delle Idee Politiche e Sociale* 36 (2003): 3–25.

Thane, Pat. "Social Histories of Old Age and Aging." *Journal of Social History* 37 (2003): 93–112.

Thomas, Keith. "Age and Authority in Early Modern England." *Proceedings of the British Academy* 62 (1976): 205–48.

———. *Religion and the Decline of Magic*. New York: Scribner's, 1971.

Tiziano e Venezia, Convegno Internazionale di Studi. Venice: Neri Pozza Editore, 1976.

Toscan, Jean. *Le carnaval du langage: Le lexique érotique des poètes de l'équivoque de Burchiello à Marino (XVe–XVIIe siècles)*. 4 vols. Lille: Atelier Reproduction des Thèses, Université de Lille III, 1981.

Trexler, Richard C., ed. *Gender Rhetorics: Postures of Dominance and Submission in History*. Binghamton, NY: MRTS, 1994.

———. "La prostitution florentine au XVe siècle: Patronages et clienteles." *Annales ESC* 36 (1981): 983–1015.

———. *Public Life in Renaissance Florence*. New York: Academic Press, 1980.

Trumbach, Randolph. *Sex and Gender Revolution*. Vol. 1, *Heterosexualtiy and the Third Gender in Enlightenment England*. Chicago: University of Chicago Press, 1998.

Turner, James Grantham, ed. *Sexuality and Gender in Early Modern Europe: Institutions, Texts, Images*. New York: Cambridge University Press, 1993.

Turner, Victor. *From Ritual to Theater: The Human Seriousness of Play*. New York: Performing Arts Publications, 1982.

Tylus, Jane. "Theater and Its Social Uses: Machiavelli's *Mandragola* and the Spectacle of Infamy." *Renaissance Quarterly* 53:3 (2000): 656–83.

Varesi, Claudio, ed. *Prosatori volgari del Quattrocento*. Milan: Riccardo Riccardi, 1955.

Vickers, Nancy J. "The Body Re-Membered: Petrarchan Lyric and the Strategies of Description." In *Mimesis: From Mirror to Methos, Augustine to Descartes*, edited by John D. Lyons and Stephen G. Nichols, pp. 100–109, 261–62. Hanover, NH: University of New England Press, 1982.

Viroli, Maurizio. *Machiavelli*. Oxford: Oxford University Press, 1998.

———. *Il sorriso di Niccolò: Storia di Machiavelli*. Rome: Laterza, 1998. Translated by Antony Shugaar as *Niccolò Smile: A Biography of Machiavelli* (New York: Farrar, Straus and Giroux, 2000).

Waddington, Raymond B. *Aretino's Satyr: Sexuality, Satire and Self-Projection in Sixteenth-Century Literature and Art*. Toronto: University of Toronto Press, 2004.

Walters, Jonathan. "'No More than a Boy': The Shifting Construction of Masculinity from Ancient Greece to the Middle Ages." *Gender and History* 5 (1993): 20–33.

Weinstein, Donald. *Savonarola and Florence: Prophecy and Patriotism in the Renaissance*. Princeton, NJ: Princeton University Press, 1970.

Weintraub, Karl Joachim. *The Value of the Individual: Self and Circumstance in Autobiography*. Chicago: University of Chicago Press, 1982.

Weisner, Merry. *Women and Gender in Early Modern Europe*. Cambridge: Cambridge University Press, 1993.

Weissman, Ronald F. E. "The Importance of Being Ambiguous: Social Relations, Individualism, and Identity in Renaissance Florence." In *Urban Life in the Renaissance*, edited by Susan Zimmerman and Ronald F. E. Weissman, pp. 269–80. Newark: University of Delaware Press, 1989.

———. *Ritual Brotherhood in Renaissance Florence*. New York: Academic Press, 1982.

Woodbridge, Linda. *Vagrancy and Homelessness in English Renaissance Literature.* Urbana: University of Illinois Press, 2001.

——. *Women and the English Renaissance: Literature and the Nature of Woman-kind, 1540–1620.* Urbana: University of Illinois Press, 1986.

Woods-Marsden, Joanna. *Renaissance Self-Portraiture: The Visual Construction of Identity and the Social Status of the Artist.* New Haven, CT: Yale University Press, 1998.

Wunder, Heide. "Considerazioni sulla costruzione della virilità e dell'identità maschile nelle testimonianze della prima età moderna." In *Tempi e spazi di vita femminile tra medioevo ed età moderna,* edited by Silvana Seidel Menchi, Anne Jacobson Schutte, and Thomas Kuehn, pp. 97–103. Bologna: Il Mulino, 1999.

Yates, Francis A. *Giordano Bruno and the Hermetic Tradition.* Chicago: University of Chicago Press, 1964.

Zarri, Gabriella. *La sante vive: Profezie di corte e devozione femminile tra '400 e '500.* Turin: Rosenberg and Sellier, 1990.

——. *Recinta: Donne, clausura e matrimonio nella prima età moderna.* Bologna: Il Mulino, 2000.

Zorzi, Andrea. "Giustizia criminale e criminalità nell'Italia del tardo medioevo: Studi e prospettive di ricerca." *Società e Storia* 11 (1989): 923–65.

LaVergne, TN USA
16 December 2010
208940LV00002B/1/P